Troubled Waters

Troubled Waters

CHAMPION INTERNATIONAL
and the
PIGEON RIVER CONTROVERSY

Richard A. Bartlett

Outdoor Tennessee Series
Jim Casada, Series Editor

The University of Tennessee Press • Knoxville

Library of Congress Cataloging-in-Publication Data

Bartlett, Richard A.
        Troubled waters: Champion International and the Pigeon River Controversy /
    Richard A. Bartlett.—1st ed.
        p.   cm.—(Outdoor Tennessee series)
    Includes bibliographical references and index.
        ISBN 0-87049-887-8 (cloth: alk. paper)
        ISBN 0-87049-888-6 (pbk.: alk. paper)
    1. Paper industry—Waste disposal—Environmental aspects—Pigeon River (N.C. and Tenn.)
    2. Water—Pollution—Pigeon River (N.C. and Tenn.)
    3. Champion International Corporation.   I. Title. II. Series
    TD428.P35B37   1995
    363.73'942'09768—dc20   94-18741
                                                             CIP

Contents

Illustrations

Editor's Foreword

The sad saga so skillfully chronicled in this work is, for me, an intensely personal and in many ways painful one. I acknowledge as much at the outset, for the tale of the Pigeon River is not one which I can contemplate from the viewpoint of a disinterested observer. After all, in one way or another the Champion mill in Canton, North Carolina, and the Pigeon River, which long has been the recipient of effluent from its production of paper, have repeatedly touched my life.

I grew up close by, in the small town of Bryson City in Swain County. This high-country county is adjacent to Haywood County, where the Champion paper mill is located. On certain days during my childhood, when lowering clouds and southwesterly winds combined, the stench emanating from Canton found its noxious way across the Balsam Mountains. Locals would shake their heads in dismay even as they muttered sympathetically about "the smell of money," and though a carefree youngster I wondered why a part of the world that was so breathtakingly beautiful had to be befouled.

There was ample reason for my concern, poorly informed though I unquestionably was. After all, at that time Bryson City had its own version of the polluted Pigeon River. The Tuckasegee River flowed black and ugly through the heart of the mountain hamlet, carrying with it the outpourings from a Mead Corporation plant upstream as well as untreated sewage and who knows what else. The contrast between the Tuckasegee and nearby streams such as Deep Creek and the Nantahala River could scarcely have been more striking, particularly to a lad who loved to fish. Then, too, both my father and grandfather had told tempting tales of a once-clean Tuckasegee, recalling as they did so a time when the stream teemed with smallmouth bass, trout, and even the occasional "jack" (muskie).

Dad even related the time when a local preacher caught a massive brook trout, or "speckle" as we knew the species, from the Tuckasegee. Speckled trout are synonymous with cold, clean, and pristine water, and in my mind's eye I harkened back to what must have been a stream to dream about.

Then, in the 1960s, after I had gone off to college and moved on to a wider though not necessarily better world beyond the comforting embrace of the Appalachians, a miracle happened. Faced by tightening economic regulations, the Mead Corporation closed its papermaking operation on the Tuckasegee near the upstream town of Sylva. Outflows of untreated sewage also ceased, and in the intervening years what was once a filthy eyesore has undergone a wondrous renaissance. Nature's healing powers have "taken holt," as my grandfather would have put it, and once again the Tuckasegee runs clean. Smallmouth bass and brawny brown trout, redeye bass and muskie—all fish that demand high quality water—now call the river home. The Tuckasegee has become a haven for float tubes, kayaks, and canoes, and today anglers catch spunky game fish rather than catfish marked with sores. Among those who live along its meandering course (Tuckasegee is taken from a Cherokee word that means "moves slow, like a turtle"), one senses a quiet pride in the pristine face it now presents.

For those who have long known both the Pigeon and the Tuckasegee, comparison is inescapable. The former remains an environmental nightmare, an eerie, earthly version of the hellish Styx. Laced with toxins and laden with PCBs, it defiles sections of two states. The Tuckasegee, by way of contrast, has come back from the dead (thanks to a larger volume of water and a smaller paper plant, and it was never as bad as the Pigeon). Today it is vibrant and vital, a lovely natural attraction enhancing the economies of both Swain and Jackson Counties. Time and again I have wondered, as someone whose roots run deep in the Great Smokies and who loves the mountain fastnesses in their matchless natural glory, why the transformation that gave the Tuckasegee new life cannot be repeated on the polluted Pigeon. Every time, an answer echoes back: "Unbridled greed."

Frankly, I find it impossible to be as dispassionate on the subject as Richard Bartlett has been. In addition to my intimate familiarity with the Pigeon River and its environs from a geographical standpoint, I personally know a number of the people, all of them staunch advocates of Champion, who are mentioned in these pages. They are basically good folks, hardy high-country types who possess an abundance of the cardinal virtues we as Americans have long prized—independence, self-reliance, honesty, and industry. Yet these individuals are also, in my view, singularly misguided. Unconscious or unthinking prisoners of a powerful corporate giant that clutches them tight against its materialistic maw, they have turned their backs on the good water that is earth's lifeblood.

In the halcyon days of my youth—and in retrospect the shining promise of a mountain childhood far outweighed any adversity presented by the region's hardscrabble lifestyle—the town of Canton and the river that ran through it evoked the occasional derisive comment and my unvoiced concerns but little more. Our high school basketball team laughingly talked about playing the "Canton Stinkers." We hoped the wind would carry the plant's pervasive odor away from us when we made occasional forays to see a world-class fast-pitch softball team sponsored by Champion play the likes of the Clearwater Bombers. And always, as one motored along U.S. Highway 19, windows were rolled up tight.

Then for years I more or less forgot about Canton and its Stygian stream; I was reminded that air and water pollution still reigned supreme in Haywood County only when I visited my parents or returned to the Great Smokies for a few days of trout fishing. On every such occasion, though, the stench was there, moderated only a bit by stiffening environmental regulations. Each time I saw the river, black with acid and covered with scudding foam anywhere there were rapids, it troubled my soul. More than once I fished the Pigeon's lovely headwaters, pausing to ponder, even as I joyously hooked wild rainbow trout, on humanity's shameful penchant for dirtying its own nest.

Then came a powerful moment of truth. The revelation was a striking one, but in looking back it is all too abundantly manifest that my personal experience typified the Champion management mentality. I was a budding outdoor writer, with no more than a score or so of published articles to my credit. In a standard "where to" piece for a regional magazine, I mentioned the upper reaches of the Pigeon River as part of a survey of prime fisheries in western North Carolina. After discussing what the angler could expect in the way of angling bounty on the upper Pigeon, I noted that below the Champion plant's outflow the stream was a fishless "river of the dead."

Within a few days of the article's appearance, the magazine's editor received a blustering, threatening letter from a Champion spokesman. It condemned me in no uncertain terms and threatened to initiate legal action through authorities with the North Carolina Wildlife Resources Commission. No direct mention was made of what I had said about Champion; instead, the letter pointed to the fact that I had noted that the "yellarhammer" was a traditional fly pattern used to catch mountain trout. The correspondent suggested that I was encouraging fishermen to kill an endangered species in order to fashion trout-deceiving flies (yellarhammer is the local name for an endangered species of flicker that furnished the feathers from which the pattern was originally tied). Never mind that suitable substitutes for flicker feathers have long been in use or that I set off mention of the pattern in quotation marks. The intent of this particular minion of materialism was clear—resort to threats and intimidation to deflect my criticism of Champion.

Given my inexperience as a free-lance writer, the strategy would have worked had it not been for the magazine's editor. He took a straightforward, simple approach, asking Champion's spokesman a single question: "Does the article contain anything which is untrue?" That ended the matter forthwith, but it also revealed a great deal about Champion's *modus operandi.* You will encounter examples of this tactic repeatedly in the pages below. Over decade after environmentally destructive decade, Champion has silenced critics when it could, run roughshod over local folks who dared challenge its policies, and used its fiscal might to derail one legal challenge after another. As these pages also reveal, Champion has had plenty of company, ranging from its employees to the highest levels of state government and even into the federal bureaucracy.

Only here and there, at least in North Carolina, were dissenting voices, most notably that of Dick Mullinix, raised. In North Carolina, for the most part, these voices crying *in* the wilderness about the importance *of* wilderness and pure water were ignored.

In neighboring Tennessee, on the other hand, growing alarm about the possibility of the Pigeon being deadly led to activism. Increasingly, Champion faced challenges that could neither be ignored nor readily deflected. This book is, in large measure, the unfolding story of those challenges. As such, the work is in many senses a cautionary tale for our times, and the message it conveys far transcends the Pigeon River's predicament.

Champion's ongoing befouling of the stream, along with the controversy swirling around it, is a microcosm of the environmental problems our being wed to so-called "progress" at the expense of plain common sense has brought us. No one wishes to go back to the simplicity of that preindustrial world we have long since lost. Yet surely there is a middle ground where crass materialism can be tempered by care for the natural world around us and a determination to share its beauty and bounty with generations yet to come.

Dick Bartlett does not directly show us the way to that middle ground. Rather, employing the seasoned historian's research skills and savvy, he delves into the complex history of Champion and the Pigeon River in a fashion sure to cause consternation in certain corporate quarters. For all of Bartlett's careful devotion to fairness, in the final analysis the book he writes is a scathing condemnation, one in which the sheer weight of accumulated evidence speaks far more eloquently than any amount of outraged railing or righteous rhetoric would have done.

If ever a book was tailor-made for the Outdoor Tennessee Series, this is it. The author focuses our attention on the dilemma of the Pigeon River in gripping fashion. The chronicle is one that goes to the heart of what can happen when people allow shortsighted avarice to outweigh soul-sustaining devotion to protection and preservation of the natural world. No one who cherishes the purity of the earth we call home should ignore this work and its implicit message. It reminds us, in quiet but penetrating fashion, that the time for a season of environmental reason is at hand.

One thing is certain—whatever your perspective, you cannot read this tale of the polluted Pigeon and remain unmoved. To me the story is tragic, yet as I leave these pages it is with a fervent if muted hope that somehow, some way, someday, the Pigeon will undergo a transformation that is magic. On that glad morning, sparkling pure water will replace putrefying pollution, and fish will once more fin through ripples and runs that are now home to naught save flecks of unsightly foam. For now, we have a sobering study of a shameful story. Read it and weep or wonder. Most of all, though, pause to ponder what the Pigeon River tells us about the difference between the use and the abuse of water, and as you do so be reminded that it is water that sustains life.

Jim Casada
Series Editor
Rock Hill, South Carolina

Preface

The paper upon which this book is printed, the news-paper read this morning, the *TV Guide* consulted last night for the evening's program listings, the carton in which the new VCR was delivered, the toilet tissue used in the privacy of the bathroom, the diapers for the baby, the "personal products" used by women between puberty and menopause, the adult diapers that save embarrassment from incontinence, the towels that wipe the grease off the frying pan, the duplicating paper used for interoffice memos, the bond paper the company uses for its formal correspondence, the paycheck, the bills, the wrappers, the milk and juice cartons—all these and ten thousand times ten thousand other items are made of paper. It is all around us; it is so ubiquitous, so omnipresent, so much the mastic that cements civilization together that rarely a thought passes about its source.

But paper has to originate somewhere. For many, awareness of its source arises with an unpleasant olfactory experience in the presence of mill effluents. A passenger plane comes in for a landing and flies through paper mill smokestack emissions and the cabin is filled with an odor like that of a thousand outhouses. Or one drives past a mill along an interstate in the South, in New England, in the upper Midwest, or along the Pacific Coast and the stench permeates the car. Soon, however, the mill is passed and the unpleasantness goes away. The experience is forgotten.

Should one stop at the mill town and ask about the stench, the reply will be "What odor?" Or "It smells like money" or "It smells like ham and eggs to me." If a visitor is critical, the native bristles. The stranger hears something like this: "Want to go back to corn cobs in the bathroom?" Or "That baby of yours use cotton didies?" The businessman might be asked if he wants to return to wooden crates for packing and shipping. Any complaining tourist could be asked "You read the newspapers, don't you? Wouldn't be any newspapers if it weren't for this mill and others like it."

In the United States over six hundred mills are involved in paper production; all but seven states have at least one such mill. Some mills extract from wood the raw materials for paper by separating the cellulose from the lignins. These mills are often called pulp or fiber mills, the words being, for all practical purposes, interchangeable. Today most mills carry the raw materials through the papermaking process so that a finished product rolls off their machines; they are often called pulp and paper mills. Thus, Champion's huge mill at Canton, North Carolina, which was first called a fiber mill and shipped its product to the company's paper mill at Hamilton, Ohio, was producing finished paper at Canton within a decade of opening. Whether they just produce fiber or refine the fiber into finished paper products, these factories are voracious consumers of a raw material, trees, and of the environment: they empty millions of tons of toxic pollutants into the atmosphere—to say nothing of their stench—and pulp and papermaking use vast quantities of water. If this processed water does not go through an expensive treatment procedure, it is released into rivers, lakes, or bays as a nearly black, foamy, smelly liquid. If this water is disgorged into a huge river like the Ohio, the water mass of the river soon absorbs the polluted liquid; if into a lake or bay, it is now known that terrible damage is done to the fish, crustacea, and the plants of the lake or bay bottom. If dumped into a river that is too small, that river is befouled and is unusable for miles downstream.

We use paper. We have ignored, forgotten, or been blasé about the cost to the environment.

Those days are ending. With a rapidly increasing population that demands and absolutely must have potable water, with the world's civilizations consuming ever greater quantities of raw materials, with landfills topping out and additional space hard to come by, with indications of a widening ozone hole and the possibility of global warming, many societies are taking a new, serious look at major polluting industries. Paper manufacturing is high on the list: it ranks third in toxic emissions, surpassed only by makers of chemicals and primary metals.

The industry is not unaware that it is being targeted. Increasingly, it is recycling. It is beginning to allot a little more of its research and development funds—never very impressive in terms of total revenue—to antipollution methods and a little less to product development, speed, and efficiency. Pulp and paper industrialists are learning that public relations, no matter how expensive and sophisticated, can accomplish only so much when a citizenry has had enough of a mill's stench in the air or pollution in a waterway. An increasingly educated populace that reads about toxic carcinogens, such as chloroform, furans, and dioxins, will only buy the public relations arguments for so long. On occasion, this populace will throw out of office a politician who is backed by polluters. There are even limits to how far a loyal, well-paid work force can be manipulated to support the industry in the face of hostility from neighbors increasingly concerned about their environment. Courts are more sensitive to strong environmental standards imposed by governments. Today, in lawsuit after lawsuit, adverse decisions are being handed down to the paper companies.

This book is a case study of one pulp and paper mill, of the river it has polluted since 1908, and of the battles waged to force the company to clean it up. It is the story of the Canton, North Carolina, facility of Champion International Corporation, an industrial giant with assets of over six billion dollars, and of economically depressed Cocke County, Tennessee. It is also the story of the county seat town of Newport, through the center of which flows the polluted Pigeon River.

Historians speak of "the milieu of the times" or "the climate of opinion," and they strive to present history that embraces these concepts. Thus, in order to be fair one must present an event, such as the construction of a pulp and paper mill, with an understanding of the way people thought about it at the time. In 1908 did anyone care about the destruction of one small river in southern Appalachia? Or did they think instead of a payroll that would bring prosperity to a depressed valley? As decades passed, was there a change in the climate of opinion? If so, what were the reactions of the company and its employees, and of the residents of the surrounding area?

Because the subject is the struggle to get the Pigeon River clean, a bias is implied. If efforts are made to have the river flowing clear and pure, then someone must be resisting those efforts. That someone has been Champion International Corporation, including its nearly two thousand employees at Canton, their families, and the businesses that serve them.

With a bias, can one still be fair? One can try. Fairness begins with understanding. Next to life and love and health, what is more important to a person than steady employment? How does one react when one's job is threatened? Anyone who has ever had a livelihood placed in jeopardy must have sympathy for Champion's employees and their families.

But fairness should be spread equally. The residents of Cocke County and the county seat of Newport believe the Pigeon River that runs through the heart of Newport should flow clean. For more than eighty years, they have put up with a dark, foamy stream that emits a constant stench over the whole town. It has harmed the citizenry economically, socially, and quite possibly physically. Has this been fair?

The long struggle to clean the polluted Pigeon River is a complex story. This work attempts to present the history of the struggle as much as possible through the words of the participants. They tell the story through their quotes in newspapers, through propagandistic flyers, by testimony at hearings, in legal actions, and through interviews with the author. The struggle has produced its share of confrontations, and harsh words have been said by both sides.

At this writing, near the end of 1993, the river is cleaner than before, thanks to Champion's expensive modernization program. However, opponents remain adamant in their condemnation. They insist that Champion has not done enough, and—no question about it—the river still flows dirty. These opponents want the Pigeon's waters clean enough and clear enough for fishing, swimming, and rafting; they want the river to smell as fresh as an unpolluted mountain stream; they do not want dangerous toxins dumped into it. They want tourists to use the river. At the same time, the mill is still operating twenty-four hours a day, and the payroll remains in excess of a hundred million dollars a year. No one has won a clear-cut victory; no one has suffered a major defeat.

And progress has been made.

Acknowledgments

T his story begins on one of those cloudy, sultry summer afternoons one experiences in Appalachia, the kind of day not mentioned in tourist brochures. Sporadically it rains, but mostly it just tries to. I was escorted into the chamber of commerce meeting room in Newport, Tennessee, after having been given a brief tour of the town. Facing me around the table were Charles Lewis Moore, an impressive person whose attire would have been appropriate in a Wall Street conference room; he was Cocke County's executive officer. Then there was Bob Seay, in early middle-age and dressed in jeans and a sports shirt; he was executive director of the Newport-Cocke County Chamber of Commerce. A third person was Seay's secretary, slim, bright Fran Ketterman. Dick Mullinix, the fourth person, introduced me as a retired historian "who is going to write about our fight to clean the Pigeon River."

He was not quite accurate. I had told him that I was *thinking* about writing such a book. But never mind. I wanted to hear what these people had to say.

Usually a discussion takes awhile to heat up, but this one started off already hot. Their anger at the injustice of that polluted stream running through the heart of their town, and their common conviction that *this time* Cocke County residents were going to succeed in forcing Champion to clean the Pigeon, combined to give these people the adrenaline necessary to carry on a spirited discussion. Soon, five o'clock was approaching, and it was time to break up the meeting.

Yes, I would write the book. The sincerity, dedication, and enthusiasm of Moore, Seay, Ketterman, and Mullinix had convinced me that their cause was just.

In my bibliography I have listed nearly fifty people who have helped me by giving personal interviews, by responding to correspondence, by allowing me to engage them in telephone conversations, and by providing duplicated material that I otherwise could not have obtained. Each one deserves more than a mere listing at the back of the book, but space precludes my mentioning all of them here. I want to thank especially Dick and Lucie Mullinix. Dick's newspaper files presented me with the basis for this book. In addition, Bob Seay, Gay Webb, Jim Harrison, and Nelson Ross have helped me substantially. Special notice—and thanks—should be extended to the *Newport Plain Talk* and the *Mountaineer* (Waynesville) for their extensive coverage of the Pigeon River issue. Gilbert Soesbee of the *Newport Plain Talk* has applied the highest standards of journalism to the Pigeon River assignment, and he has given me a lot of assistance. As the reader will discover from the notes, I have used both newspapers extensively. Larry Clark, TVA manager of Reservoir Water Quality, made available archives pertaining to the Pigeon River at his office at Chattanooga. Paul Davis, Tennessee director of Water Pollution Control, gave of his time on the very day he was clearing his desk for a vacation to Hawaii. Richard Watts, historian of the Canton Area Historical Museum, helped me better understand Haywood County's attitudes. Anne E. Gometz at the Robert Manning Strozier Library at Florida State and Edwin M. Schroeder at the Florida State University College of Law Library gave of their expertise above the call of duty. My thanks to Susanne E. Green of Florida State University for helping me with the glossary. Fran Schell at the Tennessee State Library and Sue McGinnis at the Tennessee Supreme Court Law Library were extremely helpful: Ms. Schell allowed me to have microfilm of the *Newport Plain Talk* on interlibrary loan after I had quintuple bypass surgery. To several individuals whose material I was unable to use, please be aware that your contributions were appreciated even though space precluded my using the information.

The people at the University of Tennessee Press have been patient and helpful; Director Jennifer Siler, Managing Editor Stan Ivester, and Copyeditor Scot Danforth deserve special mention. Dr. Clyde Voigtlander, a scientist with TVA, trained to be precise, corrected many errors. To my wife, Marie Cosgrove Bartlett, who thought I really meant it when I retired, go my thanks for her patience and support. And finally, the bottom line of every such little essay is something like this: I wrote the book and I am responsible for its errors.

Chronology,
May 1985–April 1994

May 14, 1985:	The North Carolina Division of Environmental Management (DEM) issues a discharge permit to Champion without incorporating color standards recommended by EPA.
July 19, 1985:	EPA rejects the permit issued to Champion by North Carolina, leaving the Canton mill without a valid permit.
August 6, 1985:	In a letter to state DEM director Paul Wilms, EPA regional administrator Jack Ravan states that a 50-color-unit level is necessary in the Pigeon River at the state line, and that the issue must be resolved in the state permit within ninety days.
November 6, 1985:	Wilms responds to the letter by asking the EPA to reconsider its demand that a numerical color standard be established in the permit.
November 8, 1985:	EPA assumes authority for issuing Champion's wastewater permit from North Carolina.
January 17, 1986:	Champion files suit in U.S. District Court seeking to prevent EPA from regulating the Canton mill's discharge.
March 11, 1986:	EPA notifies Champion that it must file a wastewater permit application by March 31 or face civil or criminal penalties under the Federal Clean Water Act.
March 24, 1986:	The state of North Carolina files a motion in district court seeking to block the EPA's authority over the permit.

March 26, 1986:	U.S. District Judge David Sentelle denies Champion's motion for a temporary restraining order against EPA.
April 11, 1986:	Champion complies with Sentelle's order, filing an application with EPA to discharge treated wastewater into the Pigeon River.
May 2, 1986:	Sentelle denies a motion by EPA seeking to dismiss the Champion suit that challenges the agency's authority over the discharge permit.
May 12, 1986:	Champion announces that a million-dollar ultrafiltration test facility failed to live up to expectations, removing only about 45 percent of the color in the mill's effluent instead of the projected 75 percent.
July 14, 1986:	In response to another EPA motion, Sentelle declines to reconsider his decision in May not to dismiss Champion's lawsuit. But he allows three additional parties—the state of Tennessee and two environmental groups—to join the side of EPA in the suit.
September 22, 1986:	Champion says it is prepared to spend two hundred million dollars to increase profitability and reduce color in its discharge, contingent upon approval by regulatory agencies.
December 1, 1986:	Sentelle grants a summary judgment in Champion's lawsuit in favor of EPA, ruling that the agency acted properly and with reason when it took over the permitting process from the state.
January 14, 1987:	EPA issues the preliminary draft of the wastewater discharge permit it is proposing for the mill. The permit would require Champion to meet a 50-color-unit standard not only at the state line, but also just downstream from the mill.
January 27, 1987:	The U.S. Supreme Court rules that Tennessee can sue Champion in its own courts to force a river cleanup, but only if North Carolina law is applied. The ruling overturns a Champion victory in the Tennessee Supreme Court.

February 27, 1987:   At a forum sponsored by the town of Canton,
                        Oliver Blackwell, the mill's operations manager,
                        says publicly for the first time that if the EPA's
                        permit were approved as proposed, the mill
                        could close.

March 4, 1987:   Champion announces it is appealing Sentelle's
                        December 1986 ruling allowing the EPA to take
                        over the permitting process.

March 16, 1987:   Governor Jim Martin, at a meeting in Canton,
                        rallies to Champion's support, contending the
                        Pigeon River "is not an environmental prob-
                        lem."

March 20, 1987:   EPA issues the final version of the draft permit,
                        which has no major changes from the prelimi-
                        nary version. Dates for public hearings in Can-
                        ton, North Carolina, and Newport, Tennessee,
                        are set for May 14 and 16, respectively.

May 12, 1987:   EPA postpones the public hearings, saying it
                        needs more time to review technical and eco-
                        nomic data submitted by Champion.

May 22, 1987:   The public comment period on the draft permit is
                        extended until September 16.

September 16, 1987:   The comment period ends without EPA having
                        set new hearing dates.

November 2, 1987:   EPA reschedules public hearings on the draft
                        permit for January 14 in Asheville and January 21
                        in Knoxville. The agency says that the 50-color-
                        unit standard in the original draft permit will not
                        change.

November 6, 1987:   In his sharpest remarks to date, Oliver
                        Blackwell tells a local civic organization that
                        critics of the mill may force it to leave and that a
                        consensus of support is needed for it to remain.

December 1, 1987:   EPA issues the revised draft of the discharge
                        permit, maintaining the 50-color-unit require-
                        ment for the river downstream from the mill but
                        incorporating a five-year compliance schedule.
                        The previous permit required color compliance
                        by Champion upon issuance of the final permit.

December 2, 1987:   In a public notice making official the reschedu-
                      uled hearing dates, EPA opens another written
                      comment period, to extend through February
                      22.

December 4, 1987:   Champion announces that it will not proceed
                      with its proposed two-hundred-million-dollar
                      modernization program because the plan will
                      not bring the mill into compliance with the re-
                      vised draft permit.

December 11, 1987:   A meeting in Stone Mountain, Georgia, be-
                      tween officials of Champion, EPA, and the states
                      of North Carolina and Tennessee outlines the
                      position of each party, but produces no change
                      in the draft permit.

January 11, 1988:   At a press conference in Asheville, Oliver
                      Blackwell says that while Champion will apply
                      for a variance from the color standard, the com-
                      pany also will not rule out further legal challenges
                      to the permit.

January 14, 1988:   Hearing is held at the Asheville Civic Center.
January 21, 1988:   Hearing is held at the Knoxville Civic Center.
February 12, 1988:   EPA announces a permit, with variances, which
                      EPA, North Carolina, and Tennessee are ex-
                      pected to approve. Eighty-five color units are
                      to be allowed at the North Carolina–Tennes-
                      see state line.

March 14, 1988:   EPA releases test results showing dioxin in the
                      Pigeon River in Tennessee.

March 30, 1988:   The North Carolina Champion Variance Com-
                      mittee issues its report.

April 9, 1988:   Governor McWherter signs legislation making
                      variances legal in Tennessee.

June–August, 1988:   Greenpeace, followed by the state of North
                      Carolina, posts signs warning of dangers of con-
                      suming fish from the Pigeon River.

July 13, 1988:   North Carolina grants permit with variances.
August 18, 19, 1988: Hearing held in Newport on the variance.
September 20, 1988:   Tennessee Governor Ned McWherter paddles
                      the Pigeon River, investigating need for a
                      cleanup.

December 23, 1988:   Tennessee Governor Ned McWherter refuses
                      to grant the water quality variance.

January 25, 1989:   Champion Chief Operating Officer L. C. Heist announces a phase-down of operations and reduction of up to one thousand jobs at the Canton mill.

January 31, 1989:   EPA proposes new discharge permit requiring Champion to meet—within three years—Tennessee's water color standards at Tennessee state line.

February 7, 1989:   Champion clarifies its plans, claiming that it will spend two hundred million dollars on upgrading the plant but will still reduce the work force at the Canton mill to about fourteen hundred workers.

August 17, 1989:   Hearing held in Newport.

August 24, 1989:   Hearing held in Asheville.

September 25, 1989:   EPA grants five-year NPDES permit.

October 24, 25, 1989:   Champion and LEAF both file briefs requesting an evidentiary hearing.

August 30, 1990:   Groundbreaking ceremonies at Canton for Champion's Canton Modernization Project.

January 4, 1991:   A five-billion-dollar class-action lawsuit by residents along the Pigeon River and Douglas Lake filed against Champion.

April 15-16, 1991:   Evidentiary hearing held in Atlanta.

February 12, 1992:   EPA administrative law judge dismisses all challenges to the permit.

October 16, 1992:   Class-action suit ends in a mistrial.

January, 1993:   Champion's fiberline No. 2 goes on line, but observers notice little change in the Pigeon River.

March 12, 1993:   Settlement of class-action suit provides a total of $6.5 million for plaintiffs' attorneys' fees and remainder distributed to plaintiffs.

March 27, 1993:   Activist protesters organized by Foundation for Global Sustainability rally and throw Pigeon River water over fence onto Champion property.

May 12, 1993:   North Carolina extends color variance for three years.

August 1993:   *Canoe* magazine runs article on whitewater canoeing in the Pigeon River gorge.

October 12, 1993:	Plaintiff class-action lawsuit filed with Sixth Circuit Court of Appeals.
April 14, 1994:	Champion announces that all the water color at or near the Tennessee line does not exceed an average of 50 platinum cobalt units.
June 11, 1994:	To advertise a cleaner river, Champion sponsors the U.S. Olympic kayak team in a "Whitewater Shootout" below Walters powerhouse on Pigeon River.
June 15, 1994:	Champion announces implementation of new bleaching technology at a cost of up to thirty million dollars.
June 17, 1994:	Champions announces a 20 percent reduction of work force, eliminating 210 jobs.

SOURCES: *Mountaineer*, Jan. 13, 1988; *Asheville Citizen-Times*, Oct. 17, 1992; *Knoxville News-Sentinel*, Sept. 13, 1993, and author's notes.

CHAPTER 1

The Mill, the Setting, and the Problem

Western North Carolina and East Tennessee constitute a region of misty mountains, lush pastures, fertile gardens, rippling streams, and abundant forests. Its people are, for the most part, genuinely friendly, decent, American folk. But the lush greenery and beauty hide a spotty prosperity. Haywood County, North Carolina, for example, has an excellent economy for an Appalachian county; Cocke County, across the line north-northwest into Tennessee, has one of the lowest per capita incomes of all Tennessee's counties. The difference between the two is that an industry was established in the first and the effluent from that industry flows through the heart of the other. The industry is the Canton, North Carolina, mill of Champion International Corporation.

Champion's Mill Today

As the traveler leaves Interstate 40 about fifteen miles west of Asheville at the Canton exit, the stench of the paper mill will already have made the mill's presence felt; the cloud of smoke and vapor rising to the southwest will verify the existence of the mill. The source soon comes into sight. In a slough of the Pigeon River embedded in the center of Canton— a small town of four thousand people—are the tall smokestacks, the high silo-like digesters, blow towers, and evaporators, the bleaching machines, and the cleaners. All of this massive machinery plays a part in turning wood chips into pulp suitable for processing into paper. The pulp, in a stew that is more than 99 percent water, is laid on Fourdriniers, the name for the endless screens and felting over which the substance is molded. Then the pulp is pressed and the water is squeezed out of it until

Structures of the Canton mill of Champion International Corporation reflected in the tranquil waters of the Pigeon River. December 1981. Courtesy Jim Harrison.

it is of a consistency capable of carrying itself unbroken over the heated rollers in the drying sections. Soon the paper (or paperboard, if milk and juice cartons are being made) reaches the slitter and winder. A roller expands until it is carrying up to twenty-two tons of the finished product. Workers methodically use specially made, stationary cranes to remove a roll and insert an empty one. The process continues twenty-four hours a day. The finished roll, whether it is paperboard or envelope paper, may be shipped directly to a manufacturer who will further process it—by cutting it or by applying a coating, for instance—or it may go to Champion's own cutting room where it is sliced and assembled according to the orders of that day. The bleached paperboard will be sent to Champion's nearby Waynesville facility, where polyethylene is applied; from there, the paperboard will be shipped to one of Champion's five regional distribution centers. In addition, millions of envelopes are made from Champion stock produced at Canton. Business papers and uncoated printing papers are also produced at the plant.

The public relations officer who guides the visitor through the mill will say that the basic system of papermaking has not changed since the 1790s, but modern technology has certainly crept in. Instead of standing or sitting near the noisy machines, the papermakers now sit in an air-conditioned, darkened room, studying television monitors that show changing statistics about the process going on outside their enclosed cubicle. At one point along each lengthy paper machine, a two-by-two-foot box glides back and forth across the paper; its sensitive devices convey information to the control room. Less fortunate employees, who wear ear protectors and safety goggles and sometimes hard hats, work outside the control booth, and they scan monitors attached to structural beams. Despite some of its modern comforts, this is heavy industry: it is noisy, smelly, and, if chlorine is being used for bleaching, dangerous. Despite modern technology, chlorine has proven difficult to control. If splattered on a worker or released as steam or as a gas, it can cause injury and even death. Safety is stressed at Champion, and through its many years the Canton mill has chalked up an enviable safety record.

Anyone not familiar with heavy manufacturing will be struck most of all by the immensity of Champion's Canton facility. From a hill east of the plant, an observer can see the tall smokestacks spouting black smoke; lesser vents spew white steam. A big eighteen-wheeled semi is being manipulated by a device that tilts it at a precarious angle as if it were a child's toy, dumping out its loads of wood chips onto an already impressive mountain of the same raw material. The device then gently

The immensity of mill operations is demonstrated by the way eighteen-wheelers carrying wood chips are unloaded at the Canton plant. 1980s. Photo by Gilbert Soesbee. Courtesy Newport Plain Talk.

lowers the truck to ground level, and it is driven off as other trucks are positioned for the same operation. Railroad freight cars seem always on the move, as are the white, sparkling clean Champion trucks, which are conveying paper to buyers far away. The constant movement, the noises, the smells, the old red-brick office building, the chain-link fence surrounding the plant, the security boxes here and there, and the occasional sight of hard-hatted personnel methodically going about their tasks all make for a favorable, even awe-inspiring impression. At night, the floodlit plant—still just as busy, noisy, and smelly—creates an eerie impression.

In 1959 Champion installed paper machine No. 20: it is 515 feet long. It produces more than a mile of paper every three minutes in a sheet 200 inches wide; in less than an hour, it makes enough paper to reach from Canton to Asheville. In 1965 No. 19 went into operation: it produces a continuous sheet of paperboard 246 inches wide at a speed of 1,500 feet per minute; the machine is nearly 600 feet long. It consumes 20 acres of trees in order to produce a million pounds of paperboard every 24 hours. Since 1987, when it was rebuilt, it has produced up to 800 tons of paperboard daily, enough for 11 million paper cartons; one ton can be converted into 14,500 half-gallon containers.[1]

Champion personnel reside in Canton or within a 20–30-mile radius. Many are second- and third-generation Champion craftspeople, for the plant has been a stable producer for all of its 85 years. In a precarious world, Champion's papermakers until recently have felt remarkably secure. They now fear that new technology will put some of them out of work. In fact, Champion's multimillion-dollar modernization, due for completion in 1994, will cut up to 500 employees. But attrition should take care of most of the reduction. They also worry that environmentalists, protesting the stench and toxicity pouring from the chimneys and being carried away in the Pigeon River, will force closure of the mill. The company's CMP (Champion Modernization Project) will, it is hoped, keep environmentalists at bay for years to come. At an average wage of $42,000 a year (as of 1992), even for high school graduates, there's a lot at stake for Champion's Canton personnel.[2]

The Setting

If tourists were to inquire, they would discover that residents of the Pigeon River Basin—including inhabitants of Canton, where the mill is located—are fiercely proud of the Pigeon River country and have no desire to leave it. They love it for its lush vegetation, its beauty, and the outdoors life it offers. Today residents have acceptable medical and educational facilities. Electricity and running water serve their homes. Black-topped roads lead into the towns of Canton, Clyde, Waynesville, Bethel, Lake Junaluska, and other small communities. Across the state line in Tennessee lie Newport, Parrotsville, Del Rio, and Hartford. If residents desire a larger selection of consumer goods, Knoxville lies up Interstate 40 to the northwest, and Asheville is just a few miles east. The vegetable gardens so many keep with pride, the fervor of the autumn hunting season, Wednesday night choir practice and Sunday morning church services, and family get-togethers are activities they share in common with their ancestors, four or five generations of whom likewise lived in the region.

The first inhabitants of this beautiful land were the Cherokee. They were a stationary tribe related linguistically to their northern neighbors, the Iroquois. Since at least A.D. 600, the Cherokee had lived close to this fertile land, which embraces both northern and southern flora and fauna. Their domain was blessed with forty-five inches of rainfall a year, ensuring them the dense hardwood forests in which lived deer, cougars, bears, raccoons, ruffed grouse, quail, doves, squirrels, rabbits, and mink; the rivers were abundant with edible fish—bass, bream, shiners, darters, sunfish, and brook trout. Small cultivated plots supplied the natives the maize, gourds, squash, pumpkins, and beans they needed to supplement their rich diet of game, edible wild plants, and herbs.

Since they lived in a land rich in the raw materials necessary for survival, the Cherokee had time to contemplate the world around them. Their cosmogonic myths fit well into their place in the world, explaining that the earth is a great island floating in a sea of water. It is suspended at each of four cardinal points by a cord hanging from the sky vault of solid rock. In addition, the underworld had different seasons; the Cherokee knew this because the springs, which come from the underworld in their cosmology, are warmer than the outer air in winter and colder than the outer air in summer.

And among their myths was the one about the great serpent Uktena. Its girth was as large as a tree trunk. Its horns protruded from the sides of its head. At the center of its head was a bright, blazing crest that looked like a diamond. Its scales glittered like fire. Anyone who gazed upon the crest met death. So bright and dazzling was it that hunters of the serpent became befuddled like a deer caught in oncoming headlights and ran toward it rather than away, and they were killed by the horrible creature.[3] Cherokee mythology includes the tale of a daring magician who attacked the serpent and then took refuge in a trench. The dying monster rolled over and over down the mountain, destroying the forest as it fell. Its horrible blood filled the trench. A lake of black water formed; in this liquid, women dyed splints for their baskets. "When I read that, it frightened me," recalls Jim Harrison, who grew up in nearby Waynesville and is now an employee of the Environment Protection Agency. "People of the southern Appalachians are aware of crystallized rocks on the spurs of the ridges. They know how they sometimes sparkle. That is the basis of the Cherokee serpent named Uktena." What fascinated Harrison was the detail about the horrible blood and the lake formed by it. "The gorge is the Pigeon River Gorge," he suggests, "and North Carolina Power and Light built Waterville Dam and filled the gorge with the stinking, molasses-colored foam filled waters from Champion's plant. It fits the mythology with frightening accuracy."[4]

Except for seventy or eighty thousand eastern Cherokee, the Native Americans have long been gone from western North Carolina and East Tennessee. White people trickled in. First were the explorers. Hernando de Soto ventured into East Tennessee in 1540. In 1673 James Needham ᵉᵉ

ᵉᵉ

and Gabriel Arthur were in the vicinity. Hunters and traders had traversed the region by 1776, and the highlands were becoming known as the Great Iron Mountains. One of Tennessee's great frontiersmen, John Sevier, probably crossed the Balsam Mountains during a campaign against the Erati, a branch of the Cherokee. In 1789 the name "Smoke Mountain" first appeared officially in a description of North Carolina's western boundary. In the late eighteenth century, naturalists Andre Michaux and William Bartram traveled through the region. They wrote about the botanical wonderland of the area, and they discovered one of the rarest flowers in North America: the bell-shaped, white-petaled shortia. They marveled at the mountain crests covered with colorful rhododendrons ablaze in the spring and gazed in awe at the towering forests of virgin spruce and balsam, poplar, cherry, ash, pine, oak, and tulip. Flora of southern climes prevailed at the lower elevations; a mile up a mountainside, the flora changed to that of a thousand miles north. Of 250 botanical drugs produced in the United States, at least 75 percent are gathered in western North Carolina. Springs, their waters so cold, some said, that they emerged from the earth "two degrees colder than ice" and clear streams tumbling down the mountains or flowing gently along the valley floors added to the beauty.[5]

A few bold pioneers were trickling into the Pigeon River Basin west of present-day Asheville by the last quarter of the eighteenth century. Although the basin is a relatively small area of about 660 square miles, it includes a gorge, well-timbered lands, and some tillable land in several beautiful valleys; the surrounding mountains, including the Balsams, are among the highest in the southern Appalachians. Tributary streams of the Pigeon River, particularly Richland, Jonathan, Hemphill, Fines, Cataloochee, Big, Harrison, and Shining Creeks in North Carolina and Cosby Creek in Tennessee, in essence drain the southern portion of the French Broad Basin. The French Broad River, so named because it led ultimately west into country claimed by France, rises close to the two forks of the Pigeon, but splashes down the other side of the ridge, turns east and then north for a considerable distance before curving around to the southwest where it is joined by the Nolichucky and finally by the waters of the Pigeon. These streams all enticed early settlers to their banks. As early as 1785, David Nelson was growing corn near where Canton now stands. In 1808 Haywood County was formed, and by 1811 settlement was sufficient to found a new town, first known as Mount Prospect but quickly renamed Waynesville in honor of Revolutionary War hero "Mad Anthony" Wayne.[6]

The region experienced some violence between its Native-American inhabitants and the white settlers. One casualty of the unpleasant-

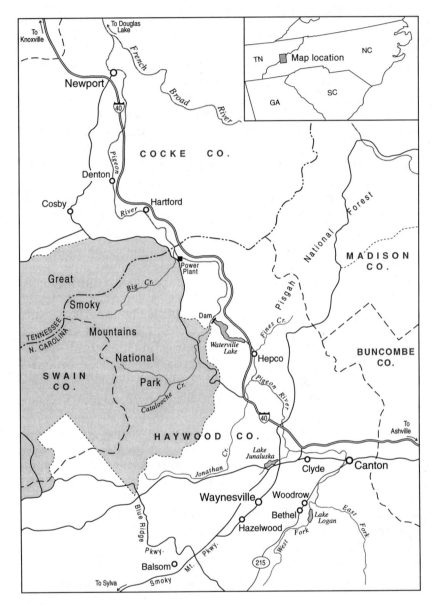

The Pigeon River flows approximately sixty-five miles through Haywood and Cocke Counties to its junction with the French Broad, close to Douglas Lake. Map by Peter Krafft.

ness was a man named Fines, who was killed in a skirmish in the cold of winter. His companions hid him in the ice of a nearby stream, planning to return in the spring to bury him. When they returned, they could not find the body. Thus did Fines Creeks acquire its name. In August 1776, Gen. Griffith Rutherford set out to chastise the Cherokee. He crossed the Pigeon River on his way to the Overhill towns, encountering sporadic opposition. By a treaty concluded in 1798, the Cherokee ceded the headwaters of the French Broad and its tributaries, the Big and Little Pigeon Rivers. (Occasionally throughout its history, the Pigeon River has been called the Big Pigeon, but the United States Board of Geographical Names considers "Pigeon River" to be the accurate term. The Little Pigeon flows through Pigeon Forge, Tennessee, into Douglas Lake.) In 1812 the great Shawnee chief Tecumseh is said to have visited Waynesville, trying to persuade the Cherokee to join him in his war against the whites.[7]

Those who settled along the Pigeon and its tributaries or along the Nolichucky or the French Broad were sometimes called Overmountain Men. They were affiliated with the pioneers settling north of them, along the Watauga and the Holston Rivers. When North Carolina in 1784 ceded its western lands to the United States, the pioneers in the many little settlements from Watauga down to the Pigeon River Basin found themselves in a precarious situation, for the national central government—the Confederation—was weak and could not defend them from Indian attacks. They decided to create their own state. At first it was known as Frankland, but later it was changed to Franklin, in hopes that the pioneers could appeal to Benjamin Franklin's ego and that he would intervene in their cause. In August 1784 representatives from the western counties met at Jonesboro (just west of Johnson City on today's highway 11E) to create their new state. The plan of government was drawn up by a frontiersman named William Cocke. He traveled as the embryo state's representative to Philadelphia but was rebuffed, and after a complex but ludicrous series of events, the state of Franklin ceased to be. William Cocke, however, remained a local leader. When he was sixty-five years old he enlisted as a Tennessee Volunteer to fight in the Seminole War. Little wonder that Cocke County is named for him.[8]

The Pigeon River Valley, which one enters between fifteen and twenty miles west of Asheville, was sparsely inhabited by farming people who were isolated from one another. Two forks, the east and west branches of the Pigeon, tumble in a northward direction from high on Black Mountain where they originate. After about fifteen miles, the two forks have merged and the stream enters a floodplain. Here, where the river widens and becomes shallow, was the sensible site for horses, buggies, and wagons to ford the stream.

It was also a logical place for settlement. In 1803 a major religious revival took place there. Probably as a direct result, the Locust Field Baptist Church was established just east of the Pigeon and close to the ford. Over the next fifty years, the site was variously known as Pigeon River, Pigeon Ford, and Ford of the Pigeon.[9]

Although the population remained sparse, growth did occur and with growth came more activity. By 1856 the Western Turnpike had advanced from Asheville across the Pigeon at the ford, led through Waynesville to the Tennessee line; there, it linked with a Tennessee wagon road to Newport. By 1870 a weekly stage carried people and mail all the way from Asheville to Murphy in extreme southwestern North Carolina.[10]

As the population slowly increased, changes inevitably took place. The little settlement of Clyde, three miles west of Canton, took form in 1877 and was incorporated in 1889. Waynesville, another ten or so miles west of Canton, was the only real town in the North Carolina section of the Pigeon River. It was the seat of Haywood County, and by 1865 it boasted a courthouse, a jail, and twelve or fifteen houses. The village of Waynesville was incorporated in 1871. The White Sulphur Springs Hotel was constructed, its owners hoping to profit from the expansion of the tourist industry out of Asheville. A railroad had reached the community in 1882.[11]

Haywood County embraces 543 square miles; the southwest section of the Blue Ridge, the Great Smoky Mountains, and the Tennessee border define its northwest boundary, and the Balsam Mountains bound it on the west. Farming, grazing, lumbering, tourism, and manufacturing constitute the county's economic base. Its similarities to Cocke County across the Tennessee line are striking. It is linked to Cocke County by I-40, by the same geographical terrain, and by the Pigeon River.

Cocke County's principal town is Newport, slightly more than seventy miles north by northwest of Waynesville. Cocke County was formed out of adjoining Jefferson County in 1797. Today it embraces 500 square miles of rivers, farm and grazing land, small valleys, and mountains. Mount Guyot, at 6,621 feet, is the highest point in the county, which is bordered on the south by Great Smoky Mountains National Park. Another landmark is the glistening sandstone eminence once known as White Rock, but since changed to Mount Cammerer in honor of a director of the National Park Service. The Nolichucky River constitutes Cocke County's northern boundary, and the French Broad, which receives the waters of both the Pigeon and the Nolichucky, flows through the county to its junction with Douglas Lake. Douglas Lake was created when the Tennessee Valley Authority (TVA) built Douglas Dam in the early 1940s.

In earlier days the natural wealth of Cocke County was noted by travelers and was a subject of pride to the residents. Substantiated stories tell of grape vines with trunks 60 inches in circumference, of a magnificent chestnut tree 12 feet around. Today 40 percent of the county remains woodland in spite of massive lumbering during the last hundred years. Apples grow well in Cocke County: the Fugate apple was developed there.[12]

Then there were the hogs. In the nineteenth century, Cocke County hogs were described as "the ugliest of their species with long thin heads, long legs, arched backs, large flapping ears, lank bodies, and long tails and they are among the filthiest of the filthy. . . . The hog of England" wrote a visiting Englishman, "is much superior. . . ." Hog driving was a major chore in many a Cocke County farmer's year. Every August as many as 40 droves of 400 to 500 hogs from Cocke, Greene, and Jefferson Counties assembled near the hamlet of Del Rio (originally Big Creek) along the French Broad and started the 125- to 150-mile drive to the markets of South Carolina.[13]

Farming, including fruit growing and livestock raising, was and remains the principal industry of Cocke County. Among early farm families were the Stokelys. Their progenitors settled in Cocke County in Colonial times. Many Stokelys married members of other large farm families, a happening not unusual in a time of limited communications, sparse population, and lonely, isolated farms. The Stokelys are important in Cocke County history; it is, in fact, the county's leading family. The canned vegetables the family made have graced millions of dining tables. The company eventually purchased Van Camp's brand, before being purchased by Quaker Oats. The influence of the Stokely family upon Cocke County's economy has been tremendous. The company had a long history of purchasing from the lonely little farms off in the hollows, giving cash income to those hard-working people.

From very early times, Cocke County was dotted with little settlements: Big Creek, later Del Rio (the birthplace of the 1930s opera singer Grace Moore), Cosby, Newport (first known as War Ford and later embracing Clifton), Denton, Edgemont, Edwina (formerly Taylorsburg), Hartford, Parrotsville, and others. Through the heart of Newport flows the Pigeon River, which has been dubbed the Black River by the county's historian because of the pollution from the pulp and paper mill.[14]

Newport's early history is confusing. The village got its name when early settlers launched rafts on the Pigeon and, by way of the French Broad and the Tennessee Rivers, made their way into more settled lands where they could sell their produce. This early success bore promise that Newport would become a bustling city. An extreme case was that of William Faubian, who, in the early 1800s, attached a paddlewheel to the stern of his raft and, with a blind horse for a companion, floated all the way to New Orleans. When the railroad bypassed the community by three miles, Newport residents simply dismantled their wooden buildings and moved lock, stock, and barrel to a site by the steel rails. They enveloped the nearby settlement of Clifton in the process.[15]

In its early days Newport was not very inviting. In 1811 a traveler from North Carolina into middle Tennessee found the settlement difficult to find because it was hidden in a deep valley. "It is," he wrote, "the most licentious place in the State of Tennessee, containing about twenty houses of sloth, indolence, and dissipation." The Cincinnati, Cumberland Gap, and Charleston Railroad arrived in 1857. When it went bankrupt it was taken over by the East Tennessee, Virginia, and Georgia Railroad; today the county is served by the Southern Railroad. Railroads were also constructed by lumber companies, and some of their lines crossed into North Carolina.[16]

Cocke County's people were agricultural, not very well educated, very religious, and possessed of rural humor. One-room schools often obtained their light by removing logs at the right height to aid young eyes in focusing on reading, writing, and arithmetic. Pokeberry juice made good ink, goose quills usable pens. Churches were the anchor of rural social life and morals; to be "churched" could be a chastening experience. Parishioners were censured for "getting in a passion"; wayward girls were condemned for having illegitimate progeny.[17]

It was a well-drained, humid, mountainous region sparsely inhabited for generations by mountain people, of Scotch-Irish ancestry for the most part. They were fiercely independent and possessed plenty of basic intelligence. They were just as woods-wise for survival in the Pigeon River country as a Brooklyn resident is streetwise for survival in a big city. Although schooling was minimal, mastery of the three R's was common. They could and did read the Bible. They had and still retain their own code of the hills, a code that can be and often is violent. For some, the environment was overwhelming, and they retrogressed. Isolation engendered genetic deterioration, and a poor economy led to bootlegging and other means of survival outside the law. Despite this harsh life, however, many Cocke County residents have lived long lives.

One anecdote tells of a local who lived to be 110 "before coffee and tobacco killed him." Their talk is colorful. Asked by an interviewer to spell an unusual word, one semiliterate replied, "Oh, just put it down without spelling it."[18]

Their farms are concentrated along the streams. Until recent times, when they cast their eyes toward the high mountains to the northwest, west, and southwest, they were nearly as ignorant of what lay in the mountains as the tourists who occasionally visited the county. Writing in 1933 about the Great Smoky Mountains that fringed the region, a historian said that "it is a little hard to realize that it has hardly been a decade since this was a land almost wholly unknown, save where the lumberman was pushing his operations back into the virgin timber. Only a limited number of hardy spirits had climbed the peaks and penetrated the deep valleys, and many were spots that the human eye had never looked upon."[19]

The two counties, Haywood in North Carolina and Cocke in Tennessee, with only artificial boundaries, blend beautifully into one area. Both should be beneficiaries of the Pigeon River drainage, both are mountainous, and both are inhabited, although in neither case very heavily, by Americans of largely Scotch-Irish and English lineage; some German and French ancestry is mixed among them. Family ties are strong, and a remarkable percentage of the inhabitants choose to reside, generation after generation, in the beautiful region. In 1920 Haywood had a population of 21,020, less than 2,000 more residents than Cocke at 19,399. By 1990 Haywood had 46,942 residents to Cocke's 29,141. With exceptions, the population constitutes a solid, hard-working, churchgoing, decent citizenry.[20]

Today historians and sociologists are questioning the stereotypes of the southern Appalachian people before and after industry entered the region beginning in the 1880s. The conventional view of preindustrial Appalachia, historian Ronald Eller argues, is one of little farms that produced corn, beans, squash, and other truck. The farms had poultry, hogs, and possibly a cow or two. Some farms produced fruits—apples and peaches especially—with the larder supplemented by game and berries taken from the forest. Their cabins were crude, and modern amenities hardly existed in any rural areas. Admittedly, the people were poor, but few starved. Of course, they were always short of money, but what historian Crandall Shifflett calls "rural itinerancy"—working away from home but rarely more than fifty miles from it—brought in small amounts of cash. There was also moonshining, which brought in outside money.[21]

The stereotype of these Appalachian dwellers is one of fairly contented family units, never rich but rarely starving. The reality, as Shifflett suggests with convincing documentation, was somewhat different. From settlement in the early nineteenth century to the 1950s, the mountain people were incredibly fecund. Large families and shrinking patrimonies ensured a smaller and smaller agricultural base per person. The shortage of cash was far more serious than has been depicted; moreover, lack of educational, recreational, and medical facilities insured ignorance, disease, and a brutality to their existence. It was hardly an idyllic way of life.[22]

As for the towns, many appeared prosperous, but they consisted of an elite, usually local large landowners, and a middle class of doctors, lawyers, and merchants. It was a cliquey and class-conscious society in which "poor white trash" was an accepted phrase that those who were better off used to describe impoverished farmers and town-dwelling day laborers. But the wealth of the town's elite and middle class was a relative quantity: there wasn't much wealth in any of preindustrial southern Appalachia.[23]

So when a timber company, for instance, began operations in the Pigeon River region, taking employment at the sawmill or contracting as a timber cutter on company land was looked upon as a godsend. The work was hard and dangerous, but it meant cash to purchase a little more land or another mule, cow, sow, or a boar. At a later time, these jobs could mean an electric refrigerator or a washing machine, a new gas or electric stove, or even a new house.

And the lumbermen came. In the early 1880s in Cocke County, a Scottish businessman named Alexander A. Arthur founded the Scottish Carolina Timber and Land Company with its headquarters at Newport. He placed booms at several points along the Pigeon River, planning to float timber, controlled by these booms, downriver. Natives predicted that just one big freshet in the Pigeon would wipe out the booms, carry away the cut timber, and destroy Arthur's ambitious plans. In 1886 it happened, and Arthur was wiped out.[24]

In 1903 the Unagusta Furniture Manufacturing Corporation began operations in Waynesville. It was later known as the A. C. Lawrence Company, which also produced leather products using tannic acid purchased from the Champion Fibre mill.[25]

After 1900 Cocke County was the site of a large lumber company operated by West Virginia entrepreneurs and later by various Pennsylvania interests. It was at first known as the Mount Sterling Lumber Company or the Cataloochee Lumber Company, and it had operations in both Tennessee and North Carolina. The company built the Tennessee and North Carolina Railway to serve its holdings. Later it was called the Pigeon River Lumber Company and finally the Champion Lumber Company. (It had absolutely no affiliation with the Champion Fibre Company.)[26]

In 1917–18 the Boice Hardwood Company established a mill at Hartford capable of cutting fifty thousand board feet a day. The company made use of two railroads to carry its logs to the mill and its finished lumber to market. One was the old Tennessee and North Carolina, which ran from Newport down the Pigeon to Big Creek, a Pigeon tributary; it then followed Big Creek as it ran up to the sawmill town of Crestmont, North Carolina. (Crestmont is now embraced by the Great Smoky Mountains National Park.) The other railroad, the South Atlantic and Western, was purchased out of bankruptcy by Boice. Its narrow-gauge rails ran up Snowbird Creek to the first cut. A third rail was added so that the rolling stock could use the standard gauge of the Tennessee and North Carolina to carry logs to the mill at Hartford.[27]

Until the company finished the cut in 1928, Hartford enjoyed a brief period of prosperity. During the sawmill years, the community that today consists of little more than a single building that houses a gas station, general store, post office, and a few homes had a population of more than two thousand and supported a barber shop, a dentist, a pool hall, and a motion-picture theater. Although Hartford was somewhat larger than most sawmill towns in southern Appalachia, the pattern of life and the mill routine were much the same. The company policy was, of course, to cut out and get out. Everyone knew it; fatalistically, everyone accepted it.

By 1931 the mill had been dismantled. Earlier, the owners had dammed the Pigeon and built a hydroelectric station. They had joined other companies in the endeavor, and in 1926 the Waterville project—the reservoir, dam, and power station just inside the North Carolina border—was underway. This is their lasting contribution to the region's economy.[28]

Historians may quarrel over whether or not the inhabitants of southern Appalachia were better off than before with the new industrialism, but no one denies the cost to the environment. The southern Appalachians were abused and then deserted by the exploiters. Millions of acres of virgin hardwood were cut with no subsequent reforestation. Damage to the land, the watershed, the rivers, and their valleys was passed over without an expression of sorrow, regret, or guilt.

Smoke belching from smokestacks, water leaving mills carrying putrid, toxic wastes, workers breathing, touching, and being exposed to what we now know to be dangerous carcinogens—these were the accepted criteria of a dynamic nation on the move. The milieu of the time,

Artificially created Waterville (also known as Walters) Lake has served as a settling pond for Champion pollutants since the late 1920s. When full, the view of Waterville Lake and Dam is imposing. Courtesy Carolina Power and Light.

the climate of opinion, accepted spoliation and environmental damage without a twinge of conscience or a backward look at what had been and what industrialism had done. The mountain folk accepted, encouraged, and participated in this exploitation. When rumors that northern capitalists were considering a pulp and/or paper mill somewhere west of Asheville, most residents welcomed the possibility.

Picture the region today. The 106 miles of Interstate 40 between Asheville, North Carolina, and Knoxville, Tennessee, splice the region with miles of countryside on either side of the highway to spare. As one drives west along the four-lane artery from Asheville, the road gradually enters the mountains. As is typical of interstates, the highway passes on the outskirts of towns or is often out of sight of them altogether. I-40 misses Canton, Clyde, and Waynesville and skirts Newport. As the highway continues west-northwest, the mountains grow steeper, and west of the Waynesville exits the curves are more numerous and the grade accentuates. Ordinary travelers are very aware of the innumerable eighteen-wheelers cannonballing along at seventy miles an hour on this road—so aware of them that rare is the driver who dares to do any sightseeing. To the left of the highway is a steep, forested gorge. Occasionally, a body of water can be glimpsed. It is Waterville Lake, which is really a reservoir. Beyond Newport the land levels off and the road straightens; Knoxville lies ahead. Douglas Lake, the reservoir created by TVA, can just be seen from I-40 where the freeway crosses the French Broad.

The Course of the Pigeon River

The Pigeon River is important: its watershed embraces 666 square miles, 544 of them in North Carolina and 122 in Tennessee. Its headwaters begin 15 or 20 miles west-southwest of Asheville, at nearly 6,000 feet on the north slopes of Black Mountain in the Pisgah National Forest. This places the origin of the river at the southern boundary of Haywood County and very close to the Blue Ridge Parkway. Tourists driving state Highway 215 may stop to observe the waterfalls of the West Branch of the Pigeon tumbling down the steep mountainside, under the highway, and into a gorge. They will rarely catch sight of the East Branch, which is across the gorge, and during spring, summer, and fall, it is nearly hidden from view by thick foliage. The West Fork flows north until it is impounded, as it has been since 1931, by Champion's artificial Lake Logan. Prior to construction of this reservoir, the site was known as Sunburst, a lumber camp also owned by Champion. Down to and including the lake, the West Fork is an idyllic Appalachian mountain stream. It flows clear and clean, and it is swimmable and fishable. Champion's Lake Logan, heavily posted as private property, has guest cottages along its shores for the use of company officials and their friends, clients, and politicians. When he was vice-president, George Bush tried his luck with the fish there.[29]

The West Fork continues downstream from the spillway at Lake Logan, receiving waters of the Pigeon Little Fork along the way. After six miles it is joined by the East Fork, still clear and clean, at the small settlement of Woodrow. There, the state of North Carolina maintains Sample Station One, where it tests the water for temperature, color, dissolved solids, and insect and fish life. Then the swollen Pigeon River, forty yards wide, flows six miles to the intake at Champion's mill. Until then—a distance of perhaps sixteen miles from origin to intake—the Pigeon, enlarged by tributary waters, has been an ever more beautiful stream, with deep, sandy holes where fish thrive. Occasional large boulders interrupt the stream's flow. From the boulders, anglers cast their lines and frolicking boys and girls dive into the clear, clean waters or loll in the sun. The tree canopy is reminiscent of an earlier day; at many spots, no sign of civilization is present. North Carolina classifies the Pigeon to the mill intake as an A-2 stream, meaning that, with minimal treatment, its waters are satisfactory for human uses.

By springtime in a normal climatic year, the clear, pure waters of the Pigeon flow into the Canton plant at forty-five to fifty million gallons a day. After being used in several of the steps leading from pulp to paper, the liquid reenters the streambed via a large conduit hidden underneath the stream's surface. In local parlance, nearby residents speak of the outlet as being "at the pipe." In addition to the pollution from the pulp and paper processes, it carries with it the treated sewage of the municipality of Canton. Often, however, especially in late summer and fall, the Pigeon does not flow at fifty or even forty million gallons a day. During those periods, Champion has used everything in the river plus the waters of Lake Logan to keep the mill running. (The company's new system, on line since 1993, is claimed to use one-third less water.) The fluid exiting at the pipe once flowed warm, black, foamy, and smelly; even in 1994, after an expensive modernization, the river is not clear, nor free of foam and smell. Granted, however, it is much improved from conditions of the past.

As one advances downstream from the mill along a graveled road, one views sylvan scenes reminiscent of an earlier era. The tree cover is heavy and green, and the Pigeon, forty or more yards wide, splashes against boulders; here and there are eddies and pools. Again the river narrows and rapids appear. It is a perfect mountain stream for rafting and fishing. Farmhouses, many of them substantial and well kept, occupy lands bordering the streambed. But nowhere is there a boat dock or a picnic table. The river, even with today's improvements, still exudes an odor.

The little town of Clyde, just below Canton, and the more substantial community of Waynesville, including Lake Junaluska and Hazelwood, empty sewage from their secondary treatment plants into the Pigeon. The resort community of Maggie Valley dumps the waste from its secondary treatment plant into Jonathan Creek, a Pigeon tributary. The state of North Carolina designates the river below the pipe as a Class C stream, "suitable for fish and wildlife propagation; also suitable for boating, wading, and other uses requiring waters of lower quality." It has not been suitable for fish and wildlife propagation, nor has it been wise to wade or swim in, nor have boating and rafting been very pleasant.

The Pigeon's route from the pipe is six miles nearly due west, and it is mercifully diluted with waters of a tributary, Richland Creek. A few miles above its mouth, Richland Creek has been dammed to create 250-acre Lake Junaluska. It is the focal point around which the Southeastern Jurisdiction of the Methodist Church has built its headquarters. In 1956 it was the site of the Ninth World Conference of Methodist Churches.

About six miles from the pipe, the Pigeon veers northwesterly and flows unimpaired for sixteen miles. Then, below the mouth of Fine's Creek, the current slows as the stream enters Waterville Lake, created in 1926 by the so-called Walters Project and operational since 1930. It consists of a concrete arch dam 185 feet high, 390 feet long at the river-bed, and 900 feet long at the crest. The dam backs up the Pigeon for 5.2 miles, creating the 340-acre lake. Upstream from the dam on the left bank of the Cataloochee Creek arm is a concrete intake structure, which diverts the Pigeon through a 6.2-mile tunnel to the powerhouse about 12 miles downstream from the dam. This leaves 12 miles of the Pigeon riverbed dry—except during very wet years and apart from a little water from a tributary or two. The dry streambed is to the right of the lake, down the embankment from Interstate 40. When Pigeon water is released through the turbines, it flows another mile in North Carolina before it crosses the state line into Tennessee.

At that point the water has flowed about twenty-six miles since leaving the pipe. It has been temporarily halted in its flow by Waterville Dam. It would be logical to suppose that a twenty-six-mile flow plus temporary storage in Waterville Lake would result in a cleaner river. But—at least until Champion's plant modernization of 1992–94—this has not been the case. As it leaves the lake, the Pigeon River is in worse condition than when it entered. Eleven miles farther, the Pigeon joins the French Broad, which by this point is flowing into Douglas Lake. The Tennessee portion of the Pigeon River is 25.9 miles. Out of Douglas Lake flows the Tennessee River, the source of Knoxville's water supply.

Industry came to the region in 1906 with the construction of the Champion fiber plant. This plant handled the first stage in the process of converting wood chips to paper; within a few years, the company expanded its operations to carry the process to the final paper product. No question about it, the plant was a boon to the entire region. Champion's mill created stable, well-paying jobs; moreover, the demand for timber gave employment to others within a substantial radius, and most of the money was spent in the region. Businesses at Canton, Clyde, and Waynesville

Foam froths from rapids and riffles as the Pigeon River flows below the Canton mill, September 1987. This view is upstream from the bridge at Fine's Creek about fifteen miles from the mill. Photo courtesy Jim Harrison.

profited; to a lesser extent, so did businesses in Asheville and even East Tennessee, where Champion had timberlands.

Unfortunately, there were negative aspects to this industry. Unlike Appalachia's emerging coal business, which cost the health and lives of the miners, the paper industry was (and still is) most injurious to the environment. The reasons involve the way the industry developed and the technology that evolved as the most economical and feasible for the making of paper.

A Thumbnail History of Papermaking

It is not disparaging to comment that typical papermakers, like typical assembly-line workers at an automobile plant or at a factory making computer chips, are ignorant of the long, detailed history that lies behind the technology they are using. But unlike chips, which are an invention of the late twentieth century, and the automobile, which got its start hardly a hundred years ago, the history of papermaking goes back thousands of years. If papermakers knew a little more about their

Nearly dry natural channel of the Pigeon River below Waterville (Walters) Dam in May 1992. When water is not being released from the power plant or spilling over the dam, the Pigeon's only waters are from small springs and tributaries such as Cold Springs Creek and Hurricane Creek. Courtesy Jim Harrison.

product's history, they might better comprehend what has brought the industry into a collision course with the environmental movement.

Certainly their product will not cease to be necessary, at least not in the foreseeable future. Telecommunications involving computers still demand printers that consume paper by the thousands of reams. Further, it is hard to conceive of anything replacing the human demand for paper-based personal products. However, with population growth, environmentalism, and the growing problem of waste disposal, drastic changes in the paper industry are inevitable. Paper development has progressed along with civilization; it can be said that paper has helped civilization progress, and the industry can and will adjust as civilization changes.

Egyptian papyrus, the source of the word paper, is not paper but a laminate (a layering of thin sheets made from the fiber of the papyrus plant); still, it was used to write on, which was the original use for paper. Real paper dates from its invention in China, perhaps by Ts'Ai Lun, in about A.D. 105. The Saracens had brought it into Europe by the eighth century. For several hundred years thereafter, Spain, dominated by the Moors, was the principal paper-producing country in Europe. By the fourteenth century, however, the process had spread to Italy, Austria, and Germany. Paper had overcome an initial prejudice in favor of parchment. As would be expected, the demand for paper increased greatly with the invention of movable type.[30]

Paper was first made from linen or cotton and linen rags. The process was lengthy and labor intensive. Using lots of clean water, the rags were macerated (softened in liquid) into a pulp, which was spread onto a screen within a wooden frame. A layer of felt was added, then more pulp, until several layers were accumulated. Pressure was applied to squeeze out the water and to further flatten the sheets. Then the paper was taken off the screens, the felt layers removed, and the paper hung up to dry. Once dried, it was cut to the desired size and packaged.

William Rittenhouse was the first papermaker in the British colonies of America, founding his paper mill in 1690 near Germantown, Pennsylvania. Although the colonists did not have any great need for paper, supplies still fell short of demand. This was partly because the British mercantile system discouraged colonial industrial growth, including papermaking. When the colonists rebelled, the few colonial papermakers were encouraged to expand production with such rewards as guaranteed monopolies and, during the American Revolution, by exemption of paper mill employees from military service. The paper shortage became serious. In New York in 1781, the legislature decreed that the governor and legislature needed no more than six reams of writing paper for the year.[31]

Even when paper mill production approached demand, the shortage of rags restricted output. Occasionally, contests were held to increase rag collections, and suggestions appeared in newspapers to encourage women to collect their rags. A Vermont paper mill urged the ladies to come and inspect the plant "so that they might thereby be influenced to save rags."[32]

Well into the nineteenth century, with demand constantly rising and although rags were imported from Europe and Asia, shortages were common. Tin peddlers often exchanged rags for their wares, singing out as they pushed their vehicles down the street:

> Sweet ladies, pray not be offended,
> Nor mind the jest of snearing [sic] wags;
> No harm, believe us, is intended,
> When humbly we request your rags.

The scraps, which you reject, unfit
to clothe the tenant of a hovel,
May shine in sentiment and wit,
And help to make a charming novel.[33]

Chemicals began to be used. To make their raw materials go further, papermakers accepted calicoes, worn-out sail, rope, bagging, and
the refuse from cotton mills. Such flotsam was bleached with chlorine
gas, chloride of lime, alkalies, or lime and soda ash to neutralize its
color. Sulfate of lime and gypsum, it was discovered, could add 10 to 12
percent weight to the paper. Still there was not enough paper to meet
demand. The U.S. Senate purchased its paper from Europe, the local
supply being so unpredictable. Developments in printing by the 1830s
brought on the penny press and increased the demand for still more paper. A raw material cheaper and more abundant than rags was needed,
as was more labor-saving machinery.[34]

Beating machines were in use by about 1800. They ended the task
of the beaters, who, after years of leaning over the vats, became stoop-
shouldered and whose hands became permanently red from being in the
mixture so long. In time, methods were developed to dry the paper, first
with a fire contraption and then with steam. Finally, the Fourdrinier
machine molded the paper and dried it. Apparently, the inventor, a
Frenchman named Nicholas-Louis Robert, developed the machine as a
labor-saving device to dispense with some of his cantankerous employees. The Fourdrinier brothers of England improved the machine and
promptly went bankrupt, but their name for the device stuck. It consisted of an endless wire band carrying the pulp, passing it between two
squeezing rolls. A lesser-used cylinder machine also came into use; it,
like the Fourdrinier, created a continuous sheet of paper. The technology has improved and the size of the machines of today dwarf the origi-
nals, but the basic concepts remain unchanged.[35]

By the 1840s the industrial revolution had swept through the paper
industry. Efficiency, that American phenomenon so noticed by Euro-
pean travelers prior to the Civil War, had also swept the industry. The
New York Journal boasted of how its paper, received at 9:00 A.M., had
been rags just 24 hours before and 150 miles away. Still, an abundant,
workable raw material was needed—not that the industry was lacking
in ideas. Any fibrous vegetable material could be transformed into paper: cabbages, corn stalks, peat, tule, wiregrass, blackberries, even frog
spittle (the filamentous algae floating on the surface of ponds). Eco-

nomically, of course, problems arose with all of these. Eventually, in the first half of the nineteenth century, the number of possible raw materials for papermaking in the Western Hemisphere was reduced to four staples: rags, straw, wood, and jute. (In the Orient, however, still other materials were used.)[36]

In the early nineteenth century, research concentrated on wood. A persistent story, possibly a myth, is that inventors simply could not accept that wasps could build paper nests of wood but human beings could not develop a usable, economically feasible process for making paper from the same raw material. By 1851 two Englishmen, Hugh Burgess and his partner, Charles Witt, finally succeeded in making paper by boiling wood in caustic alkali at a high temperature. Unsuccessful in marketing his technology in England, Burgess came to the United States and in 1854 obtained a patent. Within a decade at least one firm, the American Wood Paper Company, was producing twenty tons of wood pulp a day and use of the methodology was expanding.[37]

Meanwhile, in Germany a process had been developed consisting of grinding the wood fibers mechanically and adding water; a rough paper was obtained. By the late 1860s, this experimentation had resulted in the production of a practical, usable wood-pulp paper.[38]

Beginning in 1857, an American inventor named Benjamin C. Tilghman experimented to try to improve wood pulp. He knew the problem was to remove the intercellular matter of the wood—the lignins, as they are now known—that bind the cellulose in the wood, leaving the fibers to be turned into a usable pulp suitable for papermaking. Tilghman used sulphurous acid to accomplish the task. He succeeded in producing pulp, which was a major breakthrough, and was awarded a U.S. patent for the process in 1869. However, the problems involved had to await further research and experimentation to allow pulp making from wood to become economically feasible. In the 1870s Carl D. Ekman, C. A. Catlin, and others improved the process still more. By 1887 this sulfite process was rapidly being adapted in the United States. Newspaper publishers quickly grasped its advantages and purchased newsprint made by this process.[39]

Then, in 1884–85, the *kraft* (German for strong) process was developed by Carl Dahl in Danzig. Today more than 60 percent of all paper is initially kraft, produced by the sulfate process. Kraft is tough paper—an advantage—but only about 50 percent of the wood is used in the process. This can hardly be described as efficient use of a raw material, yet it is considered a cost-effective process for making tough paper. Benjamin Tilghman, Dahl, and those who experimented with and perfected the sulfite and sulfate processes had done the paper industry a great service. A cost-effective way of processing a readily available raw material into paper had appeared just when the industrial revolution demanded it. However, along with wastefulness of the raw material, the processes had other disadvantages. They stank and they polluted—but a hundred years ago, few challenged the papermakers. Champion's Canton facility is a kraft mill.

The Nagging Problem: Pollution

This is not to say that the new kraft mills did not run into trouble with communities suffering from paper mill effluents. As early as 1907 a U.S. Geological Survey report suggested a new way of disposing of paper mill wastes that had the advantage that "residents along the streams will be relieved of a steadily increasing nuisance, while the mill owners will avoid the almost constant expense and vexation of lawsuits and injunction proceedings, which in some cases have caused the closing of the mill." While officially the industry ignored pollution, *Paper Trade Journal,* the primary industry news organ from 1872 until its merger in 1986 with *Pulp and Paper,* is dotted with items about litigation involving pollution. Rather than attempting to solve the problem with scientific research—sanitizing the papermaking process, so to speak—the industry fought protesters legally and politically. This is as true today as it was a hundred years ago.[40]

Still another reason paper companies have failed to address the problem with the resources necessary to make a difference lies in the location of the mills. Pulp and paper mills tend to be in small communities. Writing in 1984, Robert H. Zeiger, an authority on pulp and paper mill workers, noted that 90 percent of pulp and paper factories are in cities of fewer than 100,000 people, and one-third are in towns of 2,500 or less; for 137 communities, the paper mill was the sole source of employment. These communities, by their isolation and dependence on the mills, stifle any opposition that may arise; Champion's Canton facility is located in a town that has fewer than 4,000 inhabitants, and it is far and away the largest employer in town. For such small communities, mill closure means economic hardship for the entire citizenry.[41]

Moreover, in the years following the breakthrough by Charles Holmes Herty that made the resinous, young southern pine a viable raw material for paper (1931), the industry revolutionized large elements of southern life. Millions of acres below the Mason-Dixon Line were converted from scrub or debilitated cotton and tobacco fields to tree farms. Along with the simultaneous proliferation of pulp and paper mills, this mini industrial revolution deserves equal credit with the Second World War for bringing the South out of the Great Depression. Understandably, such a promise of economic rejuvenation prompted southern state governments to ignore the pollution that came with the industry. Often, laws were not on the books; if they did exist, variances were granted or authorities looked the other way.

After browsing through *Paper Trade Journal,* one must conclude that pollution difficulties, although they have caused litigation, have not been considered a major problem by the industry. Like a little dog biting at one's heels, pollution has been a nuisance to the industry, but until recently it has not been considered a danger to its operations; it has not affected growth and profits. Even today, *Pulp and Paper* devotes surprisingly little space to pollution problems.

Beginning in the 1880s with the sulfite and sulfate processes in wide use, the industry expanded at an astounding pace. At long last, four processes—the soda method, the groundwood method, the sulfite process, and the sulfate process—seemed capable of supplying all the paper needed by an expanding civilization. (In its eighty-five years, it should be noted, the Canton plant has used all four methods.) "A paper frenzy ensued," writes Professor David Smith, historian of the paper trade. "Battery jars, house insulation, door and window frames, coffins, oil cans, chimneys, bathtubs, pots, skating rink floors, railroad wheels, [and] pipe were all constructed of paper. A store in Atlanta was entirely constructed of paper; a piano exhibited in Paris [was] manufactured of paper, and the ceiling of the Assembly Chamber at Albany, New York, was made of paper. . . . The list is endless."[42]

While much of this enthusiasm came to naught, other unexpected uses materialized. When World War I ended, the use of cellulose wadding for sanitary napkins opened a new market for the pulp and paper makers; today disposable diapers have added still more avenues of profit for the industry. Corrugating machinery and the process for cutting and creasing cardboard into boxes brought on a revolution in freight and express shipping; wooden crates and boxes went into decline. Rayon, a fiber made from cellulose, had also come into its own; it received the name in 1924, but was first developed in 1907. "The invention of wood yarn for clothing," commented *Paper Trade Journal,* "inspires some thoughts on Adam and Eve in the original State, since the forest will again, as of yore, furnish fig leaves."[43]

The American Paper Manufacturers' Association was founded in

1878; shortly thereafter it changed its name to the American Pulp and Paper Association. It holds well-attended meetings. A "good old boy network" has existed in the industry for well over a hundred years. A Bible of the industry, *The Chemistry of Paper Making*, was first published at about this time. By 1899 there were 763 mills in the United States, improvements were being made with breathtaking rapidity, the price of paper had declined drastically, and consolidation was taking place. Improvements were primarily in the machinery; the industry blithely accepted the basic methodology, which used chemicals and produced malodorous effluents in the form of solids, liquids, smoke, and steam.[44]

The pulp and paper industry is enormous. In 1987 (the latest year for which census statistics were available for this study) pulp and paper mills in the United States employed in excess of 129,000. In that year the average pulp worker received $37,683 in wages, and the average paper mill worker $35,541. In both categories the hourly wage exceeded $16. The industry uses massive quantities of sulfur, chlorine, sodium hydroxide (caustic soda), sodium carbonate (soda ash), and sodium sulfate (including salt cake), sodium chlorate, titanium dioxide, aluminum sulfate, rosin sizing, and lime. Pulp and paper and related industries consume 22 percent of the water used in all industries in the United States. In 1993, according to *Business Week*, papermaking was a 131-billion-dollar industry.[45]

Convention speeches and seminars reported in *Paper Trade Journal* and *Pulp and Paper* reveal the concerns of industry executives through the years. Early on, they were terribly concerned about forest depletion, for obvious reasons, and much verbiage was devoted to the subject. Some industry executives, including Reuben Robertson of Champion, were pioneers in promoting forest conservation. New pulp and papermaking machinery were discussed and heavily advertised in their trade periodicals. Methods of solving problems inherent in the papermaking process were exchanged. But very little space in trade journals and very little time at meetings, as reported, were devoted to pollution problems. These issues were not involved in cost cutting or efficiency, both of which could increase profits. Pollution problems rated a very low priority.

The most recent historian of the paper industry lists its problems in the post–World War II world as being land ownership and forestry, labor relations, safety, education, and technical change; pollution and the environment are not mentioned, although possibly the category of "technical change" embraces pollution problems. Professor Smith states categorically that not until the 1930s did chemists come into their own in the pulp and paper industry; he goes further, observing that on the eve of World War II chemists were the orphans of the industry. Since then, the larger companies, including Champion, have established chemical laboratories equipped with small papermaking machines. Little research has been done on the kraft (sulfate) process, whereas in sulfite pulping—for reasons that do involve pollution—there has been a tendency to use magnesium and soda base in place of limestone. Finally, the author states that "looking back on the last century the observer is forced to say that the one place in which the industry has not made great strides was in the field of pollution control."[46]

For the most part, Professor Smith observes, communities simply endured the pollution. Not until 1924 did articles begin to appear on the problem, "and the evidence is that the industry at this stage spent almost all of its time in defeating antipollution legislation, rather than attempting to control it through research." After World War II both state and federal antipollution legislation began to be passed in spite of powerful industry opposition.[47]

As early as 1950, some farsighted executives realized that the days of unbridled pollution were coming to an end. By the late 1960s, "air and water control standards" were mentioned in an American Can Company advertisement with regard to the company's kraft mill at Halsey, Oregon; however, even today the subject remains secondary in advertisements of suppliers to the industry and in the industry proper. Pulp and papermakers insist that they have spent millions on pollution control and swear they are doing everything that can be done. Many unsolved technical problems remain, they say, insisting that they are continuing research and allotting millions to solve the problems.

Yet, in 1983 T. Marshall Hahn Jr., chief executive officer of Georgia Pacific and president of the Technical Association for the Pulp and Paper Industry (TAPPI), chided the industry for lagging in research and development. "The American chemical industry dedicates 3.6% of its net sales to R&D, while the communications industry spends twice that much. In comparison, the paper industry devotes less than 1% to R&D," he reminded his audience. Apparently the industry failed to heed his suggestions: in 1992 the paper industry was allotting just 1.1 percent of its percentage of sales on R&D, while the closely affiliated container and packaging industry was spending just 0.9 percent. In billion-dollar corporations, this amounts to millions, but the small percentage indicates how little R&D money is allocated to pollution control.[48]

Slowly in the fifty years since World War II, litigation has increased and the seriousness of the threat posed by the industry's unrestricted pollution has accelerated. The city of Reno, Nevada, protested construction of a mill by Crown Willamette at Floristan, California. The plant dumped its effluent into the Truckee River, which flows through Reno. "The Biggest Little City in the World" sued Crown Willamette and won; the mill was abandoned. In 1969 a mill at Ticonderoga, New York, moved to a new location and installed new equipment, all as a result of litigation. More recently, a court case involving a mill on the New York side of Lake Champlain, which polluted Vermont air to the east, was won by Vermont. The Mead Paper Company pulp mill at Sylva, North Carolina, closed because of pressure brought to bear for its pollution of the Tuckasegee River. This pretty stream flows into TVA's Fontana Lake, a body of water noted for its recreational facilities. What has the pulp and paper CEOs worried today is the reality that more and more of the lawsuits are being won by the environmentalists.

The industry is suffering from its early success with the sulfite and sulfate processes. These chemical methods for manufacturing paper are technically and economically feasible, at least so long as unrestricted pollution is allowed. The industry accepted the pollution, and for decades a mute public by and large put up with it. Rather than spend millions to control pollution in the processes, in the smokestack emissions, or in water effluents, pulp and papermakers have concentrated on faster and more efficient machinery, on more and more profitable products. Certainly, intensive competition has influenced policies along with industry success in the marketplace.

Simply put, that bane of American industry, the quarterly statement, as well as corporate lethargy and the tendency to keep things as they are—to say nothing of the industry's good-old-boy understandings—have coalesced to prevent research and development in pollution control that is now called for.

The Current Conflict

Increasingly bitter litigation has resulted in tougher stances being taken by both the industry and environmentalists. The terminology of the lawsuits has taken on a sophistication that, at the level of filing briefs before a judge or presenting a case to a jury, has left amateurs in the dust. A lawyer for the environmentalists no longer issues a brief that insists, in clear English, that the water leaving "the pipe" be potable, swimmable, fishable, and boatable; that dioxins, furans, chloroform, ammonia, and other dangerous chemicals should be eliminated; that the stench (which even today science cannot measure) constitutes a public nuisance that must be eliminated. Instead, an environmentalist lawyer must insist that the water must contain just so many platinum cobalt "color units" per million parts, and even this measure is divided in two: "true" color or "apparent" color. Regulations do not specify that the liquid flowing from the pipe be at the same temperature as it was when it entered the mill. The precise temperatures allowed—a high and a low measure—must be stated, and these measures sometimes differ from winter to summer. Dissolved oxygen must be replaced. The percentage of solids in the water must be calculated and limits established. If chloroform, furans, dioxins, and other suspected carcinogens are present, the amount of their presence must be established and a limit placed on them. That most dangerous of dioxins, 2,3,7,8 TCDD, must be reported if the effluent contains levels of more than one hundred parts per trillion. (North Carolina standards are even stricter at .013 parts per quadrillion.)

The industry protests that it is being overregulated, but the very intricacy of the laws also constitutes a wonderful bramble bush for the industrial hare. Federal water acts, with amendments, take up hundreds of pages in *U.S. Statutes At Large;* the states have their own complex laws; and water and environmental legislation is increasing. Then there are the enforcement agencies. The federal Environmental Protection Agency was created in 1970, consolidating activities from fifteen federal agencies into one. During its history it has been heavily politicized and has grown at an almost geometric rate. The state agencies are often heavily politicized also. Finally, the story must include the environmental activists. They range from members of such respected organizations as the Izaak Walton League to activists who may or may not be members of such organizations as Greenpeace or, in Tennessee, a local group called the Foundation for Global Sustainability. Then there are the local groups that form to protest a specific situation: the Pigeon River Action Group (PRAG) and the Dead Pigeon River Council (DPRC) are prime examples and apropos to this study. Finally, there are the lawyers: the high-priced ones hired to defend the pulp and paper companies; the gentlemen representing respectable organizations such as the Sierra Club, the Izaak Walton League, and the Legal Environmental Assistance Foundation; and the hungry ones who anticipate higher income tax brackets if they can win lawsuits for their clients. Indeed, big money and big stakes have entered the fray. Finally, there are the public relations firms. Their six-figure retainers and their campaigns on behalf of the corporations are on occasion as cost-effective as the lawyers.

The Pigeon River story is unique in several ways. First, the river is small and has been totally polluted, and the pollution has been from one primary source, the Champion pulp and paper mill at Canton. Second, the pollution of the mill has demonstrably affected the social and economic health—if not the physical health—of a downstream county that lies in another state; the polluted Pigeon flows through the heart of Newport, the county seat of Cocke County. Finally, the company has promised to clean up the river again and again over the past eighty-five years, and it has failed again and again. Like the boy who cried wolf, the company has claimed that it will clean up the river once too often: opponents refuse to believe its promises.

Most local protest groups had lasted for very short periods of time, but in 1985 Charles Dickens Mullinix, a former packaging engineer who had retired to a rustic cottage within smelling distance of the Pigeon, protested. He formed the Pigeon River Action Group, and he refused to quit. Eventually people heard his protest, especially in neighboring Cocke County. Beginning about 1986, their opposition coalesced; it crested in 1988, and it has not declined much since then. As of this writing, their position is to wait and see. New litigation is brewing, even though Champion claims to have made a massive cleanup.

But we are getting ahead of the story. The history of the Champion mill needs to be traced in order to understand what brought the situation to its status today.

CHAPTER 2

Enter Champion

T he breakthrough in technology that brought on the
frenzied growth of the paper industry in the late
years of the nineteenth century prompted a search
by paper moguls for sources of pulpwood. Rumors about possible pulp
mills, with consequent employment, spread throughout southern Appalachia where lumbering was already a heavy industry. How else can
we explain one Colonel S. A. Jones of Waynesville securing the passage
through the North Carolina General Assembly in its 1901 session of an
"Act to encourage the building of pulp mills and paper mills and tan-
neries in the counties of Haywood and Swain."[1]

Chapter 660 of the act makes interesting reading:

> Section I. That every corporation, company or firm who may expend
> one hundred thousand dollars in establishing a factory to convert wood
> into wood pulp . . . shall not be subject to any criminal prosecution for
> the pollution of any watercourses upon which such factory or factories
> are located, and the measure of damages to the owner or owners of lands
> over which the water flows from such factory or factories shall be con-
> fined to actual damages, to be ascertained as provided by law.

Section 2 provided that in case of a lawsuit, the company could file
a bond and in so doing was relieved of any threat "of restraining order
or injunction"; in other words, while a lawsuit was under way, operations could continue. Section 3 delineated the area in which the law was
applicable: Haywood County below the mouth of Jonathan's Creek on the
Pigeon and in a specified part of Swain County, which bounds Haywood
to the extreme northwest.

Clearly, such favorable legislation came about because rumors were rife of a pending pulp mill; although the specific company was as yet unknown, it was common knowledge that pulp and paper industrialists or their emissaries were taking the lay of the land and evaluating the forests, the rivers, the railroad network, and the people.

The Arrival of Peter G. Thomson

Sometime in the early years of the twentieth century, an Ohio paper manufacturer named Peter G. Thomson was one of those interested men who came into the region bounded by Asheville on the east and Murphy in the extreme southwest corner of North Carolina. Some authorities place him in the region as early as 1904, visiting a son enrolled in a private school at Asheville. Geo. Smathers (he used the abbreviation of his first name in all his written communications), who was hired by Thomson as an attorney but whose primary task was to serve as Thomson's land broker, first met him at the Dickey House in Murphy in February 1905.[2]

Smathers had met in Thomson a man whom *Paper Trade Journal* described in 1908 as "one of the most picturesquely successful" men in the industry whose "success has been due to his indefatigable and untiring energy no less than to his keen judgment." His portrait shows a distinguished looking, dark-haired man with a thick mustache, who was perhaps a little above average height.[3]

Thomson was an unusual entrepreneur; he was something of a Renaissance man. His beginnings, however, were in strict conformity with the Protestant ethic and the Horatio Alger tradition. Born in Cincinnati in 1851 of Scottish and Welsh immigrant parents, he began his education in the Cincinnati public schools and attended business college. His formal education was curtailed when his father died in 1864, leaving Peter the only male in the family. His first job was as a shipping clerk in a bookstore. He married in 1875, and two years later opened his own bookstore and publishing business. A few years later, he sold out for one hundred thousand dollars. When he heard of a new process for making coated paper, a product in increasing demand, he built his own factory at Hamilton, Ohio, along the banks of the Miami River. His factory was in production by April 1894 as the Champion Coated Paper Company. It was immediately successful and the firm grew rapidly.[4]

During its first few years, Champion purchased its paper from suppliers, but as the business grew, Thomson saw advantages in producing his own. In 1902 he opened his first paper factory close to his coating mills. Now he needed a steady, reliable source of fiber (or pulp), the material from which paper is made. He knew that fiber mills should be located close to their raw material, and he was aware that it was in the South, especially in southern Appalachia, that fiber mill owners had discovered an enormous source of pulpwoods. This was especially true of spruce wood, which was needed for good quality paper. The presence of an enormous acreage of spruce is why this intelligent, energetic man was exploring western North Carolina—and probably East Tennessee.

At least Cocke County, Tennessee, in 1905 and 1906 was full of rumors about a coming fiber mill. Assuming the rumors were true, many Cocke County residents were discussing the merits and demerits of such an operation. Even in those early years of the twentieth century, people knew the bad aspects of fiber mills. Charles Moore, formerly a Cocke County executive officer, recollects statements made by scions of the older, more affluent, landholding Cocke County families—the Huffs, Burnets, and Sams—that Thomson had approached them with generous offers for land along the French Broad. Certainly, as a much larger river, it would have been the industrialist's first choice. Environmentalism as such was not yet known, but the landowners knew of the stench and the dirtying of streams that mills produced, and, so the story goes, they wanted none of it.[5] This handed-down hearsay rings true. In contrast, it is certain that Newport's business community wanted the mill. An article in *Plain Talk* in early 1906 held out hope that the "million dollar pulp mill" might be located along the Tennessee and North Carolina Railroad in Cocke County "if the people act promptly. The entire county would be greatly benefited," stated the article. Cocke County's Board of Trade was urged to pursue the possibility "with all haste and energy possible." Geo. Smathers's published recollections do not, however, record Thomson ever expressing an interest in Cocke County as a mill site.[6]

The meeting of Thomson with Smathers at the Dickey House in Murphy marked the beginning of a long business relationship. Thomson was indeed contemplating construction of a million-dollar pulp mill and extract plant (the extract was tannin for leather preparation, a byproduct of the pulp process). At the time the towns of Andrews and Murphy were vying for the mill. Thomson informed their leaders that he must be assured of a sufficient supply of pulp and acid woods within a radius of one hundred miles to supply the mills for at least twenty-five years. The principal drawback to both Murphy and Andrews was their lack of a nearby supply of spruce. When Thomson learned that Smathers, whose

law office was in Waynesville, had settled boundary disputes for the Cherokee and was well acquainted with the timberlands of western North Carolina, Thomson drew him aside and questioned him about what he knew
about the area's woodlands. Smathers told him about forty thousand
acres, much of it in spruce and hardwoods, on the east and west forks
of the Pigeon River, about spruce timber at the head of Richland and
Jonathan Creeks, and about stands in other western North Carolina
counties. Thomson hired Smathers as a land buyer.[7]

Smathers introduced Thomson to a big hulk of a man, S. Montgomery Smith. "I think without exaggeration," Smathers recalled, "it
can be said that Smith knew more about and had gone over more timber tracts in Western N.C. than any other living man." To show
Thomson the Pigeon lands, Smith took him to Shining Rock (a magnificent vista in south Haywood County), and Smith was hired on the spot
for two hundred dollars per month. His charge was to locate a place for
the pulp and extract plants. It was Smith who took Thomson to Canton. The industrialist decided to build there, provided he could purchase sufficient land for the plants, obtain forty thousand acres of Pigeon lands, and secure a favorable shipping contract with the Southern
Railway Company. He had one other reason for choosing the Canton
site: Smith had persuaded him that it was technically feasible to build a
flume from the three forks of the Pigeon, near where the timber would
be cut, to Canton, so that the expense of moving timber to the plant
would consist of little more than the cost of building the flume.
Thomson hired Smathers to help acquire the necessary tracts.[8]

Canton did not amount to much. When, in 1894, the town fathers
decided to change its name from Pigeon Ford—since they had just acquired a steel bridge that crossed the river, the term "ford" had become
obsolete—the best they could do was name it for the town in Ohio
where the steel bridge had been fabricated: Canton. In 1900 the U.S.
Census listed the town with 230 residents; in 1910, after two years of the
mill, the town had 1,393 inhabitants. Years later, Thomson liked to tell
the story of his meeting with Canton's city fathers while negotiations
were still pending. One of the fathers remarked that they would like to
exempt the mill from the village tax for a period, but that this would be
impossible as the town was in debt to the extent of $17.50.[9]

A millionaire coming into an economically depressed land rich in
natural resources is usually pictured as a wealthy, worldly entrepreneur surrounded by local property owners eager to sell their lands for a pittance—a
pittance, that is, to the knowledgeable entrepreneur, but a princely sum

to the natives. But such was not always the case, and regardless of what he knew was a good price, Thomson drove a hard bargain. He was a shrewd businessman. This was apparent in his negotiations for twenty-five thousand acres of prime Pigeon River lands owned mostly by Thomas Crary, president of the Haywood Lumber and Mining Company.

In a handshake deal concluded in Cincinnati, Thomson and Crary agreed, contingent upon stockholder approval, that Thomson would purchase the twenty-five thousand acres at ten dollars an acre. One-fourth of the money was due as a down payment, and the remainder was to be paid in three equal installments in three successive years; the notes or bonds given for the deferred payments were to be paid 5 percent per annum, secured by a mortgage deed on the property. The purchase, Thomson emphasized, was conditional on acquisition of lands for his mills at Canton and a contract with the Southern Railway Company.

Crary subsequently wired Thomson that the deal was unsatisfactory. The stockholders wanted full payment in a lump sum at ten dollars an acre. Thomson flew into a rage, saying that he was going to sue Crary. He wrote him a letter described by Crary as "the meanest letter he had ever received in his life and could not conceive of any white man writing any other white man such a letter." And Thomson did sue Crary.

Thomson's intimidation ploy was probably calculated. Thomson knew that a handshake, verbal agreement would never stand up in court. But acquisition of the Canton lands was progressing slowly, and he wanted the owners to sell. He knew that when they heard that the timber deal might fall through, they would immediately fear that Thomson would withdraw his offers. This fear hastened the sale of the Canton properties at lower prices than might have been asked. Moreover, by tying up the sale of the Crary properties, Thomson prevented anyone else from buying them until he had his Canton lands. Thomson obtained the lands with his original offer, except that the bonds paid 6 percent instead of 5 percent. The deal was closed October 5, 1905.[10]

By September 1905, enough land had been purchased and surveyed to begin construction. Some lots had been acquired from W. J. "Dick" Hampton and J. N. "Nelson" Mease. They were two of the "Big Five" Canton citizens who dealt with Thomson. The other three were Parker McGhee, Turner Sharp, and J. W. Scott. Headquarters for Champion officials was the Mears Hotel at Canton. Continuing negotiations involved the purchase of still more land at Canton, of more timberlands, and of permissions necessary to allow a flume to run across many properties from the three forks of the East Pigeon—where a sawmill and shingle machine were to be located to furnish wood and shingles for the

In the early years flumes were used to bring logs from Champion lands to a sawmill or shipping point. Courtesy Canton Area Historical Museum.

plant buildings—to Canton. Meanwhile, Thomson had dealt satisfactorily with Southern Railway officials. On January 6, 1906, the Champion Fibre Company, a subsidiary of Thomson's Champion Coated Paper Company, was chartered in Ohio.[11]

People soon became aware of the immensity of Thomson's operations. The settlement at the three forks of the Pigeon soon had a hundred houses for employees; the site was named Sunburst. On his business trips to the region, Thomson always enjoyed his visit to Sunburst and the fine meal he obtained at the home of Captain W. S. Terrill near Bethel. Permissions for the flume were obtained, sometimes with minor problems. One man with nineteen children held out for more money, and a preacher got his church at Bethel shingled as part of the bargain. The flume, incidentally, was a total failure: the engineer had estimated twice over the gradient from the three forks to the Pigeon at Canton.[12]

Thomson underestimated the expanse of land needed for his operations at Canton, and he had some difficulty buying more. Suddenly, the land had doubled in value. Rebuffed by one landowner, he had his agents, beginning with S. Montgomery Smith, approach Mary Ann Patton for her fifty-five-acre tract. Smith included in his negotiations a waiver for any damages caused by pollution. Mrs. Patton was adamant. She did not like two of the "Big Five," blaming them for increasing her tax levy, and she believed they had sent Smith to call on her. She had been told that fumes from the pulp mill would destroy all timber within a radius of ten miles, as had happened from a copper smelter at Ducktown in central Tennessee, and that the polluted river would poison her live- stock. Finally, she had been told that Smith hypnotized people to ac- complish his purposes. When he called on her, she seated him at the opposite end of the porch and refused to look him in the eyes. In short, she refused to deal, requesting instead to talk with Smathers, whom she had taught in grade school. Smathers says that he told her the truth about the pollution, indicating that it would kill most of the fish; she expressed satisfaction with that because "her lazy tenants had been put- ting in part of their time in fishing . . . when they should have been working the crops on her land." Still undecided, she expressed a desire to talk with Thomson. The industrialist obliged, bringing his gracious wife along. At last, all was sweetness and light; Patton sold the fifty- five acres for one hundred dollars an acre, and her land became the site of Fibreville, the early settlement Thomson built for his workers.[13]

Requesting that Patton sign a waiver for any damages pollution might cause to her property was routine. Smathers had informed Thomson of the 1901 act that gave legal protection to pulp, paper, and tanning plants below the mouth of Jonathan Creek. (Thomson may well have already known of the law.) According to Smathers, the pulp and paper- maker did not seem to be bothered that the mill at Canton would be above Jonathan Creek on the Pigeon. After all, the act did not prohibit construction above the mouth of Jonathan Creek. In fact, Thomson looked upon the act as a advantage because it indicated public support for the new industry, and he felt that he could have it amended to in- clude protections for the Canton mill. At his request, writes Smathers, "I secured an amendment in the act through Mr. D. L. Boyd, then member of the House for Haywood County, during the year 1907." Chapter 298, Public Laws of 1907, amended the original act by deleting the section specifying waters below the mouth of Jonathan Creek with the Pigeon, substituting the following: ". . . that this act shall only ap- ply to factories or plants, erected, in course of erection, or maintained for the purposes aforesaid, in the county of Haywood, and only on Pi- geon River below the forks of the river, near the Plott Mill at the J. A. Blaylock place, and not elsewhere in said county, or State of North

Carolina." This, of course, embraced the Canton mill of the Champion Fibre Company.

The amended act still did not release Thomson and his company from liability in the damage landowners below Canton might sustain because of the pollution, but only prescribed a method of procedure that prevented injunctions or other legal means that might curtail production. Thomson and his legal advisers therefore felt it wise to secure agreements from all the landowners on the Pigeon River between Canton and the mouth of Jonathan Creek "releasing," wrote Smathers, "Mr. Thomson and his heirs and assigns from damages on account of the pollution of the waters of the Pigeon." One or two parties protested, and settlements were made; Mary Ann Patton refused to sign the release, but stated that if no harm was done to her property, she would never sue, and she never did.[14]

These agreements took care of much of the approximately twenty-six miles of North Carolina through which the polluted Pigeon would flow, but they did nothing about the situation when the river crossed the line into Tennessee. In 1937 Smathers explained how Tennessee was managed:

> I will state that during or about the year 1908 and later dates, the General Assembly of Tennessee introduced acts, authorizing the Attorney-General of Tennessee to bring a suit against the Champion Fibre Co., for damages, and to enjoin it from further pollution of the waters of Pigeon River, which resulted in Mr. Robertson's, who was then General Manager of the Champion Fibre Co., employing Mr. William McSwain, prominent Attorney-at-Law at Newport, Tennessee, to defeat such acts, which he succeeded in doing, and no further action has been taken by the State of Tennessee in reference to this matter.[15]

Thomson eventually purchased 192 acres at Canton and acquired nearly 400,000 acres of virgin timber—mostly spruce but including chestnut and other pulpwoods—in the Smoky Mountains. In time, Thomson's firm developed or purchased (and then, when they were no longer useful, let die) such lumber camps as Sunburst, Crestmont, Ravensford, and Smokemont, all within an economically feasible radius of the Canton plant. He also gained legal access to the clear, pure waters of the Pigeon River. The Southern Railroad set about digging a 1,780-foot cut from the Pigeon River through the hamlet of Canton. This railway would enable it to handle the fifty or more cars of pulp a day projected to be produced by the mill.[16]

Ground was broken in 1906 for the fiber mill. It was designed to furnish 200–250 tons of hardwood pulp a day to Champion's paper mill at Hamilton, Ohio. Twelve hundred laborers were hired to push the mill to rapid completion. Incentives were offered to hurry along construction, especially after the "banker's panic" of 1907—a brief depression that resulted, ultimately, in creation of the Federal Reserve System. The panic forced the company to lay off three hundred workers temporarily. For a brief period, Thomson, who had made expensive improvements at his Hamilton, Ohio, plant and had just finished building a million-dollar mansion for himself, was plunged into financial straits by the panic; he was finally saved by selling preferred stock in the Canton plant to Proctor and Gamble interests in Cincinnati. It was claimed that two million dollars went into construction of thirty-six concrete, steel, and brick structures. This "mammoth plant"—it was probably the largest wood fiber plant in the world when it went on line in 1908—is difficult to visualize today.[7]

Electrical energy and technology have markedly reduced the size of industrial machinery over the past century, even as more of any given product has been produced. For safety reasons, much of the energy that in 1908 was exposed in whirling flywheels and long belting is no longer visible.

Initially, the Canton facility's boiler room—two stories high with thick brick walls, reinforced concrete floors, and a concrete roof with steel trusses—contained a coal bunker capable of holding ten thousand tons feeding ten batteries of boilers each producing 632 horsepower. The reclaiming room contained a battery of twelve bleaching cells, liquor tanks, five huge boilers, and five rotary furnaces. Each building having to do with shipping and receiving was connected by railroad tracks that totaled "about a mile and a half of track trestle, and about the same surface trackage."[18]

The most prominent local newspaper, the *Asheville Citizen,* provided surprisingly little information on the mill. The newspaper did comment briefly on the ten million bricks, the fifty thousand barrels of cement, the four thousand railroad cars of materials, and the necessity of importing laborers from outside western North Carolina to build the plant. The newspaper editorialized that Canton was "now the home of one of the most striking examples of the phenomenal growth of the South."[19]

Probably Champion's fiber mill became operational in stages, which explains the several dates given for that event. *Paper Trade Journal* announced that the mill was operational as of January 13, 1908; other sources placed the date as late as March 10. Whenever it did go on line, the forty-five to fifty million gallons of Pigeon River water that flowed into the mill fresh, clear, and clean flowed out at the pipe a warm, foamy, colored, stinking mess—a mess far worse than the effluent discharged today. Did anyone protest? In Haywood County, where its citizens were profiting from the new industry, the answer appears to have been a resounding no. Certainly, no legal or governmental action was instigated. The *Asheville Citizen* ran just one minute comment about the transformation of the sparkling Pigeon into an industrial sewer: "A fish story worth mentioning comes from Clyde this morning. It is that the sight of enormous blue suckers, bass, and other desirable finny game, which was driven to the edge of the water by a combination of the deposit from the Canton mill and the warm day, was too much for the small boy on his way to Sunday School. The large fish could actually be caught with the hands. Surely it was a case of the ox being in the ditch on the Sabbath?"[20]

The real surprise is the failure of any of the newspapers in the region, and especially in Newport, Tennessee, to protest the death of the river. From the vantage point of eighty-six years, all that can be surmised is that, in so sparsely settled a region, the attitude was that there were plenty of other streams in the mountains and that they were paying good wages at the Champion mill. Many Cocke County inhabitants had relatives who took employment at the plant, and, in this depressed region, the wages were incredibly good. Perhaps there was at first an attitude of helplessness—a belief that nothing could be done about it. It took two or three years for a weak opposition to coalesce. Moreover, as Smathers later pointed out, a prominent Newport attorney was on retainer to quash any political attempt by Tennessee to restrict the pollution.

At least one person was able to reminisce about the Pigeon River before and after the mill went into operation. This was ninety-seven-year-old Charles C. "Cromer" Chambers, who was interviewed on February 6, 1984, and has since died. Mr. Chambers was born in 1887 just west of Clyde, North Carolina. The old man's memories carried him back to the glorious days of a mountain boyhood when being a lad with tan cheeks who carried a willow pole fishing rod and was ready to jump into the river at the snap of a finger was still an American reality—at least in southern Appalachia.

"From April to November I swam every day," he reminisced. "You could just drink out of the Pigeon River as you would drink out of a spring now." He recalled the clearness of the stream: "Anywhere along that river you could see anything at the bottom just as clear as crystal—even water six, eight, or ten feet deep." Ten or fifteen country boys "just lived in the river during the summertime," the old man said. "Half the nights too. Half the time." Chambers waxed nostalgically about the swimming, about the diving board they rigged with waste wood from the big lumberyard at Clyde, and about the way they could take his mother's washtub, turn it upside down, pick up a heavy rock, jump in, and walk along the river bottom for a couple of minutes until the air pocket under the tub was used up. Chambers also told stories about the fishing. "Fish all the time. I could count twelve different kinds of fish that lived in that river. Sunfish, perch, bass, trout, hog suckers, horny ears, mullets—a bunch of different kinds." Then times changed.

"I was about nineteen years old when they started to build that papermill there in Canton. . . . It never ran a week until there wasn't a fish in that river. That was the last you saw of them." The old man remembered the sight vividly:

> It was terrible. When they first turned that water on it was as black as tar, and the suds [foam] were three feet deep all the way down that river. When they turned that dad gumed stuff in there they cleaned the fish out of the river. Got them in just one day. You could go to the branches [brooks] and creeks that empty into the Pigeon and there would be fish everywhere, stuck up trying to get a little clear water. Anywhere they could find clear water they were there trying to get it. . . .
>
> That river turned just as black as molasses. Even the mud turtles couldn't live in that water. There used to be hundreds of those old muskrats and now there's none. People hollered awful about what they did to the river. They ruined all the swimming; everything. You couldn't go into the darn stuff at all. They never did even say what would happen to the water before they turned the mill on.
>
> They didn't say anything about it until it was all over.[21]

As far as Champion was concerned, the mill was a resounding success. In the early years of the century, the paper business, including Champion, was making huge profits. A paper trust pretty well set prices in those days. In 1908 the cost per ton of paper to the public went up twelve dollars. Along with its massive purchases of prime forest land in the vicinity of Canton, Champion's investment was substantial; the company was definitely in the Pigeon River country to stay.[22]

Thomson was also building an extract plant. The extract was chestnut tannin; as much as five million pounds a month of it were produced by Champion in the early years. Chestnut trees were being devastated by an Asian fungus, but for years the dead timbers were harvested for pulp and

Charles "Cromer" Chambers in September 1983. His reminiscences at the age of ninety-seven of his boyhood along the Pigeon River prior to its destruction by Champion are among the best available. Courtesy Jim Harrison.

their tannin content. Much of the tannin was sold to the A. C. Lawrence Company, a leather processor, which had a plant in Waynesville.[23]

Peter G. Thomson continued to run his company from his headquarters at Hamilton, Ohio, and he saw it continue to grow. "He was never satisfied with things as they were . . . when a thing was done well he immediately set about trying to do it better," commented *Paper Trade Journal*. "The result was that time and time again great and radical changes were made at Champion's Hamilton and Canton plants—but these changes had been studied with such care that invariably they meant increased production at a lower cost. . . . He ranked among the captains of industry who have led this machine age forward and forward to new triumphs."[24]

The Champion mill at Canton did not bring cash just into the Pigeon River valley. Timber was purchased from private stands, coal and lime were purchased from Tennessee, and sulphur was bought from Louisiana and alkali from Virginia. When World War I cut the chlo-

Champion Fibre Plant, ca. 1920. Then even more than today it was the economic lifeblood of the region. Courtesy Canton Area Historical Museum.

rine supply, Thomson built his own chlorine plant on the Canton premises and sold his surplus to other manufacturers.[25]

The Canton plant was considered one of Thomson's major achievements. As a eulogist pointed out in 1931: "Canton, when the fiber company was started was a little mountain town of 400 people—now it has a population of 6,000 with a YMCA, churches, schools, a good hotel, and an admirable country club. It is an industrial town in which North Carolina takes great pride, but as a matter of fact it stands as a monument to the enterprise and foresight of Peter G. Thomson. But for him Canton would still be a mere hamlet instead of a flourishing little city. As an employer he was described as 'both just and generous.'"[26]

His wage scale included automatic raises every five years; he established a free medical clinic for his workers and free life insurance; when the cost of living was climbing, he built a well-stocked commissary where food and various household supplies were sold at cost. Company scrip was also issued, but it was not used for exploitive purposes. "His plants are visited frequently by the representatives of other large industries who come to see how these humanitarian features work out," the eulogist noted. Canton employees sent to his funeral a blanket of pink rosebuds, one for each Canton employee.[27]

Geo. Smathers once asked Thomson why he bothered building pulp and extract mills when he was already a rich man. "To which he replied," Smathers reminisced, "that he didn't think I took the right position in the matter, as he thought that no man who had wealth should lay down and live an easy life, and that the man who had accumulated wealth had accumulated the same either directly or indirectly by the labor of other people. . . . He believed the construction of the pulp mill and extract plants at Canton would prove a great blessing to the people of Haywood County and Western N.C. in that, it [they] would . . . give employment to people who were out of work and wanted to make an honest living."[28]

And what did local business people—the establishment, as it is sometimes called today—think of Thomson? Geo. Smathers was perhaps typical (although it is true he worked for Thomson), and here is what he wrote in 1937 of Thomson's accomplishment:

> In going from Canton for a distance, say, of 100 miles either east, west, north, or south, on the Southern Railroad or the highways, you will find pulp and acid wood piled up at all railroad stations and along the highways about three-fourths of which is shipped to the Champion Fibre Co. at Canton. Parties who own small tracts of land, when they need money to pay taxes with or to buy groceries and supplies, can go out and cut a lot of dead chestnut and convert the same into acid wood that could not be sold to anyone else and sell or ship the same to the Champion Fibre Co. and realize money on it for the payment of taxes, and for purchase of groceries and other supplies. Hence I say that the construction of the plants at Canton has provided a better market for wood products in Western N.C., and either directly or indirectly given employment to more labor and provided greater blessing to the people of the State than any other enterprise in the State, and the officials and employees of the Champion Fibre Co. have a right to feel proud of the fact that they have contributed so much to the support and welfare of the people of the State of North Carolina.[29]

Pollution of the air and water was not even considered a drawback.

Reuben B. Robertson's Years at Canton

Thomson died in 1931 and was survived by three sons and two daughters. One son, Alexander, became a Champion vice-president; his youngest son, Logan, was president from 1935 until his death in 1945 (Lake Logan is named in his honor), and two sons-in-law achieved entrepreneurial status within the company. The son-in-law who rose highest and was most affiliated with the Canton operation was Reuben Buck Robertson; he married Thomson's daughter Hope.[30]

Born in Cincinnati in 1879 and graduated from Yale in 1900, Robertson studied law at the University of Cincinnati and was admitted to the Ohio bar in 1903. By 1907 he was assigned by his father-in-law to the Canton plant then under construction; when it became operational, he was made its general manager. Robertson rose steadily in the Champion constellation: he was a vice-president of Champion Fibre from 1918 until 1925 and its president until 1935. When the companies merged as Champion Paper and Fibre Company in 1935, he became executive vice-president; he was president from 1946 to 1950, and chairman of the board from 1950 to 1960. He died in 1972.[31]

Regardless of his obligations to the larger Champion Corporation, Reuben Robertson chose to live and raise his family in Asheville. He loved the southern Appalachians and their people. His portrait reveals a handsome, decent man with a slightly cherubic face. He must have loved people because Robertson was a joiner: his civic consciousness and organizational talents led him to be chosen head of Asheville's Community Chest, president of the North Carolina Forestry Association, chairman of the Southern Conference [on] Human Relations in Industry, chairman of the Board of Trustees of Western Carolina Teachers College (now Western Carolina University), trustee of the University of North Carolina, and so on. He was selected "Man of the South" for 1951. The list of his appointments to paper trade and industrial organizations is equally impressive.[32]

Robertson is warmly remembered by Canton's longtime employees and their families. He continued many of his father-in-law's humanitarian policies and built the splendid YMCA building at Canton (which is now closed). He represented the epitome of late-nineteenth- and early-twentieth-century industrial paternalism. A Champion employee's family struck by tragedy was likely to receive some largess from the company, which in Canton meant that it would come from Robertson. His philanthropy extended to scholarships, aid to local groups trying to raise money for worthy causes, financial aid to the town of Canton, its schools, and its infrastructure. His generosity and helpfulness were considered genuine.

He was one of that rare breed of businessmen who could be found in the factory talking shop with his employees, and he was not superficial about it, but talked and listened with knowledge and concern. Old-timers insist that Robertson let it be known that his office door was open to

Champion President Reuben Robertson was popular with the company's employees. Here he and associates are holding a scroll listing the names of Champion scholarship recipients, ca. 1950. Robertson is third from left. Courtesy Canton Area Historical Museum.

any employee who had something to say, good or bad, and the employees insist that the story of this open-door policy was true, not a legend that has grown with time.[33]

Champion's commitment to and investment in the local community has been long standing and not limited to the actions of executives like Robertson. When Canton suffered from a typhoid epidemic in 1915–16, it was Champion that bought the Episcopal school and converted it into a hospital. Besides helping out in short-term emergencies, the company helped plan for its workers' futures: Robertson continued Thomson's policy of training employees and ensuring their competence with new technologies. This policy of continuing training has been maintained to this day.

When the mill opened in 1908, the company built sixty small dwellings to house some of the laborers. Known as Fibreville, some of the abandoned structures existed until 1991. In the early 1920s, Champion invested sixty-five thousand dollars in Canton property, which was then sold, on very easy terms, to employees through a Home Builders Improvement Plan, a kind of company-run savings and loan. Borrowers repaid their mortgages on a monthly basis. By the end of the decade, about 35 percent of Champion's employees owned their own homes. The *Log of Champion Activities,* the local company journal, ran photographs of some of the houses built and financed by employees with the Champion plan. (It also ran photographs of employees' newborn babies.)

Employees' children were offered vacation days at Camp Hope, up the Pigeon River. The name was in honor of Robertson's wife, who, among other accomplishments, formed Canton's parent-teacher association. Retirees were given the premises of an old house in Canton where they could meet, play cards, drink coffee, and reminisce; it was named Snug Harbor. When it was dedicated on January 25, 1953, Robertson, who had come down from headquarters at Hamilton, gave the retirees' president a mammoth key to the building. In the *Log* for September 1940 is a photograph of the Champion Old-Timers' baseball team. One among them is dressed just slightly differently from the others; wearing a baseball cap and obviously a welcome part of the camaraderie is Reuben B. Robertson.[34]

All this paternalism does not answer the question of the company's attitude toward labor with regard to working hours and conditions, wages, grievances, etc. Generally, throughout its nine decades at Canton, labor relations have been good at Champion. This is not to say that jurisdictional disputes between unions or conflicts over the use of outside artisans to do electrical or pipe-fitting work have not occasionally flared up. The one major labor dispute was in 1924 when the Canton plant was shut down for almost a month because of a union organizing campaign. Management resisted and broke the union's attempt; not until 1965, by which time the Thomson family was no longer active in the corporation, did the plant become unionized—without much company opposition.[35] (Parenthetically, it is worth noting that, in reporting on the termination of the strike, the *Newport Plain Talk* observed on February 29, 1924, that "during the time the mill has been closed Pigeon River began to clear up and was taking on its old-time color, resulting in much comment.")

It was said that Reuben Robertson liked to drive up to Lake Logan and "just sit and whittle." Certainly he was a good businessman. He is credited with being the first paper company executive to start a tree farm, which he undertook in his early years at the Canton mill. "As a result," according to his obituary in the *New York Times,* "the third southern pine crop is being harvested." He is also credited with using the three million dollars the company realized from its sale of woodlands to the federal gov-

Champion plant and much of Canton in the 1950s. Courtesy Canton Area Historical Museum.

ernment for Smoky Mountain National Park toward furthering the research of Charles Holmes Herty. Herty, a chemist, developed the technology for making the southern pine a viable raw material for papermaking.[36]

Yet, for all this deserved adulation, Robertson, like Thomson, was a tough businessman. It was Robertson who hired a Newport attorney to stifle any protests about pollution of the Pigeon River in Tennessee. His dealings with the federal government over purchase of Champion timberlands in the region projected for Great Smoky Mountains National Park reveal a negotiator loyal first to his company. Champion initially asked an impossible sum for its acreage; years after a deal had been made, a lawyer was disbarred for having accepted a bribe from Champion or someone affiliated with Champion's cause while negotiations were proceeding. The claim is still made that, once the sale was the made, the company clear-cut much of the land as fast as it could, with no thought of sustained yield or damage to what had been a virgin forest. When Wilma Dykeman, an authority on the region and Tennessee's state historian, interviewed Robertson more than thirty years ago and asked him about cleaning up the Pigeon, his reply was that the stockholders came first, and Champion would not act until it had to.[37]

No corporation has had as much impact upon western North Carolina as has Champion, and it would be a distortion to assume that controversy involving the mill's pollution has not erupted from time to time. But Michael Frome, author of *Strangers in High Places,* does not make a scoundrel of Robertson. After talking with him, Frome felt that Robertson "plainly felt he could share in celebrating the preservation of the Smoky Mountain Forests."[38]

One cannot help being impressed by such outstanding paper industry entrepreneurs as Thomson and Robertson. They developed enormous smokestack industries, exploited raw materials, and gave employment to thousands of people. On the other hand, their business acumen often bordered on the unethical. Always there was that blind spot: pollution. Rarely do we read about it; it was the great unmentionable. And that blind spot continued into the 1960s, when environmentalists began to protest the stinking emissions from industry chimneys and the obnoxious, toxic effluents being poured into the nation's rivers.

Champion officials soon discovered that Peter Thomson's choice of Canton for his fiber mill was extremely wise except for one deficiency. On the plus side, not only had he purchased some of the finest pulpwood—especially spruce—forests in the nation, but also he had a willing and complacent work force at hand. Mountaineers who liked regular hours working for a paternalistic company could take employment at the plant. Independent mountaineers who did not want to press a time card could cut timber on their own acreage and sell it to the mill, or they could take employment cutting Champion's own forests. The Southern Railroad provided good transportation. Suppliers from as far away as Virginia and Louisiana supplied everything from felting to boilers to this big corporate customer in the South that paid its bills on time. On the minus side was one serious problem: the river. The Pigeon could not absorb the pollution, and on occasion, generally at the end of a dry summer, the river did not even supply enough water to run the mill.

This situation did not, however, deter Champion officials from steadily increasing the Canton mill's production. Although it was initially built as a fiber mill to service the Hamilton facility, the economic practicality of carrying the fiber process on through paperboard and paper manufacturing right at Canton was not lost on Thomson and Robertson. The beginning of paper manufacture brought the use of chlorine, a chemical element that has always been known to be dangerous. It is now known to combine with other compounds, especially organic ones, to form toxic or carcinogenic compounds. Steadily the plant expanded production.[39]

By 1921 (some sources say 1922), with a process whereby not just kraft quality papers but book quality papers as well could be manufactured from the available wood supply of southern pine, Champion installed the first book paper mill in the South at Canton. As a company promotional pamphlet puts it, "Champion . . . perfected a means of making from pine wood the kind of smooth, white paper for which the company is noted, the kind of paper that Peter G. Thomson had visualized years before."[40]

The Canton facility was one of the principal paper providers for *Life* magazine in its heyday. At present, the plant produces bleached paperboard for an estimated one-third of all the milk cartons and half the juice cartons used in the United States. In addition, the Canton plant produces "uncoated free sheet printing papers," business papers, and envelope papers. Four enormous paper machines have an annual capacity of 255,900 tons of uncoated paper and 284,300 tons of bleached paperboard. The mill produces 14 grades of paper; each has a trademark, such as Champion Bond, Dairy Pak, Chamfold Opaque, and Keystone Poster. In 1992 the company employed 1,714 men and women at Canton and another 251 at the Waynesville facility; with the modernization program, employment was down to about 1,650 by October 1993, and it will probably bottom out at about 1,450.[41]

Through the years, other changes have taken place at Champion. The death in March 1960 of Reuben B. Robertson Jr., who had succeeded his father as head of the company, marked the decline of the Thomson-Robertson control of Champion Paper Corporation. From then on, it became a corporate behemoth. Employees recognized the changes gradually: much of the paternalism disappeared, and today the Robertson YMCA, opened in 1965, is closed. The old Snug Harbor house is no more. Employees increasingly realize that they are just a small part of another huge international conglomerate. This does not mean they will not fight for their jobs, but that is not exactly the same, they will tell you, as standing up for Champion. The changes at Champion are reflected in its name changes over the years. In 1935 the name was changed from the Champion Coated Paper Company and the Champion Fibre Company to the Champion Paper and Fibre Company; still later, it became Champion Papers, Inc., and finally Champion International Corporation.

Another aspect of change at Champion has been the company's long-standing interest in innovation and research in the papermaking industry. The company is proud of its research department, which was organized in 1927. Its Technical Center since 1962 has been located in West Nyack, New York. A descriptive brochure of the facility begins by explaining the center's role in providing "technical information and services that Champion requires to maintain its competitive posture in products and processes." It strives "to improve the quality and cost effectiveness of our existing paper grades, . . . to introduce into our mills the most cost effective materials, and to provide the technical input . . . for the purpose of lowering cost or improving quality." A pilot paper plant is maintained "to realistically test our ideas on a small scale."[42]

Environmental technology is not emphasized. It breaks into the brochure as a result of a consent order invoked in litigation involving Champion's Pensacola plant. "Members of the environmental technology team," the brochure says, "will describe efforts to reduce the cost and increase the effectiveness of effluent color reduction technologies." Certainly any major breakthroughs in color reduction would quickly be applied at the Canton mill.[43]

Champion is rightfully proud of its new Ultratrace Organic Analytical Laboratory, which opened in West Nyack in 1990. It was "specifically designed and built for dioxin analysis at a cost of $2.2 million." The laboratory routinely analyzes "pulp, food board, sludge, aqueous and fish samples from all Champion mills. . . ." It is a state-of-the-art facility, as the description makes clear: "The current detection levels are 1 ppt (parts per trillion) for solid and 5 ppq (parts per quadrillion) for aqueous samples. To give an analogy, 1 ppt is one second in 32,000 years and ppq is one second in 32 million years. All ultratrace dioxin analysis methods stipulate sample specific compounds of large sample size, several clean-up steps to remove interfering compounds and a high resolution gas chromatography/mass spectrometry analysis."[44]

In 1958 Champion acquired a Brazilian paper company in the state of São Paulo; today, it is a profitable part of the corporation. Champion also owns 84.6 percent of Weldwood of Canada. In the 1970s the company expanded rapidly, and it diversified and became a conglomerate. As early as 1937, it had merged with U.S. Plywood; in 1968 it merged with Arrow Transportation and Drexel Enterprises. Such acquisitions continued in 1984 when, at a cost of $1.6 billion, Champion acquired the St. Regis Paper Company in a leveraged buyout; Champion then became the nation's largest forest products company.

As early as 1984, Champion's CEO, Andrew C. Sigler, observed that many of the companies that Champion had purchased were not earning sufficient revenues to warrant ownership. He therefore began a

policy of divestiture, disposing of eighteen companies in a two-year period. Sigler's aim was for Champion International to become a leader
in three main areas: paper products, building products, and packaging
materials. Even with such consolidation, it is difficult to comprehend the
massiveness of a corporation that, as of 1992, owns more than 6,400,000
acres of timberland in the United States and Canada and in addition has
landholdings in Brazil. Champion has mineral, oil, and gas rights on
3,324,000 acres, of which about 914,000 acres are in the Southeast. It
also owns or controls an estimated 740 million tons of lignite coal reserves
in Texas, 30 million tons in Alabama, and 100 million tons in Kentucky; in
these states, an estimated 80 percent of the coal is recoverable.[45]

A brief profile of Sigler in the *New York Times* portrays a man capable of taking a long view, a man who can see beyond the next quarterly dividend. Yet, in the late 1980s, a lot of things went sour with
Champion International, and investors have worried about its small earnings. In 1989 and 1990, Wall Street raiders Warren Buffet, Laurence Tisch,
and John M. Templeton purchased hundreds of thousands of shares of
Champion stock, raising fears of an impending takeover.[46]

Champion's Policies Today

There can be no doubt about it: Peter G. Thomson was a successful
late-nineteenth-century tycoon, a man of considerable vision with the
courage and ability to forge ahead successfully. Certainly, the large size of
his industry did not frighten him. His son-in-law Reuben B. Robertson
carried on Thomson's policies. He was an innovator, cultivated good labor relations, and made useful contacts with the politically powerful in
North Carolina. During much of its history, Champion has been a pace-
maker in developing new technology and adapting state-of-the-art procedures in its huge mills. It has manufactured or marketed such byproducts
as tannin, tall oil, and caustic soda in liquid form for other manufacturers;
it has produced turpentine, printers' ink, and insecticides; it has sold surplus chlorine.

When Champion lost the Thomson-Robertson leadership, the corporation adapted more closely the policies and procedures of mainstream
American businesses. Soon it was acquiring other corporations, the bottom line was stressed as never before, and paternalism toward employees faded. But Champion still ranks as a good employer: it pays well,
has an excellent safety record, and provides numerous fringe benefits.
Andrew Sigler is active in the Forest History Society and the Business

Round Table, an organization not yet thirty years old that grapples with the problems of big business in American society. In a speech given to the Third National Consultation on Corporate Ethics in 1988, Sigler underscored "Acceptable Behavior." He emphasized ethical behavior with employees and suppliers, and then said about local communities: "With a company like ours, if we're in town, everybody knows we're there. We're a very big factor in the area. And if you don't deal with all of the community issues, the environmental issues, etc., in a straight up acceptable way, you won't exist for long. The community will make sure that you either change, or you're put out of business. So good ethical values, acceptable values, are an essential ingredient of good business."[47]

On paper Champion professes loyal adherence to Sigler's expressed philosophy. In a one-page statement the company summarizes the "Champion Way." Most of its aims show concern for its work force: "We are committed to providing equality of opportunity for all people, regardless of race, national origin, sex, age, or religion. We actively seek a talented, diverse, enthusiastic work force." Moreover, "Champion wants to be known for its interest in and support of the communities in which employees live and work. . . . Champion wants to be known as a company which strives . . . to use and dispose of materials with scrupulous regard for safety and health. We take particular pride in this company's record of compliance with the spirit as well as the letter of all environmental regulations." How close does Champion come to achieving its expressed standards?

A cynic might call the "Champion Way" a mass of glittering generalities, yet in many ways Champion lives up to its corporate philosophy. Pay is very good at Champion. Champion dispenses funds for good causes. When Waynesville has a street fair, the paperboard waste containers are "Courtesy Champion International." Ironically, the corporation gave more than seven hundred and fifty thousand dollars to the 1992 United States Canoe and Kayak Team, a sport that implies the use of clean water.

Cynicism enters with Champion's statement about taking "pride in the company's record of compliance with *the spirit* as well as the letter of all environmental regulations" (italics mine). The company, along with other members of the pulp and paper industry, assumes a defensive, almost fortresslike mentality toward any and all attacks upon its effluents. "We are doing all we can," they all say. "The technology does not exist to do more." In the fall of 1983, according to *Paper Trade Journal*, Sigler made a speech in New York City in which he expressed doubt that American business would be spending millions of dollars to clean up the environment if it were not for government regulations. "There's no way that any single company could deal with these issues . . . could maintain a competitive position and do that." When corporation moguls feel that environmentalists have driven them to the wall, they have reacted by fighting back. The story of Champion's pollution of the Pigeon River is but one example of many throughout the nation.[48]

It is almost accurate to say that the industry's reply to criticisms about smokestack effluents or liquid discharges are met with innocent-sounding questions—"Pollution? What pollution?"—just as employees react when questioned by visitors about the odor and effluents. A key to understanding the industry attitude is contained in Sigler's statement in a *New York Times* article. He refers to Champion as a "smokestack industry." Elsewhere he describes it as a "process company." Implicit in the statements is a recognition that the paper industry is a polluter—always has been and always will be. To pulp and papermakers, stench and pollution are as much a part of the industry as hamburgers are to fast-food restaurants. And so the blind spot continues. The industry's relatively good labor record, high marks for community support, excellence of products and safety count for nothing when it comes to pollution.

But forces beyond the companies' power to control are forcing a change in attitude. A nation with a population of 250 million and growing has less space, less air, less water, less land, and less permissiveness to dispense. The companies, including Champion, are learning that not even politics, PACs, high-powered public relations agencies, and expensive lawyers can prevent an inexorable movement toward clean air and clean water. The more enlightened companies are facing the issue. Is Champion one of them?

CHAPTER 3

Pollution at Will
The First Seven Decades of the Canton Mill

W hen Champion's Canton plant went on line early in 1908 perhaps the milieu of the times—a world of offensive odors, poor hygiene, the excrement of horses, billions of flies, muddy or dusty streets and roads—allowed the company to befoul the air and destroy the waters of the Pigeon River with no serious opposition. Sparse population contributed to the indifference. The reality of good wages and steady employment were obvious factors. An item in the *Newport Plain Talk* noted that "the effect of the use of the Big Pigeon [as it was called locally at that time] by the fiber company can be felt nearly or quite to Knoxville." Yet no mass outpouring of protest took place. Pollution that was accepted in the early twentieth century would today have people protesting in the streets.[1]

The Economics and Politics of Pollution

Throughout most of the industrial age, entrepreneurs—for the most part intelligent, educated men—have accepted pollution as a concomitant of business. According to their economic theories pollution had plenty of justification. To Peter Thomson and Reuben Robertson, the economic and social good of a pulp and paper mill so heavily outweighed the environmental bad effects that there was no contest. However, according to Robert Heilbroner, "Nowadays, even the staunchest supporters of [Adam] Smith's vision agree that the effects of private economic effort are not always in the public interest. Economists," he writes, "speak of 'bads' that emerge along with the 'goods' from the system of output, such as the smoke that accompanies a flow of production." And he states further: "The difference between bads and goods lies in the failure of market systems to count the full costs of producing things, such as the higher health or laundry costs imposed on those who live in the vicinity of the smoking factory. Thus, the system's heralded efficiency is in part the consequence of fobbing off the cost of bads onto the hapless public, instead of billing the guilty producer for them. . . ."[2]

Vice-President Al Gore expresses similar thoughts in his overview of the environmental crisis, *Earth in the Balance.* He describes our economic system as being "partially blind." It sees its products and its bottom line—its profit and loss—but is blind to things "harder to buy and sell: fresh water, clean air, the beauty of the mountains. . . ." In its financial ledgers, there is no category for the loss of income to people living downstream by a factory-polluted river, or for the loss of topsoil year by year due to poor agricultural practices. So mercenary are some companies that decisions about pollution control depend upon their best judgment as to whether the environmental movement is here to stay or will soon fade away. Vice-President Gore cites paper companies that hesitate to build recycling plants because they are not sure the pressure to do so will be sustained.[3]

This is not to say that paper companies have not had to deal with an occasional irate citizenry. Through the years these companies have faced costly litigation, and Champion is no exception. Most often, the plaintiffs have insisted that the effluents constitute a public nuisance. In defending themselves, the companies have resorted to science, especially to chemistry, to help them identify what constitutes an acceptable smokestack discharge or an acceptable waterway. To the layman, if a smokestack does not belch a heavy or odorous discharge it probably releases an acceptable level of effluents into the atmosphere; if a stream flows cool and clear and the water is potable, it is considered a clean river. But for legal and regulatory purposes, such simple criteria are unacceptable. If there is pollution, industries have asked (never openly admitting that pollution even exists), then what level of pollution is acceptable? Just how much chloroform, furans, ammonia, dioxins, color, foam, and odor will be acceptable to society? Stipulate the tolerable amount, the industry has said, and we will try to achieve that limit.

In order to set limits, criteria must be established; there must be gradations of the various types of pollution. Color, therefore, is rated by aluminum cobalt color units—that the stream flows black or brown is not a sufficient criterion. In reality, it is still more complicated. "True" color is the measure after the turbidity of the water has been removed; "apparent" color is the measurement including substances in solution or as suspended matter. In the story of the Pigeon River, the criterion of 50 aluminum cobalt color units will be discussed repeatedly. Once measures of coloration have been determined, the company suggests a "reasonable" color standard under which it can continue to operate (here is where companies have traditionally complained and propagandized, always requesting very high color limits on the grounds that they can do no better).

The same logic applies to the temperature of the liquid leaving at the pipe, a mile downstream, or at a state boundary: once temperatures have been classified, the company can then argue for a temperature that the company can comply with. Dissolved oxygen also flows into the river from the company, so again the water is tested at given places at given times, and the company brings about a compromise by determining how much the company can abide by. Chloroform, ammonia, furans, dioxins, and other chemicals are in the water. Their quantities are measured down to the trillionths if necessary, then a limit is fixed that the company cannot exceed. Once such limits are established by a state water quality bureau or the Environmental Protection Agency, the company can pollute and still adhere to regulations.

Always, and for the most obvious reasons, the company uses its lawyers and lobbyists to influence state legislatures, regulatory agencies, and the federal government for leniency—regulations it can live with—always insisting that it cannot do more. For the paper industry, the refrain is always the same: when a new, less polluting method for producing paper is discovered, the company will adopt it. A convenient catch 22 situation is created: the company, aware of public pressure to control pollution, lobbies and gets the most lenient regulations; when the pollution is protested, the company insists that it has abided by all the rules and regulations. And it has.

Through the 1960s Champion assumed a stance of arrogance and hauteur approaching, says Paul Davis, Tennessee's director of Water Quality Control, a "fortress mentality." A trickle of letters to the company protesting the pollution was a constant, an accepted part of doing the paper business. People who wrote Champion relate how their letters were seldom answered. The company, if it did reply, did so probably with a form letter politely explaining that it was doing all it could to clean up the mess. Meanwhile, although faced with the reality of a water source that was not sufficient to clean itself when the plant effluent poured back into the stream, Champion went right on increasing its production at Canton—which elevated the level of pollution. Certainly this policy of expansion indicates a callousness toward defilement of the Pigeon River and the situation of those living along its banks all the way to its junction with the French Broad.[4]

That the pulp and paper trade, subject as it is to taxation and regulation, would be politically active is to be expected. Indeed, the industry has constantly worked the politicians to protect its interests. Much of this lobbying is above board; it is generally accepted as the American way of doing things and can be documented. Thus, supplying fish for a fish fry at a get-together of North Carolina legislators or entertaining then Vice-President George Bush at Lake Logan are widely known events and are passed off as part of the corporate scene. A little less acceptable is the way three or four lobbyists, usually lawyers, make appointments, which are nearly always granted, with a governor, legislator, representative, or senator, and they make their pitch for or against (usually against) pending legislation. Unmentioned but obvious are threats that if the Honorable Whatever-His-Name does not support the industry's position, the industry will not support him for re-election. Nor is any secret made of the fact that a company gives campaign funds to friendly legislators, governors, congressmen, and senators. Again, this is a part of modern corporate life. The payoff comes when pending legislation is killed, or, conversely, when a regulatory agency gets too strict, in the company's view. The word comes down from Washington or from the state capitol—and strangely, a change takes place in a regulatory commission's attitude.

The extent to which Champion has played the political game is apparent to anyone who has observed the parade of politicians who have appeared at the regulatory hearings. That a local congressman, both of North Carolina's United States senators or their surrogates, the governor, and the local state legislator would consider it expedient to appear at out-of-the-way Asheville in January 1988 to make a pro-company statement at an EPA-sponsored hearing in spite of their busy agendas is no surprise to the student of realpolitik.

Unfortunately, we cannot enter the boardrooms of the big paper companies. We can only surmise at the gist of the conversations between the CEO and his associates. We can observe the results of their discussions, such as threats to close the mill, press releases insisting that the technology does not exist to abide by a given regulation, legal campaign funds allotted to bring a politician or two onto the industry side, the hiring of a high-voltage public relations firm to frighten employees and coerce the EPA or a governor or a state regulatory agency. We can observe what is done; we can understand the rationale, but much of the factual material is denied us.

Such is the corporate side. What about the local, state, and federal governments? Why have they succumbed to the most flagrant, transparent lobbying activities? The answer is for the most part obvious, but historically much of the story has been forgotten.

Governor Hooper's Response

Take Tennessee's government from the time the Canton plant went on line in 1908 into the 1970s. A large portion of the Volunteer State's electorate has always been politically active; its politicians have been hyperactive, and many of them have been corrupt. Memphis had its Boss Crump, and most Tennessee counties have had their political machines. In the first twenty or thirty years of this century, Tennessee's government was heavily blemished, placing it in company with many other state governments. The Republican and Democratic machines brought out the voters, but many of the politicians they elected were not only dishonest but widely known to be. One historian of Tennessee describes the period from 1900 to 1920 as one in which "there was an amazing restlessness and dissatisfaction in some social and political and industrial matters which at times bade fair to lead to conditions akin to chaos." We now know that during these years, Champion had a prominent Newport attorney on retainer to quash any move to limit Champion's pollution into the Pigeon. Such unethical activity was commonplace, and certainly bred dissatisfaction.[5]

Yet it should be remembered that such statesmen as Cordell Hull and James F. Byrnes of Franklin Roosevelt's New Deal came from Tennessee (as did Senator Kenneth D. McKellar in the same period). Senator Estes Kefauver in the 1950s exposed the national connections of the Mafia. During this period, Tennessee was the state where John Scopes was brought to trial for teaching evolution and was found guilty (July 21, 1925). And it was a state in which during the first two decades of the twentieth century the sale of Demon Rum—well, in Tennessee, whiskey—was the hottest political issue at least until passage of the Eighteenth Amendment. Drys versus Wets dominated Tennessee politics during most of the first two decades of the twentieth century. The governors were pretty much run-of-the-mill, which is not to say that they were not colorful. One governor stands out.

His name was Ben Hooper. He was born October 13, 1870, a twelve-pound bundle to a seventeen-year-old unwed mother, "in a cabin," he wrote, "on a foothill of the Great Smoky Mountains, overlooking the beautiful valley of the Big Pigeon River." When he was eight, his father, a Newport doctor, claimed him, gave him his name, and began raising him. In November 1885 young Ben was baptized in the Pigeon, which was in its "winter flush and high with winter tide, and brush and logs were floating downstream."[6]

From 1910 until 1914, Hooper, a Republican, was Tennessee's governor. His autobiography tells much about the party battles, most especially with regard to laws controlling the liquor trade. Hooper was a prohibitionist. He wrote that his father, a big man at 235 pounds, occasionally went on drunken sprees and became violent. This, explained Hooper, convinced him of the dangers of alcoholic liquors. As a Republican, he believed in laissez-faire economics and hated big government, but at the same time was quite willing to restrict personal freedoms. Thus he denied that people had the right to drink alcoholic liquors on the grounds that no man is an island and a drinker affects his neighbor disastrously. Hooper possessed the colorful southern politician's rhetoric: he denounced "somnalescent political hacks" and once compared Kenneth McKellar, against whom he ran unsuccessfully for the United States Senate, with a rooster that had been made into a capon. The governor later built his home just outside Newport on the Carson Springs Road and made Newport the base for his activities.[7]

If any Tennessee governor during the period from 1908 to 1920 should have taken steps to restrict the Pigeon's pollution, one would expect it to have been a chief executive from Cocke County. And, indeed, Governor Hooper did take initial steps. According to the *Newport Plain Talk,* antipollution agitation had been sufficient in 1909 for the state's attorney general to bring suit against Champion, "but for lack of funds to pay litigation, nothing was done." The following year (1910) the legislature had appropriated a larger sum to instigate proceedings, and finally, in November 1911, under Governor Hooper's administration, steps were taken to sue the company. A news item explained that it would be a federal suit, following the logic of a case recently won by the state of Georgia against the Tennessee company that ran the copper smelter at Ducktown, southeast of Chattanooga. The toxic fumes from the smelter had wafted into Georgia where they had destroyed the flora. The courts had ruled in favor of Georgia. The company installed an apparatus that made sulfuric acid from the fumes instead of discharging them, enriching the company and eliminating the effluent. "I recently took the matter [of the Pigeon River] up with the attorney general," the governor was quoted, "who will begin to make preparations for the suit immediately." Hooper had also discussed the problem with the state chemist, Dr. Lucius P. Brown, who was to study the toxicity of the Pigeon River.[8]

Two months later, in January 1912, a news item appeared bearing information that would become familiar in years to come: "Additional time in which to perfect a chemical process for the purifying of the Pigeon and French Broad rivers was granted Wednesday by Governor Hooper to the Champion Fibre Company of Canton, N.C. . . ." It further stated that Prof. C. W. Dabney, formerly of the University of Tennessee, accompanied by Reuben B. Robertson of Champion, had appealed to the governor for more time. Dabney said he had been studying the polluted Pigeon and French Broad Rivers "for more than a year" and that he "had perfected a process that would make them harmless."[9]

On April 14–15, 1912, the British White Star liner *Titanic* hit an iceberg and sank with the loss of 1,503 passengers and crew. That was certainly big news, but it had to take a second-page location in the April 18 Newport paper. The lead story on page one was Champion's announcement that it was in process of making massive changes that would cut the pollutants entering the Pigeon. "The Champion Fibre Company is making every effort to stop the pollution of the Pigeon River which is carrying its black waters into the French Broad and Tennessee rivers," the story began. The company insisted that, as of April 1912, it had already cut the total waste dumped into the river by one-half. Now a new electrochemical plant costing $750,000 was being installed, which would take care of bleach sludge wastes. Admitting that sulfites and sulfates were still being released, the company stated categorically that "they are harmless to all life in large dilution," and that the lignin solution dumped into the river is "entirely sterile . . . and harmless to every living thing." Further, in a statement made over and over again, the company's announcement insisted that "you may be sure that all manufacturers, including ourselves, will continue to work at this problem until it is solved." Experiments were also being made to end the dumping of black ash, "which, though perfectly harmless, has discolored the water of the river."

Not until February 1913 was the Pigeon the subject of another newspaper article. This time the news came from Knoxville, where that city's legislators, it was said, were going to take measures to have the Tennessee River "freed from pollution which is reaching into it from the Pigeon River. . . . For several years," it continued, "there has been complaint about the water which the people of Knoxville are compelled to drink. In many instances it has been claimed that the refuse from the Canton, N.C. pulp works has been responsible for sickness. . . . It is known that the Pigeon river and even the French Broad river over seventy miles from Canton is [*sic*] so black that it is almost impossible to see a hand in the water and forty and fifty miles from Canton it is impossible to penetrate the dark waters."[10]

As proof of the dangerous pollution, the article noted that fish had been driven from its waters, that even catfish, "which love a filthy stream, cannot exist in the river below Canton and this should be sufficient proof that the stream is not a fit one to furnish the water supply for a big city like Knoxville." The article ended by implying that politicians were in bed with corporations over this issue. It was noted that a bill had been introduced in the legislature to prevent pollution of Tennessee streams by out-of-state corporations, but it had died. Now, it was suggested, if the Knoxville legislators could line up the support of other counties, perhaps something could be accomplished.[11]

Between 1909 and 1913, then, Tennessee legislators were aware of the polluted Pigeon, and beginnings were made in the legislature and in the attorney general's office, with gubernatorial blessing, to take action. But nothing happened. In his autobiography Governor Hooper says nothing about efforts made during his administration to clean up the river. Whatever Champion accomplished—and apparently it did make some improvements—the Pigeon still remained polluted. Too many "somnalescent political hacks" encouraged official lethargy, or corporate pressure was too strong to fight. One is tempted to speculate on what condition the Pigeon would have been in after 1914, when Governor Hooper stepped down, if he had shown the same vigor toward cleaning up the Pigeon as he had in fighting the liquor interests. As a believer in laissez-faire, his support of those advocating a clean river may have been less than enthusiastic in spite of his residence in Cocke County. Did he know that his fellow Newport lawyer William McSwain was on retainer for Champion? Did this affect the vigor of his clean the Pigeon campaign? No one will ever know.

The Pigeon continued to flow black, foamy, and smelly. Improvements had indeed been made, but they just emphasized the incredible pollution Champion was creating in the stream. Residents of Cocke County could see little difference.

Cocke County residents assumed that it could not get worse, but on occasion it did. During Governor Austin Peay's administration (1923–25), Champion either accidentally or purposely released large amounts of acid into the Pigeon. "Since Monday morning tons and tons of [dead] fish have floated down the Pigeon River," noted *Plain Talk*, "and . . . it is estimated at least five two-horse wagon loads have passed the Newport mill." At first residents blamed dynamiters and called the game warden; indeed, setting off dynamite in a body of water will kill the fish, and they float to the surface to be collected. It was soon apparent, however, that the fish kill was not due to explosives. It was blamed on acids dumped into the Pigeon by Champion. Petitions protesting the dumping were drawn up to be sent to Governor Peay, East Tennessee Congressman Brazilla Carroll Reece, and the state's senators. *Plain Talk* then editorialized, "It was argued that an enterprise of the magnitude of the Fibre company would be worth more to the people of this section than all the fish that would ever be in the river, and the statement still goes unquestioned." But it suggested that water that will kill fish "will kill stock along the stream and the poisoned fish have already created a stench which carries hundreds of yards from the river bank."[12]

One reason for the continuing pollution, in spite of Champion's claims about cleaning it, was the company's ongoing expansion of its Canton facility. In 1931 the company announced plans to increase output by 75 percent and added that a new half-million-dollar paper machine had been ordered. But this was only the beginning. In 1959 North Carolina Governor Luther Hodges helped launch Champion's No. 20 machine, which was almost as long as the building housing it. In 1965 the company put on line its No. 19 machine, which produced a paper sheet 246 inches wide at 1,500 feet a minute. These were major expansions; minor changes, most designed to improve efficiency, were constantly underway at the mill.[13]

Coexistent with expansion came some improvements in waste disposal, dictated, one suspects, more by problems accompanying expansion than by any desire to clean the Pigeon beyond its status at any given time. In 1960, for example, the company's new primary waste-treatment plant went on line; it was said to have cost 3.4 million dollars. As a result, twelve five-ton truckloads of muck a day were being carried to a landfill. A modernization program inaugurated in 1963 probably resulted in some improvements because the new equipment was designed to recover chemicals in the pulp-making process. In 1972 a still larger waste-treatment facility was built.[14]

Meanwhile, Newport struggled on. By 1940 the town, which obtained its water supply of four hundred thousand gallons a day from wells and springs, was suffering a water shortage. Although the Pigeon River runs through the heart of Newport, it was so polluted that the community had to pipe water from the French Broad, six miles away and over a ridge.

Scientific Studies Begin

Studies of the river's pollution have been conducted throughout Champion's tenure on the river. The real key to rising interest, which began in the late 1930s or early 1940s, was the coming of the Tennessee Valley Authority. This bureaucracy, which was created as one of the New Deal's great experiments, came into existence in 1933, but federal interest in the region dated at least from the development of Muscle Shoals on the Tennessee River during the First World War. The Tennessee Valley, barely six hundred miles long, had suffered from deforestation, unwise agricultural practices, erosion, and social deterioration for decades.

President Franklin Roosevelt's concept of planning included programs to improve the standard of living of the inhabitants as well as conservation measures to protect the environment. By the late 1930s, TVA administrators, who were designing dams (more than thirty were built) and indulging in social planning, had become aware of the pollution problems posed by industry, by inadequate municipal sewage systems, and by farm runoff into the Tennessee River and its tributaries. Moreover, the reservoirs created by the dams were receiving this polluted water, restricting TVA's aim that the reservoirs should be teeming with fish, that they allow swimming and boating, and that they should be attractive for settlement along the banks. High on the list of polluted streams were the French Broad and its tributary, the Pigeon River. If it could do nothing more, TVA could at least conduct studies and surveys using its professional staff.[15]

From 1941 on, the Pigeon has rarely been free of scientific studies. Sometimes they are TVA conducted; occasionally Tennessee and even North Carolina have authorized investigations; more recently, the Environmental Protection Agency has been involved; and Champion itself cannot be omitted from the list.

In 1942 TVA aquatic biologists A. D. Hess and C. M. Tarzwell published "A Study of the Biological Effects of Pollution on the Pigeon River Watershed," which was based upon research conducted in 1941. The frontispiece of this report shows the Pigeon River above Crabtree Bridge, "Showing Excessive Foaming Produced by the Pollution of the Stream with the Canton Paper Mill Wastes." Collections of biological specimens—considered better indicators of pollution than chemical tests because biological specimens provide information over a considerable period whereas chemicals indicate pollution only at the time observations are made—were conducted between November 4 and November 7, 1941. Collections were made from sixteen stations.[16]

Hess and Tarzwell had done their homework. They noted that in its last forty miles, the Pigeon falls just thirteen hundred feet; that the only record of fish collections prior to the opening of the Canton plant was made by a person named Jordan at Newport in 1877. Bass, sun perch, walleye, pike, and suckers had been the principal fish caught at that time. They said that when the plant opened in 1908, dead fish by the wagon load were collected at bends in the river, although the scientists gave no source for that information.[7]

Sampling stations four through seven were located between the pipe and Waterville Lake. The river, they wrote, "presents a condition of gross pollution, with only pollutional or very tolerant organisms present." As for Waterville Lake, they described it in 1942 "as an immense septic tank, with an abundance of rat-tailed maggots and other pollutional forms; in it, a large portion of the solid pollutants [from the Champion discharge] are settled out." They observed that below the power plant, the Pigeon began to show signs of biological recovery, "although pollutional forms are still present. . . . At Hartford local residents reported catching suckers and carp." Even after flowing the sixty miles from Canton to Newport, the water still retained a high oxygen demand caused by the presence of chemical reducers in the paper mill wastes. "It is significant," they commented, "that the tolerant organisms at Hartford and Newport were collected only in well-aerated ripples, where the dissolved oxygen was temporarily increased." Hartford residents reported that in times of hot weather and low water, even the carp and suckers died. Hess and Tarzwell could see that, as the Pigeon entered the French Broad, which had a flow four times that of the Pigeon and over twenty times that of the Pigeon at Canton, and despite the great dilution from tributary streams, "the water retains an abnormal color and odor." The two aquatic biologists concluded that "the desirable food and game fishes have been eliminated from the Pigeon River from Canton to the mouth of the stream."[18] It is of course true that anyone who had come in contact with the river could experience their findings, but, as has been pointed out, when efforts are made to force a cleanup, specifics about a stream's chemistry and biological condition are necessary. Hess and Tarzwell had made a beginning.

In 1943–44 the Tennessee Stream Pollution Study Board made its report on the Pigeon River. Its authors blamed the Champion mill for 90 percent of the river's pollution. They wrote that the water at Newport was of no use except for cooling purposes in industrial plants and that "the effects of this pollution are felt as far downstream as Knoxville." The authors lamented that the aesthetic value of surface water could not be evaluated objectively, but they added that obviously "floating scum and objectionable odors make adjoining sites undesirable and lower the relative attractiveness of such waters."[19]

Post–World War II Activity

When the Second World War ended, civilian activity roared back into America's hinterlands like a tidal wave. Newspapers, including Newport's *Plain Talk,* ran editorials with the theme of "What can we do to improve our town." One of the answers in Newport was to clean the Pigeon River of its pollution. "That has been one of the suggestions for many years," the editor commented. The same column asked if Newport and Cocke County could be developed as a tourist center.[20]

Reversion to civilian activity highlighted the deteriorating condition of the nation's infrastructure. After a frenzied five years of all-out war production, highways, schools, city streets, and water and sewage systems came up wanting. Regulations had been suspended while wartime industries strove to break production records. Now that society was back on a peacetime basis, municipalities were confronted with outdated, insufficient services. Cleaning up water pollution, or at least guaranteeing municipalities pure drinking water (which carries a slightly different emphasis), became something of a national issue.

The Army Corps of Engineers and the United States Public Health Service both got into the act, receiving federal largess to make studies of the problem. HEALTH OFFICIALS TO LOOK INTO POSSIBILITY OF CLEARING PIGEON FROM ACID TAINT, ran one article in *Plain Talk*; GOVERNOR McCORD PROMISES MORE LIBERAL LAW IN CLEARING STREAMS OF POLLUTION the newspaper announced a few months later; NEWPORT'S RIVER POLLUTION PROBLEM TO BE OFFICIALLY PRESENTED TO [U.S. ARMY] ENGINEERS WHO WILL CONVENE IN ASHEVILLE, ran a headline of May 4, 1950. It was noted that Newport's efforts "have always been 'stymied' by the fact that Tennessee laws could not reach the pollution source that is situated across a state line. In our case, the one that is situated at Canton, N.C., the Champion Fiber Company." A December 17, 1950, issue noted that Tennessee was receiving U.S. Public Health Service funds to research pollution, but that it was Champion, in North Carolina, "who is hesitating to spend the necessary money for a cleanup until they are made to do it."

A 1960 headline stated that the Pigeon would be "75% clean by 1961," quoting Fred V. Doutt, a Champion chemist interviewed by a *Plain Talk* reporter. "But he [Doutt] emphasized that science would still have to find a way to take all of the 'blue coloring' out of the water." He insisted that the blue was what country boys called "stump water." The reporter's article continued:

> "You mean that's the kind of water that we have always heard would remove warts?" I asked cagerly [*sic*].
> "Exactly," he replied, "and that wasn't superstition either. It did actually cause them to shrink away. It was the tannin in it."
> Champion's Mr. Doutt said that the water "would be fit for livestock use, for sporting fish, for irrigation purposes, and for swimming, if any local youngsters should want to take a dip in it."[21]

Because it was spending some money and making some improvements, Champion's claims were given the benefit of the doubt. Cocke County residents, however, became increasingly skeptical. In spite of the paper mill's pollution-control innovations, they knew that the river remained colored, foaming, scummy, and smelly. Nor can anyone say that they accepted it without protest. Every so often, a contributor would wax nostalgic over the Pigeon as it had once been:

> The old timers who remember Pigeon River before it turned black, say there never was a more beautiful stream anywhere. Along its many cliffs and bluffs pigeons were plentiful, and that is how the river received its name. The reflection of the high cliffs on the crystal clear water was a sight to behold. The day the black mother liquor (or acid as we know it) started to pour into the river at Canton, N.C., must have been a dreaded day for those who recognized the beauty of the river. At this time, the river supports suckers, rock bass and perch or smallmouth bass. Fishing then was not as sporty as it is today. When a man wanted a mess of fish, he simply went down to the river and caught them. The fish didn't disappear at once, but gradually vanished. . . .[22]

Chronicling Cocke County's continuing protests about its polluted stream is simply to repeat a litany. Rarely did a month pass, and never a year, without complaints being registered about the smelly, polluted Pigeon River. Locally it came to be known as the Black River. Local legislators carried their constituents' protests to the halls of government at Nashville, but until the 1980s no sustained drive was ever mounted by Tennessee's government to force Champion to clean up the mess.

Champion officials say that the late 1960s marked a turning point in the company's record of pollution control. The time had arrived to upgrade the plant to state-of-the-art standards, and, they continue, the

massive changes being wrought today are the normal result of a continuing policy of upgrading that takes place every thirty years or so.[23]

Others see a more cynical, pragmatic explanation for Champion's
interest in pollution control. They say that Champion officials in the
1960s noted the rising environmental movement, especially the push for
clean air and clean water, and decided to stay a step ahead of criticism.
Even their friendly host, the state of North Carolina, went after Champion in the mid-1960s when the North Carolina State Stream Sanita-
tion Committee required the company to proceed with design and construction of secondary treatment facilities. These facilities were to reduce
the average five-day, 20 degree BOD discharge to twelve thousand pounds
per day, to that extent protecting river quality standards. Whatever its
motivation, Champion, as stated above, installed additional antipollution equipment in the 1960s.

In the 1960s increasing concern about pollution was apparent throughout the nation. It was reflected in state and federal actions involving
water and air pollution. Regardless of measures they had taken to clean
up the Pigeon, Champion was going to bear the brunt of studies that
were critical of its day-by-day operations at the Canton mill, studies indicating that the company had not done nearly enough to cope with the
pollution.

Mill officials must have been aware of a mobile lab that was sta-
tioned for a time in Canton in the summer of 1965; federal bureaucracy
had arrived. The lab was operated by employees of the Biological and
Chemical Unit of the Federal Water Pollution Control Administration
out of Cincinnati, Ohio. The operators were taking samples of the Pigeon. And they were thorough: samples were collected around the clock
at six-hour intervals for four days; in addition, the two sample collection teams were kept busy determining temperature. Chemists and bac-
teriologists worked in twelve-hour shifts, measuring dissolved oxygen,
BOD, turbidity, total coliform, fecal coliform, and Salmonella.[24]

In February 1966 the Biological and Chemical Unit's report was released. It was entitled "Effects of Pollution on Biota of the Pigeon River,
North Carolina and Tennessee," and it was authored by two aquatic biologists, Lowell E. Keup and R. Keith Stewart. Their conclusions confirmed
in a scientific way what everyone already assumed. Champion wastes
polluted the Pigeon, reducing "the growth of both the desirable suspended planktonic and bottom attached algae in twenty miles of the
Pigeon River and in Waterville Lake." The effluent also "stimulated the
growth of undesirable slime organisms . . . from Canton . . . into the
State of Tennessee"; and "it reduced substantially the desirable sensi-

tive fish food organisms, from Canton . . . downstream to Newport . . . (including Waterville Lake), a total distance of 40 miles." Keup and Stewart also reported that the pollution "increased in numbers the tolerant bottom associated organisms including many disease vector and nuisance insects such as mosquitoes and midges." The pollution also destroyed the fisheries for twenty miles downstream and "caused the waters that entered Tennessee to contain a fish population dominated by large rough-fish such as carp and suckers."[25]

Three years later, in February 1968, another document, "Report on the Pollution of the Interstate Waters of the Pigeon River" was prepared by the Federal Water Pollution Control Administration of the Department of the Interior. The study was led by C. E. Runas, a sanitary engineer, and L. E. Keup and R. K. Stewart, biologists under the direction of A. W. West, acting chief of the Pollution Education Section. Although the recommendations were, as usual, to clean up the river, the reasons set forth marked the beginning of one of the major environmentalist arguments. According to the report, "Realization of the Pigeon River['s] potential future development for tourist and recreational activities requires restoration of all stream reaches for fish and wildlife, boating and other recreational uses and for aesthetic appeal." The authors were also critical of the sewage systems at Canton, Clyde, Waynesville, Lake Junaluska, and Newport, and they found fault with the A. C. Lawrence Leather Company at Newport; it has since ceased operations.[26]

In TVA's files, this report dovetails into yet another report, entitled "Biosystem Character of the Pigeon River in the Preliminary Stages of Recovery." This study had as its supporting institute the University of North Carolina at Asheville, and the participants were graduate students; their faculty advisor was John Christian Bernhardt, professor of biology. Between May 20 and August 12, 1973, five biologists and five chemists studied the river from its headwaters to Waterville Lake. The headwaters of the Pigeon, clean and potable, were their control and "served as an indication of the aquatic existence the river could obtain under ideal conditions." As for the Pigeon below the pipe, "it is known and documented," they wrote, "that before the Champion plant put any water pollution abatement equipment into operation, circa 1962, the river was a 'dead river.' Until 1970, the year the secondary water treatment equipment was placed into operation, there were periods when, because of very low dissolved oxygen and large pH fluctuations, no life other than bacteria could have existed in the water."[27]

After 1970 it had been assumed that the river had recovered, and this is what the young researchers set out to determine. On a fixed schedule, students monitored the water for acidity, alkalinity, ammonia, chemical oxygen demand, chloride, dissolved oxygen, residual chlorine, lignins, nitrates, phosphates (total and ortho), pH, settleable solids, sulfate, sulfide, temperature, and turbidity. Their report stated that the Pigeon River below the mill was "stuck" in a state of radical contrast to its condition above the mill. The young scientists emphasized that, as of 1973, no regulations existed to control temperature, color, and turbidity, although in the Pigeon these were the major disrupting factors. Other aspects of water quality met federal regulations.[28]

In spite of Champion's claims, improved pollution control methods proved insufficient. In 1978 the company paid a $45,000 civil penalty in settlement of a water pollution suit brought against its Canton paper mill by the United States Environmental Protection Agency. EPA had sought fines of up to $10,000 a day, and Champion had been faced with the possibility of a maximum penalty of $1 million. In the out-of-court settlement, Champion insisted that it had spent $13 million on waste treatment since 1965 and its operation of the facilities cost the company $10,000 a day. Indeed, in 1960, 1965, 1970, 1972, 1975, and 1977, the company had upgraded its wastewater treatment facilities. Clearly, though, these efforts were not enough. (Parenthetically, one might comment on our age of inflation and big money: whereas Champion spent a few millions in the 1960s and 1970s, the corporation's upgrading in the early 1990s is costing the company, so it says, $330 million.)[29]

In October 1978, North Carolina issued a draft statement of its own Pigeon River investigation; the final report was issued a year later. It considered the "black liquor" discharged from the plant to be a major concern. From a kraft mill such as Champion's, wastes could contain "such highly toxic constituents as hydrogen sulfide, mercaptans, resin acids and soaps." The researchers noted gill damage in fish below the pipe, and they were especially concerned about the turbidity and color of the stream. The excessive turbidity, they said, reduced light penetration in the water column, which in turn reduced photosynthesis by planktonic organisms, attached algae, and submersed vegetation. These communities are important because many species of fish are bottom grazers; if the plankton are gone, they have no food. Champion, they wrote, dumped thousands of tons of wastes into the river: "A buildup of settled solids is extremely damaging to gravel and rubble-type bottoms, such as the Pigeon River. The materials fill the interstices between gravel and stones thereby eliminating the spawning grounds of fish and the habitat of many aquatic insects and other invertebrates."[30]

The North Carolina report stated categorically that Champion's discharge was affecting the entire length of the Pigeon River to Waterville Lake. "Organic enrichment, habitat destruction due to solids, and increased turbidity are factors of major concern," the scientists emphasized. As for Waterville Lake, it appeared to be a catch basin for the solids and organics—sort of a septic tank. This North Carolina study made thirteen recommendations. Among them perhaps the most important were:

1. use hydrated lime to clean up the River
2. install cooling equipment to meet state requirements for temperature [which implies that Champion was not meeting state water temperature specifications]
3. reduce Champion's mixing zone (the mileage from the pipe accepted as a zone in which the waters were theoretically mixing with tributary waters and becoming cleaner: tests were made below this zone, to Champion's benefit)
4. reduce allowable dissolved solids
5. include limits on tannin and lignin
6. require bioassays by both the company and the division [of Natural Resources and Community Development, division of Environmental Management] to monitor high inorganic metals and toxic substances
7. initiate a scheduled detailed review of the self-monitoring data provided by Champion Paper Co. [numerous violations were noted in the data review for this report]
8. reduce the suspended solids limit from 79 ng./l to 25–30 ng./l to protect the aquatic life of the stream.[31]

Although nothing came of this report, which was devastating in its analysis of the Pigeon and what Champion had done to it, it is significant that the study was conducted by a North Carolina agency. Environmentalists believed that the state had dragged its feet when it came to regulation or even criticism of Champion International. It was hoped that this study was a portent that the state was going to tighten its regulations and enforce them more stringently. In addition, the company was suddenly faced by the fourfold threat of intervention from North Carolina, from Tennessee, from the Environmental Protection Agency, and from TVA.

The Fourfold Threat

That threat developed in 1980 when conferences took place between water quality officials from each of these government entities. A draft work plan stressed that cooperation was necessary from all of them in order to document adequately the present status of Champion's water treatment, the impact of the discharge on the river, possible "refinement of the wasteload allocation for Champion Paper Company's discharge," and the "adequacy of North Carolina and Tennessee water quality standards for protecting the designated use of the Pigeon River."[32]

The study undertaken by these officials was the most thorough testing of the Pigeon River yet. It included a fish survey and fish samples tested for trace organic and metal analysis; benthos (plants and animals living along the river bottom) samples to be collected and analyzed; static bioassays to determine toxicity of Champion's wastes; and in situ bioassay tests, in which live fish and organisms would be placed at selected points in the Pigeon to see how they reacted to the water. Capable, qualified scientists would conduct all the tests.[33]

Tennessee issued its own report from these investigations, entitled "Biological and Chemical Investigation of the Pigeon River, Cocke County, Tennessee, October, 1980." Biologists David Melgaard and A. David McKinney were the authors. They reported that the Pigeon inside the Tennessee line "continues to be degraded by pollution originating in North Carolina," primarily from Champion's plant. The company's advances, they wrote, have resulted in "a slow improvement in some areas of water quality," but color, solids, odor, and foaming remained serious problems. They also pointed out that the draining of the Waterville Lake for company repairs resulted in the discharge of tons of organic muck from the bottom of the lake into Tennessee, with obvious but undetermined damage.[34]

Two years later, in 1982, both North Carolina and Tennessee issued statements about the Pigeon River. North Carolina published a briefing paper, and Tennessee released a document entitled "Position Paper: Restoration of the Pigeon River." The North Carolina report noted that, even though the Pigeon below the pipe was designated a Class C stream, "many of the uses assigned to Class C waters including fishing and fish and wildlife propagation can not be fully attained because of the river's poor quality." The study found that the accepted 2.8 degrees Celsius temperature increase allowed by Champion's permit was exceeded, even six miles below the pipe, by a temperature reading of up to 6.5 degrees Celsius. The report stated that violations of the dissolved oxygen standards for Class C waters of 5 mg/1 DO occurred regularly. As for color, a product of tannin and lignin compounds, it was resistant to degradation until diluted in Lake Douglas. It was perceived that approximately 80 percent of the dissolved solids dumped into the river are salt compounds, which increase the river's salinity and thus affect the freshwater habitat. As for the fifteen thousand pounds of suspended solids also released, they hindered light penetration and settled to the bottom, where they clogged the substrata with silt and altered the benthic community. The report acknowledged that since 1965 some improvement was apparent as a result of Champion's wastewater treatment efforts; however, the water did not approach the condition of the pure water above the plant. Over the distance from the pipe to Waterville Lake—even in 1980 after Champion had installed sludge dewatering belt presses—poor to very poor conditions prevailed. It was noted that when Carolina Power and Light drew down Waterville Lake 123 feet in 1980, thick deposits of organic mud were exposed; these had accumulated since the dam and power plant became operational in the late 1920s. The report noted, as had the Tennessee report, that during the month that it took to make repairs on the dam, the river carved a channel forty feet deep through the sludge. The resulting turbidity violated Tennessee's water quality standards for six weeks.[35]

Champion's permit from North Carolina expired June 30, 1981, but because EPA had not yet formulated certain criteria required for a new one, the company continued to function under the old permit. However, even North Carolina wanted a few changes, some of which Champion agreed to, but the company objected to others on cost-benefit grounds. For example, the company insisted that it would cost the company $96 million, and annual operating costs estimated at $5.7 million, to comply with the water temperature limit of 2.8 degrees Celsius above the river's normal thermal reading. It should be added that North Carolina's attorney general suggested that Champion, instead of requesting a variance to the temperature limit, should request a revision to the state's water quality standard involving temperature. The report stopped with the facts; it made no recommendations beyond the suggestion regarding temperature.[36]

Tennessee's position paper was not so neutral. It emphasized that Champion had failed to comply with its North Carolina permit, which had expired June 30, 1981. By implication, the paper suggested that North Carolina had been negligent in enforcement. It said that the Pigeon, after it entered Tennessee, violated the Volunteer State's more stringent antipollution regulations. And, finally, it stressed that the Tennessee problems of the Pigeon were not the result of violations of National Pollution Discharge Elimination System (NPDES) permit limits for the simple reason that Champion's permit—the one that had expired in June 1981, but was still in force pending issuance of a new one—did not control any of the conditions of color, solids, odor, and foaming. Perhaps it is worth noting that, by this point, no scientific Pigeon River investigations had raised the issue of the effect of the pollution upon human health. This would change before the decade ended.[37] (The NPDES is the legislation that empowers EPA to issue permits for the discharge of pollutants.)

It was the oral presentation based upon McKinney and Melgaard's report in April 1982 that triggered the legal challenges to Champion's continuing pollution. If business as usual had prevailed, then Champion would have received its permit, and the Pigeon River would have continued to run polluted without penalty; there would have been very few changes. Possibly a few new, innocuous restrictions or requirements would have been inserted, but residents of the region assumed that the company would continue as usual. They knew that when Champion decided to do more toward eliminating pollution, the company would do it; until then, the river would continue to flow at the state of pollution that existed in 1981.

The residents of Cocke County and the state of Tennessee had never had input into any changes that had taken place. They accepted Champion's promises of improvement; yet, no matter how much the company did, it was never enough. The smell, the color, the foam, the scum—they still remained a part of the river, even as it flowed through the heart of Newport and on to its junction with the French Broad.

But changes—major changes—would take place in the 1980s.

CHAPTER 4

Who Is
Charles Dickens Mullinix?

M omentum is difficult to quantify, but it is a fact that by the 1970s, environmental concerns had mounted sufficient drive to have entered the national psyche. Greenpeace, the Sierra Club, the Izaak Walton League, the Environmental Defense Fund, the National Parks Association, and the Audubon Society, to name just a few of many national organizations, kept up a drumbeat for environmentalism that could not be silenced. Hundreds of local groups were publicizing regional environmental problems as never before. There can be little doubt that Champion officials who possessed foresight knew that it would not be long before criticism of their Canton facility, with its excessive pollution of water and air, would become a major company problem.

In the late fifties and early sixties, as we have seen, Champion undertook some pollution control measures. It is a fact that the Pigeon River of the 1980s was in better condition than it had been in years past. Yet it still foamed, stank, and carried away tons and tons of solids. The color remained. At times of low water—often in late summer when the climate was at its warmest—the water flowed almost black, and the odor was at its worst. Cocke County residents complained, of course, just as they had since the fish and wildlife supported by the river were killed off in 1908. But there was much lethargy. Who could combat Champion? Protest tended to be like criticizing the weather: it made for casual talk, but it never changed the temperature or the day from rain to shine, and everyone thought criticism of Champion would make no difference. Truth is, no one liked the odor: not the employees at Canton or their families who had to live nearby and smell it twenty-four hours a day; not the occasional executive who flew down from corporate headquarters in Stamford, Connecticut; not the residents along the stream as it flowed through northern Haywood County; not the Cocke County inhabitants who had to smell the river along Newport's main street. But it was a given. All pulp and paper mills pollute the air and water. Nothing could be done about it.

But there were factors that made Champion's Canton facility more vulnerable to criticism than most pulp and paper mills. First and foremost, the Pigeon was a small river. It could not absorb the toxic wastes and the black liquid dumped into it because it was too small a stream. Years ago, even Champion officials acknowledged—and still do—that today no contemporary paper executive in his right mind would build a mill along so small a river. Nor would a company be likely to build a facility along a stream of beauty that in its pristine state was one of the finest fishing streams in the southern Appalachians. Few doubt that if it were restored, the Pigeon could produce such game fish again, and it could offer the added attractions of swimming, boating, and rafting. Profits from tourism would soar. And certainly the CEOs would think twice before building along a river that, while still polluted, flowed across a political boundary into another state. They would think again when they realized that the pollution would run through the center of the business section of a county seat. And they would probably think twice if that same river supplied some of the water for a city the size of Knoxville. But in 1908 none of this appears to have bothered Peter Thomson or Reuben Robertson. Champion developed a momentum of its own: instead of reducing its productivity to better fit the capabilities of the Pigeon River to accept the discharge, the company increased the mill's capacity, boasting of setting production records right up into the 1980s. Until recently, the mountaineers of Cocke County had not constituted much of a threat to Champion's activities.[1]

Originators of the Clean Pigeon River Crusade

It depends upon who one asks to determine who began the drive for a clean Pigeon River, a drive that has continued unabated. According to Jim Harrison of the EPA, it was Steve Tedder, who was the head of North Carolina's Surface Water Department in the mid-1970s. Champion had paid the state a forty-five-thousand-dollar fine for polluting, and Tedder suggested, successfully, that the money be used for a state investigation of the Pigeon. Tedder subsequently took employment with

EPA. "From that time on," says Harrison, "the Pigeon River has been a prime subject of contention."[2]

In her master's thesis, Margaret Corwin gives the real credit to Tennessee biologists David McKinney and David Melgaard, who tested water in Waterville Lake prior to a company drawdown of the Pigeon River for repairs and again afterwards. Their report, referred to briefly in the last chapter, was issued both orally and in writing to the Tennessee Water Quality Control Board in 1982. The two biologists were aware that, in the 1960s and 1970s, the state of Tennessee had toughened its environmental laws, forcing a number of industries to clean up their disposal systems and even prompting a few companies to leave the state. To McKinney and Melgaard, it was only fitting and proper that a neighboring state with a river flowing into Tennessee should enforce equally tough environmental laws. And it was clear that Tennessee's neighbor to the east, North Carolina, was badly remiss, at least with regard to the Pigeon River.[3]

The inequity of Tennessee enforcing its environmental laws against its own industries while North Carolina lagged with its legislation and, if laws were on the books, resisted enforcement has not been lost on citizens of the Volunteer State. Disturbed by McKinney and Melgaard's report, Tennessee's Water Quality Control Board drafted a resolution that was sent to Champion, the Tennessee attorney general's office, the Tennessee Manufacturing Association, and the Tennessee Scenic Rivers Association. Some of these organizations also wrote Champion and the governor of North Carolina, citing the findings in McKinney and Melgaard's report. Something, the statements all insisted, had to be done. The upshot of all this was a meeting between Tennessee and North Carolina officials on February 1, 1983, and an agreement drawn up in October 1984 that still did not meet Tennessee's requirements. Meanwhile, because of North Carolina's failure to cooperate—and now with provisions of the Federal Clean Water Act to back up its demands—the state of Tennessee went to court. This litigation is discussed in Chapter 5.[4]

Besides Steve Tedder's investigation for North Carolina and McKinney and Melgaard's work for Tennessee, Charles Lewis Moore, Cocke County's former executive officer, tells a story that involves Cocke County residents in the crusade from at least the fall of 1982. Once again, Cocke County was in the headlines for criminal activity carried on within its borders. This time, its sheriff had been caught engaging in business with drug dealers. Moore had been working with the chamber of commerce to improve Cocke County's image and attract industry to the depressed county. He was beside himself with frustration.

"The drug scam was making the news every fifteen minutes," he recalls. "TV was flashing it across the state. So I called Channel 10 in Knoxville and explained to them the terrible unemployment problem we were having." Then he asked for help. "Couldn't you give us some positive reporting?"

"What's positive about Cocke County?" asked the reporter.

"I said, 'Well, we need some help to clean up the river over here.' He said, 'What river?' and I told him and he replied he'd think about it."

As a result, a TV reporter and a cameraman came down to Cocke County. With Moore and Bob Seay, executive director of the Newport-Cocke County Chamber of Commerce aboard, the TV crew flew by helicopter to Canton and landed at Pisgah High School's football field. Unbeknownst to them (as they were unbeknownst to Champion), the company had invited a TV team to come down to shoot some footage for the seventy-fifth anniversary celebration of the Champion plant at Canton, and that TV team was scheduled to land at the same place.

Champion had one of its limousines and a van on the field to take the journalists around, give them lunch, and treat them royally. Waiting near a limousine were two vice-presidents. In an accompanying van were two well-dressed young men, who were supposed to follow the limo with dignitaries of lesser note.

The helicopter landed, and the TV technician with an audio apparatus said to one of the Champion men, "We want to see where you put the discharge back into the river."

"Aww," replied one of the company men, "you don't want to see that messy stuff."

"I don't think you understand why we're here," the TV man began.

"Aren't you here for the seventy-fifth anniversary?"

"No, we're here because of the pollution of the river."

Abruptly the two vice-presidents climbed into the limousine and drove off, leaving the TV crew to talk to the two young men entrusted with the van.

"They didn't know whether to take us down to the river or jump in the van and drive off," Seay adds, laughing. "And we walked down and looked at the river and then we did everything we wanted to do—in fact we hovered over the pipe where the water comes out. And all this was aired on Channel 10 in Knoxville."

Of little significance in itself, this incident marks the beginning of the Pigeon River problem as an ongoing story in the Knoxville media. By bringing the polluted Pigeon into Knoxville residents' minds over and over again, sentiment in the city has built up against Champion.

Yet, during all the years of the 1980s, the Pigeon ran as black, smelly, foamy, and sterile as ever. Litigation was nothing new to Champion. Public nuisance charges were old hat to it. A few protests were to be expected; this was a constant with the company and its lawyers. Nothing to get worried about.

But, much to Champion's chagrin, times had changed. The climate of opinion was turning against polluters and in favor of strictly enforcing government regulations. Perhaps most significant of all was the element of persistence. Heretofore, protests had arisen and faded like summer storms. Now protesters appeared who would not stop their clamor. The media listened to them and reported on their activities. A greater and greater number of citizens were getting involved. Unlike earlier times, people just wouldn't "shut up."

The story of the fight to clean the polluted Pigeon changes in the mid-1980s for all these reasons. Champion was confronted with more than the usual amount of litigation involving its Canton plant. More regulations were being promulgated by the Tennessee and North Carolina bureaucracies. Environmentalists were insisting that legislation long since passed be enforced. The Clean Air Act and the Clean Water Act that EPA was empowered to enforce gave additional ammunition to those insisting that corporations take care of their toxic wastes in environmentally sound ways: these acts allowed protesters to pressure EPA "to do something." Thinking people, even some industrialists, when confronted with population growth, diminishing acreage for landfills, destruction of the ozone layer, and global warming, came to realize that changes must come. But environmentalists and industrialists parted company over the reality of the dangers, the costs for industry, and the extent that technological developments made such massive cleanups economically feasible.

Charles Dickens Mullinix and PRAG

Of all the gnats buzzing around Champion's Canton plant, the new protesters were the most aggravating. Many will say—though on balance they are probably wrong—that it was the persistence of these few protesters that forced Champion to launch a massive cleanup of its Canton plant. (Champion will deny this, insisting that it had planned the changes all along.) One protester stands out above the others. If he did not instigate the crusade to clean the Pigeon, he has at times kept the crusade alive by sheer tenacity. He will not give up.

His name is Charles Dickens Mullinix, known to his friends as Dick. Mullinix has been the principal gadfly, the most persistent individual rousing people from their complacency. Among his many virtues are courage, tenacity, integrity, decency, and compassion. He is the person a reporter for a national newspaper, periodical, or television network who is inquiring into the Pigeon River affair is advised to contact first. If the reporter can spare several hours, Dick, who is retired, will cheerfully fill in the time. He and his wife, Lucie, will jump in their car and give their guests a tour of the entire river, even on the Tennessee side. Dick and Lucie will make their case, and point to Dick's broken jaw as the price that sometimes must be paid to make that case.

After retiring at age sixty-five in 1976, Dick was still of sound mind and body. He resented the condition of the polluted Pigeon, and, as a career-long paper man—he was a packaging engineer—he knew that the river could be cleaned up and that the Canton mill could continue to operate. It was just a matter of Champion expending money and energy. To Dick, complacency rules in Canton and at company headquarters in Stamford, Connecticut, and complacency is the enemy.

Mullinix is tenacious. And because of his energy, his stubbornness, his refusal to accept defeat after defeat, he became the catalyst for the growth of more determined opposition. His letters to the editor, especially to the *Mountaineer,* Waynesville's triweekly paper, and to Champion officials, and his talks to any group that would listen to him became the headwaters for a subconscious stream of knowledge about the problem. These efforts have contributed to the realization by a usually quiescent citizenry that someone was really trying to do something about the Pigeon. He convinced people that there was hope. When Cocke County residents decided to take steps in opposition to Champion, they turned for advice to Mullinix; when the Legal Environmental Assistance Foundation (LEAF) wanted to enter the fray on behalf of the protesters, its representatives contacted Mullinix. The Pigeon River Action Group (PRAG), an organization created by Dick and Lucie, gave him still more clout in arousing opposition.

Mullinix was not responsible for the litigation commencing in 1983, which was inspired by McKinney and Melgaard's study—litigation that has continued on, one case after another, to the present—but it was Dick Mullinix the letter-writing publicist who helped make the public aware of these cases. He would not let the public forget: he detailed the progress of litigation and of regulatory decisions, and, when decisions were made, spelled out their meaning.[5]

Just who is this David battling the Goliath corporation named Champion? Mullinix had a Horatio Alger-like path to success. He was born in 1909 in the little community of Pleasant Ridge, near Cincinnati, Ohio. When he was twelve, he ran away with the Barnum and Bailey Circus. After several months of incredible adventure, he returned home. His father died shortly thereafter, and the boy quit school—he never went beyond the fifth grade—and took work in a paper plant. His father had been in the folding-box business.

Before he was nineteen, he was a traveling salesman selling boxes and labels to manufacturers. Soon, young Dick, imaginative and innovative, gifted in drawing and designing, was a top packaging engineer. Older readers may recall the cardboard boats in which Nedick's hot dogs were sold. As the consumer ate, the "boat" was squeezed with the fingers, forcing bite-sized lengths of the hot dog out one end. It worked well, except that everyone discarded the boats on the sidewalk, leading Nedick's to cancel the product. Mullinix had not only designed the packaging of this product, he had also designed the machinery to produce it.

Another of Mullinix's inventions is the bacon package with a small, peek-a-boo window in it that allows the purchaser to examine the bacon inside without opening the package. Meat packaging became his specialty: at one time, 70 percent of the pound and half-pound bacon packages used west of the Mississippi were of his design, as was the wrapping machinery. When younger engineers approached one CEO with ideas, that wise person used to say, "Let's see what our fifth-grade engineer thinks of it." Sometimes Dick approved the design; often as not, he rejected it or made helpful suggestions for improvement.

For years, Dick and Lucie were on the road selling for Crown Zellerbach out of California. Then he founded Mullinix Packaging Company in Fort Wayne, Indiana. In their travels they had always looked forward to visiting the South Atlantic states, so it was only logical that they should choose to retire in western North Carolina. This decision brought them to their present residence. It is a comfortable, well-appointed cottage offering an awe-inspiring view of Mount Sterling. It was there, in the summer of 1976, that Dick and Lucie decided to spend the late spring, long summer, and extended autumn of each year for the rest of their lives; they contemplated spending their winters residing in Florida.

They both love wildlife, especially birds. Special feeders bring the hummingbirds; regular feeders attract more birds than Lucie had ever seen before. In the gloaming, flying squirrels appear like little stealth bombers, approaching to within a foot or six inches of Dick's face, then, almost faster than the eyes can follow, they veer away.

Determined, defiant Charles Dickens "Dick" Mullinix on a bridge across the Pigeon River. Mullinix was named "Tarheel of the Week" by the Raleigh News and Observer, *September 16, 1990. Photo by Martha Quillin. Courtesy* Raleigh News and Observer.

It is easy to imagine Dick and Lucie Mullinix standing on the deck, looking out across the natural beauty of western North Carolina, satisfied that a lifetime of work has earned them retirement at such a secluded, peaceful site. He stands slim, ramrod straight, his craggy face and thoughtful eyes testifying to a life well lived. Lucie, by his side, is vivacious and alert, still busy with homemaking, church activities, and projects of her own.

But one day early in their retirement, Dick stepped outside and smelled an offensive odor. "What in hell is that?" he asked his neighbor up the mountain. "Didn't you know?" came the reply. "When the wind is right you'll smell it constantly. It's the stench from the Pigeon River down by the Interstate. It carries the industrial sewage from Champion's paper mill at Canton. That's about twenty-five miles south of here, just the other side of Waynesville."

Dick Mullinix was offended. He drove to the bridge across the Pigeon. "What a beautiful mountain stream," he had thought before examining it carefully. Now he could see the water, dark as black coffee. Foam gathered at the rocks and eddies. And did it smell.

When Dick Mullinix returned to his cabin off Panther Creek Road, he was as angry as a wet yellow jacket. "This isn't necessary and this isn't right," he said, "and I'm going to do something about it."

Thus began Charles Dickens Mullinix's ongoing, nearly two-decade campaign to force Champion International Corporation—a six-billion-dollar behemoth, the second largest landowner in the United States—to clean up its effluent.

And Dick Mullinix is still at it. Has he succeeded? The jury is still out.

The Lonely Crusade

From 1976 until 1982, little happened; these were the barren years in Mullinix's drive to clean up the Pigeon River. Unfortunately, they are also barren years for the story we have to tell. Dick did not keep copies of letters he wrote to Champion, and since the company did not answer his early letters, we must simply surmise the contents of Dick's protests. He chastised the company for committing a sin against God and humanity. He reminded Champion officials that he had worked all his life in the packaging business and therefore knew what he was talking about. Packaging is closely affiliated with pulp and paper companies and is often a part of their operations. When Dick Mullinix stated flatly to Champion officials that they could clean up their effluent and make the Pigeon flow clean and clear he was not providing just an opinion—he was providing an expert judgment. (This did not improve his popularity with the company.)

When he wrote letters to Waynesville's *Mountaineer*, he at first received little response from readers. But over time his persistence produced results. People at church, at Ingles supermarket, at the gasoline station would tell him privately that they approved of what he was doing. It was also clear that they were unwilling to help him. It was too delicate a matter in Haywood County; too many people earned their living from Champion, and too many business people feared hostility, even a boycott, if they actively entered the fray. Even so, this silent support encouraged Dick to continue his campaign.

Gradually invitations began coming in: would he speak to the local chapter of the Sierra Club, to the North Carolina Clean Water Coalition in Asheville, to a group of Knoxville environmentalists? At the age of eighty, this dedicated crusader did not hesitate to rise at 4:30 A.M., hop in his car, and drive the seventy miles to Knoxville to speak at an

pigeon river action group

P.O. Box 105
Waynesville, NC 28786

(704) 627-9774

The Pigeon River Action Group (PRAG) logo on envelopes and letterheads became a familiar sight to newspaper editors, Champion officials, politicians, and environmentalists. Courtesy Charles Dickens Mullinix.

environmental group's breakfast. He and Lucie formed the Pigeon River Action Group (PRAG) and tried to raise money and membership. In neither case were they very successful, particularly in the early days, but the PRAG logo appeared on more and more envelopes as correspondence increased. Queries about his crusade came not only from North Carolina and Tennessee, but also from all over the country. Congressmen, senators, governors, state legislators, newspaper editors, and local politicians, to say nothing of Champion officials, began to recognize that logo, sometimes ruefully. What was Dick Mullinix demanding now?

In retrospect, the years from 1976 to 1982 were years of trial and error, of discouragement, and above all a time of learning. Dick and Lucie absorbed everything they could about the Pigeon River. They traced its course from its beginnings close to the Blue Ridge Parkway to the mill, and from the pipe through Newport to its junction with the French Broad.

Whenever he has the opportunity, Dick takes interested environmentalists, journalists, scientists, and anyone else showing concern over the Pigeon's pollution on a tour of the river. Above the mill he likes to show a natural hollow in the stream bed where people have been swimming for decades. When he turns at State Road 215, he often sees an occasional fisherman. "Trout really are caught in the stream," he tells his guests. "At fifty-two degrees—the normal temperature of the water there—the river is perfect for those feisty game fish." A short distance down the river is a bridge where Dick will drop a penny into the water; it flashes in the sunlight and can be seen as it falls all twenty feet to the stream bed.

Later, he comments on the sign hung high across the river informing everyone that beyond that point is private property of the Champion Paper Company. Shortly thereafter, the road leads past heavily posted Lake Logan, Champion's artificial lake.

Then the giant buildings of the mill come into sight, and, if the wind is right, the stench is also noticed. Sounds of civilization are heard: railroad switch engines, trucks delivering tons of chips, and the muffled roar of great chemical and mechanical systems at work converting the raw material into paper and paperboard. Chimneys and vents spew masses of smoke and steam into the air.

If they reach Canton between shifts and things are fairly quiet, Dick may drive to the site of the outlet—the "pipe," as it is called. Actually, the pipe is underwater; turbulence and discoloration are the only signs of an addition to the Pigeon's flow. Then they follow a well-maintained, graveled country road, State Road 209, past Clyde into pretty farming country. The tree canopy persists, and the entire stretch is beautiful—save for the polluted water. By the time the road approaches Fines Creek, several tributaries have swollen the river until it is as wide as a four-lane highway. The contribution of the tributaries cuts down the pollution, although it is still very present. Here are rapids; there a span of smooth water. Farmhouses can be observed on either side of the river. Some are dilapidated or at least need painting, and there are cannibalized cars or abandoned washing machines in sight of the road. But others are freshly painted and well kept with neat yards. Mullinix acknowledges that there may be as many as five hundred open sewers draining directly from these houses into the Pigeon. "This is wrong," he states emphatically, "but what can you expect when they look out upon an already polluted stream?"

Continuing along Interstate 40 toward the Tennessee line, Dick turns off at the exit to the Waterville (or Walters) Power Plant. Here Mullinix and his guests get out of the car and observe the water. If the generators are in use, the water, including Champion's effluent, can be seen pouring out of the power plant gates. To the right, a splashing tributary stream spills down the mountainside and joins the main stream. To the left is the old Pigeon River bed. It is much reduced in volume since the Pigeon's waters are now caught in the lake, but some clear water enters the old bed from tributaries. As these two tributaries, one from the left and one from the right, join the main stream bed containing the polluted Waterville water, one observes a consolidated stream: the center part is nearly black and the two sides are clear, and the difference is so marked that it looks as if it were drawn with a crayon.

As the years of his struggle have gone on, Dick has accumulated stories that constitute a tour guide's running commentary. At the Waterville powerhouse, he relates how some whitewater guides proposed a "brownwater rafting trip" from the dam to Douglas Lake. "We talked with the power company and told them what we were going to do, that we'd have cameras and the press there," Mullinix recalls, "and the officials said they had no intention of closing the gates that weekend." But by the time the group had assembled, the gates were closed, and there was not sufficient water for a single raft. "The company said it never knew for sure when the power was needed," Dick adds, "but we think CP&L's six-million-dollar-per-year contract with Champion had something to do with it."

In passing, he also observes how EPA proposed that Champion take water samples 1.1 miles above the state line in North Carolina. This placed the site close to freshwater tributaries. "Too much of a temptation," Dick suggests dryly, "to take water from or near the freshwater inlet."

Dick and his passengers now start up Interstate 40, cross the state line into Tennessee, and in due time reach the exit labeled Hartford. "This," says Dick, "is Widowville." Widowville is the little ex-lumber mill town where cancer deaths appear to have skyrocketed, especially among the male citizens, thus the name Widowville. "It is all wrapped up in controversy now," Dick will say. "Some say dioxin, which is supposed to have caused the cancers, is not dangerous. Some Champion officials claim there is no dioxin in the effluent. One study says the cancer rate in Hartford is no higher than anywhere else."

The tour continues. After all, there is little left of Hartford but a small combined general store-gas station-post office alongside the river. Approaching Newport, Dick points out a sign erected for those driving in the opposite direction, toward Haywood County and the mill:

WARNING: DIOXIN AHEAD
POLLUTED BY CHAMPION PAPER COMPANY
81 YEARS IS ENOUGH

(A newer sign is much more professional looking. An unknown benefactor came to certain Cocke County residents and offered to pay for its cost—in excess of a thousand dollars a month.)

The tour is approaching its end. The party enters Newport, whose

Frustration and rage is exemplified by this billboard along Interstate 40 in Cocke County, Tennessee, February 1988. Courtesy Jim Harrison.

main street is a mile or two off the Interstate. It is a step into the 1920s. Buildings are old and of an earlier era, the street is narrow, and signs of late-twentieth-century prosperity are missing. The Pigeon flows right through the heart of the town, fifty feet from City Hall. "They say the stench is worst when the weather is at its hottest," says Dick. "Before they got air conditioning, they had a choice: keep the windows closed and perspire, or open the windows and work with the stench."

Between stops, Mullinix informs his passengers about Champion and the Pigeon and about incidents that have occurred during their eighty-five-year relationship. He reminds his listeners that today no pulp or paper company could build an enormous plant along a fifty-million-gallon-a-day river, and then he points out that Champion has increased production more than eight times since the mill became operational in 1908. He relates his experiences with company and state government officials, especially North Carolina officials, and his anger rises. Yet he tries to understand their situation. He has kind words as well as critical comments about the now deceased vice-president in charge of operations at the Canton mill, Oliver Blackwell. "He was a right nice fellow," says Mullinix. "I'm sure that if we hadn't had this river between us I would have enjoyed his friendship. One afternoon we got to talking about different grades of paper and how glassine paper is made and so forth and we just got along beautifully." In Blackwell, whom Mullinix considered a good man, he sees Shakespearean-sized conflicts involving loyalty, honesty, and corporation policy at war with a polluted river that harms the well-being of the downriver residents. Having spent his adult life in a business closely affiliated with the paper trade, Mullinix is very critical of Champion's lack of responsibility. "There are two essential ingredients for making paper," he tells his visitors. "They're both natural resources, and this is why I think the paper industry is lacking in ethics. They live by taking advantage of natural things, wood and water."

His lecture is also sprinkled with incidents involving people who have antagonized Champion or its employees. Two young Champion electricians who had criticized the company at a public hearing on the pollution of the Pigeon River had their lives threatened at work. The day following the hearing, their statements were duplicated, and copies were tacked all over the plant. At the time, they were working on a two-hundred-foot-high tank. An employee demonstrated how easy it would be to take care of them: a little innocent shove and the young electricians would topple two hundred feet to their deaths. They both quit; the threats were too serious to ignore. Mullinix tells of a man who purchased land from the company below its landfill. The water in his well gradually turned black and gave off an offensive odor. Champion told him that he would have to get rid of his attorney before officials would sit down and discuss the matter with him.

Much of Mullinix's spleen is vented on North Carolina officials. "The boys at the North Carolina Department of Environmental Management are appointed by the Governor and they do what he tells them to do," Dick explains. "And as for the Governor—he will come to Asheville to make a speech and then go up to Champion at change of shifts and shake hands with the employees as they pass through the gates."

And so the years 1976–82 passed by. Raising public awareness took time. Sometimes the crusade seemed hopeless, yet in retrospect some progress was made. But it was progress in protest, not progress in results. Champion finally replied to Dick's letters and even arranged meetings between Mullinix, the company's environmental officer, and Oliver Blackwell. Dick thinks it was his continuous stream of letters published in the *Mountaineer* that finally prompted Champion to pay some attention to him. But the obstacles to progress were enormous. Haywood County, where the plant is located, depends for its prosperity on those seventy million dollars a year in wages paid out by Champion. Such an economic reality makes talk of the pollution of the Pigeon a forbidden topic for the great majority of its citizens. Like a family scandal, it is just not talked about. Moreover, one of Dick and Lucie's frustrations—particularly during the early years—has been "sunshine environmentalists." These are people who agree with everything they say and initially display interest in joining PRAG and becoming active, yet are hesitant to stand up and be counted or to take action. "They sit around and drink coffee and eat donuts and say tsk tsk tsk," Dick complains, "but when the chips are down and some courage is demanded, they withdraw from the fray."

Other Early Crusaders

As 1983 began, Dick looked back upon the years since 1976 with feelings of frustration and of hope. The Pigeon flowed just as dirty as ever: that constituted frustration. But Tennessee had started litigation against both Champion and North Carolina. Surely that was a good sign. Moreover, during these years a coterie of dedicated environmentalists had finally gathered around Dick and his organization, PRAG. Most of them have stuck with him through thick and thin. They are the ones who, with Dick, have made a difference.[6]

One of the early PRAG members was Jim Harrison. A bright, intense man in his early forties, Harrison grew up in Waynesville, where his parents ran a small five-and-dime store. He attributes his interest in environmentalism to Earth Day in 1970. His curiosity whetted, his first opportunity to do something constructive came in 1971 when, as a senior at Waynesville High School, he did a photography project on pollution in Haywood County. He was honored by having a number of his photographs placed on the school bulletin board. No one threatened him, although Champion was then as now the county's principal polluter.

Harrison was scientifically oriented. With good grades and ambition, he was accepted at Massachusetts Institute of Technology, where he graduated in 1976 with a major in Earth and Planetary Sciences. He then worked toward a master's degree in astronomy from the University of Texas, but a summer's vacation in Waynesville changed the course of his studies and of his life. That summer, he affiliated himself with the congressional campaign of the Democratic candidate from North Carolina's eleventh district, which includes Haywood County. Although the direct connection between that summer's politicking and his conversion to the cause of environmentalism is not entirely clear, by fall Jim Harrison had decided his future. When he returned to Austin, he switched from astronomy to courses in the Lyndon Johnson School of Government.

After earning his master's degree, he returned to Haywood County for a couple of years, actively supporting the local Democratic machine. Then he spent two years with the National Resources Defense Council, followed by employment with the Environmental Protection Agency. He is still attached to the EPA's Atlanta office, although his fury at the pollution of the Pigeon has on more than one occasion placed his job in jeopardy. Jim Harrison is courageous and he speaks his mind. It would be wrong to deny that his position in EPA hasn't on occasion helped the antipollution forces in their battle against the behemoth. Jim's expertise on Champion and the Pigeon, based upon a boyhood growing up in Haywood County, has also been beneficial.[7]

Still another early member and a consistent supporter of the cause is Nelson Ross. This talkative, friendly alumni coordinator and fundraiser for Carson Newman College is capable of clear analysis and succinct writing. He has put both abilities to good use in the Pigeon River campaign. Moreover, he designed the logo for Cocke County's Dead Pigeon River Council (DPRC). Along with other protesters, he does not buy Champion's claims that the river will flow "nearly" clean after the massive improvements go on line in 1994. "A cleaner river!" he scoffs at lunch in a restaurant off of I-40. Ross takes his iced tea and water glasses and drinks half the liquid in each. He holds up the two glasses. "See the difference?" he asks. Then he pours the half glass of iced tea into the water glass and holds that glass up to the light. "Is it clear?" he asks. With this analogy, he challenges Champion's claim that the river will flow "nearly" clear.[8]

Ross's initial interest in the Pigeon River came about during a Saturday adventure with his son. They had gone mountain climbing in the Pigeon River Gorge. "Our outing was ruined by the stench coming up from the river," he says, "and from then on I was determined to help bring about its cleansing." As the Southeast coordinator of the Izaak Walton League, Ross has been in a good position to advise and, at times, to lead the effort. The Izaak Walton League works quietly through legal action or through discussions at the highest levels. The organization does not advocate direct action.

Determination to do something about the pollution was one thing; implementing some kind of action was another. Someone suggested to Ross that he attend a PRAG meeting. When he received a PRAG flyer announcing a meeting in Asheville, Ross and his daughter drove there to attend. His aim was to check out the legitimacy of the organization, meet its leaders, and determine if it should receive the Izaak Walton League's expertise. It was rainy and foggy. Night was falling over the city in the eastern Appalachians as Ross and his daughter searched for the meeting place. They found it in an old two-story house in a dimly lit part of Asheville.

Ross relates their experience with amusement. "I got out of the car," he recalls, "and I looked up a steep stairway at this old wooden two-story house. I thought I saw a light in one of the rooms, so I climbed the steps, walked across the rickety porch, and rang the doorbell. I heard footsteps and soon the door was opened by this friendly, affable elderly man who introduced himself as Dick Mullinix. He escorted me into a parlor bare except for some chairs and an old table. The only light was from a sixty watt bulb screwed into a socket at the end of a cord hanging from the ceiling." Sitting at the table were Lucie, Lucie's sister, and Millie Buchanan, an environmental activist who lives in Asheville, and one or two other persons. All of them were wearing coats because it was chilly. At one end of the room, a small electric heater tried to reduce the cold; it was old, and the fan was touching something and making a rattling noise. About halfway through the meeting, a chair broke, sending one of the ladies sprawling. Ross savors the scene. "Believe me," he says, "I felt like I was a fifth columnist or maybe a communist, meeting secretly to plan a bombing or a revolution." The feeling must have been unanimous, he adds, because "we all talked in hushed tones as if there might be hidden mikes in the walls. I did not know at the time, but members had already experienced incidents—threats to their jobs, obscene phone calls, and that sort of thing." But they *did* talk, even if quietly, about their next moves against Champion.

Ross left the meeting with positive feelings about PRAG's legitimacy and about the integrity and sincerity of its officers and membership. He became one of PRAG's strongest supporters. At the same time, he was skeptical of the organization's chances of success. Its members did not possess the expertise of officers of a national organization, like the well-established Izaak Walton League. The support of such groups is essential to succeed in a campaign against powerful vested interests. Those interests included not just Champion but the government of the state of North Carolina and, in some of its manifestations, even the federal government. It would take more than PRAG to force a cleanup; it would take strong support from interests in the neighboring state of Tennessee.

One day in 1983, Dick Mullinix received a call from Bob Seay, who introduced himself as the executive director of the Newport-Cocke County

Chamber of Commerce. Seay wanted to know if Mullinix would be willing to come to Newport and talk with a few advocates of a clean Pigeon River. Of course, Dick accepted.

He was soon meeting Cocke County residents, long-suffering recipients of the Pigeon's pollution, who were beginning to stir with righteous indignation. Unlike other periods of protest in the past seventy-five years, which had quickly ended, this wrath was destined to stay risen. A number of important individuals attended these meetings and remain committed to the clean Pigeon River cause, two of whom stand out because of their dedication, persistence, energy, and ingenuity.

The first is Bob Seay. This middle-aged Cocke County man—he was born in the nearby hamlet of Del Rio along the French Broad—received his education at East Tennessee State University at Johnson City and returned to Cocke County to become the chamber of commerce's executive director. His office is in a community building on a side street where everything from county business meetings to youth meetings are held. Seay, whose face exhibits intelligence and sincerity, is determined to get that river cleaned up now. He realizes that his position is a source of power, and in the fight to clean the Pigeon, he has not hesitated to use it. As executive director of the chamber of commerce, he represents the county's businessmen, is the spokesman for the county's interests, operates with a staff and a budget, and has a central office. He is innovative and courageous; threats have not deterred him.[9]

Down the interstate just a couple miles from the Newport exit is Wilton Springs. After leaving I-40, there is a right turn on a gravel road, and in about a mile the road comes to Wilton Springs General Store and Hardware. It is a white, one-story building that has been added to until it seems out of proportion. In the back of the same building is the residence of owner Gay Webb and his family. In his late fifties, Webb is a survivor of serious heart surgery and of a life in tempestuous Cocke County.[10]

But Webb is not the television caricature of the country yokel who stands in front of his store and waits to service flatland tourists. He is highly literate, has college-educated children (one is a physician), and continues to make a modest profit even in this day of twenty-four-hour chain stores. It is a step into the past to enter his store, where everything from a candy bar to a No. 2 washtub can be purchased. It is also a meeting place of the local gentry, which around Wilton Springs includes all the farmers.

Webb's ancestry from early in the nineteenth century has been associated with Cocke County. He tells yarns of the Pigeon River prior to Champion's excesses. It was a wonderful land then, teeming with muskrats and beaver and all kinds of bird life. Stories were told, he says, of how mothers had to watch their toddlers for fear eagles would swoop down, grab them in their claws, and fly off with them. Proudly, he tells of supportive neighbors who have encouraged him in his fight against Champion. They have helped him take threats to his own life and to the lives of his wife and mother-in-law in stride. He tells of threats to firebomb his business. But Gay Webb is not cowed. "One elderly man came in here and said, 'Gay, my last hope is that before I die that once beautiful river will be clean again.'" says Webb. Then he explains, "Someone has got to fight for it, and keep on fighting, and some day we will win."

Webb does not deny Cocke County's reputation for violence and moonshining, but argues that the people had to make a living as best they could, and bootlegging was about the only economic opportunity Cocke County mountaineers possessed. "And they made good hooch here," he adds. "I've tasted peach brandy so delicious you could just taste

Dick and Lucie Mullinix often confer with Bob Seay, the activist executive director of the Newport–Cocke County Chamber of Commerce. Photo by Gilbert Soesbee, September 1983. Courtesy Newport Plain Talk.

Gay Webb displays a deformed fish taken from the Pigeon River near his home at Wilton Springs, near Newport, in November 1988. Photo by Jack Kirkland. Courtesy Knoxville News-Sentinel.

the freshness of the fruit." Everyone in Cocke County was aware of the moonshine business, he says, admitting that he was once involved, as were so many respected Cocke County citizens. "If the river was cleaned up," he insists, "new prosperity would come to Cocke County and the moonshining, marijuana growing, chop houses, and occasional prostitution would all die down." He tells of carloads of Cocke County residents returning from a long day's toil in Pigeon Forge, so tired they can hardly move from the car to buy groceries at his store for the evening meal. "Why should they have to drive thirty to forty miles each way to make beds in motels?" Webb asks. "With a clean river the motels would be here."

Webb's insistence that no compromises be allowed with Champion places him close to Mullinix and a nuance away from Seay and Nelson Ross, who occasionally seem more willing to accept a compromise with Champion. Part of Webb's inflexibility stems from the early 1930s when Champion cut a most favorable deal with the federal government for the sale of Champion timberland for the creation of Great Smoky Mountains National Park. The story, heard again and again in Cocke County, is that once the land was certain to be sold, Champion clear-cut indiscriminately, leaving nothing but a cut-over wasteland for the federal government. "This was wrong," he says, adding that the federal government was likewise wrong in the way it uprooted families from the soon-to-be national park, paying them a pittance and forcing them out of lands that had belonged to these families for generations.

Still another supporter of the movement has been Jerry Wilde, president of the Dead Pigeon River Council. Jerry is a robust, middle-aged Cocke County realtor and surveyor. When Seay and Ross were looking for active support from a member of the business community who could speak well and make a good impression, they turned to Wilde and found him amenable. It has taken time and cost him money, but he feels that the struggle has been worth the effort. According to Wilde, the problem in Cocke County, when Seay began the drive for membership in the Dead Pigeon River Council, was convincing people that they could accomplish anything. "Believe it or not," he says, "and down in Canton they won't believe it, the most common complaint when we launched the drive for supporters was the fear that by campaigning for a clean river we would cost the people of Canton their jobs." At first, he relates, businessmen were reluctant to place anti-Pigeon River stickers in their windows. "Not until the massive caravan of Champion employees to Knoxville in 1988 did this community get behind us. When that happened," Wilde recalls, "you could almost feel the polarization."[11]

While there are other very important individuals in the Pigeon River story, Dick Mullinix, Jim Harrison, Nelson Ross, Bobby Seay, Gay Webb, and Jerry Wilde are the foundations. No fair-weather friends are they: in the face of discouragement, death threats, and the seemingly insurmountable odds of fighting a six-billion-dollar corporation that, from 1980 to 1992, enjoyed a comfortable political climate, they have stuck together.

CHAPTER 5

The Legal Battles Begin

E
ven as more formidable opposition began to coalesce, the legal problems confronting Champion in
its defense of pollution of the Pigeon River began to
accumulate. Probably this fact did not bother Champion officials, at
least at first. Litigation is part of the business of making pulp and paper.
Public nuisance lawsuits have been fought by paper companies ever since
they began polluting. Moreover, pulp and papermaking is heavy industry,
somewhat dangerous, and so lawsuits involving personnel are common.

The Regulatory Brier Patch

What is different and changing is the legislation that has been passed
in the last fifty years aimed at cleaning up the air, water, and soil. After
all, until 1970 there was no Environmental Protection Agency. Dealing
with the few environmental regulations established by most states was
child's play for astute company lawyers. These lawyers were aided by the
fact that an alert, educated public was missing. But now that public has
become more alert and more educated. Dozens of nonprofit organizations serve as watchdogs over enforcement of environmental laws.
While recent presidential administrations dedicated to "getting the government off business's back" may have looked the other way as companies disregarded rules and regulations, the public clamor to clean up
smoke emissions, polluted water, and toxic wastes has continued to
grow; politicians ignore the clamor at considerable risk.

Any tabulation of federal laws, let alone those of the states of Tennessee and North Carolina, with amendments and legal interpretations

would fill several hundred books. So complex is this maze of laws, opinions, and interpretations that the situation works to the benefit of the defendants (the companies) and against the plaintiffs. As was the case with Brer Rabbit and the brier patch, the intricate, overlapping rules and regulations are a sanctuary that can give a polluter haven for a long time. But the litigation is costly, time consuming, and the resulting publicity can be harmful to a company's image. The defendant's arguments, on the other hand, can be scientific to the exclusion of the interested layman—which can be of benefit to the defendant.

An example of the burgeoning bureaucracy created in the name of environmentalism is the Environmental Protection Agency. Dick Mullinix and Gay Webb tell of standing on the sidewalk outside EPA's seven-story regional office in Atlanta and wondering what in the world all those people do. When EPA was created in 1970 by a reorganization plan, it brought together six thousand employees from fifteen government programs in three department-level agencies, the Department of Health, Education, and Welfare (now called Health and Human Services), the Department of Agriculture, and the Department of the Interior. The largest component of the newly formed EPA was the federal Water Quality Administration from the Department of the Interior, with twenty-seven hundred employees.[1]

In 1991 EPA had more than seventeen thousand employees. Its charge has expanded as new laws have been passed and assigned to EPA for enforcement. The Clean Water Act of 1972, Safe Drinking Water Act of 1974, and the Toxic Substance Control Act of 1976 greatly expanded its activities, and amendments to all these laws keep coming. It grants National Pollution Discharge Elimination System (NPDES) permits. In 1991 EPA's budget was well over four billion dollars.

Every state, likewise, has antipollution laws and a bureaucracy to enforce them. North Carolina's agency is the North Carolina Department of Environmental Management, Water Quality Section, which has an Operations Branch. Sometimes the description of a unit breaks down even more. A 1978 North Carolina Pigeon River Investigation gave as its source the North Carolina Department of Natural Resources and Community Development, Division of Environmental Management, Environmental Operations Section, Wastewater Management, Biology Unit. Tennessee's bureaucratic breakdown is somewhat similar: Tennessee Department of Health, Division of Water Quality Control.

State and federal legislation changes constantly; so do administrations. At a given time, a state agency might be determined to enforce environmental legislation, while its federal counterpart might be allowing industries to have their way. With a change in administrations, the agencies might flip-flop. Morale in the enforcement agencies fluctuates as the political pendulum swings.

Perhaps the best way to describe the legal and regulatory situation in environmental control, protection, and regulation is to say that it is in a state of flux. It is on the cutting edge of a new field of governmental responsibilities. Which entities have the authority to regulate? One needs only read the Supreme Court decision in *International Paper Co. v. Ouelette* to comprehend the intricacy of the issues. In this complicated case involving pollution from a paper mill in New York that diffuses its effluents into Lake Champlain and, in doing so, pollutes waters on the Vermont side of the lake, the Supreme Court handed down a decision in which it affirmed in part and reversed in part the decisions of inferior courts. The judges were hardly unanimous in their decision: Justice Powell delivered the majority opinion, in which Justices Rehnquist, White, O'Connor, and Scalia joined. But Justice Brennan filed an opinion concurring in part and dissenting in part; he was joined in this by Justices Marshall and Blackmun. Justice Stevens filed a separate opinion, again concurring in part and dissenting in part, and was joined by Justice Blackmun, whose opinion in Justice Brennan's opinion was again emphasized. Under such circumstances, trial and error are inevitable. Many of the new regulations are untried, some are unrealistic, some unenforceable, and some unnecessary. Some probably do place an unwarranted burden upon industries—the result of "regulatory overreach"—as Red Cavaney, president of the American Paper Institute, calls it. Regulations are the ingredients of a melting pot of government efforts to control toxicity, water pollution, and smokestack effluents. Simultaneously, industry fights back tooth and nail, opposing controls, determined to carry on business as usual. Environmentalism costs money; it also forces new approaches.

It is, Champion officials will insist, one thing to clean Pigeon River water in a laboratory process—at least 35 to 40 processes are possible (in fact, Champion claims to have investigated 150 technologies)—but it is something else to apply that process to 45 to 50 million gallons per day of Pigeon River water.

McKinney's Presentation

David McKinney's oral presentation to the Tennessee attorney general in April 1982 constituted the beginning of the legal drive by that state to force the cleanup of the polluted Pigeon River. McKinney and David Melgaard were the two biologists assigned the task of studying the muck in Waterville Lake, and their findings formed the crux of McKinney's talk. "It was the finest presentation I ever heard," says Paul Davis, present director of Tennessee's Water Quality Control bureau. It certainly bore positive results.[2]

Specifically, Melgaard and McKinney protested Carolina Power and Light's drawdown, which, they stated, "should not have been allowed to proceed in the manner in which it was performed. No controls were imposed to lessen the severity of the discharge of tons of organic muck from the bottom of the reservoir into Tennessee." And, by implication, their indictment of the drawdown indicated that it was high time something was done about the polluted condition of the Pigeon. It should be, they stressed, "an asset rather than the current liability status it holds for Cocke County, Tennessee."[3]

The biologists offered several specific recommendations. They said that Champion should be forced to live up to the National Pollution Discharge Elimination System (NPDES) process and that North Carolina should bring the Pigeon up to the Class C status specified for it from Canton to the state line. They suggested that Tennessee petition the EPA to "uphold its regulatory authority," something it had clearly not done. Moreover, they suggested that both EPA and North Carolina should petition to establish NPDES effluent limitations—including restrictions on odor, color, foam, and dissolved solids—so that the water from the river in Tennessee would be fit for domestic as well as industrial uses. The two scientists recommended that "a reasonable compliance schedule" providing for restoration of the Pigeon be adopted. They suggested that the state of Tennessee petition North Carolina to hold a public hearing on Champion, and, finally and most important, they said bluntly that if North Carolina and EPA "failed to execute their regulatory responsibilities, the State of Tennessee should take appropriate legal action."

In justifying such a drastic response, McKinney and Melgaard cited North Carolina's own "Rules, Classifications, and Water Quality Standards" and found the condition of the Pigeon below the mill in violation "of sections headed a and b and items a, c, d, and f of Class C usage." They even quoted from a North Carolina Pigeon River investigation, which had concluded, "Under North Carolina definition, the Pigeon River from Champion Paper to [its] confluence with the French Broad River in Tennessee (some 65 river miles) is offensive."[4]

Waterville Lake during the drawdown in 1980. Scientists discovered thousands of tons of toxic muck in the lake, primarily from Champion's effluent; as a result, Tennessee began litigation against North Carolina. Courtesy Carolina Power and Light Company.

The two biologists had merely focused on what everyone knew in a general way—that North Carolina's government, by granting variances, had allowed Champion to violate that state's own antipollution laws. They also pointed out that recourse existed at the state and federal levels to force Champion and the state of North Carolina to begin obeying or enforcing that state's regulations and to abide by NPDES specifications.

The scientists did not present a detailed description of the probable toxicity of the silt and organic muck that had been released when the drawdown occurred. Had they done so, their report and McKinney's oral presentation might have had an even greater impact. The total toxicity of Champion's solid wastes is not known, but almost every scientific study reveals the presence of carcinogens and other contaminants dangerous to human health in such solid wastes. Had this fact been stressed, the citizens of Knoxville, who get their water from the Tennessee River shortly after it leaves Douglas Lake, could have demanded more drastic action.

Tennessee Takes Action

The state of Tennessee, under the direction of Attorney General William M. Leech Jr., did the right thing. Already the Tennessee Department of Health and Environment (TDHE)—now the Tennessee Department of Environment and Conservation (TDEC)—had begun discussions with its North Carolina counterpart, the Department of Natural Resources and Community Development. Tennessee Governor Lamar Alexander, TDHE Commissioner James E. Word, as well as Attorney General Leech corresponded with their North Carolina counterparts. They noted that Champion's permit had expired on June 30, 1981, but was still considered in force by both North Carolina and Champion. Perhaps a new one would be issued in the second quarter of 1983. Subsequently, Tennessee officials discovered that, although North Carolina's water quality laws did contain some restrictive provisions, that state's own NPDES permit said nothing about color, solids, odor, or foaming, all of which were included in Tennessee's laws. McKinney and Melgaard suggested that North Carolina be forced to improve its water quality laws so that they were on a level with Tennessee's.[5]

On April 28, 1982, the Tennessee Water Quality Board passed a resolution calling for the restoration of the Pigeon River. It petitioned "the North Carolina Department of Natural Resources and Community Development to establish for Champion Paper Company of Canton, North Carolina, those standards and criteria necessary to abate pollution at the Pigeon River and to provide for the Tennessee segment sufficient to provide utilization of all classified uses. . . ." Shortly thereafter, the Tennessee Scenic Rivers Association entered the fray by passing a resolution petitioning for restoration of the Pigeon River and calling for the cooperation of the governors of North Carolina and Tennessee to achieve this goal. A similar resolution was passed by the Tennessee Wildlife Resources Commission.[6]

The Water Quality Board's resolution, which was received by North Carolina Governor James B. Hunt Jr., elicited a reply. In his letter of June 22, 1982, the governor admitted "that a potential problem exists in the Pigeon River Basin." Then he turned the problem over to Robert F. Helms, the director of the Division of Environmental Management, who, the governor said, would "be meeting with Tennessee representatives in the near future to discuss mutual concerns and possible improvements of the situation."[7]

Probably Governor Hunt had also heard from Champion officials. They knew they had a problem because the Tennessee Manufacturers Association—not ordinarily hostile to industrialists—had authorized its president, Carter H. Witt, to write Champion. "By means of this letter, this Association wishes to convey its concern to you regarding water quality in the Pigeon River and the resulting impact on economic development in Tennessee," Witt's letter began. He reminded Champion's vice-president for operations at Canton at that time, R. L. Marlewski, that several association members were located downstream from Newport and needed Pigeon River water for processing and cooling purposes. They had, Witt added, "made the financial commitment to come into compliance with Tennessee's water quality law and regulations." But what good did it do them when Champion polluted the Pigeon's waters? Witt reminded Marlewski that testimony by the Tennessee Water Quality Board had blamed Champion "for the Pigeon's deplorable condition," which made it unsuitable for industrial water supply.[8]

He went on to say that association members had over eight hundred plant locations, and they certainly understood the operational problems of manufacturers "who operate under varying water quality situations." But in Tennessee, he said, the association's plants work with state water quality officials to achieve compliance. "These efforts," he explained, "take the form of numerous evaluations, compliance schedules, and good faith efforts on the part of industry." Witt implied, therefore, that the situation between Champion and North Carolina should be the same. "As a matter of regulatory equity," the letter concluded, "it seems only fair to your downstream manufacturing neighbors that substantial changes in Champion's effluent occur soon." Witt hoped Champion would keep him informed of its response.[9]

The upshot of the exchange of letters between Tennessee and North Carolina officials was that discussions were carried on through the summer of 1982. In a letter of September 2, Michael T. Bruner, assistant commissioner of the Environmental Management and Quality Assurance Administration of Tennessee, wrote to Dr. Jay L. Langfelder, who held a somewhat similar position in North Carolina, and encouraged interstate cooperation in cleaning up the Pigeon, pointing out that Tennessee industries along the river usually had to use expensive groundwater even though the Pigeon flowed close by.[10] By September 28 Dr. Lunn, head of the Division of Water Quality Control, was writing Mr. Ben Smith, executive director of the Tennessee governor's Safe Growth Committee, on the subject of restoration of the Pigeon River. Suggestions were made about what approach to take next.[11]

But the talks got nowhere.

Thus began a conflict between Tennessee and North Carolina that, as of this writing, has not yet been resolved. Litigation was not initially contemplated. It was believed by Tennessee officials—naively, as it turned out—that serious cooperation between Tennessee and North Carolina could solve the problem. But the officials were sadly mistaken.

In January 1983, Tennessee notified North Carolina that Champion's effluents were violating Tennessee's water quality standards and demanded that reissuance or modification of the 1981 permit address Tennessee's concerns. That permit had been issued without prior notification to Tennessee, which was a violation of Section 402 (b)(3) of the Clean Water Act.[12]

When the two states' officials met in February 1983 to discuss appropriate terms for the pending permit, Tennessee submitted a model for Champion that, among other items, suggested that the Pigeon carry not more than 40 color units at the state line. In May and again in June, Tennessee requested that North Carolina adopt the model permit for Champion's effluent. In July, when it was apparent that North Carolina was dragging its feet, Tennessee officials requested that the Environmental Protection Agency investigate and assist in solving the problem. Mullinix's Pigeon River Action Group separately pressured EPA for the same action. North Carolina's recalcitrance prompted Tennessee to file a case against North Carolina in July 1983 "seeking injunctive relief and asking for civil penalties against Champion."[13]

Tennesseans were incensed. Their state had led the way among southeastern states in terms of clean water policy. Tennessee factories had been closed because the industrialists claimed they could not adhere to the strict water pollution laws, and other factories had been moved to other states because Tennessee was tough on environmental issues. It was hardly fair for Tennessee industries to adhere to strict standards while a mill in an adjoining state was allowed to pollute waters flowing into their state. Tennessee authorities were angered—angered to the extent that they said, "Let's sue them." And they did.

Tennessee's lawsuit was filed in the state's chancery court (Tennessee's trial-level court) in July 1983. As Champion stated in its brief, "Tennessee alleg[es] that Champion is violating various Tennessee statutes pertaining to water quality standards and that the Pigeon River is polluted by Champion. The Complaint seeks injunctive relief and monetary penalties." Assistant Attorney General Michael Pearigen, who was involved in the case, describes Tennessee as alleging "violations of the Tennessee Water Quality Act and the Tennessee common law of public nuisance." Champion argued that Tennessee's water pollution statute had been preempted by the federal Clean Water Act and could not be applied to an out-of-state discharger of pollutants such as Champion. The court handed down its decision in February 1984. The chancery court ruled in Tennessee's favor.

Tennessee law provided for a fine of ten thousand dollars a day for water pollution violations. "I would think we could ask for that amount since the act went into effect in 1977," Pearigen said, "but what we want from them is a clean river."[14]

Champion appealed to the Tennessee Court of Appeals. On January 15, 1985, the court handed down its opinion, again finding in favor of Tennessee.[15]

In the court's opinion, written by Judge Samuel I. Lewis, the court reviewed the clean water laws applicable to the case. The judge pointed out that Champion had been issued a National Pollution Discharge Elimination permit in August of 1977 by the state of North Carolina; when the time had come for renewal, Champion applied for and was granted the second permit, which expired on June 19, 1981. Before its expiration, Champion had applied for renewal again, and that permit, at the time of the judge's decision, was still pending.[16]

The opinion in this case explained that the Clean Water Act establishes the National Pollution Discharge Elimination System (NPDES), which is applicable nationwide. Without an NPDES permit, the discharger is subject to substantial penalties. Enforcement is in the hands of the Environmental Protection Agency. EPA is empowered to authorize states to issue their own permits if the state has water antipollution requirements at least equal to those promulgated by the EPA pursuant to the Clean Water Act. Such a permit satisfies both EPA under the Clean Water Act provisions and the state. Both North Carolina's and Tennessee's clean water regulations had met these requirements, and they were authorized to issue their own permits.

But there was a problem: water quality standards vary from state to state. Those of Tennessee were markedly tougher than those of North Carolina. In fact, Tennessee's standards exceeded the federal standards as set down under the Clean Water Act and EPA. "The regulations of the Tennessee Department of Health and Environment," wrote Judge Lewis, "place limits on the amount of dissolved solids and foam which may be discharged under a permit and the degree to which the water may be colored or an odor created by a discharge. *Neither the State of North Carolina nor the Federal government place such restrictions upon their discharge permits*" (italics mine). And, the judge added, it was these solids, foam, odor, and color, which had destroyed the Pigeon River "for any useful purposes."

Judge Lewis went on to cite Article 6, Clause 2, of the Constitution (known as the Supremacy clause) that preempts state laws only when congress has so intended, and he began his discussion "with the basic assumption that Congress did not intend to displace state law"; the Constitution demands that congress's intention has to be unmistakable. But Champion insisted that congress, by enacting the Clean Water Act, precluded the application of Tennessee law "to discharge into interstate waters occurring in another state."

The complexity of the decisions was increased, as always happens, by precedent. Heavily cited was the 1972 decision in the case of *Illinois v. City of Milwaukee,* which involved one jurisdiction polluting another that had more stringent antipollution laws. In that decision the United States Supreme Court indicated that "a state with high water-quality standards may well ask that it not be compelled to lower itself to the more degrading standards of a neighbor." But, the Supreme Court opinion added, "there are no fixed rules that govern. These be equity suits in which the informed judgment of the chancellor [judge] will largely govern." The highest tribunal also stated that lower federal courts did have jurisdiction under federal common law. The problem did not end there. Illinois had sued again. This time, the Supreme Court had ruled that congress, by passing the Clean Water Act and subsequent amendments, had eliminated recourse to "federal common law" and had "automatically prevented resort to state law remedies."

For Judge Lewis, this was too much. He disagreed, believing that the Clean Water Act had been interpreted "in a strained manner." As Judge Lewis interpreted it, a state most certainly does have the right to sue another state that is polluting its waters. By the Clean Water Act with its amendments, he concluded, "The states are invited, and we think encouraged, to adopt water quality standards more stringent than those set by the Federal Government under the act." Tennessee could sue North Carolina, under provisions of Tennessee's Water Quality

Control Act of 1977; the judgment of the earlier court was reaffirmed, and Champion was to be assessed the costs.[17]

Champion appealed again, and in August 1985 the Tennessee Supreme Court agreed to hear the case. On April 21, 1986, the Tennessee Supreme Court handed down its ruling. As an indication of how justice can be blind, the court ruled against its own state and in favor of Champion. Judge Harbison handed down the majority opinion; a minority opinion was filed by Justice Drowata.[18]

In his majority opinion, Justice Harbison noted immediately that there was no question as to the material facts of the case; i.e., of course Champion polluted the Pigeon River and of course the effluent flowed into Tennessee. However, the court ruled that environmental agencies of one state may not take official action against a permit holder in another state except as authorized by federal statutes. Thus, a state such as North Carolina, with mild antipollution regulations, can (and indeed does) allow polluted waters to flow into Tennessee, which has far more stringent controls. Tennessee has no legal recourse. Federal legislation is preemptive of both states' rights. Insipidly, the opinion reminded litigants that the affected state (Tennessee) was to receive notice of each application for a permit and have an opportunity for public hearing. Moreover, Tennessee could submit to North Carolina written recommendations, and North Carolina had to notify Tennessee officials "in writing of its failure to do so [carry out the recommendations] together with its reasons for so doing." Finally, the majority decision suggested that any other ruling would "lead to chaotic confrontation of sovereign states." As if this was not enough, the Tennessee Supreme Court defended North Carolina and Champion. "A duly authorized permit from the Environmental Protection Agency or from an authorized state should . . . afford some protection to the holder thereof, who frequently has obtained it at enormous expense."[19] Tennessee, it should be remembered, had submitted recommendations, but to no avail. One reads the majority decision and wonders if the justices live in the real world.

The blow to Tennessee environmentalists was somewhat alleviated by Justice Drowata's minority opinion. Granting that it was "a difficult case," he felt that under the Tenth Amendment to the Constitution— "The powers not delegated to the United States by the Constitution, nor prohibited by it to the States, are reserved to the States respectively, or to the people"—Tennessee had jurisdiction. Tennessee, he argued, suffered from pollution from just one facility in another state; it was not like the situation along a major waterway such as the Mississippi or

Ohio. And it was primarily Tennessee, not North Carolina, that suffered from the pollution. Moreover, Champion did business in Tennessee and owned property there; for most other purposes Champion would be subject to the regulatory powers of Tennessee as well as North Carolina, just as many corporations were subject to the laws of many states.

"In effect," reasoned Justice Drowata, "the Majority is permitting the State of North Carolina to dictate the policy of this State [Tennessee]." North Carolina's law and policy remains "unfrustrated" while Tennessee's is "frustrated"; but if Tennessee were granted the power to regulate, "the law and policy of both States would be enforced." Tennessee was not suing North Carolina, he added, but was seeking redress from a private party, Champion. He cited the words of the Federal Water Pollution Control Act (FWPCA) to substantiate his argument that the state not only had the power to enforce strict pollution laws on another state, but also was actually encouraged to. In fact, uniformity was not to be encouraged. Relegating the higher standards of one state to the lower standards of another, wrote the dissenter, "transforms the minimum federal standards into the maximum standards for many interstate streams."[20]

Further, if Champion were forced to comply with Tennessee's laws, then it would be forced to comply with just one standard since Tennessee's embraced North Carolina's standards plus additional requirements. Justice Drowata insisted that Tennessee's case was "wholly consistent with the objectives and obligations of the Federal Water Pollution Control Act [FWPA]." To deny Tennessee the power to regulate pollution in waters that enter the state "reduces the State to an administrative arm of the Federal Government," a violation of the Tenth Amendment. On the other hand, if the state were successful in its suit against Champion, a private party, "its action would not only incidentally benefit North Carolina, but it also more fully serves the purpose of the FWPCA to eliminate pollution." Judge Drowata also found it "incongruous that North Carolina would ever defend as its public policy a right to pollute on the part of Champion." Any fair and liberal interpretation of the Tenth Amendment would give "scope and meaning" to Tennessee's case, the judge concluded, and so he dissented from the majority opinion.[21]

Tennessee's reaction was to petition the U.S. Supreme Court to review the Tennessee Supreme Court's decision. At the time, the U.S. Supreme Court was considering the case of *International Paper Company* v. *Ouelette*. This case originated in Vermont, where International Paper was polluting Lake Champlain. The Court accepted Tennessee's petition, then vacated the decision "with instructions that the Champion case be considered in light of the *Ouelette* decision." To quote Attorney Michael Pearigen:

In *Ouelette,* the U.S. Supreme Court decided that the federal Clean Water Act preempted a downstream State's statutory water quality law (but not its common law of riparian rights or public nuisance) in an interstate water pollution situation, with a downstream State's water quality being protected by the interstate water pollution provisions of the federal Clean Water Act. Upon remand of the case to the Tennessee Supreme Court, the State voluntarily dismissed its case in order to concentrate on the interstate remedies in the federal Clean Water Act.[22]

In layman's terminology, the *Ouelette* decision says that a state could not sue a polluting upstream neighboring state even though the former state had a law that would prevent such pollution from occurring within its own borders. The recourse would be to enforcement of the Clean Water Act. This recourse, including issuance of NPDES permits, is in the hands of the Environmental Protection Agency. However, aggrieved individuals had a right, under the common law of riparian rights and public nuisance, to sue the source state—New York in this case—on grounds of violation of New York's own nuisance law. Vermont, therefore, could sue in Vermont courts but had to apply New York's law, not Vermont's. The state of Tennessee dismissed its case, determined instead to resort to the remedies specified by the Clean Water Act. (The problem—since politics is always present—was to get EPA to act against Champion and North Carolina.)

North Carolina and Federal Cases

Tennessee's officials refused to give up. When Attorney General Leech resigned and W. J. Michael Cody took his place, the pressure remained constant. Tennessee's next recourse was in the courts of North Carolina. It filed suit against the North Carolina Environmental Management Commission in Wake County, North Carolina Superior Court (Raleigh) to set aside the state's water quality permit on grounds that, under the federal Clean Water Act, it infringed upon Tennessee's rights as an affected downstream state. The suit was dismissed but was reversed on Jan. 21, 1986, by the North Carolina Court of Appeals [23]

To this point, nothing had been heard from the Environmental Protection Agency, which, with its charge to enforce the Clean Water Act and issue National Pollution Discharge Elimination System permits, should have been involved. Now the clean water proponents—Dick Mullinix of PRAG and Tennessee officials—began applying pressure to this massive agency. On May 14, 1985, North Carolina had issued a new permit to Champion, with the usual variances. On November 13, EPA rejected North Carolina's permit and announced that it would take control of the permitting process because the permit issued by North Carolina violated state and federal pollution laws. Until a new permit was issued, the state permit would remain in effect. On January 17, 1986, Champion filed a brief in the Federal District Court for Western North Carolina against EPA. The agency had failed to approve of North Carolina's permit, and Champion's claim alleged that EPA had unlawfully denied it; in fact, EPA, asserted Champion, had no power over North Carolina's permit.[24]

Federal District Judge David Sentelle's opinion in this case was to be a blow to both appellants, Champion and the state of North Carolina through its regulatory agency, the Department of Natural Resources and Community Development. Their adversary was EPA; appearing as its defendants were its Region IV administrators, Lee M. Thomas and Jack E. Ravan. Intervenor defendants were the state of Tennessee on behalf of the Department of Health and Environment and the Tennessee Wildlife Resources Agency represented by lawyers from the Tennessee attorney general's office, including W. J. Michael Cody, Frank J. Scanlon, and Michael D. Pearigen. The Pigeon River Action Group (PRAG) and the Legal Environmental Assistance Foundation (LEAF) were likewise intervenor defendants and had a lawyer at hand. Also present was PRAG's founder, Dick Mullinix.

Champion's opposition looked formidable. The company had its usual band of highly paid counselors. They were bolstered by Alan S. Hirsch and Daniel C. Oakley, North Carolina's assistant attorneys general. The presence of North Carolina lawyers sitting at the same table with lawyers for a polluting industry, and supporting that industry, seemed utterly shameful to environmentalists. They just wanted Champion to clean up its act, so to speak.

This case dealt with far more precise details of water pollution than had the previous ones. While the subject could have involved water temperature, dissolved oxygen, dissolved solids, foam, stench, toxic wastes, or still other matters, Judge Sentelle limited the question to color. It must be emphasized that a stream that is colored does not receive sunlight as does a clear stream; its photosynthetic activity is curtailed. This affects literally everything in the river—plants, insects, and fish. Moreover, the measurement of stream color has been perfected with the platinum cobalt measure defined in units. Champion's effluent into the Pigeon River at the pipe (at least until January 1993) ranged from 700 to 900 color units with occasional situations, such as low water, when it exceeded 1,200 color units. It was such heavy coloring that led Cocke County residents to refer to the river for over eighty-five years not as the Pigeon but as the Black River.

Michael D. Pearigen was involved in most of Tennessee's litigation against North Carolina during the 1980s, first as a member of the Environmental Division of the Tennessee attorney general's office and later as deputy attorney general for the Environment. Courtesy Michael D. Pearigen.

Indeed, color has been the prime consideration throughout much of the Pigeon River controversy, whereas toxic wastes, BOD, foam, stench, ammonia, chloroform, and even dioxin have commanded lesser consideration. From the environmentalists' point of view, this has had a negative effect on their campaign because Champion and its defenders, including North Carolina Governor Jim Martin (a chemist by profession), have insisted that people were just objecting to a colored river, and, therefore, they were expressing an aesthetic feeling. It is, these Champion supporters argue, hardly worth risking an industry that was pumping one hundred million dollars per year into the local economy just to have a prettier river.

North Carolina's laws said nothing about color tolerances, whereas Tennessee's mentioned color restrictions, but unfortunately never mentioned specific color unit limits—a point often made by the Volunteer State's Tarheel adversaries. It follows that Champion's permit that expired June 30, 1981, had no color restrictions placed upon the company. Indeed, as Judge Sentelle noted in his decision, "Neither North Carolina nor Champion requested the public hearing provided for, . . . and North Carolina failed to modify the permit in accordance with EPA's objections. . . ."

That decision was not handed down until December 1, 1986, with the motion for withdrawal of mandate rejected on February 3, 1987. The decision was clear, persuasive, and devastatingly thorough. In Sentelle's opinion EPA had never acted in an "arbitrary and capricious" way. He proved, citing federal statutes, that 1) EPA had a right to apply the numerical standards of 50 color units even though Tennessee's regulation was a narrative one; 2) North Carolina failed to reply to EPA's objections to the permit within the ninety days following that objection, and when the state did reply, it was in the form of a letter, not as a revised permit; and 3) EPA had the expressed right to intervene in a dispute between two neighboring states.[25]

Judge Sentelle found that Champion opposed EPA on three grounds, two of which dealt with color. He acknowledged that North Carolina had finally adopted an EPA-approved color standard, one specifying that color was allowed in only such amounts as would not harm public health, secondary recreation, aquatic life or wildlife, affect the palatability of fish or the "aesthetic quality or impair the waters for designated uses." Trouble was, Champion's permit "did not contain an aesthetic requirement." Nor did it contain conditions whereby the requirements could be achieved. This alone made the permit "outside the guidelines and requirements of the Clean Water Act." The permit also failed to describe the "methodology to be used by the [North Carolina] Environmental Management Commission to judge compliance. . . ." So the permit, emphasized Judge Sentelle, failed to "ensure" compliance. "Clearly," the judge added, "unless there is some method for measuring compliance there is no way to ensure compliance." EPA had committed no error in judgment.[26]

The judge made quite an issue of compliance—unequivocal compliance. The failure of the permit to insist upon this was, Judge Sentelle wrote, EPA's second reason for asserting its authority. He examined with a magnifying glass, so to speak, the Environmental Management Commission's use of the word "may," noting that, according to the permit, if Champion failed to meet the color requirement, "the Commission 'may' in the future require some unspecified 'additional action' to achieve 'appropriate' color removal." Champion had to make only "all reasonable efforts." With reference to Champion's demonstration facility—a pilot antipollution program Champion was touting at the time—the permit stated that if it was found unsuccessful, the "commission 'may' in the future require some unspecified 'additional action' to achieve 'appropriate' color removal." In other words, the judge found such wording the work of a Philadelphia lawyer, the kind of attorney the dictionary defines as a lawyer of outstanding ability at exploiting legal fine points and technicalities; the difference between 'may' and 'shall' is considerable. Judge Sentelle was not fooled. He found the language of the Champion permit from North Carolina "to be clearly permissive." He noted that if the demonstration project failed, Champion was not *"required"* (Sentelle's emphasis) to make any further efforts to eliminate the color. Again, EPA, in denying the permit, had made no error in judgment; it had not acted in an arbitrary or capricious manner.[27]

Then there was the matter of the 50-color-unit standard. As has been noted, color became the most contentious item in the Pigeon River controversy, at least until the dioxin scare came along in 1987. EPA had noted that Champion's permit failed to require compliance with Tennessee's requested color standard. EPA had, therefore, found the permit outside the guidelines of the Clean Water Act. Champion and North Carolina contended that Tennessee had just a narrative color standard, not a numerical one, but Judge Sentelle brushed aside this argument. In a footnote he added that Tennessee had imposed a 33 color unit increase limit upon Bowater Southern Paper Company in 1984.

He described briefly the history of color regulation by the EPA. In 1974 EPA had identified color as a pollutant peculiar especially to the pulp and paper industry and had promulgated national color limitations, but in 1982 had concluded that color matters should be determined on a case-by-case basis. Thus, EPA's selection of the 50 color units for the Pigeon "was in line with that stated policy" and was not arbitrary or capricious. The only way Champion could comply with a color standard, the judge emphasized, was by a numerical standard—there was nothing arbitrary or capricious about that. The 50-color-unit figure was likewise logical; North Carolina and Tennessee representatives meeting with the EPA at an earlier date had agreed to a number of between 40 and 50 units. "There has been no clear error of judgment," reads the decision, "and this court will not substitute its judgment for the informed, technical judgment of the EPA." Moreover, Tennessee had finally accepted 50 color units as constituting its numerical standard, and it was not arbitrary or capricious for it to do this.

Finally, the question remained of EPA's permitting authority. This was what Champion and the state of North Carolina contested; even if EPA had jurisdiction over color, they insisted, the agency should have authority over nothing else—toxins, oxygen, chemicals, stench, etc. Judge Sentelle cited the various federal water acts, with amendments and additions, to prove that EPA had the specific powers it had used in rejecting Champion's permit. He showed that when a state fails to reply to an objection within ninety days, EPA has the stated power to issue its own permit, a permit that meets "all applicable requirements."

The Clean Water Act has no provision for partial permits. And so EPA was "entitled to summary judgment"; it did have the power to both issue or reject a permit.[28]

Champion's lawyers then cited the recent United States Supreme Court case, *International Paper Company* v. *Ouelette*, and Champion moved for "withdrawal of mandate" on the basis of the decision in this case. *Ouelette* was, however, a case involving a common-law nuisance action, and Judge Sentelle failed to see a connection between *Ouelette* and *Champion* v. *EPA*. Judge Sentelle let the decision stand.[29]

The Litigation Continues

As is so often the story involving litigation in the United States, this did not end the controversy. Champion appealed as plaintiff appellant, North Carolina as plaintiff.

The case, *Champion International Corporation* v. *United States Environmental Protection Agency,* with the Tennessee departments, PRAG, and LEAF also represented, was argued on October 5, 1987, before the Federal Circuit Court, and the decision was handed down on June 24, 1988.[30]

Most of the court's discussion was similar to the background given by the district court. Rather quickly, the Federal Circuit Court made one thing clear: the district court had acted within its delegated authority in objecting to the draft state permit and assuming issuing authority, but it did not have the right to conduct further review—because of "lack of subject matter jurisdiction." That, wrote Judge Widener, was within the jurisdiction of the Federal Circuit Court. Nevertheless, Champion lawyers could have found little solace in the court's statement that "EPA has been much too hesitant to take any actions where States have approved permit programs." The result, the court speculated, "might well be in the creation of 'pollution havens' in some of those states which have approved permit programs." Congressional intent was emphasized, especially the intent behind amendments to the Clean Water Act in 1977.

The circuit court pointed out that judicial review of the EPA permit could not yet take place because the permit had not yet been issued.

Litigation certainly did not end here. During these years from 1982 to 1988, while these actions were reported in the press and thus kept in the public's psyche, Dick Mullinix and his Pigeon River Action Group continued to protest. Now Cocke County entered the fray.

CHAPTER 6

Cocke County
Takes a Stand

L egal issues involving a renewal of Champion's permit, the positions regarding the permit taken by North Carolina and Tennessee, and the intervention of EPA all created constant exposure that surely Champion was not used to and certainly did not covet. Never before had the Pigeon River been the subject of so much litigation and media attention. The publicity influenced the activities of Dick Mullinix and members of his Pigeon River Action Group. As local activists, they were more determined than ever not to allow the media to forget about the polluted Pigeon. They had positive indications that East Tennessee was aroused. As for North Carolina, save for a few brave environmentalists, the publicity was not welcomed.

"There is no chance and never has been," says Jim Harrison, who grew up in Waynesville in North Carolina, "that the movement to clean up the Pigeon River will ever come from Haywood County, or even from North Carolina, for that matter."[1]

But it could be different across the line into Cocke County. In Tennessee Champion lacks the influence on state and local government that it wields in North Carolina. It is true that the company owns thousands of acres in the Volunteer State. By no means, however, does Cocke County benefit from Champion's mill as does neighboring Haywood County. Some timber sales bring a little revenue to Cocke County's people, and a few workers commute to work at the mill. One small factory in Cocke County manufactures the heavy rollers upon which are wound tons of paper produced at the Canton facility. But the sum total in dollars Champion has meant to Cocke County has been paltry compared to the damage done to Newport and its surroundings by the polluted Pigeon.

"About every four years," says Bob Seay, executive director of the Cocke County-Newport Chamber of Commerce, "there has been a flare-up of resentment against Champion, but it has always been of brief duration. The populace literally gives up."

In 1983 a change took place. Cocke County residents again rose up in protest, but this time the flare-up remained; instead of dying out, the resentment grew. It is still there and is still vigorous.

Certainly Charles Moore, who was then the Cocke County executive officer, considers 1983 the crucial year in which Cocke County began to be heard, and the heat began to build up against Champion. "In the very beginning they [Champion officials] would not speak to us," he recalls. "I can remember calling them and asking for a meeting, and I couldn't talk to anyone. I mean, no one returned my calls." But after the helicopter and TV crew incident in 1983, when Moore, Seay, and a TV crew from Knoxville embarrassed Champion officials by showing footage of the polluted Pigeon, the company began to show concern. Out of the blue, according to Moore, the phone rang one day. It was a Champion official asking for a meeting with Moore. "I agreed to it," Moore recalls, "but I had representatives of the county commission, the city, the chamber of commerce—about twelve or fifteen people in all—waiting in the room at our big conference table."

"And we had the press," Bob Seay adds.

Long experience has taught lobbyists the coercive power of an impressive entourage. Champion had learned that lesson as well. Its retinue was made up of seven people, including Mary Lee Ransmeier, its environmental specialist, and Oliver Blackwell, then vice-president in charge of operations at the Canton plant. He led the charge. Charles Moore smiles at remembering the scene. "They almost flipped out when they saw us," he recalls.

"We thought this was supposed to be a private meeting," the company's spokesman said.

"What you gotta say to me, you can say to the world," replied Moore.

Bob Seay recalled the results of the meeting. "What they said was the usual pap. It was technologically and economically unfeasible to clean up the Pigeon; they would do it when the technology was available and it was economically practicable. To force Champion to close would throw thousands out of work and depress not only all of western North Carolina but parts of East Tennessee, including Cocke County."

"Nothing was accomplished," concluded Moore.

Nothing was accomplished from the meeting insofar as Champion was concerned, but the significance of the power of Cocke County's officials, if they could work together against the corporate giant, was not lost upon Bob Seay, Charles Moore, or the others present. That meeting, along with the helicopter incident and the resulting publicity about Cocke County's plight, made Cocke County's government officials more determined than ever to keep the problem before the public.

The Crusade Begins

For the next three years, Bob Seay, his industrious secretary, Fran Ketterman, Charles Moore, Johnny Teague, then president of the chamber of commerce, and Jeanne Wilson, Newport's mayor, kept alive the county's interest. They were aided by Pigeon River Action Group publicity, by Mullinix's continuing letters to the editor and his availability as a speaker, and, above all, by the ongoing news of the progress (or lack of progress) of the litigation making its way through the courts. The failure of North Carolina's Department of Environmental Management to expedite the permit process, the obvious initial reluctance of EPA to intervene, and pressures from Tennessee officials and the Pigeon River Action Group to force the issue gave Newport's award-winning, tri-weekly newspaper, *Plain Talk,* plenty of newsworthy material. News editor Gilbert Soesbee, who had grown up in Canton, and his wife, fellow journalist Nancy Oberst, made the most of it. Their incisive articles kept Cocke County citizens informed and prevented them from forgetting their polluted Pigeon River.

This is not to suggest that they succeeded; after all, the river still flows dirty. All of Newport's activists worked hard and met with frustrations equal to those experienced in earlier years by Dick Mullinix and the Pigeon River Action Group. They learned that the wheels of bureaucracy turn slowly, most especially if, for political reasons, the bureaucrats are reluctant to act. They knew that politics was indeed present. "EPA's part in this thing stinks," Moore was saying in 1988, to which Bob Seay added, "and you know, the State of Tennessee's not been a big help either." He paused, contemplating his next statement. "Really, we've tried to deal with two states. North Carolina let them [Champion] have their way for eighty-three years. But in essence, Tennessee has too."

At the start of their sustained campaign, Charles Moore, Bob Seay, and Jeanne Wilson contacted officials at EPA and Tennessee's top political officeholders. In the latter category were Senators Al Gore and Jim Sasser, their congressman, East Tennessee Representative James H. Quillen, their governor, Ned McWherter, and their local state representative, Ronnie Davis. All have been supportive, but to different degrees. McWherter came through when his support was critical. The two senators and Congressman Jimmy Quillen have campaigned in—or visited— Cocke County, each one speaking in favor of a clean Pigeon River. Probably the toughest, most consistent stance has been taken by Congressman Quillen, whose home is in Johnson City.

While litigation crawled through state and federal court systems from 1983 to 1987, Cocke County residents, Dick Mullinix and the Pigeon River Action Group, the Legal Environmental Assistance Foundation (LEAF), and the Sierra Club kept up a modicum of pressure. Big and little environmental groups came to their aid. Even large-circulation newspapers, such as the *Atlanta Journal*, the *Los Angeles Times*, and the *Christian Science Monitor* ran feature articles on the controversy. Because adverse publicity is a basic fact of life in the pulp and paper industry, a well-paid public relations department is a fixed part of the industry's corporate system, and such departments are supposed to counteract negative publicity. But rarely have situations arisen in which the opposition has dragged on and on. After dealing with North Carolina and its Division of Environmental Management, Tennessee and its attorney general, the Newport-Cocke County Chamber of Commerce and its uncompromising clique of executives, Dick Mullinix and his Pigeon River Action Group, and the EPA, to say nothing of living with worrisome litigation that was making its way through the courts, Champion International's executives had to realize that something major must be done about the situation involving the Canton mill.

As for the Newport-Cocke County environmentalists, they were galvanizing support for their clean Pigeon River campaign. As time went on, they learned more and more about how to use newspapers, radio, and television to advance their cause. Long before, they had contacted Dick Mullinix, who had encouraged them to be organized and not give up the fight. Then, Johnny Teague, president of the chamber of commerce, suggested that they get help from an old college friend of his, Nelson Ross. Teague knew that Ross was the southeastern coordinator of the Izaak Walton League. Moreover, Ross knew how to launch campaigns; he could help the Cocke County opposition in establishing some kind of organization and give it useful tips on how best to promote its cause.

The Izaak Walton League has had a long and respected role in the environmental movement. It was founded in 1922 in Chicago by fifty-four sports fishermen. They were concerned over the deterioration of their fishing streams caused by industrial pollution, untreated sewage, and soil erosion. Today the league has more than four hundred chapters and a membership of fifty thousand. It has been a consistent advocate of strict water quality laws. It campaigned relentlessly for passage of the Clean Water Act. The league rarely makes headlines because its working style is characterized by quiet lobbying and occasional legal actions. Nelson Ross's personality fits that style. He is a friendly East Tennessean, affable, intelligent, and dedicated.

Ross accepted Teague's invitation and drove down from Jefferson City to Newport to meet with the activists. He helped them found the Dead Pigeon River Council. Its acronym, DPRC, has become widely known throughout East Tennessee and western North Carolina. One day as he contemplated the group's problems, he found himself doodling. Before he knew it, Ross had sketched the Dead Pigeon River Council logo: an upside-down dead pigeon hovering over a river. Charles Moore used his influence to obtain modest funding for the council's activities from the county budget, listing the council as a charitable organization.

The DPRC came into existence toward the end of 1986. The years since 1983 had been punctuated by news about the river. Now the community of Newport and the surrounding county were showing interest as never before. Meetings of the council were best attended prior to impending actions, such as a hearing, or following a legal decision or decisions made by EPA.

In 1986 Nelson Ross, Johnny Teague, and Bob Seay met at a local restaurant in Newport to plan future action. It was a special year for Tennessee, proclaimed by Gov. Lamar Alexander as "Tennessee Homecoming '86." Alexander's campaign aimed at encouraging citizens of every community to plan for the celebration of Tennessee's two hundred years of statehood, which will occur in 1996. The year was now drawing to a close, and Newport's citizens had made no plans for the bicentennial.

Nelson Ross, Charles Moore, and Bob Seay came up with an idea. Why not highlight the clean Pigeon River fight in the county's bicentennial agenda? Have a bell-ringing ceremony on New Year's Eve, 1986. Call it "The Bells Toll for Champion." Let the world know that by 1996 the Pigeon River would flow clean, and the campaign would continue until it succeeded.

"We wanted to let Champion and North Carolina know that we viewed this as a ten-year fight, that we know this is not a short-term struggle, and we are ready for the long haul," Seay explained.

They were determined that the program be impressive and success-

An upside-down dead pigeon over a river struck Nelson Ross as the perfect logo for the Dead Pigeon River Council (DPRC). Courtesy Nelson Ross.

ful. On New Year's Eve, at least a hundred people, some of them from Jefferson and Sevier Counties and a few from North Carolina, gathered on the McSween (North Street) Bridge at Newport over the polluted Pigeon. At midnight in this ordinarily quiet little town, fire and police sirens whined and church bells tolled as supporters of a clean Pigeon River rang handbells and cowbells, serving notice that Champion International's days of having its way with the river were coming to an end. Bob Seay was master of ceremonies.

"There's a reason for our gathering here tonight," said chamber of commerce president Johnny Teague Jr., "and that is to improve our quality of life." He announced the creation of the Dead Pigeon River Council, a coalition, he said, of area individuals and conservation organizations dedicated to seeing the pollution of the river stopped. The council logo was imprinted on the programs, with assurances that in due time T-shirts and other paraphernalia bearing it would be for sale in Cocke County.

Nelson Ross told the audience that it was time "to counteract the foot-dragging in the courts" and the "obstinance" [*sic*] of the corporation with pressure from the people who live along the river and with the education of students from public schools to colleges about pollution. Another speaker assured Cocke County residents that the Jefferson County and Morristown chambers of commerce were giving them its full support. Dr. Gary McKenna, president of Morristown's Bill Kiefer Chapter of the Izaak Walton League, also spoke; he was at the time a member of the board of the national organization.

The local state representative, Ronnie Davis, expressed his delight at such a midnight turnout, adding that success depended on "how much public pressure we can exert."

Then, in unison, the crowd read "The Pigeon River Resolution": "We now serve notice that the Champion mill can no longer peacefully pollute the Pigeon, depriving the citizens of this region of the recreational, aesthetic, and economic values of a clean Pigeon River. We will not rest until our river again runs clear."

The Reverend Tom Mooty prayed that the Pigeon River be treated "as it was intended to be treated. . . . You created, Lord, a beautiful stream and man has polluted it."

Then, as a physical manifestation of their hopes and determination, members of the assemblage placed lighted candles on shingles and sent them floating down the dead river.

A hundred dedicated people at midnight on a chilly New Year's Eve may not seem that impressive, but it was the strongest manifestation of displeasure with the Pigeon's condition ever displayed by Cocke County's citizenry. It was a portent of rising opposition to the six-billion-dollar corporation, to the policies of the state of North Carolina, to the on-again, off-again support of Tennessee's government, to the foot dragging of the courts and the EPA.[2]

The Dead Pigeon River Council was operational. Now the problem confronting its officials was how to maintain the momentum. In February 1987, the organization held a fund-raising kickoff breakfast almost in the lion's mouth, at a restaurant at Lake Junaluska in North Carolina. Mayor Jeanne Wilson and Newport's aldermen all promised to attend. Newport city hall contributed $425 to help fund the event, and about a hundred people were invited. A goal of $15,000 was set for the DPRC's war fund. Also, a petition addressed to the EPA was passed around requesting that a hearing slated for Canton in April be held instead in Asheville.[3]

As a testament to the civic support for the fight against Champion, the Newport Kiwanis Club contributed two plaques depicting the county's fight for a clean Pigeon River. Each had etched upon it the Pigeon River Resolution that had been read at the New Year's midnight meeting. The plaques were to be cemented prominently on the McSween Bridge.

Two days later, the mayor and aldermen of the mill town of Canton held their own breakfast at Junaluska's Lambuth Inn. Three hundred Champion supporters were expected to attend, according to Canton's mayor, C. W. Hardin, himself a Champion employee. Their mantra was the Champion company line: the company had already spent over seventy million dollars to clean up the mess; the technology did not exist to do more; the ruin that would come over western North Carolina if the plant was closed would be catastrophic—and a plant closing, they insisted, was a real possibility. Four or five members of the Dead Pigeon River Council were allowed to attend the Canton breakfast.

On a more substantive level, the DPRC enlisted the help of two professors in the Business Division of Walters State Community College at Morristown, some thirty miles north of Newport. Orville E. "Butch" Bach Jr. is an associate professor of economics and William H. Barnett II is an assistant professor of accounting. Barnett is also a member of the Lakeway Chapter of the Izaak Walton League. So that it can receive the company's annual reports, this chapter owns a bit of Champion stock. The DPRC wanted Bach and Barnett to make an impact study of the river's influence on Cocke County; the impact study would require a way to measure Champion's economic stability, and Barnett's membership in the Lakeway Chapter allowed him access to Champion's annual reports.

Walters State Community College serves ten counties of East Tennessee. Of the ten, Cocke is the most depressed. It suffers from high unemployment, which hovers much of the time around 20 percent, and from poor economic development. An investigation of the impact of the polluted Pigeon upon the county's economic potential and, conversely, the positive results of a clean river, fell within Bach and Barnett's purview. They agreed to make the study.

Bach and Barnett's Report

In May 1987 Bach and Barnett released their report. It was in two parts. Part I consisted of projections of Cocke County's economy if the river were made to flow clean. Part II was an analysis of Champion's activities based upon the company's annual reports and other sources and estimates of the technological and economic feasibility of Champion's cleaning up the river.[4]

In Part I Bach and Barnett painted a convincingly realistic picture of a prosperous Cocke County if the Pigeon flowed clean. They emphasized recreational potential. They pointed out how studies of Tennessee's Hiwassee and Ocoee Rivers and North Carolina's Nantahala River—all three of them flowing clean through scenic mountains—had demonstrated the economic rewards of swimmable, raftable, fishable streams. But, they pointed out, "the Pigeon River has been rated as having even greater potential if cleaned up." They quoted from a canoeing and kayaking guide that described the Pigeon and surrounding scenery as being "exceptionally beautiful." The Pigeon's upper five mile run, beginning just below the CP&L power plant, offered thrilling whitewater rafting, while the next six miles offered a calmer, less exciting form of boating and rafting; it was more acceptable for family sports. The authors noted that the Pigeon's accessibility from U.S. Interstate 40 made it much more convenient than the popular Hiwassee, Ocoee, and Nantahala Rivers. They emphasized the Pigeon's proximity to Great Smoky Mountains National Park, with the Big Creek campground just two miles from the floaters' put-in site for the upper whitewater run.

Using TVA studies of the dollar impact of recreation on the Hiwassee, Ocoee, and Nantahala Rivers, Bach and Barnett structured their analysis of the Pigeon's potential. Recreation days were evaluated in two categories, general and specialized. Picnicking, hiking, riding, cycling, fishing, and hunting were general amusements; the specialized category included whitewater rafting, kayaking, and canoeing.

Statistics produced by the two professors for the Pigeon were probably conservative, but even so they made impressive, thought-provoking reading. Commercial rafting alone, they estimated, would involve 17,280 raft trips at an average cost per person of $20, which in 1988 would have come to $345,000—a good income spread among small entrepreneurs. Again, based upon estimates of the business on the three aforesaid rivers, growth would be at an average rate of 19 percent, leveling off at 110,000 visits. Bach and Barnett estimated that 50 percent of all floating would be of this commercial type.

As for recreational fishing, they predicted that, if the river flowed clean, in 1988 some 12,597 fishermen would fish the Pigeon. They would spend an average of $17 each for fishing tackle and everything else a fisherman might want. The total benefit to the area would be $214,149. And what about those visitors who viewed all this activity as spectators? They had to eat, too, and they would purchase souvenirs and stay overnight in motels. Figuring 15,115 visits in 1988, each one spending an average of $4.47, the take amounted to $67,564. Estimates rose each year for the next ten years, the limit of the projections.

Next, Bach and Barnett examined the rippling and multiplying economic impact of this income upon the local economy. Economists estimate a multiplier of four; thus, a direct expenditure of $20 would have an overall impact of $80. With this multiplier, the estimates became

Orville Bach Jr. (l.) and William H. Barnett II (r.), professors in the Business Division of Walters State Community College, Morristown, Tennessee. Their carefully researched reports demonstrated how Cocke County would profit from a clean Pigeon River and showed that Champion could clean the river without seriously damaging its bottom line. Courtesy Bach and Barnett.

truly impressive. Total benefits, 1988 to 1997, came to $18,332,803, while the total impact on the economy amounted to $73,331,212, or an annual impact of $7,333,121 per year in 1987 dollars.

Such an economic jolt would raise Cocke County to an equal status with other prosperous Tennessee counties. The spin-off effect would be simply wonderful. New industries would be attracted to the region. As with Pigeon Forge on the Little Pigeon River (in a less beautiful setting), vacation-intensive businesses would flourish while recreational real estate would jump in value. Moreover, Cocke County could take advantage of its proximity to Great Smoky Mountains National Park. All told, Bach and Barnett concluded, "this development [real estate] alone would have a substantial multi-million dollar impact on the local economy."

Not included in their evaluation were the incalculable advantages to the inhabitants along a clean Pigeon River. These ranged from ending the fear that carcinogenic wastes in the river create a time bomb of cancer to the economic opportunities opened to them. Of what value is a clean-smelling stream rather than a twenty-four-hour-a-day stench? Certainly it is worth something, but a dollar value alone cannot be placed upon it.

To the residents of Cocke County, Bach and Barnett's economic analysis made plenty of sense, and the reality was that it just substantiated what they had always known. The polluted river is a drawback; a clean river would be a wonderful asset. More damning to Champion was the second part of the report, "Financial Analysis of Champion International Corporation's Ability to Provide for a Clean Pigeon River." The authors were hampered in preparing this phase of their report because there is no such thing as an "open" company. Certainly, Champion's books are not open to its critics. Bach and Barnett had to depend upon published statements of company earnings, expenses, sales, debits and credits, and annual reports for their facts and figures. They could not sit in the CEO's spacious offices in Stamford as he and his aides conferred about problems at the Canton plant and set policy. Nevertheless, Bach and Barnett were able to compile impressive statistics that furthered their argument that Champion had the financial resources to clean up the Pigeon River and still pay substantial quarterly dividends.

They began this aspect of their report with an explanation of a graph of "supply and demand with externalities." They wrote that "Champion's pollution of the Pigeon River is an example of what economists refer to as an *external diseconomy,* which occurs when one firm's use of a resource damages other people who cannot obtain proper compensation" (italics mine). And they went on to say that "when this happens our free market economy malfunctions somewhat because the firm bears only part of the full cost of that resource, and the outcome is usually not in the best interest of society as a whole."[5]

Bach and Barnett's graph shows that for Champion's Canton plant, the dollar amount of social damage done by pollution exceeds the marginal cost of abatement. In other words, Bach and Barnett proved to the satisfaction of economists at least that the dollar return of a clean Pigeon River would exceed the costs incurred by Champion in bringing a clean river about.

Always when writing about Champion there exists a wild card, an unknown factor: What does Champion really know about the costs of cleaning the Pigeon? Why has it been unwilling for so long to allot the necessary funds and instigate the procedures to bring a clean river about? After reading Bach and Barnett's report, understanding Champion and its motives becomes still more difficult.

Further, Champion is in a worse position to do something about the polluting of the Pigeon than it was when Bach and Burnett's report was released. The report was issued first in May 1987; it was updated in January 1988. By the end of 1993, significant financial changes have taken place at Champion. In this short span, the company has faltered. Its stock, which in the mid-1980s was in the forties, has ranged from around $23 a share to $34 a share. In recent years company earnings, while enormous, have been moderate considering the capital investment of between $5 and $6 billion dollars. It is not beyond the realm of possibility that a merger or takeover by other huge conglomerates or another enormous paper company could occur, even though Champion remains a profitable company.

Based upon company earnings in 1987, the Bach and Barnett report begins by stating that Champion ranks among the nation's top hundred industrial firms; between 1977 and 1986, its net reported earnings were $1.28 billion, and $621 million was paid out to stockholders. As with most great corporations, its board of directors has voted its CEOs and other top executives huge pay raises and stock options. In 1987 most of its product lines were described as being "in good shape," and there is no reason to believe that they are not still doing well.

Beginning with the basic assumption that the technology does exist to clean up the Pigeon, the two professors pointedly admit that a cleanup of the Pigeon River "will not be cheap." But in the very next paragraph, they suggest that Champion possesses the capital to accomplish the job. They base their conclusions upon *Value Line* financial projections as they appeared in the May 1, 1987, edition. Net earnings were estimated at $250,000,000, adjusted net earnings were $242,245,000. Bach and Barnett estimated the percentage reduction in those earnings from an investment in cleaning up the Pigeon to be 3.1 percent. The predicted primary earnings per share came to $2.65; adjusting the primary earnings to include the costs incurred in cleaning up the river reduced the per share earning to $2.57—a loss per share of just eight cents.

These projections, it must be recalled, were made in the flamboyant 1980s when Champion had announced (in 1986) plans to spend between $425 and $450 million per year for several years on capital projects, with most of the capital funded from internal resources. During the Pigeon River controversy, its statements about cleanup expenses of the Pigeon changed, but as of 1987 Champion had committed $120 million over the next five years to reduce coloration by 50 percent. (Millions of dollars are bandied around: as of 1987 Champion had expended $48 million on an improved boiler system and subsequently would be announcing an expenditure of upwards of $200 million for an oxygen delignification process. By 1993 these costs had reached, said the company, $330 million.) The bottom line was, and always is, very important, and Champion usually adds the caveat that antipollution expenses would not increase company profitability. Bach and Barnett suggested that it was not unreasonable to expect Champion to "invest in such a project which, though not highly profitable to the company, benefits a substantial societal interest—clean water."

By the time the Bach and Barnett report was issued, Champion was already arguing that if it were forced to adhere to the 50 color unit rule, it would have to close its Canton operations. Any study of the capital-intensive pulp and paper industry, with concentration on Champion's Canton mill, raises strong questions about the validity of such a threat. Bach and Barnett devoted a segment of their report to the probability of the company taking such action. They pointed out that Champion controls about one-third of the coated paper market, most of which is produced at its Canton mill. To maintain market share, it would have to have another facility on line, ready to fill the gap instantly; otherwise, competitors would fill the gap in failed deliveries, and it could take Champion years to regain lost clients. This fact alone ruled out closure.

Furthermore, as Bach and Barnett pointed out, what would Champion do with the closed plant? The environmental problems would discourage another company from purchasing it. Who would want to buy into such a problem? The fixed costs of a new plant plus the expense of maintaining an idle facility would far exceed the costs of cleaning up the Pigeon River. Another factor: pulp and paper machinery is so huge, complex, and expensive that moving it is rarely done; it is not cost effective. If the Canton mill closed, all the millions invested in machinery at Canton would remain there, deteriorating and declining in value at a frightening pace.

Champion has also argued that large expenditures and pollution control would prevent the company from receiving significant returns on its investment. Bach and Barnett pointed out that in the many decades that Champion's pulp and paper mill has been in Canton, it has reaped enormous returns. They estimated that the 1986 gross operating margin was equal to $37.3 million. "The traditional view," they wrote, "that investment precedes return does not always apply. In the case of Champion's use of the Pigeon River, the return has already been received, but no significant investment in the river has yet been made."

The two business professors concluded that Champion could clean up the river and still remain in the top one-fourth of U.S. corporations in terms of profitability. And they end their study with a quotation from Champion's 1986 annual report: "If change has a most valuable lesson to offer perhaps it is that we need not be victims of it if we can accept it as an opportunity to grow and achieve. In this sense, we believe the best companies are the ones with operating styles flexible enough to make necessary changes without compromising commitment to producing a quality product at a fair price."

Excerpts of Bach and Barnett's report were sent to Tennessee Governor Ned McWherter. On Izaak Walton League stationery, the two professors mailed Patricia L. Stoddard, Champion's director for Administration, a letter listing the league's major concerns with the company's operations at Canton. Barnett even flew to Champion's headquarters at Stamford to speak at the annual stockholders' meeting.

Barnett is no shrinking violet; he likes confrontation. When he arrived, he found Champion personnel filling the room, because most corporations like a full house even though hardly any stockholders attend outside of the on-site officials. When Champion's directors noticed his presence and found out who he was, they became noticeably nervous. But Barnett had a right to be there: he had proof of ownership of one share of Champion stock. What was he going to say? Who was he going to embarrass?

Barnett was allowed to speak. From Tennessee he had carried two Mason jars of water, which he set before him. "This," he said, holding up the jar containing clear water, "is a sample of the water taken above the mill. . . . The Pigeon is a beautifully clear mountain river—a Class A trout stream." The audience listened attentively.

Then he held before them the other jar. The liquid was dark and murky.

"And this is a sample of water taken below the mill. The river is coffee colored, foam covered, and foul smelling. It has a Class C designation and is unfit for human contact."

In transporting the water with him on an airplane, however, something had happened to the foul odor: it had disappeared. Moreover, he was not allowed to give a slide presentation showing the Pigeon above and below the plant. But he was able to make the point that cleaning the Pigeon by 50 percent, which at that time was Champion's announced goal, would not be acceptable "in the long run." He chided Champion for violating the "Champion Way," its avowed ethics policy. Because his presence followed the company's great propaganda campaign of late 1987 to early 1988 against Tennessee, Cocke County, and the EPA, he was able to inform them with honesty that "the public image of Champion in Tennessee (especially East Tennessee) is horrendous."[6]

Other Council Activities

The Bach-Barnett report gave legitimacy to the Dead Pigeon River Council's arguments. No longer could the organization be viewed as an assemblage of malcontent hillbillies from a depressed county in East Tennessee. No longer could Champion counter with arguments implying ignorance of facts. The DPRC's statements were now backed up by facts, statistics, research, and careful analysis.

All the while, Bob Seay and his cohorts kept up the pressure. They were aided by the *Newport Plain Talk*. Reporter Gilbert Soesbee was now assigned permanently to the Pigeon River story. Rarely did a week pass in which at least one of the three issues did not carry a Pigeon River article, an editorial, or both.

In May 1987, the DPRC launched a fund-raising campaign. Dubbing it "Cocke County Dollars vs. Champion's Millions," the campaign included a mailing of eleven thousand letters urging every family to contribute five dollars or more. Charles Moore, meanwhile, was getting a mailing underway to EPA and Tennessee officials urging that they move to clean up the Pigeon. Seay felt that the DPRC had raised public awareness within a three-hundred-mile radius of Cocke County, and the issue had finally resulted in a "very positive press."

On May 8, 1987, Newport held a Dead Pigeon River parade. Local students were given a partial holiday. Twenty-one floats were entered in the parade, and local students competed in poetry and poster contests. Festivities closed with second-graders tossing flowers into the river from the McSween Bridge; some also released blue, helium-filled balloons into the air. It was at this time that the local Kiwanis Club unveiled its two plaques, which had been shown at the New Year's Eve celebration. They were now installed at each end of the bridge.

In the same month, Cocke County schoolchildren, with the cooperation of teachers and administrators, participated in the Pigeon River conflict in still other ways. Seventh- and eighth-graders from Judy Webb's class awaited Governor McWherter's arrival at the local Holiday Inn. They held aloft banners demanding that the Pigeon River be cleaned. Eighth-grader Theresa Runnion looked up at Governor McWherter and presented him with a thick manila envelope. It contained the script of a play she had

Judy Webb turned her eighth-
grade students at Bridgeport
Elementary School in Newport
into environmental activists.
Courtesy Judy Webb.

written entitled *Trial of the Pigeon River.* Included also was a cassette tape upon which the youngsters asked questions of local, Tennessee, and North Carolina officials about pollution. These were then answered with snippets from popular rock 'n' roll, country, and gospel songs. "Some of the answers," according to the newspaper, "were not exactly flattering." For example, North Carolina Governor Jim Martin was asked what he thought of Champion's pollution; the dubbed song snippet was "Lovin' Every Minute of It." Newport Mayor Jeanne Wilson's reply to what she thought of Champion's officials was a snippet from Janet Jackson's "Nasty Boys." The final comment was from a group known as Twisted Sister: "We're Not Gonna Take It Anymore!" In addition, the tape contained thirty-two students' separate requests for Governor McWherter's help in stopping the pollution.[7]

On the Fourth of July and Labor Day, 1987, the DPRC staged a "Dead Pigeon Safety Break" at rest areas in Cocke County along U.S. Interstate 40. Members handed out more than thirty-five hundred brochures, served coffee, and answered questions. Council officials considered the promotion very successful. More than fifty T-shirts bearing the Dead Pigeon River Council logo were sold, and more than twelve hundred dollars were raised.[8]

Examples of DPRC-sponsored activities included a Sunday fishing expedition. In August 1987, a small army of expert bass fishermen, including members of the National Smallmouth Bass Association and the Tennessee Smallmouth Bass Association, descended upon the Pigeon from about seven miles below Waterville Lake to seven miles above it. "We've heard stories that a lot of people in North Carolina fish the river all the time and say there are fish in there," Nelson Ross was quoted, "[but] we've never been able to put any names to these stories and find someone who will actually tell us that they fish the Pigeon—and we've never seen anyone fishing the river above the lake—so we hope to put an end to the question."

The fishermen were testing recent statements by Champion vice-president Oliver Blackwell and North Carolina Governor Jim Martin, who had insisted that the problem in the Pigeon was merely one of color. Both men had stated categorically that there were fish in the Pigeon River. *Plain Talk* commented that yes, there were fish in the Tennessee section—trash fish such as carp and suckers. Now expert fishermen would determine who was right and who was wrong.

SPORTSMEN FIND LITTLE ON LINES IN PIGEON RIVER ran the follow-up story. Tom Rogers, president of the National Smallmouth Bass Association, complained that "this [was] the first time I've paid ten dollars to fish in a coffee pot," adding that the Pigeon was "the most despicable excuse for a river I've ever seen." Four hours of fishing hooked four bream from the Pigeon, although from the fresh water tributaries the fishermen sighted game fish, and from Fines Creek they even took two brown trout and a smallmouth bass. "So there are signs of life on the river," Rogers informed a reporter, "but when you get into the river itself, there really isn't much of anything."

All the while, *Plain Talk* continued running letters to the editor that were almost always supportive of the Dead Pigeon River Council. As Willie Ferguson of Route 1 in Cosby (which is near the river) wrote of the Pigeon, "Anything that will supposedly kill mange in a dog and cure the itch and eat the crud out of a car radiator isn't dead!" Haywood County, he added, has the gold mine; Cocke County has the shaft.

Even country music composers contributed to the DPRC's drive for a clean Pigeon River. Local musician Carl Williamson penned "Save the Pigeon," and Dave Cureton supplied the music:

> My Granddaddy used to tell me when I was very young
> About a little river that flowed whose beauty was next to none
> She rolled out of Carolina and flowed into Tennessee

Her crystal clear waters were as far as the eye could see
He'd fish along the banks at night and listen to the crickets sing
It was the early part of this century a young fella's dream
But times were a-changin and progress was to come
They put a papermill in Canton and spoiled all of granddad's fun
Then came the stinking waters that looked like coffee stain
That flowed down from the papermill human greed was its name
Some folks called it progress and others said it's OK
Who's God gave man the right to kill a river off this way?

Chorus
God help us save the Pigeon, let's bring her back to life
If it's left to human nature, we're in for an awful fight
Now Lord gave us sunshine and good water to drink
You'd think that folks would use their heads that you gave them
    to think

Now the Beautiful Pigeon River that was is the dead Pigeon now
I know that we can band together and clean it up somehow
What some folks call progress ain't nothin but human shame
If we allow pollution like this then we are all to blame.[9]

Clearly, opposition to the dead Pigeon River was not going to go away as it always had before. Along with the grass-roots opposition was the litigation that resulted in decisions adverse to the paper company. EPA, in spite of the fact that it was operating in a pro-business environment that characterized the Reagan-Bush years, was beginning to raise questions about North Carolina's environmental statutes and the lax enforcement by that state's officials. "In [North Carolina]," Dick Mullinix told a reporter, "the state officials have held an umbrella over Champion." He likened the situation to that of a bad child who repeatedly gets away with bad behavior. "They've allowed the mill so much leeway—the state has let them get away with it," he added.

Indeed, times were a-changin'.

CHAPTER 7

A Growing Conflict, 1985–1987

No question about it, the Pigeon River story in the 1980s and early 1990s is confusing. Choose any date after 1983 and ask where the issue stood, and pretty soon one loses track. It's difficult to sort out what Tennessee and North Carolina and EPA were doing. What about the litigation? It's even difficult to tell which cases were in the Tennessee courts, the North Carolina courts, the federal district courts, or the federal circuit court of appeals. And the public hearings? Up to the present, the number is approaching ten. It's hard to keep track of when they have taken place— a good question with so many postponements. And the personalities involved keep changing: EPA, Tennessee, and North Carolina officials appear to change even more often than the party in power. What of the Dead Pigeon River Council, the Legal Environmental Assistance Foundation, and the Pigeon River Action Group? So complex has the story become that newspapers occasionally list the chronology of events, as they are listed at the front of this work.

The confusion is compounded by the accusations and defenses, of public hearings and court cases, of bureaucratic actions and inactions all wrapped up in red tape and obfuscation; of press releases by Champion, North Carolina's Division of Environmental Management, its Environmental Management Commission, and officials speaking on behalf of the Tennessee attorney general's office; press releases by EPA, Pigeon River Action Group, and the Dead Pigeon River Council; and occasional speeches by Champion officials and their Waynesville and Canton supporters.

Sometimes it seemed that nothing was being accomplished on either side. One thing was a constant: Champion still polluted the Pigeon, and the wheels of change in this situation, if they were grinding, were grinding so slowly one questioned if they were turning at all. Even at this writing, opinions differ: to some the Pigeon flows colored, dirty, and polluted in spite of Champion's massive modernization; to others, marked improvement is apparent, manifested by lighter color, little foam, and less stench.

If one takes an overview of the period from 1985 to 1988, all the activity boils down to this: North Carolina approved Champion's permit, Tennessee contested it, EPA entered the fray and asserted its legitimate right to set the standards and grant a permit; Champion contested EPA's authority and lost; and EPA then proceeded, slowly and according to established procedures, to take the prescribed steps leading to the granting of the permit. These included a period set aside for the receipt of letters, pro and con, followed by hearings. The most significant and well-publicized hearings were the two EPA held in Asheville and Knoxville in January 1988. As the time for those hearings approached, Champion reacted with a massive public relations campaign that reverberated against the company. This chapter carries the story to those hearings in January 1988. Some of the ground that was covered in chapter 5 will be recapitulated, with a slightly different point of view. The time frame is about the same as that for the litigation discussed in chapter 5, but the narration concerns public relations, grass-roots controversies, and hearings.

Meetings Along the Way

Even as litigation began—and as it crept through the state and federal court systems over several years—negotiations continued. In July 1983, a meeting was held by EPA, Tennessee, and North Carolina officials at EPA's regional headquarters in Atlanta. In an attempt to be realistic yet not excessively demanding, the group came up with a three-part plan: 1) to develop permit limitations for Champion that would result in the Pigeon becoming clean in reality, not just in theory; 2) to consult with Champion officials about "assessing the technical achievability" of these limits; and 3) to try to develop a technically acceptable solution. As for the color units, after considerable research into all aspects of the Pigeon's pollution, EPA came out in favor of a top limit of 50 color units. North Carolina officials believed that just 75 percent of the color units had to be removed in order to achieve this goal.[1]

For the next fifteen months little happened, but Dick Mullinix kept busy. If Champion and North Carolina authorities believed stalling was the best way to lull their opposition into impotence, they were to be sorely disappointed. As he campaigned for a cleaner river, he acquired more knowledge about Champion and North Carolina, on the one hand, and Tennessee and EPA, on the other. When he learned that Champion's permit from North Carolina had expired on June 19, 1981, and that for nearly three years the state had failed to take action for renewal (although Champion had applied even before the old permit expired), Mullinix sensed an opportunity.

He knew that renewal was in the hands of the North Carolina Division of Environmental Management (or DEM, which is often erroneously referred to as the Environmental Management Commission, or EMC). The DEM consisted of seventeen members chosen by the governor. Three of them were from Champion country: two from Buncombe County (Asheville) and one from Haywood County, where the mill is located.

Using PRAG stationery, Dick wrote the members. "We complained to them that the water coming from the mill was too hot and the fish could not live in such water," Dick recalls. "The commission replied that it would consider this and discuss it at their next meeting, and so forth."

He informed them that he wanted to be present at the meeting, slated to be held in Raleigh. "I wanted to hear their arguments and note who voted for and against Champion's renewal, and I'm sure they knew that," he says. A member then informed him that, although he could be present, "Dick, I'll tell you, you won't be allowed to say anything. If you want to come to listen, all right, but I'm warning you ahead of time that you can't say anything."

"What kind of a deal is this?" Dick protested. "Well," he said, "these are men who know about the river and are best qualified to make these decisions."

Next he contacted the two commission members from Buncombe County, explaining to them the problems posed by the outflow. "I thought I had them on my side," he says, "that they would argue to lower the maximum allowable water temperature." This was the way matters stood when Dick learned that, unbeknownst to him, the meeting place had been changed to the little town of New Bern, on the coast, and the meeting had already been held.

Later he learned more details. The two commissioners from Buncombe County had not bothered to make the trip, nor had Haywood's single member. "The only three men who knew anything about the river weren't there at all," Mullinix says, his anger rising. "And the five attending of the seventeen members not only renewed Champion's permit but even granted the company's request for an increase in the water temperature. It was accomplished peremptorily," he adds, "without any serious discussion. A rubber stamp. Apparently Champion had been violating the temperature limit all along, and so now applied to make the violation legal." Mullinix's face contorts with anger. "That," he observes, "is the sort of thing we had to contend with."[2]

Indeed, the meeting had taken place at New Bern on Thursday, October 11, 1984, and Champion had succeeded in having the temperature restrictions changed to make legal what it had been doing illegally. Previously, the company had been prohibited from raising the water temperature above 29 degrees Celsius (84.2 degrees Fahrenheit) throughout the year. Now the DEM allowed Champion to release water up to 32 degrees Celsius, or 89.6 degrees Fahrenheit, during July, August, and September. Previously, the variation in temperature was limited to 2.8 degrees Celsius; the new regulation allowed a much larger variation of 13.09 degrees Celsius. Thus, two changes were made: hotter water was allowed for three months of the year and a greater variation in the water temperature at the pipe was allowed. In addition, the company agreed to inject oxygen into the stream where needed and to remove "at least 75 percent of the color contained in the effluent that is currently being discharged into the river."[3]

On October 26, 1984, North Carolina gave public notice of the draft permit for Champion. PRAG issued an appraisal, and it was very critical. "Pointing to the language in the agreement and phrases such as 'make all reasonable efforts' and 'subject to technical feasibility,' Mullinix said the agreement is too lenient," reported *Plain Talk*. Nor would the state of Tennessee accept the permit as it was issued with the variances. Both PRAG and the state insisted that the permit impose an *absolute* requirement of 75 percent color removal. Such provisions, they believed, would force Champion to investigate all possible alternative techniques to clean the water. And they still insisted upon 50 color units at the state line, even at low flow, where the color level in the stream had sometimes reached 1,200 units.[4]

At this juncture representatives of the Legal Environmental Assistance Foundation (LEAF) showed Mullinix how to continue the criticism. They pressured Paul Wilms, in charge of North Carolina's office of the National Pollution Discharge Elimination System, to assert his powers and call a public hearing to discuss the proposed permit. The issues, they argued, were in the public interest. He complied.[5]

Meanwhile, in January 1985, the Division of Environmental Management issued a preliminary copy of the new permit. Although it was similar to the one of the previous October, it showed evidence of change. Champion agreed to construct a pilot ultrafiltration plant. The facility would process up to one hundred thousand gallons daily (MGD) of the two million gallons daily that produced most of the color effluent. This was the company's reaction to language in the permit that asked that the company "make all reasonable efforts to achieve successful operation of the demonstration facility with color removal efficiency of 75% based on total effluent flow, at a cost of $1 million." The DEM was to inspect the pilot plant for efficiency and cost. If the commission favored it, then Champion agreed to build a plant that would reduce 75 percent of the color in two million gallons of waste water a day. The plant was supposed to be operational by October 11, 1987.[6]

The Canton Hearing

Wilms announced ground rules for the hearing. North Carolina Division of Environmental Management officials would explain the North Carolina permit procedure; public comment would be accepted written or orally, but if a statement was to exceed three minutes, three copies had to be filed. No cross examination would take place, although the hearing officer, who would be moderating the meeting, could request clarification. The hearing was to take place in the second-floor courtroom of the Canton municipal building on January 29, 1985, at 7:00 P.M. Tennessee would be represented by its attorney general, W. J. Michael Cody, Commissioner James Word of the Department of Public Health and Environment, and Gary Myers, executive director of the Tennessee Wildlife Resources Agency.[7]

Days before the meeting, some clean Pigeon River advocates released to the press affidavits they intended to file with the North Carolina Environmental Management Commission. Mayor Jeanne Wilson's statement said, "The gorge of the Pigeon River would develop rapidly as a tourist attraction were it not for the pollution allegedly caused by the Champion International plant." Charles Moore pointed out that there were virtually no agricultural uses for the Pigeon and reminded listeners that fish could not live in the Pigeon's waters. "Development is not being made because of the condition of the river and particularly the smell and color. . . . From the standpoint of Cocke County, Tennessee, the pollution of this beautiful stream by this industry is almost a criminal act and is definitely retarding the area," he added. Earlier, at a

Newport-Cocke County Chamber of Commerce banquet, President Deane Smith urged members to attend the hearing. "We need the Pigeon cleaned up; it's an environmental disaster," he said. "But if we don't get out there and make ourselves heard, there's no telling what will happen."[8]

Between January 1985 and January 1988, hearings were to become a general topic of conversation in western North Carolina and eastern Tennessee. About 140 people attended the one at Canton. It was by and large a polite, civil affair. Only when some Champion employees expressed resentment to the opposition did participants gain a portent of the bitterness to come.

Sixteen people spoke; eleven opposed the permit. Tennessee Attorney General Michael Cody made color the issue, calling it the key to cleaning up the Pigeon. Jeanne Wilson brought religion in: "God put us on earth for one reason: to be good stewards of His natural resources," she said. "We need a clean river so that our people can survive."

On Champion's side, the vice-president in charge of operations at the Canton plant, Oliver Blackwell, predicted that two years of trial and error with new processes would result in a big increase in the Pigeon's oxygen content, and Richard Wigger, the company's vice-president in charge of environmental and safety affairs, held out great hope for the success of the demonstration facility being built at the Canton plant. He predicted that it would eliminate 95 percent of the color in the water. "Champion has worked hard at this," he said. "They want it to work."

So far the talks had been logical, unemotional, and rational. Then the employees came to the rostrum. A seventeen-year Champion veteran wearing a Champion cap held up his Tennessee fishing license and theatrically tore it up. Bruce Medford of the nearby community of Bethel typified these employees' attitude. He said that for twelve years he had fished, scuba-dived, and enjoyed water sports in Lake Douglas, and had eaten fish taken from there, and he said, "I ain't broke out in scabs yet." Then his statement became meaner. "I'd like to say what I'd like to but I won't because I'm in a mixed audience. I ask you folks what's more important—family or a darned fish?" Another employee insisted that North Carolina cows drank from the river, so why wouldn't Tennessee's? Another argued that why, after seventy-five years, do the opponents want the river cleaned up "next week? Let Champion do the things they are working on," he pleaded. "No one likes to be threatened. . . . Don't demand that it be done this week, next week or the very near future."[9]

Now the agonizing wait began. The permit was still in the hands of North Carolina's Division of Environmental Management, whose new director was Paul Wilms. A decision was expected in February, but nothing was announced; on March 18, Wilms announced a postponement on the grounds that he was "snowed under."

All the while Dick Mullinix and his friends, members of the Legal Foundation, and other environmentalists had been busy. Specifically, they were pressuring EPA at its Atlanta headquarters. They had challenged the agency to live up to its charge. EPA was bound, it was argued, to enter the Pigeon River case. If North Carolina failed to meet its own requirements for a clean Pigeon River, then EPA, as a federal agency, was empowered to carry out certain provisions of the Clean Water Act that anticipated just such a situation as a state's failure to enforce its own regulations. EPA could either grant or repudiate North Carolina's permit to Champion International Corporation.

EPA Enters the Fray

Their lobbying succeeded: EPA was heard from. In February the agency openly expressed its displeasure with the permit. It doubted that the 50-color-unit standard could be achieved with just 75 percent color removal at the plant, and it wanted a provision in the permit that if Champion's experimental ultrafiltration process did not work, then the company would strive to find alternative methods until a workable solution was found. In April EPA contacted the Division of Environmental Management, and on May 10 EPA administrator Charles J. Jeter sent Wilms a letter expressing the agency's hope that North Carolina would issue a permit "that will allow the Pigeon River to be cleaned up." The letter went unanswered.[10]

To North Carolina officials, these notifications must have warned of troubles ahead. Until this point, North Carolina's Division of Environmental Management had enjoyed full state authority to issue pollution-control permits. Now the federal arm of environmental regulation was threatening. Probably that explains why the Division of Environmental Management suddenly toughened its stance toward Champion, threatening to limit production at the Canton plant until significant steps were taken to clean up the Pigeon. In doing this, according to Jim Shepard of the DEM, the agency was establishing a precedent for wastewater permits. "It is fairly routine in the air quality area. It is the first time we've ever done this in the wastewater area," he said. The threat was embodied in the discharge permit issued to Champion—finally—

on May 14, 1985. But the permit said nothing about color. In failing to mention color, it flaunted EPA's request for such a standard.[11]

Champion was meanwhile taking steps to counter the opposition. Early in May the company unveiled its pilot project, the one-year experiment with a state-of-the-art filtration system. Officials made a public relations event of it, saying that it was the first one of its kind in the United States. It represented, said company officials, an investment of $625,000 (later the company bandied about the sum of a million dollars) and a crew of four technicians.[12]

According to the *Mountaineer,* the proposed facility would take two million gallons of "almost black water daily and remove at least 75% of the murky color." This was water from the bleaching process, the principal source of the colored, polluted water. The process involved a sort of reverse osmosis, the colored water being forced through membranes with molecular side holes; when the water emerged, it was nearly clear. Of course, the pollutants had to go somewhere. They would be in a solid form, which Champion officials insisted contained the color and was not toxic. Better dumped into a landfill than into the Pigeon River. (Mullinix has related that he had a talk with Mary Lee Ransmeier, Champion's environmental officer, in which she left him with the distinct impression that much of Champion's criticism of the experimental facility was that the company did not know where to dispose of the solid waste.) Success or failure of the pilot would not be announced for at least a year.[13]

When the North Carolina Division of Environmental Management issued the permit on May 14, 1985, it offered a sop to the environmentalists. As reported in *Plain Talk,* the commission demanded that Champion inject more dissolved oxygen into the water to encourage the growth of aquatic life. The permit also stipulated that if Champion failed to meet the new color standards, it may be ordered to take steps to achieve that standard, but that if such an order were given, Champion was to be granted a hearing. The problem was, North Carolina's color standard carried no numerical stipulation while Tennessee insisted on 50 units. Implicit in the permit was a rejection of Tennessee's more stringent regulations as specified in the model permit it had submitted to North Carolina. And in granting the permit without notifying Tennessee authorities, North Carolina had violated section 40 (b)(5) of the Clean Water Act. The state had also failed to call for another public hearing, still another violation. North Carolina, however, considered the permit legally issued under Article 21 of Chapter 143, General Statutes of North Carolina, "and other lawful standards and regulations." The permit was valid for five years.[14]

Besides getting to work on its demonstration facility, Champion, as far as is known, took steps to meet the demand for more dissolved oxygen. Certainly the company and the North Carolina Division of Environmental Management hoped the renewed permit would settle things for years to come. If they thought so, they were to be sorely disappointed.

On July 18, 1985, EPA informed North Carolina that the permit was not satisfactory and was invalid, although the permit would not be officially denied until November. Champion therefore was still operating without authorization. EPA officials were angered that North Carolina authorities had not sent a copy of the permit promptly to EPA, and when EPA did receive a copy, it noted that the permit said nothing about a numerical color standard. EPA's dissatisfaction would result in the scheduling of a new set of hearings, one in Canton and one in Newport. Clearly, the agency was feeling the pressure from PRAG and the DPRC.

Tennessee's senators, Al Gore Jr. and Jim Sasser, had approached EPA about the problem. On June 28 the *Mountaineer* quoted North Carolina officials as saying they had failed to submit the state's permit for required EPA analysis because of the shortage of time: state laws gave them ninety days after a hearing to grant the permit, and the ninetieth day had arrived.

Dick Mullinix countered, "This is mostly a lot of hogwash. We tried for three months to get this issue [of color] before the North Carolina Management Commission [i.e., Division of Environmental Management]. We believe the EMC [DEM] deliberately stalled until the night before the ninetieth day so no one could object [to the permit]. Also we were advised we could not come to the EMC meeting on the eighty-ninth day, but a group from Champion was present." Mullinix added, "I think you can see what was taking place here. If ever a permit should be revoked, this is the one." What he was implying was collusion between Champion and North Carolina authorities. "We have worked hard and will continue to bring all pressure we possibly can to force the North Carolina Department [Division] of Environmental Management to issue an enforceable permit, one that will result in a restored Pigeon River. The report [permit] just issued," he added, "is little more than a gentlemen's agreement and was found to be unenforceable. The long history of pollution of the Pigeon River is evidence in itself to tell us restoration will never be accomplished on a voluntary basis."[15]

Champion and North Carolina officials had believed they would win out—that the North Carolina Division of Environmental Management would be allowed to issue the permit as written. They had to know that EPA had the authority to order changes in a permit if it could prove that requirements of federal law had not been satisfied. But such power had rarely if ever been used. Bob Humphries of EPA was quoted as saying that he did not think EPA had ever changed the kind of permit issued by a state environmental agency, "not in this region, anyway."[16]

Of the two major problems that EPA had recognized—water temperature and color—the problem of color predominated. It was the true cause célèbre during these years, and to a considerable degree it remains the most controversial issue to this day. North Carolina and Champion insisted that since Tennessee did not have a specific color limit, then neither North Carolina nor Champion should be required to adhere to the 50 unit limit insisted upon by Tennessee and the EPA. Tennessee's regulations imposed color restrictions as needed on different bodies of water; thus, 50 units was determined for the Pigeon, but 40 or 60—for example—could be fixed for another stream. North Carolina had inserted a 75-color-unit standard into the Champion permit, the one issued on May 14. To PRAG, the Newport-Cocke County group, and Tennessee officials, this was not sufficient. They insisted upon 50 color units, saying that Tennessee adhered to this or even stricter standards, even though Tennessee law did not contain specific numbers.[17]

The Pigeon River Achieves Notoriety

By this time—the summer of 1985—the Pigeon River was attracting attention beyond the Asheville-Knoxville region. The *Winston-Salem Journal* in August informed readers that for eighty years, the nose has "caught it first—a full frontal assault on the nasal system that smells convincingly like rotten eggs crushed in a waterlogged sneaker. . . . From several miles out of [Asheville] on the I-40 corridor that is the major gateway to North Carolina, the telltale scent of the state's largest pulp and paper mill prevails." It quoted Mullinix on the situation. "It's a damn crime against God, nature, and the people of North Carolina what they've done to the Pigeon River." The Conservation Council of North Carolina joined PRAG in calling for stricter requirements for Champion.

The *Journal* also cited Champion's environmental officer, Mary Lee Ransmeier, who insisted that the river was now "in a recreational state. When I came here eight years ago," she added, "it was horrible. People remember when they used to put ropes across the river to keep foam from floating down. There are all kinds of old stories—how the farmers used to take their dogs down and dip them for mange. It was awful." She added that since Champion had introduced a sludge removal system, a secondary waste-treatment plant, new screens, pumps, clarifiers, and other equipment, things were much better. She was correct. A lot of progress had been made, but much more needed to be done.[18]

In October the *Atlanta Constitution* ran a feature article about the Pigeon River controversy. Again, the key figure in the story was Dick Mullinix. He was pictured dropping a shiny penny into fifteen feet of clear Pigeon River water above Canton. Then he was pictured again, gazing down from a bridge below the mill as the polluted Pigeon flowed by. At that point, he described its water as being "like blackstrap molasses before they take the foam off." Trying to be impartial, the article also quoted Oliver Blackwell as saying that Champion had spent twenty-one million dollars to clean up the river and that all that was left was "an aesthetic thing." Aesthetics versus jobs, Blackwell knew, was a strong argument for jobs. Dick Mullinix reacted to Blackwell's statements by saying, "I don't know how they get up and shave in the morning, those executives, and look in the mirror and then come to work and know what they're doing to that river and feel good about it. I'd be ashamed to come to the office."[19]

During the long summer and fall of 1985, all the concerned parties awaited EPA's next move. On August 6 a letter from Jack Ravan, EPA regional administrator, was delivered to Paul Wilms, administrator of the North Carolina Division of Environmental Management. In essence, it ordered the DEM to do a better job of cleaning up the Pigeon River, or EPA would do it for them. More should be done to remove the color. Worst of all, from North Carolina's point of view, EPA accepted Tennessee's 50-color-unit limit. The agency did, however, accept the temperature variance. And it tightened up some of the terminology in the permit, changing the word "may" to "shall" in a section that outlines procedures to be followed if the river is too murky. It was a stronger stance, but Mullinix refused to comment until he had studied the letter carefully. "I don't want Haywood County to be a mixing zone for the river before it reaches Tennessee," he said. He meant by this that a 50-color-unit requirement at the state line could mean that from the pipe to the state line—a distance of about twenty-six miles in North Carolina—the water was mixing with clear water from tributaries and only gradually lightening to the specified color units projected to be leaving the pipe.[20]

EPA also set aside a ninety-day period for public comment on its proposals, and if requested by North Carolina officials, agreed to hold hearings. Jim Shepard, DEM's spokesman, said that officials "appreciate EPA's support and comments. We view the letter as supporting. We appreciate their comments and advice on the color removal problem. The EPA–Department of Environmental Management dispute is not," he emphasized, "an adversary type of thing. . . . What I want to stress is that we are working together."[21]

At this juncture, in August 1985, the prospects seemed to be for a regulation requiring not more than 75 color units at the pipe, which equated, theoretically, to 50 color units at the North Carolina–Tennessee state line. Speculating on how the river would look if this change became a reality, John Reetz of the *Mountaineer* quipped, "Diet Coke, it's not. 7-Up, it's not. But how about ginger ale?" He credited Jim Kutzman of the EPA with the suggestion that the water might look like caffeine-free Diet Coke. "It's not going to be tea-colored," he speculated, "but it's not going to be crystal clear."[22]

The waiting continued. "If there is one thing to be learned from the continuing debate over pollution of the Pigeon River, it is that the bureaucracy of government does move exceedingly—even excruciatingly—slow," editorialized the *Mountaineer*. It speculated that there would be still another public hearing. Meanwhile, opposition to the permit continued to grow. Mullinix was quoted again and again.[23]

During 1985 and 1986, when EPA was failing to carry out its mandate, the most active supporter for the cause of a cleaner Pigeon River was Senator Al Gore Jr. His interest went beyond that of a politician just concerned about satisfying his constituents. By his letters to Dick Mullinix, his statements to the press, his personal appearances at Newport, and the pressure he brought to bear upon EPA, Senator Gore made it very clear that he really did want a clean Pigeon River. In a press release of October 6, 1985, Senator Gore demanded that EPA take "immediate action" to clean up the Pigeon River. Gore's statement was in reply to a haughty letter he had received from North Carolina officials indicating that they would not demand from Champion the 50-color-unit standard that Tennessee insisted upon until Tennessee passed specific legislation decreeing the 50 unit limit within its borders. Quoting from a letter he had written to the EPA regional office in Atlanta, Gore implored EPA to deny Champion the permit right away rather than waiting until November. "It has become clear to me that North Carolina has no intention of revising its permit," Gore wrote, "[so] I see no reason to wait until November to enforce the order; the Pigeon has remained polluted too long already. I will not tolerate any further delay in cleaning it up."

On November 13, 1985, EPA informed Champion that it had assumed permitting authority. The six-billion-dollar corporation reacted swiftly. Champion did what all huge corporations do under such circumstances. It claimed EPA lacked the authority to regulate Champion. The company prepared to sue EPA.[24]

Of course, the Canton plant of Champion International Corporation did not close. Oliver Blackwell informed the *Asheville Citizen* that the company was operating under two permits, the new one in the state of North Carolina's view, and the old one in EPA's view. Jim Shepard of North Carolina's Division of Environmental Management put the matter a little differently. "They're [EPA] not rejecting it, they are saying we are not recognizing it until we put our stamp of approval on it."[25]

Even the usually Champion-supporting *Mountaineer* was critical of North Carolina's Department of Environmental Management. DEM had been involved in a dispute over increasing the capacity of Springdale's wastewater treatment plant to process another ten thousand gallons of sewage a day (Springdale is a little community that gets its water from the upper Pigeon. It wanted to increase its sewage disposal plant's capacity, which, Waynesville authorities believed, threatened the quality of Waynesville's water supply.) Then DEM had issued Champion a permit that angered EPA. "Given the Department of Environmental Management's record with the Pigeon, somebody needs to look at its work overall," the editorial concluded.[26]

What would North Carolina do? Champion insisted that it could not meet EPA's requirements and threatened curtailment of operations or even closure should the requirements be implemented. If North Carolina failed to enforce the permit, then EPA would step in. Indeed, the state was between a rock and a hard place. On November 6 Paul Wilms of the DEM made public a letter sent to EPA regional director Jack Ravan. It stated categorically that North Carolina would not abide by EPA's demands. Wilms was "dismayed that your agency continues to insist upon the inclusion of a numerical effluent standard for color in the permit." He insisted that there was no "technical or legal basis" for the state to mandate a specific color standard. Tennessee did not specify a specific number, he reminded Ravan. "If Tennessee adopts the 50 color units as a statewide standard, then we would be happy to include it in the permit," Wilms said. In reply, an EPA spokesman announced that "we will be issuing a permit based upon that [50] color unit."[27]

Wilms's letter was not entirely negative. He made reference to Champion's demonstration facility, installed but not yet operational. If the system proved successful, then the Division of Environmental Management would require Champion to make other changes. He further stated that if, after November 1990—five years into the future—a per-

manent ultrafiltration system had been in operation for three years, the
state would be willing to include a color-removal clause in a new permit;
however, it was noted that he made no promise of a 50 unit restriction.[28]

And so the story returns to November 8, 1985, when EPA assumed
the authority to issue Champion's permit; North Carolina had lost the
round. EPA officials said the procedure was for the agency to prepare a
draft permit, hold public hearings, and finally issue the permit; the procedures would take an estimated two months. As events transpired, this
was an optimistic assessment. Champion did not have to close its plant.

Events of 1986

The slow progress of bureaucracy brought the conflict into a new year,
1986. Although what transpired in Champion's boardroom at Stamford
following the EPA's intervention is unknown, it is a certainty that discussions were being conducted about the Pigeon problem. On January
17, 1986, Champion filed suit in Federal District Court for Western
North Carolina against the EPA. A few days later, clearly acting according to plan, Oliver Blackwell addressed the Waynesville Rotary
Club. He waxed at length upon the wonderful things Champion had done
for Waynesville, Canton, and the western North Carolina region. He
painted a picture of a concerned company that was planning capital improvements of $145 million at the Canton mill over the next five years.
The head of the Canton operation claimed his company had spent
$23,421,141 on stream quality since 1970, and $31,665,451 on air quality. He
said the Pigeon had been "significantly improved and is getting better.
Major advances in technology do not happen overnight. . . . No matter
what you hear to the contrary, no paper mill in the world has a colorless
effluent stream."[29]

Although Federal District Judge David Sentelle's ruling in
Champion's suit questioning EPA's right to intervene was still pend-
ing, EPA finally moved as if it did have the authority to intervene. On
March 11, 1986, it ordered Champion to file a wastewater application by
March 31 or face penalties as provided under the Clean Water Act. The
company reacted by requesting an injunction from Federal District
Court against the EPA. When Judge Sentelle denied this request on
March 31, he gave Champion ten days to comply. On April 11 the com-
pany carried out the judge's mandate, formally applying to EPA for a
permit to discharge wastewater into the Pigeon River.[30]

Shortly thereafter, the company announced the failure of its pilot ultrafiltration plant. Initially, Champion officials had said they believed it would filter 75 percent of the color from the water, but a year of operation showed that the process would remove only about half the color. Such a system, had it worked and therefore been installed for the entire plant, would, the company said, have cost forty-six million dollars and required an additional ten million dollars a year to operate. But it did not work.[31]

Oliver Blackwell insisted that "Champion gave this our best shot. We are disappointed. We wanted it to succeed." But according to EPA officials, Champion has refused to release the figures it kept on costs, color removal, and operation of the pilot plant. Some think the system was rejected because of disposal problems for the toxic solids it created; these had always before been cheaply disposed of by dumping them into the Pigeon. One company official was quoted as saying that the system was "too expensive and will not do the job." Now North Carolina's Division of Environmental Management gave Champion a year to come up with an alternative solution.[32]

Meanwhile, the litigation proceeded. Court cases lag as badly as bureaucratic policymaking. Not until July 14, 1986, did Judge Sentelle rule that the Pigeon River Action Group, the State of Tennessee, and the Legal Environmental Assistance Foundation could participate in the case in which North Carolina and Champion were trying to have EPA denied the right to issue wastewater permits.[33]

In mid-1986 the possibility existed that EPA would be denied the right to rule on the permit, North Carolina's permit would be accepted, and the company would be allowed to continue pretty much as usual; in other words, Champion would win. Yet, at no time in the Canton mill's nearly eighty-year history had so much agitation, litigation, and publicity been aimed at the plant's terrible pollution record. The company reacted to the situation with measures on several tracks. Its lawsuit trying to remove EPA from the permit procedure was one example. The pilot ultrafiltration plant was another. Blackwell's speeches to dinner clubs and civic groups represented still another defense.

In September Champion announced a two-hundred-million-dollar wastewater management project. Officials said it would upgrade production and at the same time bring the plant's waste water up to federal standards. Details revealed that—provided the present permit was issued—the company planned to spend forty million dollars a year for five years installing the equipment. The chlorine bleaching process, which releases toxic substances, was to be replaced with a state-of-the-art oxy-gen delignification process. Blackwell said it would reduce color by 50 percent. There is no question that this was a step in the right direction.[34]

Once its plans for upgrading the mill were announced, company representatives discussed them with North Carolina officials. They even journeyed to Newport, Tennessee. At a luncheon meeting at a local restaurant, Blackwell, Champion operations manager Dr. Bob Moran, and Mary Lee Ransmeier informed Cocke County residents of the company's plans. They also traveled to Nashville where they explained their plans to Tennessee authorities.[35]

But if company officials believed this would squelch the opposition, they were wrong. "We don't believe that's enough," said Gary Davis, the lawyer representing LEAF. "We don't believe that would be enough to protect the aquatic life of the river and to protect the river for its designated uses." He said that dissolved solids and temperatures were also involved and that no matter what the technology, "the only way to assure that the river is cleaned up is through an enforceable wastewater discharge permit issued by the United States Environmental Protection Agency and administered by North Carolina."[36] Mullinix was likewise critical. "We are holding our position," he said, but since North Carolina had never given the environmentalists any help, it was time the federal government stepped in. "We have to be in the position where it [the permit] can be enforced." He insisted upon an "ironclad" permit from the federal government; it was absolutely necessary.[37]

In August 1986, Tennessee Congressman James Quillen had reen-tered the fray. In a press release, he accused Champion of being "in clear violation of federal law" and of "wrongly using the court system to avoid facing its obligation to clean up the Pigeon River." In a letter to Lee M. Thomas, an EPA administrator in Washington, Quillen demanded answers to why the federal government had allowed Champion to continue. "My question to you is: Why?" the congressman asked, pointing to "feeble efforts and half-hearted remedies" to stop the pollution. "These people deserve better," he continued. "They don't need years of petty litigation in courts. They don't need promises that are not kept. They don't need to be kept on the edge of despair." It was excellent politics pitched toward the welfare of Cocke County inhabitants.[38]

Champion was succeeding in a Machiavellian maneuver—to divide and destroy. Sure enough, the company's promises led some members of the Pigeon River Action Group and even Tennessee officials to waver in their opposition. Their argument was that they had forced Champion to do something; that was sufficient for the present. Down the road, if Champion again became uncooperative they could start up again.

Paul Davis, head of the Tennessee Division of Water Pollution Control, was one of the vacillators. "I am an incrementalist," he emphasized. In the case of Champion, the implementing of the two-hundred-million-dollar oxygen delignification process would result in a river that was clean enough and lightly colored enough to be used for recreational purposes. Such a river, Davis theorized, would be sufficiently clean to support game fish such as bass and trout. Without actually saying so, Davis clearly considered men such as Mullinix, Seay, Webb, Ross, and members of the Pigeon River Action Group to be hard-liners whose obstinacy slowed the cleaning of the Pigeon River.[39]

Mullinix had a different explanation for Davis's compromise stance. He had heard that Governor McWherter, who was being influenced by Champion, pressured Davis and other involved officials—David McKinney and Michael Pearigen especially—to accept an 85-color-unit standard. This was a rumor, however, without substantiation. To talk with these officials is to be impressed with their sincerity and dedication.

It is not known whether Champion officials were surprised that the opposition, or at least some of the opposition, was critical of its an-

Paul Davis, director of the Tennessee Department of Environment and Conservation, Division of Water Pollution Control. Courtesy Paul Davis.

nounced two-hundred-million-dollar, five-year plan. Certainly the plan helped cement the feelings of the pro-company people, to whom Champion's offer appeared magnanimous, well planned, and an example of the "Champion Way." However, any final decision had to await the federal district court's verdict on Champion's case to deny EPA the power to issue wastewater permits.

Autumn 1986 dragged on; on December 1, Judge David Sentelle handed down his decision in the case of *Champion vs. EPA.*

He granted a summary judgment in favor of EPA, PRAG, LEAF, and the State of Tennessee. Champion and North Carolina had lost the case. A more detailed analysis of Sentelle's decision is provided near the end of chapter 5. The immediate reaction of the *Mountaineer* was: What effect will this decision have on the two-hundred-million-dollar cleanup? Mullinix and his group were elated. EPA was pleased, too. "We view this as significant," said EPA attorney Tom DeRose, "because it was the first judicial test of authority to take away a state-issued permit."[40]

Tennesseans may have been pleased; certainly North Carolinians were not. "We have been injured by a neighbor," raved Governor Martin, "and we don't like it." North Carolina citizens had been treated "in a tragic way" for "no good reason." Martin went so far as to suggest that Governor McWherter's refusal to compromise "with Champion International Corporation may result in retaliations against Tennessee." He suggested that North Carolina might be uncooperative when TVA or Tennessee paper mills needed to draw down water from North Carolina. Perhaps, he threatened, North Carolina should insist that Tennessee help clean up the air if North Carolina is gassed by Tennessee's auto emissions.[41]

The *Knoxville News-Sentinel* was so angered at Governor Martin's tirade that it compared him to Muammar al-Quadaffy, the Libyan dictator. "How ironic," it editorialized, "that the North Carolina governor would say all those harsh things about Tennessee while currently trying to prod a Virginia-based paper mill into reducing pollution in the Chowan River, which flows into North Carolina." (This fifty-two mile long river rises at the Virginia line and flows south-southeast into Albemarle Sound.)[42]

Senator Al Gore, visiting Cocke County in mid-December, described Judge Sentelle's ruling as a "great victory." He gave EPA credit. "At times it moves a little too slowly, but they are moving," he said. "Champion will appeal it [the decision] but they will not win it, the court's decision is too strong. . . . I look forward to the day when the Pigeon River will flow clear, pure, and clean, and I look forward to the day when the fish will return."[43]

Never before had the possibility of achieving a clean river seemed more attainable. With the state of Tennessee, Senators Sasser and Gore and First Congressional District Representative James Quillen on their side, with PRAG and LEAF giving them support, and with the public becoming more and more concerned over environmental issues, Cocke County residents looked forward to the new year of 1987 with more hope for a clean Pigeon River than they had entertained in the past seventy-nine years. To mark their new optimism, they staged the candlelight, bell-ringing New Year's Eve parade to the McSween Bridge, where they vowed to have a clean Pigeon River by Tennessee's bicentennial in 1996. Of greater significance, perhaps, was the announcement of the creation of the Dead Pigeon River Council (DPRC).

For Champion, the issue was still up in the air; EPA had not handed down its permit. Company executives were aware that they had lost one legal battle; they could always appeal. What may have bothered them most was the tenacity of the present Pigeon River issue. Always before, the flare-ups had come and gone like a flash in the pan; protests had lasted a few weeks and then disappeared. Not this time. Tennessee officials in Nashville had not been impressed when three or four well-dressed Champion officials paraded into their offices, sleek briefcases bulging with statistics. Cocke County citizens were testy as never before, unimpressed by Yankees from Stamford who spoke to them condescendingly. Dick Mullinix, that old gadfly, refused to shut up. PRAG sent out flyers announcing meetings, soliciting contributions and memberships, and damning Champion. Now Cocke County had taken the cue and formed its own pressure group, the Dead Pigeon River Council (DPRC). Little wonder that Champion was described as having at this time "a fortress mentality."[44]

Still, Champion knew it had allies. The 1980s were the most business-oriented years since the 1920s. Corporations, which as "special interests" have always had clout in Washington, now had more influence than ever to twist, bend, or ignore regulations. Everyone knew the EPA was highly politicized. Anne Gorsuch Burford, head of the agency during the early Reagan years, was but one of several EPA administrators to resign under a cloud. And below the federal level was the state of North Carolina, which had always been cooperative with Champion, treating it, said Dick Mullinix, "like a spoiled brat."[45]

Moreover, despite sometimes claiming otherwise, Champion seemed to be in western North Carolina to stay. For Dick Mullinix, Bob Seay, Gay Webb, Jerry Wilde, Nelson Ross, Jim Harrison, and other activists, news announced in the *Mountaineer* on January 14, 1987, belied

Champion's threat to close or to curtail production if it did not receive a permit. Champion announced the rebuilding of its No. 19 paper machine. If Champion planned to close, argued the clean river proponents, why would the company spend fifteen million dollars to rebuild the machine?

Although Champion officials may not have understood why the opposition failed to fade away as had always happened before, they were acutely aware that they had a fight on their hands. Champion began propagandizing its labor force. Its workers accepted the company's warnings that it would have to close or curtail production if it were forced to accept the permit with the 50-color-unit requirement. A steady wage is worth fighting for: Champion's employees closed ranks. Neither the employees nor the company were going to accept defeat without a fight. "Champion International Corporation and the City of Canton . . . are circling the wagons and preparing to battle environmentalists whose war cry is the polluted Pigeon River," began an article in *Plain Talk*. Canton's mayor, himself a Champion employee, issued an invitation to government and business leaders of western North Carolina to a breakfast at Lake Junaluska's Terrace Hotel. Saying that he did this on his own initiative, he stressed the importance of getting "first hand information about this situation."[46]

Since January 14, 1987, EPA's draft permit had been circulating among officials. Rumors were rife about its contents. The *Mountaineer*, mentioning it on January 28, emphasized that EPA had issued a "tough permit to Champion." Indeed, it was a tougher permit than anything North Carolina had ever passed; it was, in fact, stricter than the permit Tennessee had demanded. Taking the position that much of the river flowed below the mill in North Carolina as well as in Tennessee, EPA demanded water at 50 color units just one-half mile below the pipe rather than at the state line as Tennessee had demanded. "The river would have to be ginger-ale colored below the mill itself," the *Mountaineer* commented.

However, at this point, this was just a draft permit. Public input, both written and oral, and then hearings had to take place before the final permit was issued. John Marler, EPA's spokesperson, warned that "the company may have a tough time getting changes in those restrictions." He reminded readers that the permit could go into effect one month after the hearings, and, in any event, the company was to implement the standards by June 12, 1987. *Plain Talk* was elated, quoting EPA's Fritz Wagener as saying that the water would be "almost crystal clear" by the time it reached Newport.[47]

The Hearings Are Scheduled

EPA scheduled two hearings for the week of April 23, one at Canton and one at Newport, but changed the date to the week of May 11.

The optimism pervading Newport and Cocke County in those chilly winter months and early spring months contrasted perceptibly with the pessimism pervading Canton, Clyde, Waynesville, and all of Haywood County. Champion was adamant about its inability to clean the polluted Pigeon down to 50 color units by the time water reached the state line, to say nothing of having it that clean within one-half mile below the pipe. The company did continue to frighten its workers and those who depended on its workers into granting Champion their full support.

On February 20, 1987, the *Mountaineer* ran a sketch by a local artist showing a mother and child in ragged clothes outside the closed Champion plant.

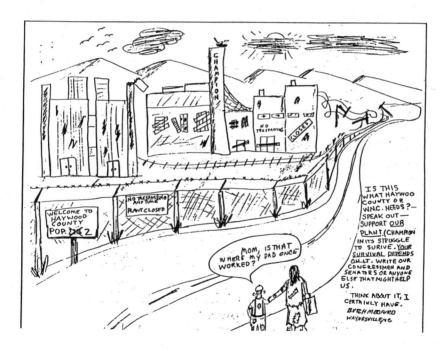

Haywood County residents harbored dreadful thoughts about the results of a closed Champion mill. This drawing appeared in the Mountaineer *on February 20, 1987. Cartoon by Butch Medford. Courtesy the* Mountaineer.

In a meeting with county officials and local businessmen, Oliver Blackwell insisted that Champion could not meet permit requirements. He insisted that the Canton mill was "a low-color mill" that "ranks with the best of the newest . . . mills." Then, perhaps as a Freudian slip, he repeated the admission: "They [company officials] would never build a mill on a river that small today." He also claimed that odor had been reduced, but "there has never been in the world a pulp mill that didn't have some odor some of the time." Since 1976 the company had quadrupled its environmental costs, he said, and these costs "are cutting into the profitability of the mill, which has been dropping steadily. It cannot be allowed to continue."[48]

Proof was lacking for Blackwell's statements (save for the admission that the Pigeon was too small to handle Champion's effluents), but neither could anyone question, with authority, what he had said. Bach and Barnett, two professors who had studied the company exhaustively, estimated that the Canton mill was extremely profitable, earning at least sixty million dollars a year; some believed that even this estimate was ridiculously low. They estimated that Champion realizes up to one hundred million dollars per annum from the facility.

The rising antagonism between Champion supporters and environmentalists can be traced in the letters-to-the-editor columns of the local newspapers. J. Aaron Prevost, who had been a member of North Carolina's Water and Air Board for eight years, wrote how he had "personally observed the total cooperation of Champion with the state in their efforts to eliminate the pollution of air in North Carolina." It is hard to believe and impossible to corroborate Mr. Prevost's statement that between 1961 and 1973 the company spent twenty-seven million dollars and from 1973 until 1985 another forty-eight million dollars on air pollution and odor control. If this is so, in view of the remaining smoke and stench, then Canton and downwind environs must have been close to hell on earth prior to the 1960s. Mr. Prevost closed his letter with this interesting statement: "I would personally hate to see the odor completely eliminated (which it almost is) since on any really foggy day just to get a faint odor from the plant reminds me of the great benefits that Haywood County gets from the presence of this fine company in our county. . . . Folks . . . Champion is Haywood's warm blanket."[49]

To champion Champion has been one of the methods by which North Carolina politicians have won the votes of the state's western citizens. On Saturday night, May 1, 1987, Senator Terry Sanford spoke to Democrats at their annual Haywood County rally. As far as is known, he was saying the same sort of thing that every congressman and governor who had ever stepped into Haywood County since the mill had opened had said. None, as far as anyone could recall, had ever criticized Champion or confronted its executives about the possibilities of cleaning the river. Senator Sanford, conservative and popular, was no exception.

"I told the Senators from Tennessee that, given a fair EPA water discharge permit, Champion would make the water so clean I would walk to the middle of the Pigeon River at the state line and take a drink from it," blustered the senator. Oliver Blackwell responded that, given three years, he would join Sanford in the middle of the river and bring along a dipper so they could both drink from it. Senator Sanford also said he would bring the Tennessee senators to fish near the plant after the permit had been issued. When Tennessee Congressman Jimmy Quillen heard this, he suggested that the senator drink the water now. "He'd better have a doctor at his side," he warned. "The river stinks terribly. It's murky and polluted; I wouldn't recommend that anyone wade in or swim in it, much less drink it."[50]

The unions also came to Champion's defense. The president and executive vice-president of Smoky Mountain Local 507, in a letter to the *Mountaineer,* expressed the "hope that EPA and the people of Tennessee will work with the company in settling this issue." A couple of months later, the newspaper ran a photograph of a big box of letters from Local 507 members to EPA, protesting the EPA draft permit. Local 128 of the International Brotherhood of Electrical Workers and Local 487 of the United Association of Pipefitters and Plumbers, on the other hand, had been involved in a bitter dispute with Champion. In their anger, they had rented a billboard in Cocke County along Interstate 40 that read, "Stop Champion Paper from Polluting the Pigeon River." When the labor dispute ended, the sign was removed.[51]

The unions certainly were not the only groups to support Champion. Pat Stewart, the YMCA director at Canton, stressed how much Champion doles out to local youth through the Robertson YMCA and Camp Hope. However, it should be noted that the YMCA was closed in 1990 for lack of funds, and as of this writing, has not reopened.[52]

Company loyalty was stressed. The *Asheville Citizen* ran three articles on the Neil McKinnish family, which could boast of sixty-four years' association with Champion. Even the churches got involved. A letter from the New Disciples Sunday School at Rockwood United Methodist Church in Canton praised Champion for the cleanup it had already brought about, accepted Champion's statement that technology for further improvement did not yet exist, and urged that if only EPA would give Champion time, it would clean up the river. On the political front, Haywood County's two state legislators introduced identical resolutions in the North Carolina House and Senate asking the U.S. Congress to persuade EPA to establish for Champion "a reasonable water discharge permit."[53]

Champion's community relations manager, Charles Curtis, prevailed upon the Asheville Chamber of Commerce to pass a resolution praising the company "as a responsible corporate citizen . . . an economic giant in Western North Carolina whose presence has enhanced the overall economy and the quality of life in the region." The *Asheville Citizen-Times* shocked Cocke County residents when it announced, in a feature article, that "the Pigeon is no longer 'dead.' Fish swim in its waters—even trout." The statements were so patently untrue that *Plain Talk* editorialized against the paper, which, it said, "continues to toe the company line."[54]

Yet, even in what might be called Champion country, the corporation did not have complete support. Take the ambivalent *Mountaineer:* On March 4, 1987, it ran a feature article with these headlines: EPA WANTS EIGHT TIMES AS MUCH COLOR REMOVED FROM PIGEON AS MILL PLANS. The article, which was full of statistics, noted that the company's discharge below the mill ran between 700 and 800 color units. Since Champion planned to reduce the color by half, that would still leave 300 to 350 units—quite a boost from the 50 units insisted upon by EPA. It also noted that the company discharged into the Pigeon some 200,000 pounds of discoloring materials per day.[55] But it was unclear whether the *Mountaineer* was being supportive or critical of the company by citing these points.

In May 1987 the newspaper ran a feature article on Dick Mullinix. It was distinctly friendly. It gave him credit for being at odds "with the 10% of the population of Haywood that is employed by Champion . . . despite crank calls, including threats to burn his house down and even shoot him, Mullinix remains a determined man. 'I'm going to fight it if it kills me,' he said, 'I know this [pollution] doesn't have to be.'" It was noted that Mullinix's livelihood prior to retirement had been in the packaging business, that he had worked in paper plants in both blue-collar and white-collar positions. The article quoted him as saying, "I watched rivers in the Northwest go to pot, but those rivers have been cleaned up."[56]

With regard to PRAG, the story continued, Mullinix emphasized that "the group is not a bunch of crazy radicals, but rather a cross-section of the community—a mixture of professionals, doctors, a preacher and several housewives. . . . They are people who are primarily interested in long-range environmental concerns." He said that the technology does exist to clean up the Pigeon, and a company in Japan already uses the system successfully. To Champion's contention that EPA's demanded cleanup would force it to close, Mullinix's reply to the reporter was that the threats are "criminal" and "cowardly." He was further quoted: "They are not going to close the mill. I wouldn't be in this thing if I thought that was going to be the final answer."[57]

Emotionalism Replaces Rational Discussion

It became evident that, unlike in times past, the protest over the polluted river was not going to go away; it also became clear that the company was going to have to take drastic measures to meet EPA's requirements or else face yet undetermined penalties. A sudden apprehension swept through Haywood County. Far from allaying the fear, Champion promoted it. People whose lives had been built around employment at the mill and business and professional people whose customers and clients were Champion employees, were suddenly fearful of their future. The mill had been so stable since 1908 that a threat of its closure or even curtailment of production affected them like an earthquake. The ability to make car payments and house payments and take vacations suddenly seemed to be in jeopardy.

It was in May 1987, as the date set for the hearings approached (it was later changed), that Dick and Lucie Mullinix received the first of what have been many obscene, threatening telephone calls. They ordinarily come in the wee hours of the morning, around 4:00 A.M. Male voices usually sound inebriated; possibly the caller has been drinking with fellow employees and has become increasingly irritated over the alleged threat to his job. It is not always a man. Wives of employees who feel threatened have expressed their feelings, too. One woman asked Dick if he had ever heard children cry. Mullinix's stock reply is that Champion is not going to close under any circumstances. If he believed it would, he would cease his campaign.

Other Champion protesters have received threats. A member of the DPRC received three death threats over the telephone and one vague warning by mail. "My wife is terrified," he told a reporter. "She feels we're dealing with ignorant people who would kill us." In the first call, the voice on the other end of the line said that "it wouldn't be surprising if I flopped 'til I died like a dead pigeon." The second was from a woman who threatened his house would be blown up while he and his family were in it. And the third call, he said, "Was from another man who told me 'I'd find myself dead, dead as the river.'"[58] In an editorial in the *Mountaineer,* reporter Dave Gerrard chided people who would issue such threats. He tried to reason with them by referring to American traditions of freedom of speech and fair play.[59]

The Incident at Meadowbrook School

Threats were bad enough, but a sixth-grade schoolteacher at Canton's Meadowbrook Elementary School, Rebecca Allen, had a much more serious experience, a real lesson in the tension between basic civil rights and job security.

Even after six years, Allen recalls the incident with righteous indignation, if not outright rage. "I basically feel that my students and I were victims of a rather uncreative 'dirty tricks' group housed in the Canton mill and long used to having absolute sway and unquestioned support from the powers-that-be in Haywood County," she writes. "Reactions do not originate with the citizenry."[60]

Her story begins on the morning of May 5, nine days prior to the scheduled hearing. Meadowbrook's principal called an 8:10 A.M. faculty meeting "to demand that we have our students write letters to EPA in support of Champion." The pitch was that a closed paper mill would throw people out of work, parents would leave, and teachers would lose their jobs.

Rebecca Allen thought the conflict between Champion and EPA was a good subject for a teaching unit geared toward civic responsibility in a democratic society. She requested permission to take her students to the hearing. Meanwhile, her informed pupils could write letters "to whomever they wanted and [could] say whatever they wanted."

At almost the same time, Champion's campaign shifted into high gear. Blue and white "I Support Champion" buttons proliferated. Expensively manufactured "I Support Champion" signs were posted on gas station walls, portable signs conveyed support of Champion, and a banner hanging across Main Street advertised Champion's message. Allen describes it all as "a visual gauntlet of support." And, she reflects, "In ignorance and parody, I drew small cartoon posters for a similar classroom gauntlet of environmental and classroom slogans." According to news stories, some bore such captions as "Don't Muddy the Water" and

Rebecca Allen encouraged discussion and dissent in her class at Meadowbrook school—and she paid the price. Courtesy Rebecca Allen.

"Don't Cloud the Issue." She wanted her students to be aware of both sides of the issue, and she envisioned the hearing as a forum in which arguments would be heard for and against Champion and its treatment of the Pigeon River.[61]

Newspapers reported that when parents at the Monday evening PTA meeting saw the placards, they protested to Haywood County Superintendent of Schools Charles McConnell. McConnell was so concerned that he asked a sheriff's deputy to visit the school, just in case there was trouble.

The next morning—with an open house slated for that evening—Allen was called into McConnell's office. When she returned with him to the classroom, he forthwith tore down the signs. "I was afraid that some folks were going to come to the school and make an effort to tear them down," he told a reporter. "There was some potential for disruption of the school." As for the issue of censorship, he said that most of Canton did not believe in it. "How tolerant they are, I have no idea," he added. "When you're looking at the loss of 2,100 jobs in the community, people's feelings are pretty close to the surface. People are very anxious, very nervous."[62]

Allen's description of the event differs slightly. She writes:

On Tuesday morning, May 12, Charles McConnell, the superintendent of county schools, accompanied by the assistant superintendent, the school supervisor, and the principal, removed the posters in view of my students who watched in stunned and silent disbelief. I was told to immediately stop my unit and to not mention Champion again in my classroom. The event was rapacious.

I see now that my posters were blasphemy to the Champion Plan, and I understand that a classroom full of children and a soft-spoken teacher were minimal sacrifices for the greater good.[63]

Allen did not shut up so easily. She charged that McConnell's actions were strictly political. She admitted that she felt Champion could clean up the Pigeon and stay in business, but she insisted that she was not indoctrinating her students. "I didn't feel they were getting all sides," she said. "The day I put up the signs, I said, 'Listen, kids, if we lived in Russia I couldn't do this. But because we live in America, I can go against public opinion and I can stand up for what I believe.'" She paused, then said to a reporter, "I feel wronged." She left Canton of her own volition, but with backing of the American Civil Liberties Union, she sued the school district. Months later, she made an out-of-court settlement.[64]

Even as she suffered humiliation, Rebecca Allen witnessed the final events in realpolitik. She learned that the hearing, far from constituting a forum with pros and cons, was to be an "in-house rally including as many powerful and political dignitaries as could be gathered." Her request for permission to take her students there was rejected. "Ironically," she writes, "the first meeting place for the dignitaries was the county's newest showplace, Meadowbrook School, where a breakfast meeting was held . . . complete with grand presentations and entertainment. The parking lot was filled to overflowing with politicians, doctors, lawyers and the like. The breakfast meeting adjourned at 11:00. . . . The EPA representatives would see how many people love and support Champion, go away, and Champion would continue pollution as usual."[65]

Tension Increases

The clean river advocates refused to be cowed. "Champion," said Nelson Ross, "is in a great position to say, 'We're doing all we can. Those old meanies at EPA and in Tennessee are pulling the nipple out of your mouths.'" The environmentalists were particularly incensed over the Haywood County Economic Commission's ill-conceived slogan: OUR

RIVER, OUR JOBS, OUR FUTURE. They quickly reminded their
neighbors that much of the Pigeon River was not in Haywood County
but in Cocke County: where did Canton get that OUR RIVER business?[66]

Nor were Cocke County residents oblivious of the significance of
the upcoming hearings. The First Pigeon River Memorial Day included
a parade and children dropping flowers into the polluted stream. It
"showed a public outcry for the future of these children," said Bob Seay.
Combined with a Cocke County "Image '87" celebration, it was the
county's largest parade ever. Some floats depicted the benefits of a clean
Pigeon River and some showed the river as it is. A North Carolina television station carried a clip of one float: a large, mock dead pigeon being carried on a small stretcher by a child. "That dead bird," quipped
Plain Talk editor Nancy Oberst, "seems to be sticking in their [North
Carolinians'] craw, because North Carolinians—from Governor Jim
Martin to the people who work at Champion—say the Pigeon River is
not dead and is not polluted to the extent Tennesseans claim."[67]

On the Champion side, the politicians were called in. In a press
conference at the North Carolina capitol in Raleigh, Governor Jim
Martin ridiculed those who protested color in the Pigeon. He said that
such color comes naturally, as in the Lumbee River in the Great Dis-
mal Swamp (the Lumbee is colored by cypress). "It doesn't make much
difference anyway except in a cosmetic sense," he pontificated. "There
are people who are entitled to worry about that kind of thing, but the
fish don't." He announced his plans to attend the hearing, set for May
14, at Canton's Pisgah High School.[68]

Every half hour, the radio stations in Waynesville ran spots paid
for by local businessmen that encouraged attendance at the hearing,
urging citizens to "show support for Canton and our continued economic health."

Governor Martin's promise to attend the Canton hearing was countered by Representative James Quillen's promise to attend the hearing at
Newport. Quillen was reported as being "fed up with delays, excuses
and foot-dragging." He would lead off as speaker when the hearing got
under way at 11:00 A.M. "There comes a point where patience ends and
action begins," he told *Plain Talk*'s reporters, "and the time for a once-
and-for-all decision on this problem has come."[69]

In general Cocke County inhabitants are skeptical of all politicians.
They feel that politicians have two faces, speak with forked tongues, and
bend with the wind. But in 1987 their politicos appeared to be on their
side. Representative Quillen is a good example. He pointed out that as
early as 1985, he had brought EPA's then deputy regional administra-

tor, Alex Little, from the Atlanta office to view the polluted Pigeon. He
followed up this action with a "stinging letter" to EPA administrator
Lee Thomas in Washington in which he requested "quick action" on
the problem. Moreover, he claims to have met twice in his Washington
office with Champion executives, once for five hours, while they explained to him their projected two-hundred-million-dollar, five-year
plan for the Canton facility. He rejected their proposal on the grounds
that it was too little, too late. He blamed the company, not its employees. "I'm sure they take no pride in knowing that their neighbors in Tennessee must tolerate such pollution, but it's not up to them. It's a decision for Champion, and I feel this company will do what is right and what
is honorable," Quillen explained. He also noted a letter received from a
Cocke County farmer whose cows would walk all the way across the pas-
ture to drink fresh water rather than quench their thirst from the Pigeon.
The farmer, commented Quillen, "says that when the cows are smart
enough not to drink the water, then it's time to improve the river. I agree."[70]

All the unpleasant emotion engendered by the company during the
early months of 1987 was uncalled for. On May 10 the *Asheville Citizen-
Times* quoted Bruce Barrett of the Atlanta EPA office as saying that even
if Champion was forced to upgrade its wastewater treatment until a 50-
color-unit goal was achieved near the pipe, the company would be granted
a reprieve while it worked toward achieving that goal. "EPA," he stated
flatly, "is not going to make it close." Newport's newspaper carried the
same story, adding that delighted Champion officials brought up the
possibility of a variance that would be beneficial to both sides: EPA
could waive its standards for water quality, especially if the polluter shows
to the agency's satisfaction that it is doing all it can do, technically and
financially.

Then EPA let fall a bombshell. At the eleventh hour, as *Plain Talk*
described it, as emotions were rising dangerously, the agency canceled
the hearings. It gave as its official reason the EPA's need for more time
to review an enormous amount of Champion material. Congressman
Quillen blasted EPA, denouncing the decision "as a ploy to give Champion more time to sell their story." Others suspected the real reasons
were death threats to Pigeon River Action Group and Dead Pigeon
River Council members and threats to bomb EPA offices and the two
hearing sites in Canton and in Newport. EPA officials, it was felt, took
the cautious view and canceled the hearings to let emotions cool.[71]

Senator Gore issued his own press release. He also regretted the
delay, reminding his constituents that "the severe problems caused by
the pollution of the Pigeon River remain. They must be remedied as

quickly as possible. I expect EPA to insist on a reasonable program to clean up the river, and Champion must comply fully with the final permit requirements." Gore's fellow senator, Jim Sasser, released a statement that was even stronger. He suggested that Cocke County's faith in the EPA was "severely strained" by the cancellation. In a letter to EPA administrator Lee Thomas, he urged that EPA "think twice" before issuing a variance.[72] Cocke County Executive Charles Moore likewise expressed disappointment. In his view, the cancellation served no purpose. "If it's something Champion's trying to pull," he added, "I think it's a shame."[73]

Whatever the reasons, the process of holding public hearings would have to start all over again. Summer arrived in the beautiful Smokies, and then the Smoky Mountains autumn set in. Colors turned, and then the trees shed their leaves and it was November; the tourists were gone. Motel and bed-and-breakfast owners and retailers of arts and crafts counted their profits and losses, set about making repairs, building additions, traveling to wholesale exhibitions where they made purchases for the next year, or took their hard-earned vacations. Only every other Thursday afternoon was activity above normal. That is when Champion's twenty-one hundred employees are paid.

But in the minds of Champion employees and residents of western North Carolina, a Sword of Damocles hung over the fate of Champion. Would EPA insist upon the 50-color-unit restriction? And, if so, would Champion be forced to abide by it? Did the company, then, really mean it when it threatened to close the plant? To Dick Mullinix, Bob Seay, Gay Webb, Nelson Ross, Jim Harrison, and other members of the Pigeon River Action Group and the Dead Pigeon River Council, all the fears were specious. Moreover, top EPA officials had stated categorically that Champion would not be forced to close if it could not abide by the color rule. Sometimes, Champion employees needed to be reminded that the 1980s were the most friendly pro-business period in the federal government since the 1920s.

Champion employees did not see it that way. Their fears were aided and abetted by the company. More and more, Champion was flexing its muscles as a powerful bully, determined to crush the opposition once and for all. The campaign assumed the proportions of the proverbial sledgehammer to kill a mosquito. The company's siege mentality led to an expensive, ill-conceived public relations campaign.

It boomeranged.

CHAPTER 8

The Programmed Asheville Hearing

One may have expected the furor to have died down after EPA canceled the May 14 hearing in Canton and the May 16 hearing in Newport. Up to four months, it was said, could elapse before the meetings were held. (It proved to be longer than that.) Why not get to work and forget about it?

But this time around, no one wanted to let the controversy go away. Champion still had that sword—the permit—hanging over its Canton facility. The company did not like the permit, insisting that the technology did not exist to implement the 50-color-unit limit. The decision was made to fight EPA. If the agency insisted, the company said, then Champion would have to restrict operations, throwing men and women out of work, or even close the plant. For employee consumption, the company minced no words: layoffs or closure if EPA prevailed. As autumn gave way to winter, the company mustered its Canton personnel. Well paid and with as permanent factory employment as could be found in the United States, Champion employees in Canton reacted passionately: they would support Champion without requesting proof of its inability to clean up the river. Some would react with blind emotion that resulted in death threats to the opposition.[1]

Another continuing Champion ploy has been to hire its own scientists to test the river. In July 1987, Champion announced still another of these investigations. Although scientists for TVA, North Carolina, and Tennessee had all conducted studies, Champion hired E.A. Engineering and Science Technology, Inc., of Maryland to probe the river from the mill to Newport. Dr. Gerald Lauer, the scientist in charge of this study, was quoted as saying that "the problem we've had is [that] various studies have been done for different segments of the river. It was sort of like comparing apples and oranges." The firm was to test the dissolved oxygen, pH levels, and algae growth. Oliver Blackwell stated that the study "further demonstrates Champion's commitment to the environment."[2]

To the opposition, the whole Champion campaign, which escalated throughout the fall and early winter, seemed unreal. Members of the Dead Pigeon River Council and the Pigeon River Action Group were convinced that the mill could operate under EPA's permit, that EPA would of course grant Champion time to make the necessary changes in operations, that no one needed be laid off, and that the mill certainly would not close. In view of the fact that then Vice-President George Bush had been fishing Lake Logan as a Champion guest in May 1986, the company's campaign seemed both illogical and unrealistic. Why keep the controversy stirred up—stirred up until violence is threatened—when there was really no need?

Champion officials were not unwilling to meet with DPRC and PRAG members and citizens living along the river and in the Douglas Lake area. On September 9, 1987, Champion officials met with about thirty of these people. Residents knew that Douglas Lake had been plagued with low levels of dissolved oxygen, which is vital to a vigorous fish population. They suspected that their beautiful lake suffered adversely from Champion's effluent. A TVA representative had said that very little work had been done on that question. In its defense, Champion reminded residents that it now deposited many solids that used to end up in the Pigeon River in its Haywood County landfill. As an indicator of the rising interest in the controversy, four television stations covered the meeting.[3]

Champion would not quiet down and neither would its opposition. Company opponents, shocked at Champion's continuing campaign, faulted the company at every opportunity. When it was divulged that Champion had paid two thousand dollars for trout consumed at a dinner for members of the North Carolina General Assembly, the opposition made sure the public knew about it. Charles "Skeeter" Curtis, Champion's community relations director, defended the company's gift. "Our local officials asked us to," he said, and "we felt like, being a good corporate citizen, it was the proper thing to do." To which PRAG's Dick Mullinix replied in a letter to the editor, "Let's let up on the 'good corporate citizen' approach and get some action on the disgraceful condition of the Pigeon River. That would appear less fishy than sending trout to Raleigh." Even the *Mountaineer* criticized Champion for paying the bill. "Environmentalists have complained and still complain that the state is too cozy with Champion and handles the company with kid gloves—a charge Champion and the state deny," wrote reporter Richard Shumate.[4]

In October the western North Carolina chapter of the Sierra Club, the Wenoca Group, issued a report calling on Champion to reduce its tannin wastes. (Tannin is a yellowish or reddish substance from tree bark.) Michael Petelle, a professor of ecology at the University of North Carolina at Asheville, braved company, community, and official wrath by writing the Sierra Club's statement. Champion, he insisted, "should be responsible for cleaning it [the Pigeon] up." He pointed out that much more than aesthetics were involved. "If an insect eats a leaf with tannins, it cannot digest it. It prevents proteins from working in the river animals. The tannins are active and not inactive as Champion has claimed." The statement said bluntly that Champion "can and should and has the resources to clean up the river. . . . A clean river and a profitable Champion are not mutually exclusive."[5]

On November 2 EPA announced new dates for the hearings: Janu-

This cartoon, appearing in November 1987, is indicative of the rising awareness in Knoxville of pollution in the Pigeon River. Cartoon by Gehring. Courtesy Knoxville News-Sentinel.

ary 14 in Asheville and January 21 in Knoxville. The agency reiterated that the 50-color-unit standard would remain in the proposed permit.[6]

If EPA had canceled the earlier dates in hopes that emotions would die down, then its officials were to be disappointed. Recriminations escalated as 1987 waned. A portent of the company's hard-line stance was revealed in Vice-President Oliver Blackwell's talk to the Waynesville Rotary Club. "If you assume, as I am now ready to assume, that the harping, the complaining, the grandstanding and the bitching by all of those who claim to know more about this [color] than we do is never going to stop, then why should we risk the money to modernize the mill?" he raved, adding that he was afraid "any permit, with any color number in it, will not stop these so-called broad-based citizens action groups, the politicians who listen to them and a news media that is hooked on controversy from complaining about our operation." He warned that critics could force the mill to leave, and that a community consensus was necessary to save Champion. He even criticized the local press. The *Mountaineer* took this as an affront and editorialized in protest, insisting that it had consistently supported Champion.[7]

Once the new hearing dates had been set, Champion shifted its crusade into the kind of high-powered public relations campaign that could be mounted only by a six-billion-dollar corporation. To manage the campaign, it hired a well-known public relations company, Price/ McNabb. Another firm was hired to handle transportation of employees to the Asheville and Knoxville hearings. Nor was the company above trying to use politicians to advance its interests.

Senator Gore Compromises

One politician who was burned by these events was Tennessee's young senator (now vice-president), Al Gore Jr. In 1987 Senator Gore was thirty-nine years old. He is the son of former United States Senator Albert Arnold Gore, a distinguished liberal who had at one time been chairman of the Special Committee on Attempts to Influence Senators. The younger Gore was born in Washington, D.C., graduated from exclusive St. Albans School, and then earned a degree at Harvard. He attended Vanderbilt's School of Religion, then its Law School, served two years in the army in Vietnam, and was a journalist for six years. In 1976 Gore entered the U.S. House of Representatives. After serving eight years in the lower house, he was elected in 1984 as United States senator from Tennessee. In 1988 he unsuccessfully sought the Democratic candidacy for president. In 1990 he was reelected as a senator and in 1992 was elected vice-president of the United States. In the introduction to his excellent book, *Earth in the Balance: Ecology and the Human Spirit*, published in 1992, the vice-president says that his interest in the environment and ecology had begun as far back as 1972.

In the autumn of 1987, he was campaigning to be the Democratic party's 1988 nominee for president. He needed money and friends—corporation friends and rich friends and political friends—from outside Tennessee. One of these "friends" was North Carolina Representative James Clarke, whose district embraced Haywood County. Senator Gore desperately needed North Carolina's support in his bid for the nomination.

In the heat of the campaign, Senator Gore breakfasted at Johnson City with some western North Carolina politicians. Precisely who attended the meeting is not clear, but the cast of characters included Representative James Clark's son, who promoted Champion, and Wallace Hyde, patriarch of the Democratic party in North Carolina. Their business clearly involved Champion International Paper Corporation. It is known that the senator met twice with Champion officials. After these meetings, his attitude toward Champion the polluter softened.[8]

According to a press release from the senator, Champion was offering a deal. It would reduce the Pigeon's water color down to between 80 and 85 color units at the Tennessee state line. Gore considered the offer "highly significant," better than any of the company's previous offers, and an excellent new starting point for new negotiations. He urged EPA to accept the offer. The press release ended with the comment that "Hopefully, Champion's recent offer represents a breakthrough that will result in the final resolution of this difficult situation." In other words, the senator favored the compromise. Moreover, a bill would be introduced in the Tennessee legislature making it legal for that state's authorities to accept a variance allowing the 85-color-unit standard as the Pigeon enters Tennessee. Gore's compromise was a major factor in Representative Clarke's decision to endorse Gore for the presidential race. "If people say he's flip-flopped, that's fine. We want him to flip-flop in our direction," said Clarke's administrative assistant; "frankly, we want to do anything to help Champion." Nelson Ross, a Gore supporter, acknowledged that Gore's position had been compromised "by the way he's been used as a political tool by Champion International and Jamie Clarke."[9]

Champion had just brought off a coup. It had driven a wedge still further into the anti-Champion ranks. The difference between 50 and 85 platinum cobalt color units is so infinitesimal as to be unnoticed by the casual observer—even by a trained one. Moreover, Senator Gore was certainly not the only one to regard the 85-color-unit standard as acceptable. As pointed out earlier, to some environmentalists, such as Paul Davis, director of Tennessee Water Quality Control, Champion's promise of 85 color units represented a clear victory for the clean Pigeon River advocates. To Davis, the 85 unit promise, as well as the company's announced plans to upgrade the plant with oxygen delignification and other improvements, denoted a change in company policy. Davis believed EPA should accept the offer.[10]

That the compromise seemed reasonable to others in Tennessee came as no surprise to such politically alert activists as Charles Moore and Bob Seay. The political good-old-boy network was involved. Governor McWherter knew of the deal and is believed to have expressed approval, as had members of the Tennessee attorney general's staff and officers in the Department of Health and Environment. It seems possible that some members of LEAF were inclined to accept the 85-color-unit compromise also.[11]

To Dick Mullinix, Bob Seay, Charles Moore, Gay Webb, Jerry Wilde, Bach and Barnett of Walters State Community College, and others, Champion's offer was meaningless. To them, Champion was the boy who had cried wolf too often: Champion had promised to clean up the Pigeon many times since 1911. Champion had never done it, and there was no reason to believe that the company was acting in good faith this time. In their view, only the force of law—and the force of a federal bureaucracy embodied by EPA—could make Champion clean its effluent. Furthermore, when the fine print of the offer was studied, those 85 color units were promised only at certain times of high water; at other times, such as at low flow in the summer and autumn, the color units would be back up into the hundreds. John Marler of EPA informed the press that a letter to EPA from Senator Gore offered nothing new—that the 85 unit number had always been the point from which EPA and Champion began discussions.[12]

Senator Gore, who thought he had made a good deal with Champion, must have been surprised at the negative reaction it received. The leaders of PRAG and the DPRC condemned it. Making matters worse, the senator committed a more serious blunder. At a Democratic party fund-raiser in Asheville where he spoke in support of James Clarke's reelection, the Tennessean reiterated that he considered 85 color units acceptable. Then he rode in a Champion limousine with Representative Clarke.

This was too much for Cocke County folk, who were locked in the struggle to get their river clean. Senator Gore received strong letters of protest. When he arrived in Newport at a later date, his constituents embarrassed him with difficult questions. He emphasized that he still favored a clean Pigeon River, however; and some if not all of his Cocke County supporters have since forgiven a young man trying to win his party's presidential nomination. After all, a politician who will not compromise is a politician out of a job. Senator Gore's subsequent statements have left no doubt of his sincerity and dedication. Chalk it up to experience. Today, one suspects, Vice-President Al Gore would not fall for such a "deal."[13]

Champion's Public Relations Campaign

On December 1 EPA issued a revised draft of the discharge permit. It would be the subject of discussion at the hearings, and it was quickly noted that the 50-color-unit limit was retained. But there was a difference: in this permit EPA gave Champion five years to achieve it. The previous draft of the permit had forced the company to comply when the permit became valid. The next day EPA announced the opening of a written comment period, which would extend through February 22. This was more than a month after the hearings, which guaranteed that the final decision would not take place until, at the earliest, sometime in the spring of 1988.[14]

News of the five-year period in which to meet color requirements did not deter Champion's campaign against EPA and the suggested permit. As a part of its campaign, the company emphasized its plans for the two-hundred-million-dollar (or more) upgrading of the Canton plant. The new oxygen delignification system, the company announced, would cut out dioxins and furans and chloroform, all of which were toxic chemicals released by the present chlorine bleaching process. Escalating the pressure, on December 4 Champion announced that the modernization plan would be canceled if the revised permit was issued. This, company officials said, was because, even with the advanced processes and new equipment, Champion still could not meet the 50-color-unit standard.[15]

By December it was clear that Champion officials had lost their good judgment. The magnitude of the public relations campaign against EPA and the permit was expanded beyond all common sense. Possibly it was frustration and irritation over Dick Mullinix and his Pigeon River Action Group, Bob Seay and members of the Dead Pigeon River Council, and the legal challenges launched by the Tennessee attorney general's office. Someone or some few in top management must have said: "Let's crush that damned opposition down there in hillbilly country once and for all." Or perhaps Champion officials were approached by a public relations firm looking for work. If so, the salesmen were persuasive and sold Champion the package.

As *Newsweek* describes these public relations organizations, they are expert at "watering at the grass roots," at creating a "'spontaneous' public uprising." One company handles all the details (the only detail left to Champion or another firm during the public relations campaign that surrounded the hearings was the transportation of employees to the hearings). The public relations team took a series of steps that guaranteed maximum publicity: it developed a theme (for Champion, the image of dominos was developed, with the implication that if Champion fell so would the area's economy); set up and operated phone banks in Haywood, Buncombe, and adjoining North Carolina counties; prepared full-page advertisements for local newspapers; drafted and parceled out television and radio spots to local stations; prepared form letters (280,000 of them were mailed to EPA); rented a warehouse to store caps, buttons, bumper stickers, decals, banners, and signs, all bearing Champion's name, logo, and colored predominantly yellow, the company color; drew up petitions addressed to EPA and the North Carolina congressional delegation; brought in the unions; and coordinated the drive with local booster organizations (such as Haywood's Economic Development Commission). Still other experts gave advice on influencing company employees. Banners, placards, and bumper stickers were to be widely distributed, appropriately placed in the communities affected. Moreover, employees were encouraged to control the hearings, especially the Asheville hearing, which was dominated by Champion. Finally, the public relations team brought in the area businessmen as allies.[16]

Residents of Canton, Clyde, and Waynesville knew something was up when strangers showed up on the streets wearing caps that sported the logo of the Minnesota Vikings football team. (It was learned that Price/McNabb, the public relations company, had just completed a promotion for the Vikings prior to bringing their personnel from cold Minnesota to the chilly mountains of southern Appalachia.) They knew their jobs and did them well. Perhaps they did their jobs too well.

"Is this good for democracy?" asked *Newsweek* magazine. Quoting Michael Graham, president of Reese Communications, *Newsweek* gave an answer: "Companies have just as much right to express themselves on issues as the NRA or the Sierra Club." As a further excuse, he says that while environmental groups (such as PRAG and the DPRC) have almost always been outspent by corporations, they have compensated with grass-roots organizing and extensive use of volunteers. "Corporations," adds *Newsweek*, "can now spend millions to neutralize the volunteer groups' main tactical advantage."[17]

The clearest indication of a programmed public relations campaign was reflected in the growing hostility of Champion employees and businesses dependent on them toward any opposition. These actions did not emanate directly from the activities of the public relations professionals, but they were certainly a direct result of the pro-Champion campaign.

Rising, Unreasoned Anger

A first case in point was the incident involving WLOS-TV, Channel 13, in Asheville. In its Friday evening news hour, the station presents a sixty-second "puff piece" labeled "personality of the week." On Friday, December 4, 1987, WLOS highlighted Pigeon River Action Group founder and Champion critic Dick Mullinix. "The story was not about Champion," explained general manager Michael Fiorile, "it was about an elderly citizen who wants North Carolina to be a beautiful place to live in."[18]

Champion employees were infuriated. Workers Bruce Holcome and Mike Israel, both of whom worked at the No. 19 machine, drew up a petition that read in part: "In order to show our displeasure we the undersigned refuse to purchase goods or services from businesses which advertise on WLOS-TV." Additional petitions were circulated at businesses and even in doctors' offices. Between eighteen hundred and two thousand Champion employees signed the petitions. Both the union and the company denied complicity, saying that the spontaneous reaction came solely from employees, some of whom made visits to local businesses, personally threatening boycotts if the businesses did not cease advertising on WLOS. The *Asheville Citizen* did not report a single business that canceled its advertisements, but the *Mountaineer* reported that Haywood Appliance and Television, with stores in Waynesville and Asheville, did cancel five thousand dollars in Christmas promotions. Even the Canton Board of Aldermen passed a resolution in which it debated "the wisdom of WLOS in its decision to confer person-of-the-week honors on such a controversial person."[19]

Outraged Champion employee Dean Free suggested that "if [Mullinix] is man-of-the-week, Gadhafy [Muammar al-Quadaffy] ought to be man-of-the-week next week. All Mullinix has done is cry about the river. The company is our life. Who is more important, our families or our fish?"[20]

On the following Monday evening, WLOS aired an explanation of its personality-of-the-week selections. It explained that it tried to choose "people who act on their own behalf to make a change in the community." Manager Michael Fiorile emphasized that naming a person does not in any way mean the station endorses that person's "cause or position."[21]

Fear in the workplace: Champion now had its employees ready to forget civil rights and the Constitution in order to preserve their jobs. "So much for freedom of speech," editorialized *Plain Talk*. "To attempt to somehow stifle the basic freedom of a television station to air, of all things, a feature story will serve no useful purpose at all." It blamed Champion, not for directly inciting the actions, which Champion insisted it did not do, but for encouraging such a response "by suggesting that the mill will have to close in light of the environmental debate. And the vote of the Canton governing board can be viewed as irresponsible at best. . . . Elected officials should be concentrating their efforts on the official business of a town. Their vote should be condemned."[22]

On December 1 Lee DeHihns, acting EPA Region IV administrator, informed the press that he wanted a meeting of mill and state officials. He said such a conference "could have an impact on [the] final permit issued to Champion," adding that "it would not change the permit before the . . . public hearings 'unless a miracle occurs.'" On December 11, at Stone Mountain, Georgia, the meeting of Tennessee, North Carolina, and Champion officials did occur. However, even though it was described as a long meeting, no substantive results were reported.[23]

On December 23 Dick and Lucie Mullinix, situated in their rustic, ordinarily cozy home above Panther's Creek Road, again received several threatening calls. The first one came at about 2:00 A.M. The male voice was low, gruff—possibly drunken—and strong. "First job lost in this state because of you, we're goin' to beat you up and throw you in the Pigeon," the first caller said. (Dick made transcriptions of the voice from his answering machine.) Later, a woman called, saying that men had left and would shortly arrive at the Mullinix house and they were bent on doing harm.

Dick and Lucie do not own so much as a pellet gun. The voices were angry and persuasive: whoever they were, they meant business. So remote is their cabin that night riders could do their work and disappear. Days could pass before anyone discovered their victims. Dick and

Lucie chose the safe alternative. Quickly, they packed, closed up, drove down the narrow dirt road, then down the wider road to Interstate 40. Only when they were speeding toward Newport and Knoxville did they breathe freely. They drove to their Florida residence—but remained away only temporarily.[24]

The first calls had come months before; over the years, they would receive many more. Some promised violence equal to that threatened the night of December 23. One such call in 1990, received about 4:00 A.M., sounded like an angry good old boy who had had quite enough to drink. "First man that loses a job at Champion and we're going to hang you up by the balls," the caller shouted. Dick has informed Haywood County's sheriff about the threatening calls, but as far as is known, the sheriff has taken no action. "Some say to just ignore these calls," says Mullinix, "but the FBI to whom I have talked says that threatening calls must always be taken seriously." To Lucie, it was a relief to have escaped to Florida after that night in 1987, even for a short while, free of feeling that she was met with icy stares as Lucie Mullinix of the Pigeon River Action Group. The threats did not prevent them from returning to the area to attend the January hearings.[25]

Oliver Blackwell kept up his own public relations campaign. He brought his cause to the Asheville Chamber of Commerce. "We've had exhaustive color technologies done," he said. "We have responded to seven alternatives suggested by the EPA, none of which were practical, technically achievable, and more importantly, none of them were economically achievable," he explained. "The draft permit issued by EPA, as written, would force the mill to close." The chamber president, Jerry Cole, admitted that "there's a lot about the chemistry involved I do not understand," but he certainly knew what it means not to have a job. Plant closure would produce a "ripple effect," he warned. "It will be a tidal wave kind of effect."[26]

As the New Year began, Champion and Price/McNabb accelerated their propaganda. A banner stretched across Canton's Main Street showed a domino and the words DON'T LET CHAMPION FALL SUPPORT CHAMPION BY CALLING 648-SAVE. White dominos were everywhere, buckets and boxes and jars of them. Each domino bore someone's name or initials. They served to remind residents of the domino effect resulting from the mill's closure, supposedly imminent if the permit was approved.

Businessmen took out advertisements in local newspapers. Canton Savings and Loan Association ran an ad in the *Asheville Citizen-Times* that reminded citizens of its estimate of the $150 million that the company generates in the region. It stated that the company had been "a loyal corporate citizen, participating in and supporting community and civic affairs," insisted that Champion "has expended more than $73 million for environmental improvements which have been highly successful in reducing said discharges," and then announced categorically that Champion could not meet EPA's draft permit requirements. Therefore, the savings and loan association supported Champion and listed the politicians to whom to send copies of its resolution.[27]

The unions have supported Champion in its battle with EPA, but not without undertones, innuendoes, and nuances. Besides Local 507, which has over eighteen hundred members, a number of trade unions have members who work at, or believe they should be employed at, the Canton facility. In May 1987, Asheville Local 238 of the International Brotherhood of Electrical Workers, Local 553 in Durham, North Carolina, and Local 487 of the United Association of Pipefitters and Plumbers protested Champion's hiring of construction-trades workers from outside the region, indeed from outside North Carolina. The company's prime contractor for construction work was B.E.&K., Inc., out of Alabama, and so, it was said, 70 to 80 percent of its employees came from other states; local union members had certainly noticed all the out-of-state automobile tags. Attempts to discuss the matter with Blackwell, Senator Terry Sanford, and Representative James Clarke had failed. What to do? The unions retaliated with an anti-Champion sign along Interstate 40. "EPA DO YOUR JOB," it read, "STOP CHAMPION PAPER FROM POLLUTING THE PIGEON RIVER." Below the statement, the unions supporting this point of view were listed.

When queried about the sign, the unions' spokesman, Jerry J. Rogers, said that the sign seemed a good way to attract Champion's attention. He added that about half the calls the unions received were about the sad condition of the Pigeon, and "we don't want a single employee to lose his job."

Suddenly, with five months of the sign lease left, the unions had their message painted over. Union representatives had met with Vice-President Blackwell. They insisted that the meeting had nothing to do with the decision to paint over the sign—although it was "a good general discussion."[28]

In January 1988, prior to the hearings, Smoky Mountain Local 507 (not one of the unions involved with the sign) ran its own announcement in support of Champion. "This Local Union," it read in part, "considers every job at the paper mill in Canton to be of utmost importance. . . . We feel the conditions and requirements of this [EPA] permit are technically and economically impossible to obtain. . . ."[29]

Behind this supportive statement lies a murky story. The union had been negotiating with Champion since August 31, 1987, for a new contract involving hourly employees. In a letter to the *Mountaineer,* some of the union members reminded Champion—which, they said, wanted to exact concessions worth thirty-three million dollars from them—that they had continued as loyal employees without a contract. At the same time, the mill had set new production records. During the outage of November 1987 (when drought forced the mill to shut down), these workers reminded their employer, "maintenance employees put in some long, hard hours under the worst conditions you could possibly imagine."[30]

But Champion was adamant about its bargaining position, finally forcing the union to vote on a contract that was, said union negotiator Arnold Brown, the company's final offer. The union rejected it, even though Champion described the contract as its best offer with an assurance that nothing new would be forthcoming. Brown accused Champion of using the threat of environmental restrictions as a way of forcing workers to accept the concessions. "They're absolutely taking advantage of our members about the water problem. They've made it an issue—a threat issue in my opinion," he said. Oliver Blackwell's reply was that a strike would not shut down the mill, but EPA's wastewater permit would. Ultimately, the union gave in. The *Asheville Citizen-Times* said that Champion had used the threat of closing due to the projected costs of dealing with environmental problems as a sword over the labor union, forcing it to accept Champion's offer.[31]

The Hearings Begin

January 14, the date of the Asheville hearing, was approaching. The Haywood County Economic Development Commission announced that it would run shuttle buses from the Ingles Shopping Center in Waynesville and from the Canton Municipal Building to the Asheville Civic Center and back. Buses would also shuttle students from Pisgah and Tuscola high schools and Waynesville, Canton, and Bethel junior highs to and from the hearing following their lunch hour. A permission slip, to be cut out and signed and given to the teacher, ran in the *Mountaineer.* On the same page, readers were reminded that if Champion closed, the school system would be out a million dollars. On January 8 the *Mountaineer*

Champion's anti-50-color-unit campaign included placards featuring falling dominos and bus schedules for free transportation to the Asheville Civic Center for the January 1988 hearing. Photo by Gilbert Soesbee. Courtesy Newport Plain Talk.

ran a full-page advertisement with a letter to be clipped and mailed to EPA. Even colored balloons were used: DON'T LET CHAMPION FALL, they read, accompanied by the image of three falling dominos.

Champion officials wearing orange armbands were present at the Ingles store on Russ Avenue in Waynesville and the Canton municipal building to load passengers and see the buses on their way. At the civic center, photographers, police, and Champion officials made sure that the program went according to plan. Jim Harrison, an EPA official who is also a clean Pigeon proponent, was incensed when photographers lured him into conversation with a shabbily dressed, hippie-like protester, and then snapped his picture. Two men known as Champion opponents were informed by the police that if they crossed the street to the civic center and tried to enter, they would be arrested. They stayed clear.[32]

The public relations firm had done its job well.

Certainly if attendance is a criterion of success, then Champion's effort at Asheville was a triumph. An estimated seven-thousand-plus Champion defenders attended the meeting—or at least parts of it—which lasted from 11:00 A.M. until 8:00 P.M. At any given time, the attendance number was probably between three and four thousand; few

Employee signing name on one of the white dominos to be placed in jar with others, all signifying opposition to EPA's proposed permit. January 1988. Photo by Gilbert Soesbee. Courtesy Newport Plain Talk.

stayed for the entire nine hours. Some, so it was said, were bused to Asheville at midnight the night before the hearing to wait at the entrances and prevent any environmentalists who might show up from upstaging the pro-Champion speakers. When supporters arrived, Champion officials at the door handed out dominos—eventually one jug on the podium contained over ten thousand signed by supporters. Champion also gave out tokens good for coffee, soft drinks, and cookies at the concession stand.

Of the hundred people—give or take nine or ten—who spoke (not including procedural statements by EPA officials), not one was openly critical of Champion, and only two or three made veiled statements that could be interpreted as critical. One can study the 330-page transcript long and hard in search of the words stench, odor, smell, toxic, dioxin, chloroform, temperature, dissolved oxygen, color, or even pollution; some of these words do appear, but they are as hard to find as needles in a haystack. Save for the moderator's opening statements, these words were not a part of the speakers' vocabulary. The pro-Champion audience cheered, clapped, and stood up to attest its agreement with the words spoken by politicians, workers, businessmen, or just plain citizens.

Bruce Barrett of EPA was moderator; he was aided by his colleague Fritz Wagener. They began the hearing by presenting the ground rules. Barrett stood at a lectern in the center of a stage. On each side of him was a lectern, so that speakers approaching from either side would not have to cross over the stage to speak. Participants were given three to five minutes to deliver their statements.[33]

Barrett set the stage for the hearing. He presented the problem very well—so well, in fact, that it was probably not appreciated by the partisan audience. He displayed five bottles of water to the gathering in the cavernous auditorium. Each bottle contained water that was colored more—and therefore darker—than the previous one. Bottle number four contained water testing at 800 platinum cobalt units. This, Barrett explained, was the long-term average of Champion's effluent as it entered the Pigeon River. The contrast with the bottle of water at 50 color units was striking. He also discussed the amount of biochemical oxygen (dissolved oxygen) and the new regulations in the permit concerning that chemical, the limits on chloroform released into the river, the possibility of the presence of dioxins, and, finally, the permit's limits on coliform bacteria from human waste, since Champion treats Canton's sewage. After this presentation Barrett assumed his duty as moderator and called for the first speaker.

He was Oliver Blackwell, the sixtyish, bespectacled vice-president in charge of operations at the Canton plant. He was valued by Champion because he was an excellent manager (he died in November 1990). To every plant employee, he was Oliver, a man to whom a worker could lodge a complaint, a man who kept tight control of the massive operation but did it with a human touch. Blackwell had assumed the job of spokesperson for Champion, defending its position by sometimes stating categorically that the technology did not exist to clean the Pigeon down to 50 color units at the pipe or by denying the existence of dioxins in the effluent.

Blackwell reiterated the statement that there was absolutely no known technology to limit the water color at the pipe to 50 color units. With the proposed two-hundred-million-dollar upgrading at the plant, Tennessee's goal of 50 units at the state line could be met 60 percent of the time. This, he implied, should be enough. After all, Champion estimated that it contributed some forty-three thousand dollars a day to the economy of eastern Tennessee.

For the next four hours, until about 3:00 P.M., politicians ranging

North Carolina Governor Jim Martin at rostrum, Champion vice-president Oliver Blackwell seated, at Asheville hearing, January 14, 1988. Photo by Gilbert Soesbee. Courtesy Newport Plain Talk.

in importance from Governor Jim Martin and Representative James Clarke to county and city officials of affected North Carolina communities paraded to the podium "like so many wooden soldiers," as Dick Mullinix described them, "obeying Champion's commands." So many of their arguments were similar that it was obvious that their statements were composed from widely distributed Champion factual material.

Handsome, robust Governor Jim Martin of North Carolina followed Blackwell to the podium. PRAG and DPRC members are puzzled by the man. They feel that if anyone should know about the thirty-five to forty methods of cleaning polluted water, he, being a chemist, should. Yet the governor always saw only Champion's side. "Champion needs a champion," he orated in his best campaign style. He insisted that the company has a good record on pollution; that the mill has been retrofitted to become the best in the world in terms of pollution technology. "Champion," he stated, "is a responsible company."

Next came Representative James McClure Clarke, whose Congressional district included Buncombe and Haywood Counties. Clarke, though born in Vermont in 1917, grew up in Asheville, graduated from Princeton, and by profession is a dairy farmer and orchardist. Representative Clarke (who was defeated for reelection in 1988) stated flatly, categorically, that trout can live in the Pigeon River—something a bit difficult to understand because trout can only thrive in water under 60 degrees, and Champion's water leaves the pipe at 80 degrees. On a more serious note, Clarke came to the defense of the woodcutters who furnish Champion with much of its wood. Their work is so hard, he said, that one seldom sees a woodcutter over fifty years old. They would be out of work if the plant were closed.

North Carolina State Representative Jeff Endow also touched on matters concerning Champion but not specifically concerning the river. He said that the company contributed to healthy forests. Timber not good enough for lumber, he explained, was still good for wood chips. He suggested that the United States Forest Service could not manage its forests save for allowing wood cutting for wood chips. Endow's colleague in the North Carolina legislature, Gordon Greenwood, defended the wood haulers, citing the seventeen million dollars a year the company paid them. The chairman of the state senate's Environmental Committee, Dennis Winner of Asheville, said that if he thought Champion was doing damage he wouldn't be at the meeting.

North Carolina Representative Cass Ballinger, a great-great grandson of "old Doughface" Lewis Cass of Michigan, was represented by a subordinate who spoke of Champion's "unselfish dedication" to the people of North Carolina. Senator Jesse Helms likewise sent a surrogate, who insisted that the Pigeon River below the mill consisted of nontoxic, harmless water that did not affect aquatic life. Senator Terry Sanford's substitute was Chancellor Emeritus H. F. Cotton of Western Carolina University. He presented statistics that the Pigeon ran at the Tennessee line with fewer than 50 color units 14 percent of the time and with fewer than 100 color units 63 percent of the time.

The loyal troops came on and on. The substitute for the speaker of the North Carolina House of Representatives blamed Tennessee for the creation of Fontana Lake and the inundation of thousands of acres of prime North Carolina land. State Senator Charles Hipps took a common line—that the company could not achieve the 50-color-unit requirement "or they wouldn't be spending so much to fight it [the permit]." He compared Champion's closing with a neutron bomb that kills the people but leaves the buildings standing. State Senator Charles Bell cited $1.5 million in city taxes paid by Champion, $12 million that it paid for electricity, and $69 million paid to regional vendors. He claimed that since 1970 Champion had spent $25 million on the Pigeon; he insisted that fish could now thrive in the river. He was also one of the very few speakers who pleaded for cooperation. Most simply stonewalled all opposition.

David C. Swan of the Wachovia Bank said that in eighty years, "Champion has never returned a check." The company, he said, reminded him of a dog. "When the dog stands still, it gets kicked. When it moves, it gets rocks thrown at it."

Champion brought in several suppliers to add to the dark picture if Champion were closed. Tommy Orr, vice-president of Western North Carolina Pallet in Candler, a settlement on the west side of Buncombe County, is a good example. His company makes pallets that Champion uses for shipping purposes and sells chips for pulping and sawdust for fuel. A total of 115 workers make their living from this little company, which sells Champion about $25,000 worth of products every month. Orr's fear was that the end of Champion would eliminate 115 jobs and a substantial payroll.

Very quickly, the theme emerged that if Champion closed its plant, absolute calamity would befall the entire region. All the speakers assumed this worst possible scenario, never suggesting compromise, never questioning Champion's unequivocal position that meeting the 50 color units was impossible. Canton's mayor said that Champion paid $691,000 in taxes to the town, 60 percent of the ad valorem taxes paid in the community in 1987. "Champion," he declared, "is the economic jugular vein of Canton and much of western North Carolina."

Some speakers addressed the quality-of-life issues that concerned Champion workers. In general, labor relations throughout the history of the Canton facility have been good. Enlightened labor policies and community consciousness paid off superbly for Champion during the recent Pigeon troubles. Canton's mayor reminded listeners of Champion's favorable policies toward men going off to war or serving a couple weeks a year in the reserves. William Branton of the Asheville City Council stressed what a good affirmative-action employer Champion had been, with 135 black workers and 293 women employed at the mill.

Jeff Ferguson, a farmer speaking in behalf of the Haywood County Soil Conservation District, reminded EPA and his audience that many of Champion's employees were small-time farmers. Because of Champion they had sufficient funds to carry out soil conservation measures. Without jobs, he warned, they would have to do more intensive farming, and that would end the conservation and, by implication, antipollution measures.

With one exception, labor unions, which one might expect to favor environmentalists, were just as loyal to the company. The president of the North Carolina AFL-CIO, Christopher Scott, said that the union ordinarily stands up for the environment, "but this [threat] is Rambo Environmentalism, and Rambo Environmentalism is when you accomplish the mission at all costs and take no prisoners." Close Champion and "Western North Carolina [will] be turned into a theme park called 'Depression Land,' a place where you could take your children to show them what the 1930s were like in the 1990s." The one exception was the statement of Robert Fraze, executive assistant to Wayne E. Glenn, president of the Paper Workers' International Union, with two hundred and fifty thousand members in the United States and Canada, and eighteen hundred members at Smoky Mountain Local 507. He issued a veiled threat to keep up the pressure on Champion to do something about the pollution.

Some speakers defended the company's environmental record. Roland Leatherwood, the mayor of Clyde, declared the river to be 100 percent cleaner than it had been years ago. Robert H. Phelps was able to speak of positive steps Champion had taken over the years to maintain a good environment. He reminded listeners that Dr. Shane (actually Dr. Carl A. Schenck), the Biltmore Estate's first forester (he was really the second), was later hired by Champion. "They [Champion] have been concerned about raw materials, the streams, the whole gamut, ever since the beginning," he insisted. Phelps then narrated how, when he first worked for Champion in 1947, one of his first assignments was to accompany a graduate chemical engineer to "test, monitor, and evaluate" the vents at the mill, and when leaks were found, to do something about them. So new was the practice that they had to make their own instruments or else send to Germany for them. When he took employment, he narrated, Champion already had monitors on the Pigeon River, "testing the [water] samples for such things as pH, BOD, color, dissolved oxygen, and various other things." And this, Phelps reminded his audience, "was prior to the public awareness of pollution in our streams, and also it was prior to establishment of EPA." He described an expensive pilot trickling system tried by Champion, which had not worked; he also addressed changes in bleaching procedures and different cooking processes designed to reduce pollution, "and many more, certainly too many for me to mention here, in an effort to improve the Pigeon River. . . . All we ask, all we ask," he repeated, "is that you use reason, and understanding, and you kind of put yourselves in our place."

Max Bradburn, a third-generation employee, deviated from the disaster scenario so many speakers used. He confessed to remembering a river into which a person with a case of poison oak might plunge or where a mangy dog might be thrown to be cured of their afflictions. He remembered foam five feet deep at the plant's railroad trestle and barrels strung across the river "to beat the foam down." Indeed, he admitted that, thirty-five years ago, the Pigeon was a dead river. But now things were different. As a diver, he claimed to have examined the riverbed. He denied the existence of a sludge layer. He believed the foam in the river now came from Waynesville's sewage outlet. Bradburn may have been the only speaker who used the word "odor" in his presentation.

Charles Taylor, chairman of North Carolina's State Parks Council, stressed the need for balance and fairness. He disputed Senator Gore's statement that the Pigeon's discharge is health threatening. "Untrue and irresponsible," he said.

The hearing must have become dull; the litany of horrors if the plant were to close—the unemployment, the economic catastrophe, the "spiritual impact" upon the region (as the pastor of Canton's Free Will Baptist Church warned)—was repeated over and over. Only a few speakers tried to instill a bit of levity. One who did was Ralph Saunders, regional commissioner for American Youth Soccer, which has received Champion funding. "Tennessee's like in a joke I know," he began. "They're kind of like a pre-teen boy, and Champion is like the pre-teen girl. Tennessee is saying I want what I want when I want it. And Champion's saying you'll get what I got when I get it." Haywood County's superintendent of schools tried the same approach. "I feel like Elizabeth Taylor's seventh husband on their honeymoon," he said. "I know what's expected, but I don't know how to make it interesting."

Some speakers, rather than predicting catastrophe, chose to damn the opposition. Jesse Ledbetter, Buncombe County commissioner, went after the federal government. "Quite frankly," he pontificated, "we are getting tired of federal government arrogance in our beautiful mountain region." Nancy Autry, a teacher at Pisgah High, chided the DPRC for asking drivers at a rest area on Interstate 40 to sign a petition against Champion "for a cup of coffee and a doughnut." She insisted that travelers had no idea what they were signing.

The audience perked up when eleven-year-old sixth-grader Andy Plemmons, a young scientist-to-be, discussed his four-month science project with the audience. He conducted two experiments to determine whether the Pigeon River was poisonous. In the first, he obtained two house plants called peace lilies, as identical in size and shape as possible, and placed them side by side in a window. Plant A was watered each week with five tablespoons of tap water; plant B with five tablespoons of Pigeon River water. After four months the plant given Champion water was just as healthy as the one receiving the tap water. He also tested Wandering Jew vines, nearly identical samples each in a small glass, one filled with Pigeon River water and one with tap water. Both plants developed roots. After forty-five days, he planted the vines and continued watering the one with Pigeon River water and the other with tap water. He could tell no difference between the two vines.

Andy Plemmons's other experiment involved fish: three bream, one catfish, and one crawfish in one five-gallon tank of tap water and the same number and species in a five-gallon tank of Pigeon River water. The crawfish in the tap water died after eight days. The catfish in the tap water died after nineteen days. The only fish that died in the Pigeon River water was the channel catfish, which lived eighty-six days. "As of today," the young scientist announced proudly, "I have a bream and a crawfish that have been living in water from the Pigeon River for four months. . . . I think this proves the water in the river below Champion is not poison. Fish and other animals like crawfish can live in it."

Other schoolchildren were dutifully paraded to the rostrum. Lydia Manley, president of the student body at Pisgah High, said: "We are literally scared to death of our future." Molly Cooper, president of the Tuscola High School Student Government, described Nova Scotia streams of a similar color to the Pigeon, teeming with trout.

Even the state of the Haywood County hospital was mentioned; one statement argued that if its twenty-five hundred Medicare patients had to go to Asheville, as it was implied they would have to if Champion closed, the cost would be 28 percent higher than at the Haywood facility. Again and again, the talks ended with the presentation of letters—hundreds of them—and dominos—thousands of them—to the EPA.

If the premise that Champion would have to quit production at Canton if EPA's permit were enforced was hard and fast, then the most impressive of the talks were those by suppliers, officials of timber-cutting operations, railroad agents, machine and boiler makers, and authorities of the towns of Canton, Clyde, Waynesville, and Asheville. Taken together, their statements add up to a composite view of the economic impact of the huge manufacturing facility upon western North Carolina. Speaking for the wood-chip suppliers, for example, was David Lieser, general manager of the western Carolina region of Champion's Timberland Operations. This company furnishes six hundred and forty thousand of the eight hundred thousand cords of raw materials consumed annually by the mill; this involves full-time employment of thirty-five log-

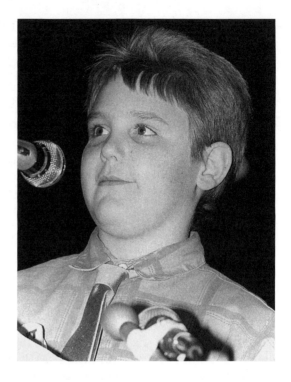

At the Asheville hearing, eleven-year-old Andy Plemmons described his experiments that "proved the Pigeon River is not poison." Photo by Dan Maxhimer. Courtesy *Asheville Citizen-Times.*

ging crews, each employing fifteen or more men supporting at least five hundred families. Speaker Earl J. Rayburn said there were twenty-eight sawmills in Tennessee and forty-eight in North Carolina serving Champion. The Norfolk Southern Railroad's director of pricing services, Herbert R. Stewart, reminded the audience of the two round trips made daily between the Asheville yards and the Canton plant eighteen miles away, of the twenty-eight thousand carloads a year hauled—twenty-two thousand of chips to the plant and six thousand of finished products from Canton. He said it brings the railroad thirty-three million dollars a year. Norfolk Southern has invested one hundred million dollars in freight cars to service Champion alone.

After nine long hours, the National Pollution Discharge Elimination System public hearing came to an end. Champion and its supporters must have felt happy and confident. The meeting, carefully orchestrated by the company and Price/McNabb, with cooperation from the Haywood County Development Commission, had progressed smoothly. No one had contested the company stand.

People left the hearing convinced that if EPA insisted upon the 50 color units, a mill earning Champion between sixty million and a hundred million dollars' profit a year would be closed. Western North Carolina, and especially Haywood County, would become a depression-stricken region of ragged children, shabbily dressed men, forlorn women, crime, old cars, boarded-up businesses, atheists, child molesters, and wife beaters.

Nothing, in those nine hours, was said about the damage inflicted for eighty years upon neighboring Cocke County. Nothing was said about the potential economic enhancements to Haywood County through tourism if the river ran clear, if it was swimmable, fishable, and raftable. Questions about toxic wastes and health hazards from the pipe to Douglas Lake and beyond were, if mentioned at all, vehemently rejected. That it was all just a matter of aesthetics was often mentioned, but rarely if ever was the phrase "public nuisance" heard. No one asked Champion what systems of water purification had been the subject of research in the company's laboratories. No one asked whether the company was conducting research on the pollution problem. No one asked why the company had rejected all seven of the proposals submitted to it by EPA for cleaning up the river. No one cross-examined company officials about when an antipollution technology might be feasible, how the system might work, or whether the company had an estimated date of placing such an operation on line.

Appraising the Asheville Hearing

They were good people, those who spoke and those who attended the hearing at Asheville. They were citizens, family people, taxpayers, breadwinners concerned for jobs. They were concerned for jobs that provided them their food, clothing, and shelter—and, for most, for jobs that left over enough for pickup trucks and good hunting rifles and time off to go hunting or fishing, to vacation, to provide for health and dental care for their families, to dress their children well and send them off to college.

They had all seen the color and the foam in the Pigeon River; they all knew about the temperature of the water; they had all smelled the stench. They all knew the river flowed through the heart of Newport and on to Douglas Lake, which is, ultimately, a source of Knoxville's water supply. Perhaps every one of them knew that the members of PRAG, the DPRC, and the citizens of Cocke County had valid complaints. Yet they ignored or rejected those complaints. They denied the reality of a polluted river, and they denied guilt. They disavowed the existence of a problem. Why?

The economic reason is clearly predominant. Regardless of wrongs done to citizens downstream, Champion, including the river it pollutes, meant a stable living, and that one fact superseded all else. It prevailed over honesty, integrity, morality, and just plain decency. The economic factor cannot be overstated. Anyone who has seen his or her employment placed in jeopardy should recall the emotions engendered by the threat. Remember the feelings: this is how Champion's people felt, and they were desperate about it.

The public relations campaign is another explanation. The citizenry of western North Carolina was subjected to a propaganda barrage that would have been the envy of Hitler's propaganda minister, Joseph Goebbels. Radio, television, newspapers, signs, banners, bumper stickers, decals, badges, hats, petitions, speeches, and company rumors were presented to people concentrated in such a small area that soon everyone coasted along with everyone else: they were for Champion. That terrible EPA and those evil minions of PRAG and the DPRC, the Izaak Walton League and Greenpeace and the Sierra Club, and everyone in Cocke County, were threatening to force Champion to close.

The paperworkers' ignorance of chemical processes played a part. Most have no chemical training. They work their eight-hour shifts in a massive factory, and, without an education in science, they cannot envision a system that would eliminate the tannins and toxic wastes and color and chemicals from the discharge. They might well think it is impossible. To them, Champion's statement that the color could not be removed was taken as holy writ. If Champion said it could not be done, then it could not be done.

Finally, peer pressure silenced those thinking souls who knew in their hearts that for reasons of its own Champion was resisting a realistic, achievable permit. Many knew that 50 color units was attainable, but the cost would be high. They knew that a six-billion-dollar corporation could accomplish the goal—especially in the five years given it by the permit—but that, for reasons known only ultimately to Champion's managers, the company had decided to resist. One does not want to be a pariah among one's friends and neighbors; an employee does not want to get on the wrong side of a supervisor at the plant by letting it be known that the employee thinks Champion is not telling the truth.

The *Asheville Citizen* was fair enough to run a lead article, along with its extensive reporting of the hearing, presenting the environmental side. In a press conference, an environmental coalition spokesperson, Millie Buchanan of the Clean Water Fund of North Carolina, suggested that the company cease using the chlorine bleaching process (which,

in fact, it has now done, although the new process uses chlorine dioxide). She also proposed that it cease bleaching the paperboard, leaving
it a light brown—a decision that has already been made in some Scandinavian countries and, to a degree, is being applied in Canada. "The
citizens of North Carolina have the right to both good jobs and a clean
environment," said Buchanan. "If we accept a choice that eliminates either,
we are accepting unnecessary limits on our own creativity and initiative."[34]

CHAPTER 9

Overkill

The Knoxville Hearing

C hampion officials dispute this, but representatives of the Pigeon River Action Group and the Dead Pigeon River Council and even EPA insist there was a clear but unwritten understanding that the Asheville meeting belonged to Champion, and the Knoxville hearing was the domain of the opposition. The opposition groups were shocked when they heard—almost (but not quite) too late to change their plans—that Champion planned to bus two thousand or more of its supporters to the Knoxville hearing. The Champion supporters were even to be supplied with a box lunch. The event was scheduled for Thursday, January 21, from 1:00 P.M. until 10:00 P.M. at Knoxville's civic center.

The Champion Caravan

DPRC and PRAG activists hurriedly corralled as many supporters as they could roust up to attend the hearing. Already they had programmed the order of speakers and, some say, had checkmated Champion's public relations crews, which had tried to wrest control of the program by arriving early. Since they suspected, correctly, that Champion partisans would be wearing the same big yellow buttons saying DON'T LET CHAMPION FALL, as well as yellow caps, Bob Seay and his aides hurriedly had big buttons made saying LET CHAMPION FALL, and they distributed these to their supporters.[1]

The day arrived. In Canton Governor Jim Martin appeared at the assembling grounds, and in his limousine led the caravan of between forty-five and fifty-two chartered buses filled with Champion's defenders up Interstate 40 toward the Tennessee line. The distance is about thirty miles. The mountains in January are destitute of leaves so that the white wooden houses, the mobile homes, and the remains of the previous summer's gardens are displayed nakedly; in spring, summer, and autumn, these homes are protected from prying eyes by the dense foliage. Here live the fiercely independent timber cutters, sawmill workers, artisans, and farmers of southern Appalachia. At the shabbier habitations, the Champion forces viewed the old pickup trucks and occasional cannibalized washing machines and refrigerators set grotesquely out of place in front yards. However, many homes are of brick veneer, sport grass-covered yards set off with clipped shrubbery, are free of clutter, and convey an image of prosperity and middle-class gentility in glaring contrast to the run-down dwellings. Some of the bus riders undoubtedly pointed out their own homes or homes of friends and relatives as they drove by.

Shortly after passing Highway 276, which links I-40 with Maggie Valley and Waynesville, the interstate begins climbing and curving along first one side then the other of the Pigeon River gorge. It is beautiful scenery, but so rapid is the traffic, so prevalent are the eighteen-wheelers whose drivers ignore the Department of Transportation's mandate of fifty miles an hour, and so twisting is the highway that few dare take their eyes off the road to enjoy the view; the highway is an engineering achievement, but it is still dangerous. Serious accidents are a common occurrence. Only occasionally, even in the bleak months of winter, can one catch a glimpse of Waterville Lake and Dam and, about nine miles farther on, Carolina Power and Light's Walters powerhouse. Less than a mile more and the river and the highway cross into Tennessee.

At or near the state line, Governor Martin's limousine swerved aside. Whether or not he waved them Godspeed as the caravan of buses and their two thousand or more occupants passed by, all were aware that their governor had driven up from Raleigh to show his support. Certainly the political payoff of such an action was not lost upon North Carolina's chief of state.

Another fifty miles ahead lay Knoxville with a population of 165,000. First, however, the gorge is left behind. The caravan passes the Hartford exit, then the outlets for Newport. The exits give little hint of the town, which is about a mile north of the Interstate. Newport proper looks like an American town caught in a time trap of the early 1930s.

On sped the caravan, past the exits with highways leading to Morristown and Jefferson City to the north and Douglas Lake to the south. The buses passed the connection with Interstate 81, which leads toward Johnson City, Kingsport, on to Bristol, Virginia, and the Shenandoah Valley. Exits to Pigeon Forge probably reminded some passengers of happy days spent shopping while their children thrilled to rides, water slides, and other amusements. Some might have recollected newspaper articles concerning Pigeon Forge's search for more water, and how the town fathers are wary of tapping into Douglas Lake because of its pollution from the Pigeon. It may even have occurred to some of the bus occupants that population pressure alone might force the cleaning of the Pigeon and other streams of equal or greater flow.

They arrived at Knoxville's civic center as an aggressive but reasonably well-behaved mass of humanity. Photographers from the *News-Sentinel* and the now-defunct *Journal* were on hand to record their arrival. The yellow Champion hats and three-inch round CHAMPION badges made a distinct impression. Tennesseans, a thousand to fifteen hundred of them, were somewhat cowed. Had their state been invaded by neighboring North Carolina?

It was soon apparent that company boosters were under the watchful eyes of delegated leaders. While these stewards helped keep order and prevented violence, they also led in cheers, boos, and standing ovations. For DPRC and PRAG members and supporters seated in the midst of the throng of yellow hats and yellow badges, it created a distinctly uneasy feeling.

Hearing Preliminaries

The ground rules were similar to those established for the Asheville hearing. The moderator was again Bruce Barrett. Sitting with him and co-chairing the meeting was John Marler, chief of the Facilities Performance Branch of the Water Division of EPA. Present also was Fritz Wagener, water quality standards coordinator of the Water Management Division of EPA. Barrett began the hearing by stating that Champion has maintained that it cannot afford the level of treatment required by the permit, even suggesting that it might have to close the mill or reduce the level of operations, which would result in decreased employment. Champion maintained this position, Barrett emphasized, despite the fact that the permit had been revised twice based upon changing information submitted by Champion.[2]

Before proceeding with the speakers, each of whom was limited to five minutes, Barrett turned the meeting over to Wagener, who encapsulated the history of the permit. He mentioned the Clean Water Act and North Carolina's and Tennessee's clean water regulations. A highlight of his presentation, which may have passed unnoticed by most of the audience, was his reminder that Champion was violating North Carolina's own water quality standards and had to operate with a variance from that state.

As at Asheville, five one-gallon bottles of water with various color unit levels were displayed because color was the principal sticking point in the permit. Water in bottle number one was taken from the Pigeon above the mill; it was rated at just 10 platinum cobalt units. The second bottle contained water at 50 platinum cobalt color units and represented what the water should look like at the Tennessee state line according to the EPA permit. The third bottle held liquid at 130 units; this was the estimate of the color at the pipe in order for it to have declined to 50 color units at the Tennessee line.

From Champion's point of view, the fourth bottle was the devastating one. Heavily colored at 800 platinum cobalt units, it represented Champion's pollution at the Tennessee line at the time a report was issued in 1986. The fifth and final bottle was somewhat lighter than the fourth. It contained just half the color—400 platinum cobalt units—and indicated the color of the water if Champion reduced the units by half.

Wagener pointed out other permit requirements. Biochemical oxygen and dissolved oxygen discharges were specifically restricted. Champion was instructed to monitor the discharges and ordered to install two streamside oxygenation facilities. And there was more sound information in Wagener's presentation—details concerning other conditions embraced in the permit—although he was losing his audience's attention. Chloroform, a suspected carcinogen, was to be restricted; a limitation on in-stream water temperature was imposed; the pH of the effluent was not to vary over a specified range; and the effluent must meet North Carolina's own standards for aquatic toxicity. Not addressed was the matter of dioxin, which had already been proven to exist downstream from kraft pulp and paper mills. He reminded his audience that once studies had been completed and the results ascertained, further restrictions might be inserted in the permit. Also, Wagener suggested, any future changes in Tennessee's or North Carolina's clean water laws would likewise result in permit changes.

Then the hearing was opened. First to speak was Oliver Blackwell. In recent weeks he had seemed to have lost all self-control, chastising Haywood County residents and the local newspapers for lack of support and threatening mill closure if the permit was enforced. Now he had regained his composure—as indeed was necessary in view of where he was—even though Champion had packed the civic center with two thousand or more supporters. He began his talk in a conciliatory vein. "We come humbly and in the spirit of neighbors visiting the home of friends," he began. Then he returned to the Champion line. "Now some have said, and will say today, that they don't believe Champion has done all that it can do," he lectured them. Champion had done its best, he insisted. "The draft permit as written will cause the mill to close. We have . . . studied every conceivable color removal technology, including those suggested by EPA. In fact, we have procedures to evaluate every suggestion and recommendation, no matter what the source. We know more about color in a kraft paper mill discharge than anyone in North America, if not [in] the world. We are recognized as an authority on this issue." Defending Champion's counterproposal, he insisted it would meet Tennessee's requirements of 50 color units at the boundary 60 percent of the time.

Then Blackwell gave the mantra of dire predictions of the impact on the region if the mill closed. It would "have a greater impact on the people of this region than any document, any law, any election, any storm or natural disaster we have faced in many years." He said the closing would affect six thousand families in western North Carolina, three hundred fifty in South Carolina, and five hundred in East Tennessee. He received enthusiastic applause from his two thousand supporters.

After Blackwell's speech, and for most of the remainder of the ten-hour hearing, those defending the permit had their turn. First to speak was Paul Davis, director of the Water Pollution Control Division of the Tennessee Department of Environment and Conservation. "The Pigeon," he reminded his listeners, "flows through one of the most beautiful mountain areas in the country," but the color, the odor, and the foam virtually ruin the scenery. Trying to be conciliatory—too conciliatory according to some Pigeon River activists—he suggested that a schedule of compliance with enforceable interim requirements be established, that EPA make the necessary revisions in the permit and then issue a draft that Champion could live with but which would still require constant stream improvement.

The orchestrated Asheville hearing had consisted of arguments for allowing Champion International to continue polluting the Pigeon; the Knoxville hearing was a 180-degree reversal of that position. Although it was not as well planned by PRAG and the DPRC as the public relations experts had programmed the Asheville meeting, and although two thousand and more Champion supporters crowded the Knoxville civic center, the Pigeon River boosters nevertheless made their points. They refused to be intimidated by the sea of yellow hats and yellow badges they looked down upon as they spoke from the podium.

Tennessee's public officials had first say, as had North Carolina's at

Asheville. They all emphasized that they did not want Champion to discharge a single employee. But they also referred to the political and economic power Champion wields in North Carolina. David McKinney, who with David Melgaard had made the tests at Waterville Lake at the time of the drawdown and who now headed the Department of Health and Environment in Tennessee, noted that his state and North Carolina shared a long record of working in harmony with each other in protecting the environment. The Watauga River, the Nolichucky, and the French Broad, he noted, had all profited from this cooperation. The one exception was the Pigeon River. "In fact," he said, "the Pigeon has remained grossly polluted before and after passage of the Clean Water Act and North Carolina's State Water Quality Act." And, he added dryly, "it has also been grossly polluted, both before and after the passage of the Tennessee Water Quality Act." It is time, he pleaded, "to resolve interstate disputes and bring this resolution to an end."

McKinney expressed some concerns about the leniency of the very permit that Champion was fighting. It was based upon estimates of wastes that decayed within a five-day period, but, he warned, evidence existed that Champion's wastes into the Pigeon did not decay until fifty to one hundred days. The variation is because of the changing flow of the Pigeon and the time the wastes are in Waterville Lake. "We are concerned," he explained, "that much of that degradation may take place in the state of Tennessee, either in the Pigeon River or in its ultimate fate in Douglas Reservoir."

He speculated that the confusing language of the draft permit with regard to color would make the standards unenforceable. He warned that the results of a dioxin study of Pigeon River water, not yet completed, would find the levels of the carcinogen unacceptable. "In our first round of sampling [for dioxin] last week," he added, "we regret to report that we had a good deal of trouble finding enough fish in the Pigeon River to fill out our commitment. . . . However, we will continue that effort."

Acting as an information officer, McKinney told of the meeting of North Carolina and Tennessee governors the week before, a meeting in which the Pigeon River problem was discussed. He narrated how in 1982—five years and more prior to the present hearing—the Tennessee Water Quality Board, acting under its Water Quality Act, had petitioned North Carolina "to bring to a resolution the issue of long-standing pollution in the Pigeon River. Five years back—and now the proposed permit gave Champion another five years to clean it up, with the usual variances being granted in the meantime. Five years," he said, "to the State of Tennessee seems unreasonable. We would suggest that the time frame be shortened significantly."

One of the points Champion's adherents had made in Asheville was that the Pigeon was not a dead river, that fish flourished in it, that the river bottom was not covered with toxic wastes—that, in essence, the Pigeon was a perfectly good river except that it had color. And the river's color, it was argued from Governor Jim Martin down, was just an aesthetic matter, hardly worth considering when two thousand jobs and a multimillion-dollar economy were at stake. To listen to Tennessee's supporters detail the fish condition, however, was to wonder whether the same river was being considered by both sides. Wayne Schacher came to the podium, representing the Tennessee Wildlife Agency; Schacher is a fisheries biologist. First, if the river were clean, he described how it was capable of supporting an excellent smallmouth bass, rock bass, and trout fishery when it enters Tennessee. But now? "Folks," he stated unequivocally, "there are no viable populations of game fish present in the Pigeon River in Tennessee."

The scientist explained how a fish population survey is made. Two methods were used in the Pigeon: explosives and electricity. "If the fish are present," he emphasized, "those two methodologies will bring them to the surface." For the first survey, Schacher chose "excellent pool and ripple habitats." Of fifty-two fish taken, not one was a smallmouth bass or a trout. One lone six-inch rock bass was collected, but all the other fifty-one fish were so-called rough fish: suckers, stone rollers, and shiners.

For his second survey, Schacher and his aides went above Newport—and therefore still farther away from the pipe—below the junction of U.S. Highways 70 and 25. There he chose "some of the most prime pool and ripple habitat with regard to holding and sustaining smallmouth and rock bass fisheries. . . . Fishermen that pursue those species," he added as an aside, "their mouths would have watered" to have seen the fishing sites he had chosen. For two hours and forty-five minutes they fished there using the electroshocking method. They did not take a single smallmouth bass or trout. "We couldn't even find the lonely rock bass we had found upstream. What did we find?" Schacher answered his own question. "We found one thirteen pound carp. We found one three pound buffalo. We found two spotted gar. We found a bullhead. The game species [for they did find some] included . . . four blue gill, six red breasted sunfish, three spotted bass, and three largemouth bass." They were all small; none exceeded seven and one-half inches. "There was not a keeper in the bunch," he stated. His conclusion was predictable: Tennessee's portion of the Pigeon River was "useless as a fishery, useless as a recreational source," and Champion's discharge was the reason. Ominously, Schacher warned that his agency was concerned about the contributory effects of Champion's pollutants as they move down the river system and about the negative effects they may have on the waters in Douglas

Reservoir and on toward Knoxville and Fort Loudon. EPA, he said emphatically, should insist that Champion accept the permit as written.

A surrogate spoke for Knoxville's mayor. "No one wants to live, work, or play next to a dirty river," he said. "Though there are economic considerations involved," he granted, "Tennessee should not, and must not, be polluted." Newport's gracious Mayor Jeanne Wilson tried to be firm but conciliatory. She had received threatening letters and phone calls. "We do not want to see one North Carolinian lose their [sic] job," she said, "but yes, we do want Tennesseans to be able to work also. We do not want to see, again, 30 percent unemployment in our county." Referring apparently to a cartoon and apocalyptic statements made by the opposing side, she added, "I, too, have witnessed starving children, rats and roach infested homes, and a stench that makes people feel ill."

Newport City Councilman Harold Allen was not so gentle. He questioned Blackwell's statements and added bluntly that "he is using employees as a pawn to force the issue, and to me that isn't cricket. Let's not give an inch." Sheriff Tunney Moore told the audience that he had lived within two hundred feet of the Pigeon and had smelled it all his life. "I've seen the time when our silverware and jewelry would turn on account of the Pigeon River," he said.

Finally it was dignified Charles Moore's turn. "Is it wrong," he asked, "that we are concerned about the color, and condition, of the river called Pigeon . . . about the dirtiness, the black, of this river that so affects the people?" Was it wrong, he continued, to be worried about the health of Tennessee citizens living along the river and having an unexplained high number of cancer cases? Was it wrong to be worried about dioxin? How, he asked, could Tennesseans be accused of impatience? They had waited more than eighty years for a cleanup. Boldly, he added, "I am totally and completely convinced that the river can be cleaned up, and the technology does exist to do so today." He accused Champion of being more of a "cannot do" than a "can do" corporation. He suggested that the company was more concerned about huge profits; he noted the enormous salaries of its highest executives. And he reminded North Carolinians that "if the river was flowing from Tennessee into North Carolina . . . the people of North Carolina would feel the same way we do." He reminded Bruce Barrett, the EPA administrator, that Newport, with almost ten thousand inhabitants, has to pipe its water six miles over the mountains from the French Broad River because the Pigeon, which runs through the heart of Newport, is filthy and dirty. He urged Champion to clean up the river and keep the jobs of its employees too. It could be done, he insisted.

In this composite photo, Newport Mayor Jeanne Wilson appears with a background of those attending the Knoxville hearing, January 21, 1988. Photo by J. Miles Cary and News-Sentinel *staff. Courtesy* Knoxville News-Sentinel.

Moore was followed by his counterpart in booming Sevier County, County Executive Larry Waters. He read a resolution passed unanimously by the Sevier County Commission that endorsed EPA, urging it to enforce the permit and clean up the river. All fifty thousand people in Sevier County want it cleaned up "because at some future date Sevier County most probably will be going to the Douglas Reservoir for water. And when we do, we want to get clean water out of the Douglas Reservoir." Waters could not resist chiding the Champion employees present. He suggested that EPA had never heard a company say, "We won't close down if you make us clean up the air, [but we will] if you make us clean up the water." He added that the citizens of Sevier County did not want North Carolinians to lose their jobs. "I'd be here too if somebody came and said, 'You're going to lose your job if you don't get on a bus and go to Knoxville, Tennessee.' I don't blame you a bit." But he argued that Champion could clean up the river. "You're talking about profits, not jobs," he said.

The list of politicians and bureaucrats slated to speak lengthened. Jim Graham spoke for the Cocke County Soil Conservation District Board of Directors. He stressed how, for thirty-five years, these people have tried to beautify the county; they had, for example, cut erosion to

almost zero. Then he lamented the river, flowing through "this beautiful county in a deplorable and ugly state caused by industrial pollution."
He described his two-hundred-acre field with the Pigeon on one side
and the French Broad on the other. "Even though the Pigeon access is
easier," he said, "the cattle go to a waterhole on the French Broad. . . . I
feel that Champion is just blackmailing the public and EPA with their
megabucks."

County officials were blunt and conciliatory at the same time. Almost
all of them went out of their way to emphasize that they did not want to
see a single job lost at Champion. At the same time, they quickly rejected
the statement that the river could not be cleaned up, damned Champion
for the problem, and urged EPA to stick to its guns.

Elected and appointed officials were followed by Wayne Bruckner,
president of the Newport-Cocke County Chamber of Commerce. Speaking directly to Champion employees in the audience, he stressed his
pride in being an employee of the Baptist hospital at Newport where
doctors, nurses, and other employees strive to save lives. And he acknowledged that Champion employees were proud to work for their
company, that Champion was in many ways a model corporate citizen
that paid taxes that support community services, that helped to build
recreational parks and sponsor YMCAs. He paused, then added: "and
they pollute the river. Are Champion employees really proud of their
company?" Bruckner paused again, letting his question settle in; then
he issued a challenge to the company "to make [its] employees really
proud" by cleaning up the river.

Dr. Kenneth Hill, a Newport doctor, talked about cancer. He said
it is unforgivable when it is due to another person's behavior, and he
implied that such was the case with many cancer patients in the communities of Hartford, Denton, Wilton Springs, Newport, Rankin, Dandridge,
and even Knoxville. He mentioned dioxin. "I have seen the agony of someone dying of cancer," he said soberly. "I have also seen the agony of someone losing their job. Both are terrible experiences, but there really are
no comparisons of the two. Unemployed people get new jobs. Cancer
victims do not get a second life."

Keith Ketterman, director and immediate past president of the Newport-Cocke County Chamber of Commerce, cited articles from *Plain
Talk,* with dates, as proof of Champion's duplicity. Although he could
have begun with the issue of April 18, 1912, the date of the *Titanic* disaster, which carried a news items about Champion purportedly cleaning
the river, Ketterman began with a news item from October 12, 1934. A
committee from Newport had traveled to Canton to protest the pollution,

and the company "made liberal promises of immediate relief." Again, on August 11, 1941, the paper ran a story about how the city of Knoxville had requested the support of Newport and Cocke County "to help in their efforts to solve the problem [of] pollution [being] so great at that time that the Knoxville Water Department feared the effect on the drinking water." But nothing was done.

Ketterman continued. In 1960 Newport sent another committee to Canton. A July 4 article quoted a Champion spokesperson as "assuring the citizens that about the middle of 1961 the river would be 75% corrected. . . . The water would be fit for livestock use, for sportfish, for irrigation purposes, and for swimming if any youngsters want to take a dip in it."

But no change took place in the river. "What," asked Ketterman, "does it mean when a corporation makes statements that are incorrect?"

Next came Nelson Ross, representing the Izaak Walton League. Organizing his presentation with the care of an experienced politician, he began in a conciliatory tone. "I'm for Champion and I'm for Champion cleaning up the river." Then his demeanor changed. "We resent the large number of people in North Carolina last week [at the Asheville hearing] that characterized us as a group of wild-eyed environmentalists that wouldn't rest until the mill was closed." He paused, then went on: "We have never taken that position. We feel that the people in Canton, North Carolina, have earned better than the fear that has been placed upon them this year with threats to close the Canton mill."

On several occasions, Oliver Blackwell and North Carolina's Governor Jim Martin had displayed water samples that were aimed at downgrading support of the 50 platinum cobalt units. Ross, an energetic individual, was determined not to let them get away with it. He had his own samples. The first was of the water above the mill, clean and potable with a color unit of just 10. Next came a water sample taken below the mill, with 800 color units. Governor Martin had insisted that the water in the Pigeon was no darker than the naturally black waters of east Carolina rivers. So Ross next produced a water sample from the Blackwater River; its average color was 80. (The Blackwater rises in southeastern Virginia and flows into North Carolina, where it is known as the Chowan River.) Ross chided North Carolina's chief executive, formerly a Davidson College chemistry professor. "He should be more responsible than to make statements like that," he said, taunting Martin for statements he had made at Canton that Tennesseans wanted to enforce the 50-color-unit standard in order to throw North Carolinians out of work. "That's an incredible statement and one that we absolutely

Nelson Ross of the Izaak Walton League and the Dead Pigeon River Council compares Pigeon River water with that of east coastal rivers at the Knoxville hearing, January 21, 1988. Photo by Gilbert Soesbee. Courtesy Newport Plain Talk.

refute and are embarrassed for the Governor of North Carolina for making public," said Ross.

He was not finished. A speaker at the Asheville hearing had compared the Pigeon's waters with Nova Scotia's lake waters. Not to be outdone, Ross contacted someone in Nova Scotia, probably another Izaak Walton League member, and had that person ship a sample of the water from one of those lakes. Proudly he displayed the jar containing the water of Pug Lake, Nova Scotia. It contained 154 color units, far less than the 700 to 900 units common to the polluted Pigeon. Another speaker had compared the Pigeon's waters to Yellowstone's Firehole River. Ross had to announce that a jar of water ordered from there had not arrived.

So much for misconceptions about water. Ross then reminded EPA's Barrett of the necessity for the agency to have the real facts about the problem. He expressed his distaste for "the scandalous tactics" used by Champion. Among them, he included Vice-President of Environmental Affairs Dick DiForio's announcement that Champion was funding a $250,000 private study of the Pigeon. It was unethical, Ross suggested, for such a behind-the-scenes study to be conducted without informing Tennessee officials; he made it quite clear that, in his mind, such a study would not be worth the paper it was printed on. Unfortunately, his presentation was cut off after five minutes.

Besides Ross, the Izaak Walton League was represented by David Dixon. "In a sense," he said, "we all live downstream from the Canton mill. When one body of water is allowed to be degraded, America's water resources are degraded. . . . The people who seek a strong permit," he argued, "are not 'Rambo environmentalists.'"

Next came Gary Davis, a Knoxville lawyer with LEAF. Davis, a quiet man, had appeared out of the blue at a PRAG meeting and had volunteered his services. He had been of such help in PRAG's campaign that he was equally welcomed by the DPRC when that group began its drive for a clean Pigeon River. Having on their side a capable lawyer primed in federal and state clean water laws was of great help to these two organizations.

At the Knoxville hearing, he began his five minutes by recalling how he had appeared in 1985 in Canton before North Carolina's Division of Environmental Management. He had reminded that group that Champion's permit had expired and was overdue for state renewal. "Because of North Carolina's refusal to issue a permit that adequately complied with the Clean Water Act, and because of legal footdragging on the part of Champion . . . we are now at this point where we have an opportunity once again to see a water quality permit issued to Champion that will result in a clean Pigeon River," Davis informed the audience. Now, he said, the legal formalities had been complied with, and it was EPA's obligation to issue the permit.

He said that color was the real problem because of its impact on fish and aquatic life. LEAF had submitted studies that proved this. He had also submitted technologies by which the river could be cleaned up. Davis then brought up information that had hardly been mentioned up to this time. Chloroform, a suspected carcinogen, had been found in Champion's effluent at a level of fifty-six parts per billion, which exceeded EPA's criterion for public health. He also noted a 1980 water quality sample of the Pigeon that included study of fish with eighty parts per billion of chloroform—an even more dangerous finding. Since he was right up to the moment on the status of water research, Davis brought up the matter of dioxin. He reminded the audience that the deadly substance accumulates in fish, multiplying in their biosystems by thousands, even tens of thousands of times. Moreover, toxic sludge contains dioxin—and in parts of the Pigeon, there are many feet of sludge, all of it produced by the Champion mill. How much of this, he asked, has reached Douglas Lake and Knoxville's water supply? He ended his well-constructed presentation by saying that he did not want to see one job lost at Champion and then added a statement that has split Champion's accusers. He said that a phased-in cleanup would be acceptable. Most PRAG and DPRC members, it should be remembered, did not agree. In their view, they had already waited more than eighty years; they wanted the river cleaned now.

Greenpeace was represented by Jim Vallett, who was with that organization's national toxic campaign in Washington, D.C. Vallett also brought up the dioxin situation, estimating that Champion was producing fifteen hundred to twenty-five hundred pounds of toxic organochlorines a day, most of which were discharged into the Pigeon River. Vallett then cast doubt on Champion's claim that it could not clean up the mess. He described the company's plant in Alberta, Canada, where oxygen delignification and a biological waste-treatment pond had made an enormous difference in the waters discharged from the facility. He suggested that perhaps the company was merely looking for an excuse to close the Canton plant and move its production to its Roanoke Springs mill, or even to its proposed new plant in Halifax, North Carolina. "The choice," Vallett concluded, "is not an either/or solution . . . but good management. . . . Obsolete practices by the pulp and paper industry have contaminated water resources all over the world. But now, proven technologies offer greater profit and higher yields while simultaneously reducing the industry's discharge of contaminants into the public's air, water, and soil."

Newport attorney Jim McSween presented his case with historical perspective. He related how on October 24, 1968, North Carolina Governor Dan K. Moore and Tennessee Governor Buford Ellington met at the North Carolina–Tennessee line to dedicate the opening of Interstate 40. The program described the new twenty-two-mile stretch at the Scenic Pigeon River Gorge. Later that day, while driving along the highway, McSween caught glimpses of Waterville Lake. It was, he said, like any other lake "except that its color was a startling coal black, flecked with an occasional cluster of white foam."

The interstate not only opened western North Carolina to Tennessee and the Midwest, McSween observed, but "it also opened to the world and to the millions of travelers along the highway the deep dark secret of a black river carrying industrial pollution quickly out the back door of North Carolina and flushing it upon the State of Tennessee." McSween knew what he was talking about. "I have lived along the banks of the Pigeon River all of my life," he said. "I knew that every time my family would drive along the banks of the river, I must close tightly the car windows to avoid the nauseating stench. . . . I had the childhood fear of falling into the river and being forever lost beneath the black murky surface."

When it became Dick Mullinix's turn, that irascible, tenacious campaigner did not mince words. He described the public relations drive in support of Champion as "job blackmail." He insisted that "North Carolina's greatest, most lasting asset was its rivers and mountains . . . that God created for the benefit of all mankind. . . . I have a pile of letters from NCDEM [North Carolina Division of Environmental Management] that go back through ten years. In effect they all say, 'We can't offend Champion. Take it easy.' Consequently, Champion has been given so much rope that they have hung themselves. . . . God knows that after eighty years of allowing an industrial sewer to flow through the city of Newport, these people deserve a change, not just a marginal improvement."

Ordinary citizens finally had their say. Roy Brown, who described himself as not having a job to protect or a political office, said he had lived his entire life beside "this flowing shadow of death." He suggested that chemicals carried by the Pigeon could have an effect upon the food chain—even the foods canned in Cocke County by Bush Brothers and Quaker Oats. Between one post-operative cancer examination after another, he and his wife pleaded for a cleaned-up stream. "Do not the small people have the right to live in a free environment and one that they do not fear?" he asked.

Another concerned citizen, Jim Runnion, made mention of Champion's false statements. "We have been very gullible in Cocke County and expected them to do what they said they would do and waited for the improvements, but to no avail," he complained. "And what had Champion done? It has increased the size of its plant and they have increased pollution."

Orville Bach Jr. and William Barrett II, the two Walters State Community College professors whose important economic impact study of the Pigeon River had galvanized the clean Pigeon River supporters, then took the podium. Their main pitch was Champion's greed. Bach noted the company's announced goal, "to be among the top 25% of all US corporations in terms of profitability. To achieve that goal, Champion needs to achieve a 16% return on stockholder equity." Sixty million dollars would clean up the Pigeon, Bach estimated, which would figure out to eight cents a share loss for stockholders. He also scoffed at Champion's threat to close the plant. It ranks number two in production for the company, Bach insisted, and almost first.

And so the protests went. Don't fall prey to Champion's "emotional blackmail," warned Steve Nifong of the Cocke County sportsmen's club. Another speaker suggested that Champion change from white paperboard to brown paperboard. A young Cocke County native remembered a Hartford public school fight song that began: "Way up on the Pigeon River where the stench fills the air. . . ." A representative of a Sevier County environmental organization, Axel Ringer, gave his support to environmentalists on two grounds: the pollution in Douglas Lake, from which the county was going to have to get additional drinking water, and the "moral dimension"—that no private interest should have the right to make of a river an industrial sewer "without regard to the rights and interests of those downstream that wish to derive economic, recreational or aesthetic uses from the river."

Apart from Oliver Blackwell, not until page 253 of the transcript of the hearing (of 325 pages) did someone speak in support of Champion. He emphasized the incomes of suppliers and timber cutters, and mentioned the North Carolina Search and Rescue Dog Association of Clyde, which receives a thousand dollars a year from Champion.

Aftermath of the Knoxville Hearing

So ended the Knoxville hearing. It had started at 1:00 P.M. and had lasted until 10:00. With some trepidation, Champion's opponents had stood at the rostrum, gazed out upon the sea of yellow hats and big yellow badges, and courageously presented their case. The opposition had not gone beyond jeers and catcalls—Champion had seen to it that its personnel behaved with decency if not with dignity.

In comparison to Champion's programmed presentation at Asheville, the Knoxville hearing was inferior. It was not well structured, nor did the Cocke County people have anything as theatrical as the dominos used by Champion to strike home their arguments.

At Knoxville the clean river supporters submitted, for the most part, rational, unemotional reasons for cleaning up the river. They really meant it when they stated that they did not want the mill to close and did not want a single employee to lose his or her job. In reminding Champion's adherents of the effects of the pollution on Newport's and Cocke County's economy, they were trying to strike a familiar nerve, for most of the people assembled were wage-earners either at Champion or at various places in Cocke County; it was an issue that should have established some rapport between them. The health issue, including chloroform and dioxin, loomed much larger at the Knoxville hearing than it had at Asheville. Considering the animosity that existed between Champion and Cocke County groups, the Knoxville hearing was remarkably mild, dignified, and courteous.

And yet, it had a greater effect than the Asheville meeting. It had an adverse effect on Champion.

The Knoxville hearing brought into relief what Champion and its public relations advisors had done. Boldly they had bused two thousand Champion employees up Interstate 40 across a state line into Knoxville. There, they had assembled as a loud, enthusiastic band of partisans determined to dominate this second hearing about their company's pollution of the Pigeon River. They flaunted their power in East Tennessee's largest city. There, wearing yellow Champion hats and displaying big yellow Champion badges, they had occupied the heart of Knoxville's civic center. They were, in the minds of many Tennesseans, intruders telling Tennessee to go to hell. They would continue polluting the Pigeon, and not the EPA, not the state of Tennessee, and not its citizens were going to stop them.

This was "a bit much" for the *Knoxville Journal*. Its editors did not even wait for the nine-hour hearing to begin. CHAMPION WILL HAVE TO CLOSE THE MILL ran the *Journal*'s lead editorial on that day. Nothing, it said, will settle the problem. "It has become an environmentally impossible situation." The newspaper quoted a Champion official: "No one in his right mind would build a paper plant on the Pigeon River today." It was too small, the editorial went on; in times of low water, even with added flow from Champion's reservoir (Lake Logan), the company cannot meet EPA's and Tennessee's insistence upon the 50-color-unit standard. Then there was the dioxin question. The editorial was blunt—more so than even *Plain Talk* had ever been:

> But in the meantime, regardless of the dioxin question and regrettably for the people who depend on the plant for employment and for the area of North Carolina that depends on it for economic well-being, the mill should close. Whether its operators cannot or will not make paper in such a way that the river is returned to a healthful, usable stream in Tennessee is immaterial. It is not going to happen. The company has made that clear. It should go somewhere else, where the discharges of a paper mill will be sufficiently diluted by the regular flow of water that the condition of the Pigeon River will not be replicated.

The editorial concluded by suggesting that only state or federal action could force Champion to either clean up or leave; that Champion
would draw out litigation until it had a better site to move to, which
would take perhaps three years, in which time Canton and surrounding
areas should attract another industry. "And, ultimately, Tennessee will
have its Pigeon River back, more or less intact. That's a tough scenario
to have to play out. But we're convinced that it must be. Champion officials, as we said, convinced us. No one in his right mind would try to
operate a paper plant on the Pigeon River today."[3]

Both Knoxville papers carried large front-page photographs of the
Champion crowd with its yellow hats and yellow badges. Local television stations made a point of displaying the same thing. The controversy assumed national overtones when the *New York Times* ran
a front-page story headlined INDUSTRY AND RIVER FORM
GULF BETWEEN TWO STATES. An accompanying picture
showed a DON'T LET CHAMPION FALL banner stretched
across Canton's Main Street.[4]

The bitterness, as has already been noted, became ugly. Mullinix,
Seay, Ross, Webb, Jeanne Wilson, and other clean Pigeon River boosters received profane, threatening phone calls. Moreover, they suspected
Champion supporters of damaging their cars, and one pro-Pigeon River
supporter was nearly forced off the highway. Pro-Champion supporters were particularly incensed at a huge anti-Champion sign placed by
clean Pigeon River supporters along I-40. It was vandalized, and the
words were blacked out.[5]

Certainly neither Champion, which hired it, nor Price/McNabb,
the public relations firm that waged the pro-Champion campaign, anticipated the result. A wave of anti-Champion hostility swept across
East Tennessee. The arrogance of a company that would send dozens
of busloads of its workers, all of them on company pay, to dominate a
meeting in another state was simply too much. So were the defacing of
the sign and the threatening phone calls. Company officials may have
broken into a corporate smirk at all this, but when East Tennessee's veteran Representative James Quillen ordered a congressional hearing, the
smirk changed to a frown of concern. Champion suddenly realized it
had a new and unexpectedly serious situation on its hands. It was suffering from overkill.

And, during the months leading up to the congressional hearing, a
new factor had been introduced into the controversy: dioxin.

CHAPTER 10

Dioxin

I n the files of TVA's offices in Chattanooga is a memo
from a top official, dated April 15, 1991: "Mr. Carraway
has a personal assignment from the pres. of Champion
to get them out of the mess they are in with the Canton plant."[1]

Jim Carraway was hired by Champion because he talked like what
he was, a good old boy from Mississippi. When he approached unhappy
Cocke County and Tennessee officials, they did not feel that they were
being treated condescendingly. This was a major change from the attitude of so many Champion officials, who for years had treated opponents as if they were country yokels.

The hiring of Carraway, who was subsequently promoted to Stamford headquarters, was but one of many indications that Champion and
its supporters realized they had committed overkill. They knew from
television, radio, and newspapers that they had angered all of East Tennessee, including the city of Knoxville. Quietly, Bob Seay was informed
that Champion would pay for the defacing of the sign that proponents
of a clean Pigeon River had placed along I-40—and in July 1991, out of
the blue, the Newport-Cocke County Chamber of Commerce secretary
received a check from Champion for five hundred dollars "in payment
of damages to billboard." Champion had changed tactics toward its
grass-roots opposition. For a time it quit proselytizing.[2]

This did not halt Champion's campaign to weaken the permit by
suggesting a variance from the North Carolina Division of Environmental Management. Actually, the company's plans had materialized by
at least November, prior to the hearings, when, after consultations with
Champion officials and North Carolina politicians, Senator Gore suggested a compromise at 85 color units; he did not grab this figure out of
the air. Negotiations and politicking continued from November into

February, even as the hearings took place in January. In an EPA Press release, Bruce R. Barrett, Director of the Region IV Water Management
Division, explained the situation as follows:

> EPA discussed possible solutions to the problem with representa-
> tives from North Carolina and Tennessee in February, 1988. There was
> general consensus that feasible technology does not exist to achieve 50 ap-
> parent color units at the state line with the mill at full production. Conse-
> quently the mill would not achieve water quality standards. The states
> agreed to consider variances to their water quality standards for color. If
> variances were granted, EPA would issue a draft permit requiring a "cap"
> of 85 true color units at the state line.[3]

Summary and Conclusions of the
North Carolina Variance Committees

With knowledge of EPA's action, Paul Wilms, director of the DEM,
created a committee to make recommendations about whether North
Carolina should accede to EPA's suggestion of 85 color units. This
Champion Variance Review Committee submitted its report on March
30, 1988. Another group, a North Carolina NPDES committee, subsequently met to study the report, carry on additional research, hold a required hearing, collect documents, and then deliver a final decision about
whether or not a variance should be issued. All this took until July 1988.

The Champion Variance Review Committee wrote that it had "used
all available information," including information acquired from two meetings with Champion representatives; committee members were even
shown around the Canton plant. For the technological aspects of the problem and for an evaluation of the economic burden that would be imposed
upon Champion, there is little evidence in the committee's extensive summary and conclusions that it used anything but Champion and EPA
information. As for the condition of the river and the economic impact
of a clean river upon the region's economy, it still relied primarily upon
Champion's information.

In its report, committee members explained that they were at a loss
to accurately evaluate the costs of enforcing a 50-color-unit standard:

> An extremely critical aspect of this variance evaluation comes to the
> surface rather quickly as one looks at technology options: Champion con-
> trols the economics, particularly as it relates to mill closure. . . . What is

being approached when looking at 50 c.u. [color units] (end-of-pipe or
State line) is the application of procedures and technologies that are un-
tested and unproven at a scale necessary to remove color from the Canton Mill wastewater. When this particular point was discussed on March
21st, Dick DiForio and Chris Day of Champion related the technology
issue in terms of risk and making a business decision. From an engineering view, Company officials cannot recommend using an unproven technology which might or might not result in effluent compliance. This point is
very important because it drives the decision of keeping the Mill or closing
it. . . . We must face the obvious conclusion that it is impossible to effec-
tively question costs when there is no full scale system in operation or
even under construction that can be used for comparison.[4]

With this caveat, after nineteen pages the Champion Variance Review Committee recommended that the variance be granted. Since it is
"based on a permit acceptable to EPA," the report reads, "it must be
concluded that the requested variance meets Federal requirements." the
committee recommended that the variance process continue with a required public hearing in Raleigh, which took place.

In July the NPDES committee issued its report, entitled *Final Decision.* To justify its opinion (which all parties knew would favor Champion), it dealt with fifty-six questions concerning the mill's effluent, the
costs of cleanup, and the impact of a closed mill on the region. It also
set up a system, devised by Champion, for measuring color at the state
line, and it provided for an annual report on progress toward cleaning the
river; moreover, it also provided for a triennial review of the variance.[5]

Exhibit D of this report of the NPDES committee as well as the
summary and conclusions of the Champion Variance Review Committee present arguments that demanded the attention of Champion's most
vociferous opponents. They had to ask themselves if they were being
fair. It is a fact that Champion was already one of the lower color dis-
chargers among bleached kraft mills in the United States. (Its problem
was that the color was being discharged into a river that is too small.) It
is a fact that in April 1985, the company built a demonstration color-
removal ultrafiltration system at the Canton plant; when company officials announced its failure and added that they really did want it to
work, certainly they should be believed. Sirrine Environmental Consultants (associated with a company that later carried out a major environmental upgrading in 1991-94) estimated the cost of a satisfactory ultrafiltration process at $204 million, and annual operating costs of $64
million. This, the company insisted in 1988, would result in mill closure.

EPA requested that Champion evaluate five color-removal processes; it actually tried seven, and—to its satisfaction and apparently EPA's (which has a system of determining economic feasibility called the Gross Margin test)—none were economically feasible. All seven systems, Champion insisted—if they required 50 color units or less at the pipe *or* at the Tennessee line—would require the closing of the Canton mill.

And Champion had come up with a solution that was spelled out in the NPDES report. The statement read as follows: "Champion determined that a combination of process modifications, including oxygen delignification, increased internal recycling and chemical oxidation of the lignin, can be installed and will reduce the amount of color in Champion's discharge on average of 50 percent from its present level."[6]

Translated into the terminology of the controversy, Champion was saying that it could reach 85 color units at the Tennessee line, and if EPA, North Carolina, and Tennessee would agree to that variance— just 35 units above the 50 color limit insisted upon by EPA and Tennessee—then the company would launch a massive upgrading to bring this about ($200 million was the cost estimate at the time). Suddenly, the mystery of the source of Senator Gore's 85-color-unit standard was solved.

Opponents questioned the cost estimates, insisting that a six-billion-dollar company could easily clean the river, even if the cost ran into the hundreds of millions, and they suggested that the figures were greatly inflated. They also insisted that better environmental systems *were* operational elsewhere. It is a certainty, however, that Champion officials convinced North Carolina and EPA representatives otherwise; Champion made its case that its arguments were valid and that its solution was viable and reasonable.

Other aspects discussed in the so-called *Final Decision* of the NPDES committee and the Champion Variance Review Committee report engendered legitimate controversy. Both documents made assertions about the condition of the Pigeon River, the number and kind of fish that live in it, the problem of color (which is described as "primarily an aesthetic pollutant") as it affects living organisms in the stream, and the economic impact of a clean river versus the loss of the mill. On all of these points, the conclusions of these reports were subject to dispute.

However, such formidable arguments, presented to state regulators who were already inclined toward Champion's position, were certain to prevail. A portent of the trend took place early in March, when the press announced that Tennessee officials had agreed to grant the variance—essentially EPA's and North Carolina's variance—to Champion.[7]

But there was a hitch. Tennessee's statutes had no provision for granting variances to color standards. EPA, Champion's lobbyists, and North Carolina officials urged the state to pass an amendment in its law to provide for a variance procedure. Tennessee's legislature complied, and Governor McWherter signed the variance provision into law on April 5.[8] DPRC attorney Gordon Ball told the U.S. House Subcommittee on Water Resources that "presidential politics" were involved in Tennessee's legislation. He then recounted the story of how North Carolina Congressman James Clarke had "convinced Senator Albert Gore to soften his stand on the clean-up of the Pigeon River in exchange for Clarke's endorsement of Gore during the North Carolina presidential primary." Clarke, Ball said, sought out Gore to prevail upon his southern campaign manager, who just happened to be Governor Ned McWherter, to sign the bill and accept the revised Champion permit with the variance.[9]

When Senator Gore was asked about the accusation, his aides denied emphatically that the senator had tried to influence the variance legislation. Moreover, as reported in the *Newport Plain Talk,* Gore had "never supported the 85 color-unit standard, but has called it 'a starting point' for future efforts to clean up the river." The reporter was also reminded that "it was Gore who 'built the fire under EPA' to get positive action from the agency" and this does appear to be a fact.[10]

The Dead Pigeon River Council objected when it learned of the variance provision, but to no avail. Council members protested that they had not been informed of the impending vote, thus denying them the opportunity to lobby against it. Even Cocke County's two representatives voted in favor of the amendment. (One of them, Ronnie Davis, explained that he was not aware that he had cast his vote for the amendment, which was buried in 150 pages of amendments that were passed perfunctorily all at once.) So the way was cleared for Tennessee to accept the variance, approved save for the formalities, by EPA and North Carolina.[11]

As of July 13, 1988, when North Carolina granted the permit, Governor McWherter had not signed the variance. Nor, despite all the pressure being applied to him, was he in any rush to approve it. Meanwhile, a new complaint had entered into the controversy. It may have been the reason the governor hesitated to sign.

Origins of the Dioxin Scare

Now Champion's defenders had something else to worry about. Allegations were being made that dioxin, a known carcinogen that also weakens both the immune and the reproductive systems, is produced by the chlorine bleaching process used to make paper and is carried off into the Pigeon's waters. Dioxin is a general name for a family of chlorinated hydrocarbons, best known as an element in Agent Orange, used as a defoliant during the Vietnam War. The most dangerous of the dioxin family is 2,3,7,8 TCDD, and it is the one released by pulp and paper mills in air emissions and wastewater discharges. It was suggested that the chemical could be responsible for cancer deaths along the river, most especially in the little community of Hartford, Tennessee. Because of the town's apparently high incidence of cancer among men, the village was dubbed Widowville; it was under that name that the controversy was mentioned by CBS anchorman Dan Rather on the network's evening news program on January 3, 1990.

The story begins with a conversation at the little Hartford Post Office, located at a general store-filling station alongside the Pigeon and just off Interstate 40. The postmistress at the time, Mary Woody, and her friends became aware of the many Hartford citizens, mostly men, who had died of cancer over the past several years. The percentages seemed alarmingly high—so high that someone questioned whether the cause could be the polluted Pigeon River. Could it have been caused by dioxin? Betsy Kauffman, a reporter for the *Knoxville News-Sentinel*, was sent to Hartford to interview any residents willing to talk. It may have been Mary Woody who dubbed Hartford "Widowville."[12]

The Widowville scare coincided almost exactly with the release by EPA of the results of a congressionally funded, $7.4-million study of the substance. The study had come about because of the Love Canal, New York, and Times Beach, Missouri, dioxin contamination cases. Although the primary polluters in these cases were pesticide plants and municipal waste incinerators, an unexpected discovery was the existence of dioxin as a byproduct of the chlorine pulp-bleaching process. It was especially present as an unwanted byproduct of kraft paper mills. As a result of this information, in November 1987, the DPRC requested that EPA test the Pigeon River for dioxin before it issued a wastewater discharge permit to the company. This spurred Champion to announce that it planned to conduct its own tests for dioxin, and North Carolina authorities also announced plans for testing the polluted river.[13]

In September 1987, the *New York Times* ran an article detailing research into indications of dioxin in paper products. Trace elements of the chemical were found, but the article downplayed the danger, quoting an EPA official as saying that "if [dioxin] is at the low level described by the industry, it is not something to be ignored but it is not something to break into a cold sweat about either." But Dr. Ellen K.

Silbergeld, a toxicologist for the Environmental Defense Fund, was quoted as taking a much more serious view. EPA, she said, had found dioxin levels in paper pulp at levels ranging up to 350 parts per trillion. EPA requires chemical makers to report the presence of dioxin in their products at levels of 100 parts per trillion. "Therefore," she said, "the amount found in paper pulp, which is formed into paper products, is not negligible."[14]

A few weeks later the *New York Times* discounted the risks from paper products. It quoted an EPA study as saying that "if all the dioxin assumed to be in a coffee filter were leached into the coffee, the increased risk of cancer would be one additional case for every 10,000 people who drank filtered coffee over a seventy-five year lifetime." For paper plates, disposable diapers, tampons, dinner napkins, and paper towels the risk was even lower, in the range of 1.4 and 6.6 in a million.[15]

Since those articles appeared, more studies have been conducted. A battle has raged between authorities who speak of dioxin as being the most dangerous carcinogen known—a particle the size of a grain of salt, they say, can create cancer—and those who pooh-pooh the danger, saying that dioxin is all around us and the frightening reports have not been based upon sound scientific research. An association of chlorine producers, not exactly an impartial source, stepped into the fray and issued press releases downplaying the danger. In August 1991, the *Wall Street Journal* headlined an article "The Dioxin Un-Scare—Where's the Press?" A government official, Dr. Vernon Houk, stated that low doses of dioxin do not pose a major health risk. Already the government had spent $33 million to buy up the town of Times Beach, where the streets had been laced with the chemical. Bureaucrats had accepted the Center for Disease Control's statement that ingesting of more than one part per billion posed a significant threat to human health.[16]

Further investigations have since been conducted, and the controversy remains unsettled. In 1992 one study, not released by EPA because it concluded that dioxin is dangerous in any amount, has since been questioned by still other authorities.[17]

Whatever the final conclusion may be about dioxin, a river carrying thousands of pounds of organochlorine wastes, as does the Pigeon, could not under any circumstances be declared free of endangering human health. As research has become more sophisticated, most of the news has been bad. The furans, chloroform, dioxins, and other chemicals in the river, alone or in combination, may cause cancer and other diseases to those who come in contact with the water. Causes of cancer, immune deficiency ailments, and birth defects are today being traced to sources never imagined a decade or two ago—and among those sources are rivers polluted by paper mills.

In 1988 and 1989, dioxin was indeed the fearful chemical. The residents of Hartford were convinced that the number of cancer deaths in the little community over a period of just twenty years was startling: 167 out of a population of just 780. (A later study was based upon a population of 1,095.) Since dioxin had been in the news, and it had become known it was released by Champion's chlorine bleaching process, residents were terribly worried that dioxin was flowing by their homes in the polluted Pigeon.

DPRC members noted that EPA's initial study of waterborne dioxin, the results of which were released in early 1987, revealed dioxin in the waste waters of the five paper mills tested. They noted that two area streams, the French Broad and Cataloochee Creek, had been tested as noncontaminated streams to be used to compare with polluted watercourses. But where was the Pigeon? Why, asked DPRC members, were these two streams tested but the polluted Pigeon not subject to any testing at all? Under EPA's own rules, the Pigeon was a prime candidate for analysis. David McKinney, manager of the East Tennessee Office of State Water Pollution Control, said the Pigeon "should have been at the top of any nationwide list."[18]

Whatever EPA's reason for not testing the Pigeon earlier, in February 1988, with Tennessee cooperation, it took the proper steps. The Tennessee Wildlife Resources Agency and the Tennessee State Department of Health and Environment took fish from the river with the aid of an electroshocking generator. They chose a site off Edwina Road upstream from Newport, which, in a clean river, would have been prime fishing water with deep, quiet pools where fish are always found. But the water was dark brown, and it smelled. Small wonder—to Tennesseans, anyway—that only ten fish were taken, and of those, five were carp and five were smallmouth buffalo carp. These are classified as rough fish; no game fish were taken. The researchers froze the fish they caught and sent them to EPA in Atlanta to be tested for dioxin. EPA had also collected fish from the river at Clyde and in Waterville Lake.[19]

In March EPA announced that dioxin in small amounts was found in two fish taken from the Tennessee section of the Pigeon in February (because one was a rock bass, these fish were obtained from a different source than the ones mentioned above). Their dioxin level was minimal: 1.7 parts per trillion in the bass and 25.2 in the whole body of the carp. More was in the carp because dioxin builds up in the fatty tissues in the whole fish, and the entire carp was tested; only the filet of the

Knoxville newspapers refused to drop the Pigeon River issue. This cartoon ran in the Knoxville Journal *(now defunct) on October 27, 1989. Courtesy Charlie Daniel.*

bass was tested. When one realizes that a trillion has twelve zeros, the amount found in the two fish was indeed very small. The U.S. Food and Drug Administration issues a fish advisory for fish over 25 ppt (parts per trillion) and a fish consumption limit if the level exceeds 50 ppt.[20]

At the time, in March 1988, many considered any dioxin, no matter how minute, to be dangerous (and some scientists still believe this today). Jerry Wilde, president of the Dead Pigeon River Council, noting that Champion Vice-President Oliver Blackwell had boasted that he would eat fish from the river, suggested that Blackwell be invited to a fish fry featuring carp caught in the Pigeon. Shortly thereafter, it was discovered that EPA, in its National Dioxin Study, had found the Pigeon to rank fourth among rivers with the worst dioxin pollution; only three others had a fish containing more dioxin than the carp with the 25.2 ppt. Nelson Ross noted that the carp was really not a single carp but a composite of the five taken from the river and ground up. "That means," he said, "that surely in that composite of five fish there were some fish with higher than 25 ppt and that some were lower."[21]

In June forty members of Greenpeace, armed with hammers and nails, posted a hundred signs from Canton to the Tennessee state line. "WARNING: Fish from the Pigeon River are Contaminated with Dangerous Levels of Dioxin, a Poison that can Cause Cancer, Miscarriages, and Birth Defects," the signs read, "Consumption of Fish or

In June 1988, Greenpeace entered the fray, posting dioxin warning signs along the Pigeon River. Photo by Paul Efird. Courtesy Knoxville News-Sentinel.

Shellfish Should be Avoided." In August North Carolina health officials followed the environmentalists with their own red warning signs; in April 1989, Tennessee health officials issued a similar advisory.[22]

When Tennessee's Senator Jim Sasser visited Newport, he listened to DPRC members and suggested that, because the validity of EPA's dioxin tests were being questioned, an independent dioxin test should be conducted, possibly by scientists at Oak Ridge, the federal research center west of Knoxville. He was told about Hartford, where some residents believed their cancer rate was ten times as high as the national average.[23]

It will be recalled that in late March 1988, EPA had drawn up another compromise permit to be approved by both North Carolina and Tennessee officials, but the permit required variances from both states. Again, the DPRC and East Tennesseans were incensed because they had not been consulted on the details of the compromise. The DPRC called for removal of dioxin and other toxins from the river as well as insisting, as it always had, on the 50-color-unit provision in the original permit. In fact, the EPA revised permit called for color reduction down to 85 color units over a three-year period—which was unsatisfactory to the DPRC—but still worse, all the permit required the company to do about dioxin was to monitor the river for the chemical's presence and notify EPA of its plans for dealing with it. To Champion's credit, the permit committed the company to spending two hundred million dollars in improvements. The principal change was the conversion of the mill from a chlorine-based pulp-bleaching process to an oxygen delignification system. Those opposing the permit in spite of these improvements could take heart, however, in the mechanics of approval: they would have a comment period and another opportunity for public hearings and, of course, variances had to be granted.

Is Hartford Really Widowville?

Hartford residents, frightened by the dioxin scare, formed the Hartford Environmental League Project (HELP) with the aid of Skip Taggart, a local activist. The notoriety of Widowville even brought representatives from Greenpeace to the scene. The State Department of Epidemiology ordered a six-week study of the situation. It was conducted by the department's Dr. Robert Taylor, who was not an epidemiologist but a veterinarian. He found that between 1977 and 1986, 19 people from Hartford had died of cancer. With a population of 1,095, or about 3.8 percent of Cocke County, the 19 deaths came to about 3.5 percent of the county's cancer deaths in that period. Actually, 21 or 22 deaths from cancer could have been expected, Dr. Taylor reported. That meant that Hartford's cancer rate was actually below the national average.[24]

Postmistress Mary Woody, her neighbor Margaret Jenkins, and many others were not satisfied with Dr. Taylor's report. "If we'd have known he was a veterinarian, we wouldn't have talked with him," said Woody. People who had lived there, had drunk the water, had frolicked in it as children, and had eaten fish from it, then had moved away and later developed cancer were not counted. Nor did the study include people who had developed the disease but did not die of it or people who had cancer but had died of other causes. Statistics, opponents of the study argued, were gathered according to zip codes, which did not accurately reflect the residents living along the river. So convinced were some people that the findings were faulty that two local physicians contemplated requesting the Center for Disease Control to run its own study.[25]

In June Dr. Taylor renewed his investigation. This time he visited four hundred households in Hartford and nearby Grassy Fork; he planned to interview about twelve hundred people, inquiring of family histories, deaths from cancer, and the types of carcinomas that killed them. Grassy Fork statistics would be used as a sample to compare to Hartford statistics. By this time, the DPRC was contemplating making its own survey, using voting records to determine residence. And a six-million-dollar "wrongful death" lawsuit had been filed. Hartford—Widowville—simply would not go away.[26]

The Controversy Intensifies

It may have been expected that the Pigeon River fight would die down after the hearings of January 1988 and the compromise variance that, in the spring and early summer, appeared to have been reached. And it probably would have died down had it not been for the dioxin scare.

Dioxin frightened people. Widowville had received national attention, and the federal EPA as well as the state agencies were involved. Since government agencies were drawn in, politicians were not far behind, especially politicians who had supported for many years Cocke County's fight for a clean Pigeon River. Jim Sasser and Jimmy Quillen were active in their support, and Governor McWherter, at least some of the time, seemed to be on Cocke County's side. The fact that 1988 was an election year, that the senator and the governor were Democrats in a Republican East Tennessee, and that Jimmy Quillen was an old pro did not in any way reduce their support of Cocke County in the controversy.

Representative Quillen asked the U.S. House Committee on Public Works and Transportation and its Subcommittee on Water Resources to investigate "the irresponsible activities of the EPA in not discovering or revealing earlier the presence of dioxin in the river." Senator Sasser, in Atlanta a day or two after visiting Newport, called for more dioxin testing of the river, this time by an independent party.

Jimmy Quillen's press release burned with righteous indignation. "After all these years of struggle to require a paper mill upstream to stop its gross pollution of the Pigeon River, I am outraged that the EPA has not until recently conducted dioxin testing in the Pigeon River. I want to know why not?" he fumed. Of course, an EPA spokesman reminded readers that dioxin pollution from paper mills had only been confirmed since 1985 and that the technology of measurement to determine parts per trillion was "relatively new." Not to be outdone, Senator Sasser insisted that similar testing of the well water at Hartford be included.

Indeed, the residents of Hartford, with the support of the Dead Pigeon River Council, Representative Quillen, and Senator Sasser, had stirred up a hornet's nest of trouble for EPA and Champion. As part of its damage control, EPA announced the expenditure of another one hundred thousand dollars for a new series of tests to determine dioxin levels at Waterville and Douglas Lakes as well as from fish caught in the Pigeon; the agency would also test ten wells in the Hartford area. True to their word, EPA officials carried out their tasks, even as they were accompanied by newspaper reporters and television crews from three states. When the tests proved faulty, they went back and tested again. Tennessee officials reacted by announcing a state policy of spring and fall testing of Pigeon River fish.[27]

It was the well water, or the water from at least some of the wells, that convinced Hartford people that the Pigeon's pollutants had worked their way into the groundwater and, therefore, into their water supply. Eighty-year-old Margaret Jenkins, who lived close to the river, had such colored, smelly well water that, for a decade prior to 1988, she had ceased drinking it and cooking with it. When EPA tested her well, it found tannins and lignins in the water. In fact, it found these pollutants in all the wells. They could have come only from the Champion mill. They are by themselves harmless, so far as is known, but the question people asked was if the water contains Champion's tannins and lignins, what other substances are in the water? The list of possible effluents included chloroform, dioxin, metals, and nitrates. Moreover, it was a fact that Margaret Jenkins's husband had died of cancer; was there a connection between the water and his death?[28]

When EPA officials reported that Waterville Lake was teeming with fish, that their catch of about forty included a thirty-inch, thirteen-pound brown trout, three other brown trout, twenty largemouth bass, twenty-four bullheads, six carp, and other fish, Champion executives were elated; environmentalists were skeptical. They recalled the expedition of members of the Smallmouth Bass Association the previous August. In four hours, fishing the Pigeon just above the lake, this group had caught just four or five small bream. There were rumors that the lake had been stocked shortly before EPA technicians arrived.[29] Indeed, the discrepancy between EPA's numbers and the fish reported in the Federal Energy Regulatory Commission's Environmental Assessment of the Walter/Waterville Project (in June 1991) is startling. The FERC stated that as of 1987 and 1988 "nongame fish comprised about 90% of the total hoop net catch in the lake." Black bullhead accounted for 61 percent, carp 12 percent, and white catfish 10 percent of the total catch. "These species," the report states, "are tolerant of polluted conditions compared to game fish species and are ecological indicators of a degraded aquatic environment." Game fish made up just 10 percent of the hoop net catch, of which bluegills constituted 8 percent; the brown trout and rainbow trout may have come from Cataloochee Creek and Fines Creek; the lone muskellunge "might have been introduced by an angler."[30]

Rumors and discrepancies: they are inevitable in controversy, and they increase as the conflict escalates. They are frequently impossible to track down. The Pigeon River story is replete with rumors. Because of rumors that begin in the mill, many Champion employees take a Chicken Little stance: they believe their sky will fall down because a closed-down, moved-away paper mill is inevitable if the environmentalists have their way. Many proponents of a clean Pigeon River, on the other hand, accept at face value any story of rascality involving Champion, its employees, and the government of North Carolina. Some suspect duplicity from EPA and even question the integrity of their own Tennessee politicians. They find confirmation of their suspicions when they hear, for example, of plans of the Sloan-Kettering Foundation (which researches cancer) to conduct a study of the Pigeon, a project that was mysteriously canceled. Some members of the DPRC and PRAG believed that EPA has concealed the results of a dioxin investigation of the Pigeon River.

Late in May 1988, EPA announced that it had found no trace of dioxin in the ten wells it tested in Hartford in April. Geological investigation indicated that most of the wells had been drilled into fractured rock and were unlikely to be impacted by the Pigeon. As for the presence of tannins and lignins, which could only come from Pigeon waters, those tests were labeled "inconclusive." Residents of Hartford did not agree. To them, there were too many loose ends. EPA had not tested the sediment at the bottom of the wells; EPA could not explain Margaret Jenkins's foul well water. Members of the DPRC and PRAG, concerned citizens, and especially residents or former residents of Hartford hoped their politicians would sit up and question the results. They wanted action.[31]

Tennessee politicians do not have an uninterrupted record of support for Cocke County and efforts to clean the Pigeon. In some politicians' minds Cocke was (and to some, still is) an inconsequential county in East Tennessee with a small population and negligible economic significance. During the nearly nine decades of the pollution controversy, a strong argument can be made with much supporting evidence that politicians have, by and large, looked the other way; they have ignored the plight of that small enclave in the extreme southeastern part of the state. Its power has been too weak.

By 1988, however, the situation showed signs of change. The media—newspapers, news magazines, television, and radio—was reporting the activities of Greenpeace, the Sierra Club, and the Izaak Walton

League. In Tennessee and North Carolina, actions by PRAG, the DPRC, the Clean Water Fund of North Carolina, and statements by activists such as Dick Mullinix, Bob Seay, Gay Webb, Nelson Ross, Jerry Wilde, and Millie Buchanan were likewise being reported. Local groups were grabbing the attention of voters. Then there was the EPA and the Clean Water Act, potentially formidable allies for those campaigning for cleaner water. Voters: they were one of the reasons why Governor McWherter and Representative Quillen and Senators Sasser and Gore expressed interest in the Pigeon River problem.

The Congressional Hearing

On June 7 Representative Quillen announced committee hearings to investigate EPA's behavior concerning possible dioxin in the Pigeon River. Although he was not a member of the Public Works and Transportation Committee or of its Subcommittee on Water Resources—under whose jurisdiction the hearings would be held—Quillen, who has been in Congress since 1963, had prevailed upon his colleagues to take the proper action to bring about the hearing. It was scheduled for 10:00 A.M., July 13, on Capitol Hill. The chairman of the subcommittee was Congressman Henry Nowak of New York.

Representatives from the DPRC, PRAG, the Izaak Walton League, Greenpeace, the Environmental Defense Fund, the town of Newport and Cocke County, Widowville (Hartford), and still others appeared. Their testimony was overwhelmingly critical of Champion. EPA, the American Paper Institute (API), and Champion International were also represented. The representatives who attended and the senators who sent prepared statements were delighted at the opportunity to take aim at EPA, and they did so with a vengeance.[32]

Representative Donald Kenneth Sundquist, whose district embraces Memphis, on the other side of the state, expressed the typical politician's anger at the bureaucracy. "I want to know . . . why EPA has allowed the tragic and environmental problems to escalate to obscenely hazardous proportions. It seems to me that EPA should have long ago been monitoring the water quality of the Pigeon River. . . . It could have prevented the excessive, lethal, toxic pollution found in the Pigeon River today." He demanded assurances of "a comprehensive, complete testing for dioxin . . . a solid commitment that our river will be cleaned up and will be kept clean."

It was James Quillen, through whose district the Pigeon flows in Tennessee, who came down hardest upon EPA. "It has failed to discharge its duty," he said. That is why he had requested the hearing, "to get some answers to serious questions which have been raised, and which continue to be raised, about EPA's handling of this distressing situation." Since Champion had built its mill, the congressman charged, "this once lovely and sparkling clean mountain river has been transformed into a foul-smelling, foaming, sludge-filled mixture that looks like oily coffee and stinks like rotten eggs. This is how Champion makes its money. This is not my opinion. This is fact." Quillen pointed out that even the health director of North Carolina had recommended that no fish caught between Canton and the Tennessee state line be eaten.

Senator Jim Sasser attributed the hearing to the high level of public misgiving about EPA's handling of the dioxin question in the Pigeon. EPA, he said, had dragged its feet in testing wells at Hartford for possible carcinogens. He said that the testing of fish in the North Carolina part of the Pigeon was done only after the state had released fish into the river. "Now," Sasser added, "these examples may strike an outsider as ordinary oversights in the operation of a government bureaucracy. But to the residents of Tennessee they left . . . a legacy of distrust." He accused EPA of failing to meet the dioxin problem head on. "And let's be clear about it," he emphasized, "there are unacceptable levels of dioxin in the Pigeon River."

At Representative Quillen's request, Bach and Barnett's economic impact report on the cost to Champion of cleaning up the river and the potential benefit of a clean Pigeon River was submitted for the record.

Dioxin, however, was the real subject of the hearing. Quillen was most critical of EPA for its failure to inform anyone of the probable existence of the chemical in the waste water from kraft pulp and paper plants. "I was floored, then outraged," he stormed. The problem had been known since 1980, but not until mid-March 1988, had he been made aware of it. Where had EPA been? (It should perhaps be noted that a method for measuring dioxin was not developed until 1985.)

Most of the testimony, both oral and through prepared statements, covered matters that had been discussed before. Nelson Ross of the Izaak Walton League presented the best denunciation of Champion's policies. The sum total of what others said added up to a bitter indictment of the company. Roy Campbell, Newport's city attorney, described how the back door of city hall opens onto the Pigeon. "The water is black and at times stinks to high heaven," he told those present. He said that from Newport's city limits to the North Carolina line, there was practically no commercial development because of stream pollution. "The blight of the river," he pleaded, "caused by one poor corporate citizen with total disregard for the rights and health of others who are less fortunate needs to be stopped." He reminded them that Knoxville obtains its water from below Douglas Dam, while the nearby town of Dandridge obtains its water supply directly from Douglas Lake.

While pollution of all kinds—color, stench, and toxins—was often mentioned, it was dioxin that dominated the hearing. The Widowville alarm also had much to do with it. Those testifying against Champion and EPA wanted to know why EPA chose a period following heavy rains to test the wells. The fresh rainwater would have diluted the well water. Moreover, since dioxin is known to accumulate in silt at the bottom of wells and rivers and lakes, why were not tests made on the silt? Further, why was the state of Tennessee's epidemiological study conducted by a doctor of veterinary medicine?

These were questions asked by Knoxville attorney Gordon Ball. He had grown up in Hartford. His grandmother was still living there at the time of the hearings; she had cancer. His father had lived there for twenty years, and by 1988 he also had cancer. And why, asked Ball, did EPA in 1985 choose to test the Pigeon for dioxin at the point where crystal-clear Cataloochee Creek runs in?

The emphasis of the hearings was not on the Pigeon River as such, however. Instead, the hearings focused first of all on technical facts about dioxin, which are frightening, and secondly on revelations of deception, duplicity, and outright collusion between the American Paper Institute and the EPA. To follow the testimony in these hearings is to challenge one's analytical powers, but it is well worth the effort. Three witnesses presented information on the hazards of dioxin. They were Ellen Silbergeld, director of the Toxic Chemicals Program of the Environmental Defense Fund; Carol Van Strum, who, along with Paul Merrell, had authored the definitive work on dioxin in the pulp and paper industry; and Renate Kroesa, International Pulp and Paper director for Greenpeace. They awakened members of the Pigeon River Action Group and the Dead Pigeon River Council more than ever to the dangers of dioxin and the enormous corporate and federal bureaucratic structure that they were fighting.

Silbergeld emphasized the dangers of the chlorine bleaching process in the pulpmaking industry. Her credentials include an adjunct faculty position at both the University of Maryland and the Johns Hopkins medical schools, membership on the executive committee of the Science Advisory Board of the EPA, and membership on the Board of Environmental Sciences and Toxicology of the National Research Council. "My research activities," she informed the committee, "concern the mechanisms of action of dioxin on nerve and muscle."

After discussing the levels of dioxin considered dangerous—and reminding the committee that EPA had downgraded the dangers— Silbergeld discussed the dangers from pulp plants. "It is our opinion that this source is, in fact, critical. It requires regulation by the EPA not only in the Pigeon River but, in fact, throughout the country." Moreover, she emphasized, "You should consider that controls on this source can be accomplished without unacceptable economic or technological dislocations, despite the threats of industry."

She then described the nature of the threat. She said that the chlorination of pulp in bleaching "results in the formation of over 100 small molecular weight byproducts." They accumulate in fat and thus are protected from environmental degradation. Some of these byproducts have not yet even been identified, but some of those that have been are known carcinogens. Ultimately, dioxins work their way into coffee filters, hygienic products, paper cups, and plates, and so on ad infinitum.

Silbergeld also emphasized the lack of regulation in the disposal of chlorine or of chemicals released by the chlorine breakdown in the bleaching process. She suggested that EPA fix a scheduled timetable for elimination of chlorine bleaching in the pulp and paper industry. The chairman was reminded that the industry "is a robust, economically healthy industry." The industry should substitute the use of chlorine dioxide and end with nonchlorine-dependent processes of bleaching and pulping, and, Silbergeld implied, the industry was quite capable of developing these technologies.

She was particularly critical of the EPA, which had "engaged in an attempt to foist off several revised risk assessments for dioxin, one [of] which would downgrade the risks of human exposure by tenfold to twentyfold." One of the assessments did not survive scientific review, and the other was not yet completed.

Most especially this scientific expert wanted to convey the enormous dangers of dioxin. From coffee filters to baby diapers, the possibilities of dioxins and furans entering the fatty tissues of humans is ever present. The bleaching process releases dioxin into the fluid flowing out of the mill, and in addition these carcinogens enter into fine solids and remain there for millennia. She deplored the use of papermaking sludges in agriculture, at the beginning of the food chain that reaches human beings. Ban chlorine bleached products, she urged; ban new construction of bleaching plants utilizing chlorine.

Finally, Silbergeld reminded the committee that substitute processes are already in operation in both Japan and the Scandinavian countries. Their production costs are lower than those of American mills, and thus they are a threat to the entire American industry, "particularly as consumer health concerns are not met responsibly and fully by the private sector and the government."

Renate Kroesa, a German-educated industrial chemist employed by Greenpeace, appeared next before the committee. Kroesa stressed the bioaccumulation of dioxin, thus checking the paper industry's argument that dioxin presence is so infinitesimal as to make all dangers ludicrous. She reminded the committee that not just Champion's Canton mill, but nearly one hundred paper mills throughout the United States use the chlorine bleaching process. About a hundred chemicals, she said (as had Dr. Silbergeld), are released by this process. Only about one-third have been identified chemically, but some are certainly carcinogenic and/or mutagenic as well as being bioaccumulative. She suggested that industry cost estimates of two hundred million dollars to three hundred million dollars for converting to oxygen delignification were way out of line. "An initial cost figure," she estimated, "would be around 12 million to 15 million U.S. dollars." She ended by posing the question of why milk cartons had to be made of bleached pulp. Brown unbleached pulp, later coated, would be just as good, she suggested.

Dr. Kroesa was followed by still another expert on dioxin, this time professional historian Carol Van Strum. For ten years she had studied EPA's dioxin regulatory program, reviewing in the process more than one hundred thousand pages of internal EPA documents. At this stage, the hearing was zeroing in on EPA and its lack of interest in enforcing regulations to limit dioxin. What emerged from the testimony was information about a case of collusion between the American Paper Institute and EPA, one of the scandals of the 1980s pro-business era. "The pulp mill dioxin problem is only the latest in a long history of inordinate delays and scandals involving EPA's semi-secret dioxin regulatory program," Van Strum stated.

Much of her argument was based upon revelations that became public as a result of a Freedom of Information Act lawsuit Strum had filed against EPA. But she had more evidence. One day a plain manila envelope appeared in the mail at one of Greenpeace's offices. Its contents were American Paper Institute files that made clear the cooperation between EPA and the institute. (Obviously, a concerned but disloyal API employee had collected the files and mailed them.) She quoted District Judge Owen M. Panner, who had presided over her lawsuit: "The documents appear to support the existence of an agreement between EPA and the industry to suppress, modify, or delay the results of the joint EPA/industry study or the manner in which they are publicly presented."

The API "Dioxin Public Affairs Plan," forty pages long, obliquely explained EPA's apparent lack of interest and activity in pushing for a decision on the dioxin question involving Champion and the Pigeon River. The Izaak Walton League's Nelson Ross emphasized the collusion, quoting from the API document obtained by Greenpeace. The goals of the plan were, first, "to get EPA to discuss the issue with the media in a balanced non-hysterical manner"; second, "to get EPA to 'rethink' dioxin risk assessment"; third, "to have EPA not to seek publicity"; and fourth, to "get EPA to issue [the] statement 'No harm to the environment or public health.'" The API statement also included an item to "improve intelligence gathering with EPA," the suggestion to "identify 'allies' within EPA," and to "obtain 'adversaries' within the same organization." How, asked Ross, do people from Cocke County take such a document? "We're bewildered. We're confused," he concluded.

The chronology of events indicates that the basic tactic taken by the American Paper Institute and the EPA in their collusion was foot dragging.

However, a five-mill study had been started, and a much larger study of paper mills was in the works. These would take time, perhaps five years. "I would like to point out here that five more years of testing means five more years of pollution," Kroesa reminded the committee, while "the possibilities to cut down the overall dioxin pollution are already available."

The hearing ended. The 404-page report contains the oral statements of participants plus extensive submitted material. Clearly, it divides into two parts: accusations of collusion between EPA and the API, which clarified EPA's foot dragging on the Pigeon River problem, and specific information about Champion's Canton mill and the Pigeon River. The hearing gave members of PRAG and the DPRC an opportunity to be heard. Perhaps it cleared the air and brought the problem into focus.

However, the hearing accomplished little else. The Pigeon River continued to be polluted, Champion continued to act as if the river was clean, clear, and sweet, and the residents of Cocke County continued to smell the stench.

Research on dioxin continues to creep along. In the summer of 1991, the paper interests could quote scientists who issued a report insisting that dioxin was not nearly as fatal as first estimated.[33] In May 1992, the final report was issued from the second of the massive studies of dioxin in pulp mills. This results are summarized cogently in the title Dr. Van Strum had given her study: "No Margin for Safety." In fact, the final report stressed that dioxin is, if possible, more dangerous than any previous studies had estimated it to be. More controversy was engendered when a class-action suit was filed against Champion and tried in the fall of 1992, which is the subject of a later chapter.[34]

Further, Widowville was not the only place where the dioxin scare made itself felt along the Pigeon River. Beginning in 1974 Carolina Power And Light (CP&L) and the North Carolina Electric Membership Corporation (NCEMC) had each petitioned for a license to run the Walter/Waterville Project, which includes Waterville Lake and Dam, and the hydroelectric plant close to the Tennessee line. As a part of the licensing procedure, which lasted until 1994 with CP&L, the Federal Energy Regulatory Commission (FERC) required an environmental assessment; this assessment was completed in June 1991.

Of three major recommendations made by the FERC, the most significant one relates to dioxin. The bottom sediments of the lake were found to be laced with dioxin and other toxics to the extent that the commission recommended the expenditure of fifteen million dollars to place a three-foot capping over the upper three to three and a half miles of the lake. The commission insisted upon this action unless fish advisories are lifted by the end of 1994. Neither of the contenders for the license disputed the need created by the toxins, although each one submitted different proposals for meeting the problem. The toxins, including dioxin, are primarily a result of Champion's effluents, which have been caught behind the dam since the dam became operational in 1930. Problems simply do not wash away.[35]

CHAPTER 11

The Governor
Rejects the Variance

The furor over dioxin and the hearings at Asheville, Knoxville, and Washington, D.C., did not put a halt to the slow-grinding wheels of administration. On July 13, 1988, the North Carolina Division of Environmental Management approved a variance for Pigeon River water allowing "a maximum level of 85 true color units . . . in the Pigeon River at the North Carolina–Tennessee state line at all times when the instream flow of the Pigeon River as measured at the Hepco gauging station is equal to or greater than 126 cubic feet per second." (The Hepco gauging station is close to the Tennessee state line.) About a month later, Greer C. Tidwell, EPA's regional administrator in Atlanta, informed Paul Wilms, director of the DEM, that the EPA was approving the variance. Endorsement was based upon EPA's water standards regulations, "which allow revisions to criteria when controls more stringent than those required by . . . the Clean Water Act would result in substantial widespread social and economic impact." In other words, more stringent controls would affect mill operations—possibly result in the mill's closing—and cause social and economic devastation in the region.[1]

All the fuss, all the energy expended by PRAG and the DPRC, the Izaak Walton League, Greenpeace, *Newport Plain Talk,* and the national press had brought about a compromise. Eighty-five color units at the state line meant a river the color of dark ginger ale. Nothing was said about stench or foam, nor was anything said about toxic sludge released into the river. Most especially, nothing was said about dioxin.

The Pigeon River continued to flow dirty.

Champion and its North Carolina defenders may have hoped the controversy was over. They were wrong. Dioxin, not color, was the new complaint, although much of the official controversy would still center around color. Fear of this dangerous toxin, and the knowledge that it was almost certainly in the Pigeon's waters and in the stream bottom and that it was deeply embedded in the sludge piling up in the Waterville Lake, had frightened Cocke County citizens, and their fright refused to be allayed.

The Newport Hearing

These citizens had a rostrum: another public hearing. Although EPA had implied that it would issue a wastewater permit if both North Carolina and Tennessee would issue a permit with the variance—and North Carolina had done so—the state of Tennessee had not. The procedure by which it could grant approval involved a public hearing. In the very week in which these discussions were to take place, five members of the DPRC filed a petition questioning the need for and the validity of the proposed variance. Their lawyer was suave, brilliant Gordon Ball, a Knoxville attorney who had grown up in Hartford, "so close to the river our baseballs sometimes fell in it," he reminisced. The variance, their petition read, allowed Pigeon River water to be double the maximum limit of apparent color units allowed under current Tennessee law,[2] and they disapproved of it. They also challenged the constitutionality of the statute, signed by Governor McWherter on April 5, which implemented Tennessee's variance procedure. Meanwhile, the governor had ordered additional fish testing. The fish would be caught in true Pigeon River water (not where a freshwater tributary flowed in) and be tested by a laboratory at Wright State University in Dayton, Ohio.[3]

A hearing was scheduled at the Cocke County High School auditorium in Newport from 3:00 to 9:00 P.M. on Thursday, August 18, and the next day, Friday, August 19, from 8:00 until 11:00 A.M. In the center section of the auditorium, 167 seats were labeled with the names of the 167 people who had lived along the Pigeon at Hartford and who, many believed, had died as a result of ingesting dioxin from the river. In addition, a plywood memorial bearing the names of more than 120 victims was unveiled outside the high school in a dedication service involving the flying of the American flag at half mast, a 21-gun salute to the victims by the Disabled American Veterans, and the playing of taps. This "Hartford Wall" was the inspiration of Rick and Wendy Knight of Del Rio.[4]

At least 400 people attended the meetings, which, despite the di-

Oliver Ford scans the commemorative wall erected outside Cocke County High School listing 167 possible victims of dioxin poisoning. Ford lost two brothers and a sister to cancer; they lived along the Pigeon River. August 1988. Photo by Nancy Oberst. Courtesy Newport Plain Talk.

oxin scare, dealt primarily with the color issue. Days before, the river had been gauged at 238 color units with a high reading of 670; a week before the hearing, the water had tested at 244 units. It was, of course, the season of low water—not a propitious time, from Champion's point of view, for color readings to be made and advertised.

The moderator, Billy Stair, was sent from Governor McWherter's office. Some speakers, and many in the audience, were incensed that the governor himself was not present. They were also angered that Tennessee officials, from their Nashville offices at least, seemed to go along with Champion. The officials hedged. Yes, Champion had a terrible record. But they defended the variance. They explained that it applied only to color, not to foam, odor, or contamination by dioxin. Paul Davis of the Water Pollution Control Division, an admitted "incrementalist," noted that 85 color units would be much cleaner than the Pigeon was then flowing, and that the variance offered "the first fixed schedule that has ever been issued for the work we want done." David McKinney of the Wildlife Resource Agency—and co-author of an important 1980 report that had given impetus to the modern campaign to clean up the Pigeon River—also advocated the variance, arguing that without it, Champion would simply continue polluting as it had always done. Even Cocke County's state representative, Ronnie Davis, urged granting of the variance as the first step toward cleaning up the river.

Senator Al Gore, in a prepared statement, stressed the necessity of Champion's understanding that the variance was to be only temporary. "It was only after years of pressure from me and other congressional and state representatives of Tennessee . . . that Champion made any effort to negotiate a settlement of the color emissions problem," the senator said.

Now it was Cocke County's turn at the rostrum, and its angry citizens made the most of it. Many wore black armbands; some carried signs. Perhaps Tennessee's involved officials were for the variance, but the people of Cocke County let it be known that they considered the deviation a capitulation. Cindie Runnion, a Cocke County schoolteacher, put the matter bluntly. "We have had enough," she stated, promising Champion that for every day the river remained polluted, "we will make every day a living hell for you." Nelson Ross of the Izaak Walton League showed political wisdom when he suggested that "to establish a variance procedure would open a Pandora's box for any industry that wants relief from these stringent standards, and would turn the waters of this great state brown." Steve Davidson of Newport said that "Cocke County has lost its share of the pot of gold because Champion has polluted the pot." And yet another protester, sensing betrayal by Tennessee officials, let them know how he felt. "If I appear to be a hostile witness," he said angrily, "it is a trait I have when someone is trying to kill me. I am appalled beyond measure that the leaders of my state, the great State of Tennessee, [should] convene a hearing and request me to make my murder legal."

Champion's Oliver Blackwell, who did not have as friendly an audience as he could have expected in Asheville (and, indeed, he was booed and hissed), made the usual statements about how the mill must close if more stringent requirements were enforced, how Champion brings millions of dollars in benefits to Tennessee, that closure would mean seven hundred fewer jobs for Tennesseans, and that just achieving the 85 color units would cost Champion thirty-eight million dollars.

Newport-Cocke County partisans had their say on August 18 and 19, 1988, at hearing at Newport High School. Here, young Shauna Stuart holds a placard. Photo by Gilbert Soesbee. Courtesy Newport Plain Talk.

The hearing took place in August 1988; now everyone awaited Governor Ned McWherter's decision: to accept or not accept a variance of Tennessee's laws, a variance similar to the ones accepted by EPA and North Carolina that had allowed Champion to continue operations.

Governor McWherter "Sees the Elephant"

Ned McWherter bided his time. It was true that he had visited Elizabethton, Rogersville, and Pigeon Forge—all in East Tennessee—within a short time after the hearing, but he had not dropped by Newport. Everyone knew he had asserted his right to issue or deny the variance. His absence puzzled Cocke County residents. Was he on their side?

When he is not holding political office, McWherter is a successful businessman—a beer distributor—and his physical bearing assures that no one is going to railroad him into a decision. Ned McWherter weighs over three hundred pounds, smokes a cigar (when not chomping on one), and on occasion chews tobacco. The Pigeon River controversy posed a major problem for him. Those interests that always have a direct line to the governor's office were pressuring him to approve the variance, as were—apparently—a number of Tennessee government officials, including Paul Davis and David McKinney. But he had promised to help East Tennesseans in their quarrel with Champion, and, envisioning the coming election, he needed their votes. What to do?

The governor decided to see the problem for himself. Without fanfare, he and one or two other Tennessee officials landed in a private plane at the Asheville airport at mid-morning of Tuesday, September 20. There they were met by Paul Davis and David McKinney, plus reporters. First the party was escorted by car to Fiberville Road, overlooking the mountain of wood chips used in papermaking. From there, the party drove up State Highway 215. At one of the bridges over the Pigeon, they halted. McWherter peered into the crystal-clear waters, flicking his cigar ashes into the river. This was the Class A stream above the mill, and it was fishable and potable.[5]

Tennessee's Governor Ned McWherter sees the Pigeon River for himself, September 20, 1988. Here he floats along a tranquil stretch in Tennessee with David McKinney on the left and Billy Stair on the right. Photo by Nancy Oberst. Courtesy Newport Plain Talk.

The party launched the canoe close to Champion property. When shallow water forced them to disembark and move the canoe to deeper water, they learned how difficult placing a three-hundred-pound man in the center seat of a canoe can be: McWherter's aides earned their pay that day. As one later said, "Don't quote me, but McWherter was a canoe fool!" The party crossed the mill site, and, on the other side, the governor observed the change in the river. Two security guards and a Haywood County deputy sheriff dropped by, curious about what a canoe was doing in the water and why several cars were parked along the road. "We're not trying to disturb the peace," the governor assured them.[6]

Below Waterville Dam they were met by two whitewater rafters who run thrill-seekers down the Nantahala and French Broad. Acting as guides, they pushed the party out into the stream and floated in a raft down to the Hartford Post Office. There, Governor McWherter purchased some chewing tobacco. They pushed off again. The water was so dirty, the governor remarked, that he could not even see his spittle after it hit the water.[7]

And so Ned McWherter "saw the elephant." Would it affect his decision about the variance? Everyone waited. September gave way to October, October to November, and November to December.

Luncheon at the Governor's Mansion

Charles Moore relates how, after considerable needling from the governor's aides, in December 1988, the governor issued an invitation to Moore, Newport Mayor Jeanne Wilson, Cindie and Jim Runnion, and Jerry Wilde of the DPRC to lunch at the executive mansion in Nashville. Initially, neither Bob Seay nor his dedicated secretary, Fran Ketterman, was asked. Moore informed the governor's aide that he would not attend unless Seay and Ketterman were also invited. Seay telephoned Nashville on his own and received an invitation; Ketterman boldly went along and was not turned away.[8]

Those attending remember how beautiful the mansion was, all decked out in its Christmas finery, and they recall that the governor enjoyed his meal. And they remember how he lectured them. For a full half hour, he explained why he should accept Champion's permit with the variance allowing the company to continue polluting the Pigeon. The governor insisted that it was in the best interests of both states for him to sign the variance.

"Even McWherter had been misled by Champion officials," says

Bob Seay. "We know for a fact that on at least three occasions he had met in Nashville with Champion executives." At least once, Governor Jim Martin had flown to Nashville to confer about the Pigeon with his Tennessee counterpart. On the other hand, Seay adds that, to his knowledge, "until the Christmas luncheon no one protesting the polluted Pigeon had ever been invited to the mansion."

The delegation was adamant. They reminded McWherter of Champion's seventy-nine years of broken promises. They compared the company to the boy who cried wolf. Champion had promised to clean up the river and had failed to do so just one time too many. For having committed these falsehoods, the company was facing a stone wall of uncompromising opponents.

Of more essential significance, these Cocke County residents proved that they could also play the game of pressure politics. McWherter, a Democrat, could use East Tennessee votes, yet East Tennessee was a Republican bastion. Moore, Seay, Wilde, and company held out to the governor a carrot and a stick: a lot of votes if he refused to sign the variance—that was the carrot—and a thinly veiled threat that if he did sign the variance, Cocke County voters would hold a news conference the very next day, protesting the move, and go public on statewide radio and television protesting what he had done—that was the stick.[9]

The luncheon ended. After they had left, County Executive Moore and his small delegation agreed that Governor McWherter was standing between a rock and a hard place. They knew that tremendous pressure had been exerted upon this Democratic but not antibusiness governor by Champion International and its allies to accept the permit with a color variance. On the other hand, to win the votes of some of the Republican mountain people of East Tennessee might tip a hotly contested election McWherter's way.

"We fought the Governor tooth and nail," recalls Charles Moore. "I mean right down to the last minute he was going to sign that variance come hell or high water. All his aides told him, sign it."[10]

The trip to the governor's mansion in distant Nashville paid off. On December 23, 1988, two days before Christmas, Governor McWherter announced that the commissioner of Health and Environment, J. W. Luna, had rejected the variance; everyone knew, of course, that the decision was McWherter's. The announcement came in a news conference held by Cocke County State Representative Ronnie Davis and State Senator Lynn Lawson.[11]

In early January McWherter explained his decision. He said that the company's financial reports indicated that Champion was sufficiently profitable to launch a cleanup. "They have had adequate cash flow dollars—profits, if you please—and in the last 10 years they've had adequate time to have done a substantial amount of cleanup to that river. . . . I made up my mind that I represented the people of Cocke County and the citizens of Tennessee, and it would be wrong for me to grant that variance."[12]

In Newport the news made the Christmas season especially joyful. On New Year's Eve, for the third year in a row, bell ringers gathered at the McSween Bridge. They had reason to be enthusiastic, for they were celebrating a victory—the first real victory in the nearly eighty-year fight to clean up the river. A Tennessee governor had finally officially sided with them. He had slapped down North Carolina, the EPA, and Champion Paper Company by denying the variance.

For still other reasons it had been a good twelve months. Jerry Wilde, president of the chamber of commerce, reminded the crowd of the ups and downs of a turbulent year. Dioxin had been found in the stream, but a congressional subcommittee had held hearings on the river, and four public hearings had kept the problem in the public's eyes. He noted Champion's busing of two thousand employees to the Knoxville hearing. "Those [yellow] Champion hats were probably the best thing that ever happened for us," Wilde noted. "Those hats galvanized the feelings of Cocke countians, and you can see what happened from there." Baptist pastor Dr. Charlie Boggan, who led the group in prayer prior to the fireworks and bell ringing, reminded the group of how much could be accomplished when people work together. "We must be guardians of nature," he urged. "There are people who are finally realizing that ecology is not just a fad. It is a reality that we must all deal with. . . . We can do things, little things, that can make a difference."[13]

And Governor McWherter won his next election by a squeaky margin: East Tennessee's support had been crucial.

North Carolina's Reaction

Cocke County's delight with Governor McWherter's decision was in stark contrast to the reaction of Champion International's numbed supporters. When their shock wore off, they were outraged. Always before, persuasion and politics had served Champion well. This time, for reasons they did not entirely understand, they had failed. In the six weeks after January 1, 1989, everyone from Governor Jim Martin and top Champion officials to minor North Carolina politicians and Champion employees vented their spleen on McWherter, the people of East Tennessee, and the DPRC. Their common complaint was that they "had been done wrong" by a neighboring but not a neighborly state. In their fury they suggested fair means, legal means, economic means, and foul means to get even.

A constant irritant to those demanding a cleanup of the Pigeon has been the consistent cozying up of North Carolina politicians with Champion. To the clean water proponents, it was bad enough that a beautiful river is polluted for twenty-six miles into another state, but that the river is polluted for thirty miles in the home state—and its government did nothing to prevent it—seemed even more reprehensible. So they were hardly surprised—but not pleased—to hear that Governor Martin and an entourage of aides had flown to Champion headquarters at Stamford, Connecticut, in a private jet loaned by a North Carolina bank to confer with Champion's moguls about the Tennessee ruling. Champion's vice-president for public affairs, Bob Turner, was quoted as having told Martin that if the rejection stood, then Champion would close the Canton plant. The governor was quoted as saying that, as soon as the formal variance rejection was received (until now, it had just been announced through the media), he would take steps to try to change the ruling. Already Champion was reacting: Oliver Blackwell had announced that plans for a three-hundred-million-dollar modernization were stalled; in less than a year, cost estimates had escalated by one-third. Eighteen hundred employees were plunged into job insecurity. He had also inserted a new element into the controversy. According to *Plain Talk*, he admitted that the company could clean up the Pigeon, but the cost would be prohibitive. All along, DPRC and PRAG members had insisted that the technology was available, but until this time, Champion had denied it.[14]

On Tuesday, January 10, Champion Vice President for Environment Richard DiForio received Commissioner J. W. Luna's three-page letter giving Tennessee's reasons for denying the variance. The gist was simply that there was no evidence that Champion International Corporation had any intention of complying with Tennessee state law. Moreover, health was now a concern; dioxins were known to be in the stream. They posed a threat to the citizenry living along the river.[15]

Not many more days passed before North Carolinians began to threaten their neighbors both officially and unofficially. First, however, came the dire predictions of economic catastrophe. Champion's chief operating officer, L. C. Heist, held a press conference at Asheville on Wednesday, January 25, and at the same time Oliver Blackwell met with mill workers at the Robertson YMCA in Canton. Both men announced plans to reduce the size of the mill. This would result in the laying off of about a thousand workers. Press releases estimated the mill's impact upon the region at $174 million a year; the annual payroll was about $100 million. The *Mountaineer*'s business editor, Greg Cook, estimated that the ripple effect of one thousand jobs lost would drain the region of $150 million; total closure would raise the loss to $300 million in 22 counties. An associate professor of economics at Western North Carolina University estimated that a total of about 4,000 jobs would be lost in the region.[16] DEM Director Paul Wilms informed the press that he felt "betrayed" by Tennessee's actions; he said EPA officials were also distressed, and he found J. W. Luna's logic "absurd."[17]

Meanwhile, North Carolinians from Governor Martin down began threatening retaliation. "From now on," the governor warned, "when Tennessee paper mills want to draw down water from our lakes to flush out their color, North Carolina will put the full force of our laws behind the landowners there." He suggested also that his state might insist upon tougher pollution control from Tennessee cars, which were "gassing our mountains." Industries might be taken from Tennessee and settle in North Carolina with its more lenient antipollution laws. The governor, who well knew that the state could not interfere with TVA's management of its lakes, was having a field day of political posturing.[18]

Champion employees noticed that locally sold Pet milk had its offices in Johnson City, Tennessee. This was enough to warrant a boycott until a newspaper informed them that the Pet milk sold locally was purchased from North Carolina dairymen and was bottled at Milkco in Asheville; more than ten thousand gallons a day of the milk came from Haywood County, and the packaging was in Champion's milk cartons.[19]

Senator Robert Swain of Buncombe County and his colleague, Dennis Winner, introduced a bill in the North Carolina state legislature to ban all Tennessee whiskey from the state's ABC liquor stores. The *Charlotte Observer* pointed out how the word "buncombe" found its way into our vocabulary. No more Jack Daniel's! No more George Dickel! Newspapers had fun with this controversy: the *Los Angeles Times* commented on the bill "to ban bourbon in a mountain feud with Tennessee over dirty branch water." Eventually Senator Swain killed the bill in the state senate. "I'm sort of like the wildcat that made love to the skunk," he said. "I've enjoyed about all this I can stand." The proposal had done about all the good it could do, he suggested. It was unpopular among Jack Daniels and George Dickel sippers, of whom there appeared to be many more in North Carolina than he had estimated.[20]

Rays of hope for North Carolina began to filter into the stormy scene. In late January 1989, newspaper headlines suggested that EPA could override Tennessee's protest on the grounds that refusal to accept the variance would create economic hardship. To this suggestion, Representative Quillen had a quick reply. "EPA," he insisted, "is a creature of Congress, and I'll land on them with both feet if they try to overrule Tennessee. . . . The people who live along the Pigeon River back the governor, and I do too." He also thought that Champion's threat to shut down was "just a threat."[21]

Under headlines of "Tar Heel Threats Will Backfire," the ambivalent Waynesville *Mountaineer* reprinted an editorial from *Plain Talk* that presented Cocke County's grievances with rare clarity. A few of its more lucid statements are as follows:

> A North Carolina paper mill has been allowed to contaminate, almost unchecked, a waterway which could be an important economic and environmental asset to Cocke countians, and we have had enough.
>
> During the past 80 years, North Carolina has repeatedly failed in its obligation to regulate the Champion International Corporation pulp and paper mill in Canton. North Carolina officials in that state have repeatedly bent the regulations designed to protect residents downstream, and turned a blind eye to the industrial sewer Champion has made of the once-scenic Pigeon River. Whatever Champion wanted it got—lenient wastewater discharge permits, variances to existing regulations, anything necessary to keep the profitable paper mill in Canton.
>
> In the meantime, the Canton plant—which currently produces a large percentage of the nation's milk and juice cartons and envelope paper—continued to gain in economic status until Champion had a choke-hold on the entire region. With that kind of clout, it is no wonder that Champion's corporate officials began to feel that no one would regulate the huge paper mill on the small Pigeon River. . . .
>
> The time has long passed when corporate and political officials in North Carolina can use threats of economic blackmail to sway public opinion in Tennessee. They've had their way for 80 years, and we are no longer asking—we are demanding—let the Pigeon live![22]

The furor died down. This was partly because Champion could remain in full operation, polluting the Pigeon, until such time as a permit was granted. On Tuesday, January 31, after its officials met with Champion executives, EPA proposed to grant Champion three years to meet Tennessee's water quality standard. As before, the proposal was by law forced to include a period for lodging discussions and conducting more hearings. Meanwhile, civic leaders in Haywood County, anticipating the worst, met at Haywood Community College and formed five task forces to try to ease the economic impact of Champion's closing. Steps were taken to change provisions in North Carolina's Free Skills Training Program so that it could grant free training to Champion workers who might lose their jobs. Clearly, the North Carolinians took Champion's words as holy script: if the corporation said it would downgrade its work force or close the mill, they believed it.[23]

Not everyone accepted Champion's statements, however. When the company announced a $475-million expansion at its Courtland, Alabama, facility, conceding that the action had been projected for some time, editors of the *Knoxville Journal* sniffed duplicity. Since the expansion would allow a shift of production of fine paper from the Canton plant, they sensed a clever ruse in Champion's lament about being forced to downsize their capacity at Canton. The company would blame job reduction on Tennessee's refusal to accept the variance, whereas the real reason was a change of production of one type of paper from Canton to another Champion facility. Why not shift the blame from company policy to the terrible Governor McWherter, the DPRC, PRAG, and those callous people of East Tennessee?[24]

By January 1989, all of Tennessee was aware of the Pigeon River. This cartoon from the Nashville Tennessean *reflects the general point of view of Tennesseans. Courtesy Sandy Campbell, the* Tennessean.

EPA Releases a New Draft Permit

In early March 1989, EPA released copies of its revised eighty-one-page draft permit. Reading the fine print, reporter Michael Weaver discovered some facts and figures about Champion's future plans for the Canton mill that included surprising new production estimates. A layoff of a thousand employees, beginning the following year, would come about, it was explained, through retirement of four old papermaking machines. These produced colored envelope paper, among other products, and were labor intensive. It took as many or more men, Champion's spokesman Bob Turner explained, to turn out eighty-three tons a day from those machines as were needed to turn out seven hundred tons from the new No. 20 papermaker. This, Turner added, is why more employees would lose their jobs, although the daily paper tonnage from Champion's mill would probably be reduced by as little as 6 percent or by as much as 36 percent.[25]

EPA's permit proposal, which included these statistics on Champion's proposed new production schedules, elicited anger because of the circumstances under which the proposal appeared to have been drawn up—in company boardrooms at Stamford with EPA officials present, but without the presence of Cocke County residents.[26]

By this time, clean river proponents were far more concerned about color and toxic chemicals, especially dioxin, than about the labor force at Canton. Meanwhile, Carol Van Strum, a Greenpeace dioxin expert who had appeared before the congressional hearing on the Pigeon River, had used the Freedom of Information Act to obtain an EPA paper industry report on dioxin. She released pertinent extracts of it to the Mossy Creek and Lakeway chapters of the Izaak Walton League, and the *Knoxville News-Sentinel* also obtained a copy from the EPA. The newspaper produced headlines announcing that the concentration of dioxins in Champion's sludge was among the highest levels found in any mills tested by EPA. Such information, the publicity given to the taking of diseased fish from the stream, and the posting of signs along the Pigeon that warned people not to eat the fish seemed to confirm the scientific reports. Such news items kept the Pigeon River problem before the people during 1988 and 1989.[27]

Meanwhile, EPA had targeted June 27, 1989, as the possible issuance date of a new permit. Concerned citizens were given thirty days, beginning March 29, in which to comment on the agency's new three-year variance proposal. Little happened until just four days were left. This was in stark contrast to a little over a year before, when, according to regional director Bruce Barrett, Champion had orchestrated the sending of a hundred and sixty thousand letters and petitions with fifteen thousand signatures to the agency on behalf of Champion; ten thousand had been hand-delivered to EPA regional headquarters in Atlanta. The contrast between the six letters received in 1989 and the mammoth mailing of the year before was not lost on reporters. "What a difference a year makes," commented reporter Michael Weaver. On the twenty-seventh day, nine more letters arrived; on the twenty-eighth day, ten more. All told, 184 comments were received. Nine letters requested hearings and nineteen requested issuance of the permit without further delay. With just forty-eight hours remaining in the comment period, the Dead Pigeon River Council presented a fifteen-page letter requesting another hearing. EPA officials must have groaned.[28]

One of those who helped the DPRC draw up the statement was attorney Gordon Ball. In justification of the request, Ball told newsmen that he did not "think Champion can be believed on any point in time. They promised us in 1912 that they would clean up the river." The DPRC found much to fault in EPA's eighty-one-page proposal: six-month status reports, to be filed by Champion, said nothing about color; the DPRC wanted interim limits that would require progressive steps toward achieving the 50-color-unit limit imposed by Tennessee; and it criticized the color testing procedure, which, the protesters suggested, could result in water below Waterville Dam being tested when polluted water was not being released—when only clear water, much of it flowing from Big Creek, would be available. The letter also suggested that the water, rather than fish, be tested for dioxin. Without these changes, said Ball, at the end of three years Champion would just say, "We're not going to do it, guys; see you 'round."[29]

On the thirtieth and last day of the comment period, Champion filed a two-hundred-page statement. In essence, it protested any change in the permit as then written and requested "a seat at the table" if changes were made. Limits on color, chloroform, dioxin, and the methodology used in testing aquatic life were questioned, with the caveat that if they did not meet with Champion's approval, legal action might ensue. Company officials found one requirement particularly disturbing: that after three years from issuance of the permit, the dioxin level in Pigeon's waters not exceed 0.1 parts per quadrillion.[30]

Another Round of Hearings

On June 21, much to Champion's chagrin, EPA announced another round of hearings, one set for August 17 at Newport and the other on

August 24 at Asheville. EPA administrator Greer Tidwell announced a new forty-five-day comment period due to the public's "high" interest.[31]

And so Champion's employees waited and worried. Bumper stickers reflected their frustration: Enough is Enough. The *Raleigh News and Observer* ran a feature article about the employees. "Champion was forever," said one. It was noted that pay was double that of the typical western North Carolina employer—the average remuneration was $13.50 an hour or $28,000 a year (as of February 1992, it was up to $42,000 a year). But disaffection was brewing. Employees were now making double payments on house mortgages. New car sales—ordinarily double the national average—were slowing. Schoolchildren, it was said, "threatened to dynamite Tennessee."[32]

It was a long, hot summer, and many things did not go well for Champion. The company supported a bill introduced in North Carolina's legislature that would have banned nonbiodegradable plastic-coated paper. Cups and other commodities made from such material would be made illegal, thus opening the way for the sale of more Champion paper products. Then someone realized that Champion itself produced nonbiodegradable plastic-coated products. The bill was hastily withdrawn.[33]

Rebecca Allen, the Canton schoolteacher who had been transferred and given a poor teacher evaluation because she had taught both sides of the Pigeon River controversy, was the recipient of the Dr. Marketta Laurila Free Speech Award. (This is an honor given by a coalition of North Carolina civil rights groups. Dr. Laurila had been denied reappointment at the University of North Carolina because she had spoken out against U.S. Central American policy.) Besides a plaque, Allen received a trophy consisting of a turtle with the inscription "A turtle never moves forward unless it sticks its neck out." The award was given on July 22 in Asheville, with full news coverage; on August 4, with the backing of the American Civil Liberties Union, she filed suit against Canton's school officials. Again, Allen received full news coverage and a favorable op-ed piece in the *Mountaineer*.[34]

Dick Mullinix commented on cattle that had been photographed drinking water out of a foamy section of the Pigeon. It was a double whammy of dioxin, he claimed; dioxin could come from the cartons manufactured by Champion and from the milk from cows that drank the polluted water. And what about vegetables grown in fields irrigated with Pigeon River water? he asked. He also reminded readers of a recent North Carolina study that indicated an increase in breast cancer in Haywood County. Are there, he asked, any connections?[35]

Finally, one of Champion's guest houses at Lake Logan went up in flames. Authorities found signs of arson, but no culprit was ever apprehended.[36]

August 1989 arrived; the dates for the hearings were approaching. This time, Champion lay low. No high-pressure public relations firm was called in to stir up emotions. The opposition, accustomed to doing things "low rent," let itself be heard. Jerry Wilde accused EPA of denying the Dead Pigeon River Council its request to participate in the permit-writing process, thus justifying the organization's request for hearings; it was the only way the group could express its views. He stated simply that it was "a Champion-written permit. . . . It's written to their advantage and the results [of required water testing] are almost entirely under their control."[37]

He listed the DPRC's concerns, some of which have been stated above. The group protested testing being conducted by the company—"it's a case of the fox watching the hen house," Wilde said. The DPRC felt that the sludge, thirty-five- to sixty-five-feet deep in Waterville Lake, as well as sludge in Douglas Lake and all the way back in the stream bottom to the Champion plant, should all be tested for dioxin. It wanted water temperature cut back; it had actually been raised to 90 degrees during the summer months, to 81 degrees the rest of the year. "No native fish can survive in that, that's bathtub temperature," Wilde protested.[38]

Shortly before the hearings, a *Mountaineer* columnist, Greg Cook, commented on the contrast between the situation in the winter of 1988 and that of August 1989. "Things are much quieter, though not silent," he noted. Back in late 1987, a Tennessee environmental leader he interviewed had called Champion officials "corporate animals," he recalled, "and the company more or less dismissed those opposed to the mill's stance as liberal environmentalists." Of course, even this time around, some paper mill workers were obtaining signatures on large rolls of paper produced at the mill to be presented to EPA, and the DPRC had called the new permit "a license to pollute." But, wrote Cook, both sides were notably quieter, Champion because it had lost, and the DPRC because it had won. He failed to add that an "EPA Response Team" had been created by Champion defenders within the past two weeks to raise money, advertise on radio, television, and in newspapers, and to bus supporters to the Asheville hearing; the company did not, however, propose to barge into Knoxville with two thousand loud supporters wearing yellow Champion hats.[39]

Because they too claimed to have been left out of the permit-granting process, Haywood County's frightened leaders requested a face-to-face hearing with EPA in order to state their concerns. Through a spokesperson, EPA said it had bent over backwards to give everyone an opportunity to present their concerns. It was added that appeals to EPA over conditions of the permit could be heard by an administrative law judge.[40]

On Monday, August 21, 1989—sandwiched between the Newport hearing on August 17 and the Asheville hearing on August 24—EPA officials sat down with community leaders of both Canton and Waynesville. The town fathers predicted dire consequences if EPA failed to accept the permit as written. A few even insisted that Tennesseans wanted Champion eliminated from the region, but most of them were tolerant of their neighbors. Barry Rogers, director of the Haywood County Chamber of Commerce, sympathized with environmentalists but added that "mankind must come first. Mankind and his or her livelihood." EPA's regional administrator commiserated, but insisted that the agency's first duty is to the environment, as its name implies.[41]

Although this round of hearings was low-key compared with the flamboyant hearings of January 1988, these sessions attracted national attention. USA Today noted that EPA had requested that Champion expend what the company claimed was two hundred million dollars to clean up the mess. It also quoted plant manager Oliver Blackwell, who repeated the claim that to build a mill like Champion's on such a small river today would be unthinkable.[42]

Only about 250 people showed up for the Newport hearing on August 17. Speakers protested three aspects of the permit: they did not want Champion empowered to make tests of its own pollution; they did not like the choice of test sites—especially the one below Waterville Dam and just below the mouth of Big Creek; and they did not like the formula suggested for determining color. The hearings had been called, DPRC President Jerry Wilde explained, because, as the DPRC had protested previously, only Champion and EPA were allowed to be present when the permit was written, and this, he protested, was not fair. Richard DiForio, Champion's environmental officer, pointed out that for two years Champion had awaited the permit prior to launching a proposed two-hundred-million-dollar cleanup; he said Champion had a right to insist upon a five-year permit. Representative James Quillen was present and insisted upon action "today . . . let's take this bull by the horns and make the tough decisions to issue the strong permit that will get this job done once and for all. . . . Any more delays would be an outrage."[43]

Senator Gore had a statement read in his behalf. Evidently, he had been informed of the provision for testing the water for color a mile and a half inside Tennessee, beyond where Big Creek with its clear water flows into the Pigeon. He insisted upon a sample taken at the state line. Wilma Dykeman, author of *The French Broad* and a Newport resident, said she had talked with Champion officials thirty-four years ago and "they asked for a little more time." Dick Mullinix urged that the final permit be written "in language that cannot be violated." Clearly, he did not trust Champion.[44]

The following week, a hearing was held at Asheville—the fifth hearing in three years, the seventh in five. About a hundred people spoke their piece. No yellow Champion hats and huge yellow badges were observed, and, instead of the seven thousand who attended the January 1988 Asheville hearing, only about four hundred attended this one. DiForio, speaking for Champion, announced what was already widely known— that Champion, by curtailing some operations and with proposed improvements, believed it could comply with the 50-color-unit regulation and that the dioxin requirements embodied in the permit may already have been met by the company. He claimed, however, that this would mean the loss of a thousand jobs and would entail enormous expense on Champion's part. But it would be done, he assured the audience, providing the permit was granted as then written. The only theatrical part of the hearing was the presentation to EPA of a huge roll of Champion paper upon which were the names of hundreds of Champion supporters.[45]

Feisty Governor Jim Martin was there, and he did not give an inch. He said he had opposed the "unduly harsh and ill-founded color removal requirements. . . . All that is at issue here is whether a thousand good people must be put out of work so that the color of the river can be reduced by a shade of difference that probably won't be noticed except in a laboratory." He reminded his audience that the color had been there for seventy-six years (it had really been eighty-one), long before most protesters moved here "and that [color] occurs naturally in our rivers and streams."[46] North Carolina Senator Jesse Helms was not so confrontational. He said such antagonisms produce no winners, only losers. He pleaded that both sides give in enough to end the controversy, which had gone on, he said, too long already.[47]

EPA hearing officer Al Smith announced that EPA hoped to issue the permit promptly, possibly in September. He also said that, unless someone contested it legally, which he did not anticipate, the permit would be immediately valid.

And thus ended the hearings. People were clearly tired of the issue. "Most [residents of Canton] agree that the anger, the energy and the enthusiasm that fueled last year's loud campaign for Champion is gone now," commented the *Asheville Citizen*. "That exhaustion appears to have drifted downstream to Tennessee, where residents still seeking changes in the permit talk of a general weariness over the issue."[48]

The Question of Layoffs

On September 23, 1989, the news came: Champion was granted the permit. It contained only minor changes compared to the major ones proposed the previous winter. The mill was given three years to comply with its terms, which included 50 color units at the state line (and the testing was to be conducted only when Carolina Power and Light was discharging water from its turbines); Champion was to conduct dioxin tests, and one of the seven testing stations was moved closer to the mill. Oliver Blackwell predicted "a remarkable transformation of Canton and the Pigeon River" within the next three years.[49]

All was fine—as long as critics did not file legal protests within thirty days. The DPRC wanted time to study the thirty-two-page permit. Blackwell said the DPRC had won. Gay Webb replied that "Champion is blowing the horn like they have lost, but they wrote the permit. EPA just approved it." Initially, members of the group were critical of the three-year period given Champion to clean up the river; that meant three more years of pollution. They did not like the fact that Champion was doing its own testing. Jerry Wilde suggested that the DPRC was going to purchase its own water-testing equipment.[50]

While the DPRC examined a permit it thought was too lenient, Canton inhabitants awaited the dire consequences of a permit they thought was too strict. The company had warned that even if it could continue operating the Canton plant, the changes forced upon it would result in the loss of up to one thousand jobs. In October the *Mountaineer* headlined the revelation that EPA had no documentation from Champion about jobs being lost due to the terms of the EPA permit. An unnamed EPA official stated that "the company . . . some five years ago, indicated to EPA that regardless of the outcome of the permit there would be fewer workers at the Canton mill. The stated reason was that the company desired to improve the mill's profitability and the best way to do that was through a major process resulting in the need for fewer employees."[51]

When two pro-Pigeon River employees were fired in September, one of them, Dana Worley, who had been with Champion fifteen years, was quoted as saying that employees were told in mid-1985 that Champion contemplated installing new and more efficient equipment that would result in substantial employee cutbacks—"that in six years the mill would operate with six hundred to eight hundred people—exactly what they are talking about now. . . . Everybody down there knew the cutbacks were coming, they just wanted somebody to blame it on."[52]

When this was revealed, the *Knoxville Journal* ran a scathing editorial:

> The files explain in general, but damning terms how Champion International Corporation lied to North Carolina and Tennessee state officials, to citizens of both states and to its own employees about its plans to make large reductions in employment at its Canton, N.C., paper plant. . . .
>
> There were wild threats made. People in cars with Tennessee tags might meet with vandalism or violence if they ventured off I-40 at the Canton exit. There was a preposterous call, seconded by Gov. Jim Martin, to boycott Jack Daniels whiskey. There was a frenzied, but futile movement to block completion of a new highway link between Elizabethton, Tenn., and Asheville, N.C., on the Carolina side. Still Champion whined and moaned that it was beset by Tennessee demons who wanted to put the company out of business and its workers and their families into the poorhouse. When Champion outlined the modifications necessary . . . it said there would be a loss of 800 to 1000 jobs. Of course, Tennessee's "unreasonable" demands were to blame. . . .
>
> That Champion was willing, indeed willful, in defiling the river and delaying imposition of any requirement to clean it up was blatantly obvious, as were the reasons of profit that lay behind its intractability. There was no doubt that its corporate conscience was as putrefied as the river it fouled. But it was not clear, not certain, until now that Champion was lying to its own people and pitting state against state with those lies.
>
> Jim Martin owes an apology to Gov. Ned McWherter and to every woman-Jill and man-Jack who lives on the watersheds of the Pigeon or French Broad rivers below. Bow deep, Gov. Jim, you were sucked in by falsehood piled on falsehood. Champion International has showed itself to be a corporation comprised of equal parts audacity and mendacity. . . . The EPA must schedule its own tests to enforce the permit. Champion will not, perhaps can not. It does not exhibit any sense of truth or consequences, save in the area of profit.[53]

It soon became clear that members of PRAG and the DPRC were dissatisfied with the permit. "If we had the money, we would file for an evidentiary hearing," said Bob Seay. Such a hearing could have resulted in some changes desired by the DPRC. Gay Webb noted that, indeed, the river would be cleaner, but still not fishable, swimmable, or potable. "After 81 years, Cocke County deserves better than this," he said.[54]

People may have been tired of the controversy, but it soon became clear that it just would not go away. On Thursday, August 31, Dick

Mullinix and Oliver Blackwell were slated to discuss the Pigeon River issue on ABC's *Good Morning America* program. Host Spencer Christian, in Hendersonville, N.C., for the annual Apple Festival, was to interview the two men for over six minutes. It did not turn out that way: there was hardly time to present the problem before they were cut off. But the publicity given the program in the Tennessee and North Carolina press helped keep the controversy before the public.[55]

Then funds to push for an evidentiary hearing became available from the Legal Environmental Assistance Foundation (LEAF). The fight was not over.

CHAPTER 12

The Permit,
the Evidentiary Hearing,
and the Lawsuit

The bombast of Champion and its proponents versus the attacks of the DPRC, PRAG, and their supporters is a story in itself. Add to this conflict the legal maneuvering involving state and federal agencies and not much space is left for subplots. Yet, incidental matters add flesh to the story along the way.

One somewhat amusing aspect of the history of papermaker pollution is the strange psychology that prompts the public relations department of a pulp and paper company to emphasize clean water. In 1954 Champion published a booklet, with state-of-the-art color printing, that extolled the company's achievements. Page 34 consists of a beautiful scene: a fisherman hip-deep in cool, smooth water, shaded by beautiful trees, is casting his line. "Pure water is of prime importance in papermaking," reads the caption. "This peaceful scene is from one of the tributaries of the Pigeon River, on which the Carolina Division is located." No mention is made of the company's use of the Pigeon River as an industrial sewer, thus destroying sixty miles of what could have been one of the finest fishing streams in all southern Appalachia.[1]

The impulse continues. In 1989 the company chose to help the U.S. Olympics by subsidizing the Canoe and Kayak Team. The specific sum to be contributed over a four-year period is not known, but is "less than $1 million for any given year." Bob Seay invited team representatives to come to the Pigeon River and "brownwater" it. Judy Webb's students from Bridgeport Elementary School sent letters to team members. Team officials, who recognized the duplicity involved in accepting the money, explained that they had argued over the contribution, but Champion was their only source of funds. Their coach asked that his salary be cut rather than come from Champion money. When the U.S. Kayak Team

The Carolina Power and Light (CP&L) powerhouse. Below the powerhouse, raft-ing, canoeing, and kayaking take place when water is released from the dam. Cour-tesy Carolina Power and Light Company.

won a gold medal in the 1992 games, Champion announced the team's achievement in a full-page advertisement.[2]

Amidst all the furor, Champion showed interest in Buncombe County scientist J. Philip Neal's process for cleaning water. The company ex-tended the hand of cooperation and granted forty-three thousand dol-lars to support Professor Neal's work.[3]

Background of Evidentiary Hearing

When North Carolina authorities granted Champion a permit on July 13, 1988, they hardly expected legal complications that would put off final permission until September 25, 1989, fourteen months later. That was the date EPA finally granted the National Pollution Discharge Elimination System (NPDES) permit. Suffice to say that the tenacity of the DPRC, PRAG, and LEAF had a lot to do with the delay. Now these groups re-quested an evidentiary hearing, and Champion followed suit. An evidentiary hearing has the same rules of evidence that apply to other judicial cases: the testimony of experts is considered, and the case is presided over by a judge. The environmental groups hoped that their concerns over Champion's testing of its own pollutants and the phase-in period could be heard impartially by a judge. In December 1989, the regional administrator of EPA "partially granted and partially denied these requests." Some of the arguments were accepted for consideration, and some were rejected. Not until April 15–16, 1991, was the hearing held in Atlanta. Administrative Law Judge Thomas B. Yost did not hand down his decision until February 12, 1992.[4]

The history of how the evidentiary hearing came about is involved. Remember that under the Clean Water Act, Champion could operate legally until such time as a new permit was fully accepted. That is why the river continued to flow dark, smelly, foamy, and polluted year after year while officials of the state of Tennessee, EPA, and the DPRC and PRAG, the Izaak Walton League, and Greenpeace fussed, fumed, and complained and took legal action. Champion knew in July 1988 that it could continue to operate until such time as the new permit was accepted by all parties. Because the permit was restrictive and, in some facets, even impossible to adhere to—according to Champion, anyway—the company lost nothing by waiting, except for the peace of mind of its Canton employees. Champion was understandably reluctant to embark upon a two-hundred-million-dollar modernization program (it should be noted that Champion has offered various figures that it says the modernization will cost—in 1993 a vice-president said the company had spent $330 million) until the company knew the terms of the permit. Opponents replied that a six-billion-dollar company could operate under any permit: it had the resources to clean up the Pigeon to the very letter of any permit, if it was forced to do so.

DPRC members knew that it would cost money—perhaps $50,000—to file a request for an evidentiary hearing. They did not have such resources. Then LEAF came to the DPRC's and PRAG's aid. Its representative was Gary Davis, a taciturn Knoxville lawyer who had been involved in the Pigeon River controversy before. On October 25, 1989, Davis, on behalf of the DPRC, filed the necessary request. The solicitation was based upon three issues: 1) Champion's questionable ability to honor the color compliance as prescribed in the permit; 2) the question of the company's ability to honor the BOD and dissolved oxygen provisions of the permit; and 3) the validity of the suspended solids provisions.[5]

Champion had indicated that if the DPRC filed a request for an evidentiary hearing, then it would file a similar demand. The company prepared for such an eventuality, even beating the DPRC by filing one day earlier. Champion cited the dioxin control and testing provisions as being impossible to meet. In a press conference, Richard DiForio Jr., vice-president of Champion's environmental division, blasted the DPRC move as an outrage and said all plans for design and construction of a new mill at Canton were once again on hold. He also used this occasion to reply to charges that Champion knew all along that it would be dismissing employees with the construction of the new facilities—a possibility that had workers nervous. DiForio insisted that the company had continually informed employees that the improvements would result in a reduction in the work force, but "the level of reduction of employment wouldn't have been close to the reductions required to meet this permit and could have easily been reached through retirement."[6]

Beyond Champion's power to control it was the dioxin scare, which was still making headlines. Greenpeace, having obtained a copy of a joint report by EPA and the paper industry, reported to the press that dioxin was found in bleached pulp and that it also contaminates paper products used by humans. Champion countered by announcing that by switching from oily defoamers used to reduce suds in the pulping process, it had reduced dioxin content of its paper by 90 percent. Oliver Blackwell said the oxygen delignification process planned for the Canton mill would further reduce the dangers of dioxins. These encouraging press releases did little to assuage fears of the populace, especially the fears of residents of eastern Tennessee.[7]

Time dragged on; 1989 blended into 1990. Certainly Haywood County residents were not happy when they learned that both the DPRC and Champion had filed requests for an evidentiary hearing. If EPA granted their demand then legality of the permit would be postponed still longer. Things would remain undecided, unresolved, up in the air. Hadn't the controversy gone on too long already? "Enough is enough," they protested.

In mid-November EPA's John Marler, chief of the agency's Region IV Facilities Performance Branch, announced that EPA would grant the hearing. There were, he said, enough arguments in both requests to warrant such a move. No date was set. First, EPA's judicial officer had to appoint an administrative law judge, who would in all likelihood set the time and date. People waited. Champion asked for an additional thirty days to prepare for the hearing even though a judge was not appointed until February; in fact, EPA did not send the necessary papers to Washington, D.C., headquarters until the first of the year. The new year had arrived, and still Champion functioned as usual, without a permit. Nor was there an end in sight: whatever the evidentiary judge decided, his decision could be appealed to the EPA administrator in Washington.

Champion Announces a Modernization Program

And then something remarkable and unexpected happened. Champion's Richard DiForio and President L. C. Heist held a press conference at Asheville on March 27, 1990. They formally announced Champion's plans to spend 250 million dollars over a three-year period, beginning immediately, on modernization of the old mill. The company said it would comply with Tennessee's water quality standard within three years, regardless of the outcome of the evidentiary hearing. "This was a far cry," noted *Plain Talk*, "from the company's angry pronouncement almost fourteen months ago that the plant might have to close and would, nevertheless, lose half of its workforce because of Tennessee's interference in enforcing its environmental laws."[8]

Besides the 250-million-dollar commitment, Heist said that the mill would "meet or exceed" all of Tennessee water quality standards, reduce water usage by 35 percent, "thereby limiting the impact of the mill on the river," reduce chlorine by using chlorine dioxide and oxygen delignification, virtually eliminating toxic dioxins, and improve air quality and greatly reduce odor. Of more interest to North Carolinians was his statement that the company had decided to keep four of its six paper machines operational, thus requiring the reduction of only about three hundred out of eighteen hundred jobs; he hoped this reduction could be brought about through attrition and retirement over a three-year period. It was less of a jolt than the company threat of a few months before of a thousand jobs lost. Moreover, about a thousand construction workers would be working at the plant during the next three years, further softening any depression in the local economy. Operations would remain nearly the same although pulp production would be reduced from fourteen to twelve tons per day. Finally, noting that the federal Wastewater Discharge Permit procedure would soon begin again, if improved technology existed by then, then Champion would implement it, Heist said.[9]

Canton employees were elated. They began buying again. Workers ran to the telephones to notify their spouses that their jobs were no longer in jeopardy. "It shows Tennessee we are committed to cleaning up the river and reducing emissions," one worker said. And it was probably just a coincidence, but the front page of the *Mountaineer* also carried a story about negotiations for a lease to open a Wal Mart store between Waynesville and Clyde. (Today the store, along with a Food Lion grocery store and smaller retailers, is open for business.)

Nearly sixty miles north, across the state line in Newport, the news made big headlines. It transpired that Champion officials, including

President Heist, had met with Governor McWherter, who expressed gratification for the modernization program but said he would follow a wait-and-see policy. Champion representatives also briefed Representative Jimmy Quillen. He too said it was a wait-and-see approach to the modernization project, but expressed confidence that Champion would push through its program.[10]

Gay Webb, one of the DPRC's most energetic members, expressed disbelief. He said the announcement was "just more of the same." Back in 1912 the company had also said it was going to clean up the Pigeon. "I don't think they . . . mean it now any more than they did then," he said. And caution was certainly the message expressed by the *Knoxville News-Sentinel.* "It will require more than promises . . . to convince Tennesseans that the giant paper manufacturing company really plans to clean up the Pigeon River," the column began. "Folks in this state, from Gov. Ned McWherter to residents of Cocke County, have their doubts about Champion's intentions. . . . The skepticism will remain until the river flows clear again."[11]

Champion remained the wild card. If the company had planned the modernization since 1985, when it first informed employees of probable layoffs as a result of the forthcoming improvements, why had the company so desperately fought the stricter standards? If technology existed that would perceptibly clean up the smokestack emissions and the water effluents, which was exactly what Champion had denied, then why the insistence that the technology did not exist? If the modernization would have cut just three hundred jobs, then why the threats of a 50 percent reduction in the work force—up to a thousand jobs—or even closure of the mill?

Outsiders can only speculate, but the publicity, the continuing animosity between Champion and North Carolina versus Tennessee, Cocke County, and the various environmental groups may have been responsible for the turnaround in the thinking of those in corporate offices in Stamford, Connecticut. At some point they realized that the environmentalists were not going to go away. Little Cocke County now had the sovereign state of Tennessee backing it, at least for the moment. Tennessee's representatives, senators, and governor were all taking sides against the papermaker. Possibly, Champion's executives admitted, for the first time, that the Pigeon River was a special case, and that ultimately they must clean it up or close a very profitable mill. Indeed, somewhere down the road, the political climate will change. A reinforced EPA will have more power. When an issue becomes so important to the public that politicians are afraid to resist, even though they may have been compromised in the past, then that corporation had better reappraise its position.

Another possibility involves the company's performance over the past ten or fifteen years. "Most dogs aren't as mangy as $5.3 billion (sales) Champion International Corporation," wrote Thomas Jaffe, editor of the "Streetwalker" column in *Forbes*. In the early 1970s Champion stock traded in the high thirties, but under Andrew Sigler's leadership, it has hit that high only once, just prior to the 1987 stock market crash; before and after, it has ranged from the high teens to the mid-thirties. "And what of its fundamentals?" Jaffe asked. "According to analyst Gary Palermo of Oppenheimer & Co., they stink." Nevertheless, Jaffe noted that three of Wall Street's heaviest rollers, Warren Buffett, John Templeton, and Laurence Tisch, had purchased lots of Champion stock. The threat of a takeover always seemed to loom, but as of this writing nothing had materialized.[12]

Details of the Canton
Modernization Project (CMP)

Whether the plant modernization cost Champion $200 million, $300 million, $330 million (their most recent estimate), or a much smaller sum, padded by accountants' legerdemain for tax purposes, there is no question about the immensity of the project. A ground-breaking ceremony was held August 30, 1990, at the construction site. Over the more than three and a half years in which the project was underway, more than a thousand artisans would be employed at one time or another. It was expected that $52 million would be spent on wages and purchased goods just in Haywood County and environs.[13]

Updating a massive pulp and paper mill while maintaining full production involves intricate, precise planning. Specialized (and therefore highly paid) engineers are essential. Employees must be retrained for new technologies so intricate that experts are hired to teach them, using special texts. Engineers run into "one time only" problems at the site that only they, using their expertise and ingenuity, can solve.

The equipment budget alone at Champion came to more than $66 million. "The complexity of purchasing equipment for the project from steel tanks and tile chests to speed switches and soap skimmers, is mind-boggling," stated the *Canton Modernization Project Update*. "Purchasing staff must also handle rental of special equipment necessary for outages and particular jobs. When quality or operational problems arise, purchasing staff must work with vendors to reach a resolution."[14]

Two companies did most of the job. The prime contractor for the conversion was BE&K Construction Company of Birmingham, Alabama. It had as many as 1,100 workers on hand at a given time, and, according to Champion announcements, the company did an excellent job, completing most of its assignments on schedule; its safety record was excellent.

Engineering was contracted to CRS Sirrine of Greenville, South Carolina. The company drew up more than 7,914 detailed engineering drawings for the project and had as many as 130 full-time engineers working at Canton at one time. By May of 1992, with 95 percent of its work accomplished, the company had invested 475,000 work hours in the project, with about 53,000 hours left. Jim Machen, a senior vice president, described it as "one of Sirrine's most complicated jobs ever. I've been in business 26 years, and Sirrine has engineered billions of dollars in projects," he said, "[but] this is one of the most complex jobs I have ever seen in my career—and we have done a lot of rebuilds."[5]

No question about it, the Canton modernization project was an enormous undertaking. Entire buildings, tanks, pipelines, electrical conduits, and other facilities connected with the pulp and papermaking process had to be demolished, new foundations laid, and new facilities erected. Hardly a facet of mill operations was exempt from major changes. A central, totally computerized control system was built. Except for semiannual pine mill and hardwood outages and cold mill outages that are regularly scheduled for every two or three years, mill operations continued unabated.

Champion tried to advertise the project, hoping that progress reports on the modernization would help improve its poor public image. The *Canton Modernization Project Update,* released from time to time, usually consisted of two sheets of information highlighting progress of the engineering and construction phases. A separate paragraph carried news of the enviable safety record, and occasionally the bulletin devoted a paragraph or two to the environmental benefits resulting from the modernization. BE&K's hiring of personnel from western North Carolina was emphasized, as was the company's own public relations program, consisting of such meritorious deeds as improving Clyde Elementary School's soccer facilities and constructing a new water system for the Bethel school. An occasional town meeting was held at the Canton town hall to update citizens on CMP progress. A CMP speakers' bureau was organized. It would furnish a guest speaker to any school, business, civic organization, or environmental group that requested it. About halfway through the project, Champion made available a fifteen-minute videocassette on "Champion and the Pigeon River" and a seven-minute one of "CMP Video Highlights." The narrator of the Pigeon River videocassette virtually admitted that Champion had been a poor neighbor, emphasizing that a new era had arrived, and, he implied, let us forget the past and look to the future.[16]

The most important change being made was the adjustment of the chlorine bleaching process to the oxygen delignification system. "Its benefits," according to the *Update*, "include reduced use of bleaching chemicals, improved pulp cleanliness, and reduced effluents from the bleach plant." It is described as "an additional process" after the initial bleaching, separating still more of the lignin from the cellulose fibers using pure oxygen, caustic, and steam. "While a dark-colored effluent is produced, it does not contain chlorine compounds and can be reused in pulp washing [or] evaporated and burned in the recovery boiler. Re-using this effluent will reduce the colored effluent treated by the Waste Treatment plant and will contribute toward the Canton mill's compliance with future color standards specified in the EPA wastewater discharge permit." Note that it does not entirely dispense with the color.[17]

Much of the work involved construction of the No. 2 fiberline building with the necessary technology; it would process pine fibers. The No. 1 line, which handles hardwoods, also underwent the necessary changes for the oxygen delignification process. Included in the plans were a large new cooling tower and three smaller ones for use with the No. 11 and 12 paper

Part of Champion's upgrade, the cooling tower—along with other improvements—reduces use of Pigeon River water from 45 mgd (million gallons a day) to 29 mgd. Courtesy Champion International Corporation and CRS Sirrine, Inc.

The new No. 2 fiberline. l. to r.: oxygen reactor; chlorine dioxide tower; extraction vessel. According to Champion officials, this new process will virtually eliminate toxicity from the effluent. Courtesy Champion International Corporation and CRS Sirrine, Inc.

machines. These, along with a vacuum pump system on the No. 12 machine, were designed to conserve water: Champion hopes to achieve a reduction from the forty-five million gallons per day it has been using to about twenty-nine million gallons, or a reduction of about one-third. A noncondensible gas system (NCG) has been erected; it is designed to eliminate much of the odor that enters the atmosphere, while a condensate stripper is supposed to reduce the odor that accompanies effluent dumped into the Pigeon River. A turpentine recovery system for both pine and hardwoods has been installed. The turpentine will be sold as a byproduct of the pulp process. Boilers were overhauled. A training scheduled was set up for employees who would operate the new equipment.

In a special edition of *Update* in March 1993, the company listed its environmental accomplishments. It boasted, as of that date, a 35 percent reduction in water usage, "at least" a 50 percent reduction in the amount of wood color discharged into the Pigeon River, diminished chances for dioxin formation through the elimination of molecular chlorine as a bleaching agent, a reduction in the unpleasant odor of the Pigeon River, and improved air quality.

Opposition Continues

All the while, occasional news items, besides information about the modernization, appeared that kept the Pigeon River controversy prominent in the regional psyche. In July 1990, Dick Mullinix, who just would not quit, whose letters to the editor never ceased in spite of threats upon his life and his wife's life, who cooperated and advised and acted as a without-fee consultant to anyone fighting Champion, was one of the recipients of the annual Dr. Marketta Laurila Free Speech Awards. They are sponsored by the American Civil Liberties Union, the Clean Water Fund, the National Organization for Women, the Asheville-Buncombe Community Relations Council, the Southern Appalachian Lesbian and Gay Alliance, and Citizens for a Responsible Government. The annual affair at Asheville, which includes a banquet, draws considerable publicity.[18]

Indeed, Dick Mullinix was a worthy recipient. It was one thing to fight the battle against Champion from the safety of residing in the state of Tennessee. But to combat Champion bluntly, fearlessly, openly, and publicly in Haywood County took courage. It was more than the threatening phone calls. It was being aware of whispers, stares, and glares, the icy attitude of citizenry he and Lucie came in contact with on the streets, at the Post Office, in the stores. Even after Champion announced its multimillion-dollar modernization, he has continued his criticism. Specifically, he sees opportunities for deception in the monitoring process. As stipulated in the permit, monitoring is to be done at the pipe according to a mathematical formula: so much color at the pipe means so much color left by the time the water reaches the state line. In truth, authorities say that Champion is whistling in the dark when it claims it can achieve the 50 color units at the state line, even with modernization. Dick, and some authorities, insist that more will need to be done. Yet, he is sincere when he says that he does not want to see the mill close or workers laid off. This gadfly, who spent his career in the paper business, is absolutely convinced that Champion can achieve a clean river with a busy, prosperous mill at Canton—if only it wants to. "What do I do?—walk away in shame or stay here and fight?" he asked a reporter. "Maybe I could run, but so far I haven't been able to bring myself to do that. The Pigeon River must be cleaned up." It is a sign of changing values that the *Raleigh News and Observer* named Mullinix the "Tar Heel of the Week" on September 16, 1990.

It was because of his determination, his insistence never to let the matter lie fallow, that Mullinix became the symbol of opposition to the Champion mill. "At times, when we would be really down and with our backs to the wall, Dick would come and speak to our group," relates Bob Seay. "We have grown to respect Mr. Mullinix as our mentor. He's a damn good motivator. He has been our spiritual leader, so to speak. We all get down in the doldrums, but somehow, just to hear his voice or to see him and his wife in person motivates us and puts us back on track."[19]

While participants waited for the slow wheels of bureaucracy to bring about the evidentiary hearing—the dates for the hearing were finally announced in October 1990—the controversy went from hot to simmering to lukewarm. Just when it was about to leave people's minds, however, something new came up. In August Senator Al Gore visited East Tennessee. He stood along the banks of the polluted Pigeon and pledged to support the DPRC in the forthcoming hearing. It would be only the second such evidentiary hearing ever held by the EPA. In his remarks, the senator made a cogent point—that the concept that a clean environment cuts out jobs is wrong. "If you look around the world," he said, "the places where the environment is degraded, those are the very places where the economy is in the worst shape." He noted the deteriorating economic states of eastern Europe, where the environment had suffered terribly from communist apathy.[20]

Gay Webb informed the senator that the monthly average color prescribed in the permit, and the place where the water would be tested, allowed virtually a thirty-five-mile-long mixing zone and a lake (Waterville Lake) to be used as Champion's settling pond. "We've had hearing after hearing on this issue," said Webb, "[and] then some bureaucrat ends up writing a permit the way he wants it."

"You've got the best side of the argument," the senator replied, adding that Tennessee's congressional delegation had worked hard in pressuring EPA to hold the hearing.[21]

The Evidentiary Hearing

The hearing did not take place until April 15–16, 1991. EPA was represented by two lawyers, the DPRC by Gary Davis, North Carolina by two lawyers, Tennessee by one, and Champion International Corporation by two. Mullinix attended, but as an observer. He was incensed that Judge Thomas Yost entered the room casually carrying an aluminum baseball bat. Administrative law judges do not wear robes; this thirty-year-old judge expressed his freedom by sporting a salmon pink tie. At times he placed his feet over the bench railing; once he tossed a government file to a clerk: it missed and spewed papers all over the floor. He was abusively sarcastic to the attorneys. He announced procedural rules with an unprofessional flippancy. Perhaps he had watched too many sitcom judges.[22]

When Judge Yost handed down his decision ten months later, on February 12, 1992, it was clear that all the issues brought up both by the DPRC and by Champion, following brief discussion in the decision, were either rejected by the judge, were dismissed, or had already been settled by being withdrawn by one of the parties. Of greatest importance, Judge Yost gave his approval to the permit. For the first time since 1981, Champion International was operating legally within the parameters of a permit.[23]

On page twenty-two of the twenty-six-page decision, Judge Yost dealt with what he termed "the meat of the regulation and the one to which all parties directed their attention," namely, color and the company's methods of treating the effluent. "The record is clear," he wrote, that "the mill evaluated, in depth, the following treatment alternatives: Aerobic lagoons, artificial wetlands, ultrafiltration, power-activated carbon (hereinafter 'PACT'), and granular-activated carbon ('GAC')." EPA and North Carolina, having analyzed these methods for efficiency, reliability, space requirements, energy/resource requirements, environmental impacts, and cost, had rejected all of them. The first two were not feasible, according to EPA and North Carolina, due to space limitations at Canton; the others, it was claimed, created more problems than they solved. (The latter two cleanup procedures involved dissolved solids, air emissions, and landfill use, all of which were apparently considered worse than using the Pigeon as an industrial sewer.)

The judge distrusted the model set up by EPA by which to monitor Champion, but "given the unique physical factors involved, no realistic alternative appears to exist," he wrote. And he added that the permit contained a re-opener clause—it could be re-examined and changed—should the mill be unable to meet the color limits.[24]

Although DPRC and PRAG members were unhappy with the judge's decision—after observing his behavior at the hearing and his general attitude, which struck them as pro-Champion, they were convinced all along that his decision would be in favor of the permit—they could take some solace in the re-opener clause. Champion would hear from them again—in court.

Mullinix Shatters His Jaw

It was during the long wait between the hearing and the decision that Dick Mullinix finally had his physical brush with pro-Champion extremists. It took place on a bright, spring Sunday at noon of May 12, 1991.

Whether his attackers were the same ones responsible for threatening telephone calls he will never know.

Dick, whose wife was in Florida, was driving their Volkswagen home after shopping. Instead of turning up Panther Creek Road toward their home when he came to the Fines Creek exit, he drove down onto the bridge over the polluted Pigeon. As he leaned over the railing looking at the dirty, foamy water, he heard a pickup truck come onto the bridge and stop. As he turned around, he saw three men get out of the old truck. Obviously they were bent on mischief. The truck was parked so close to the Volkswagen that it was impossible for Dick to enter it from the driver's side.

They did converse with Mullinix—saying things like "So you're the sonofabitch who's caused all the trouble with Champion"—but Dick does not recall the conversation clearly. He knew he was in trouble. Three burly men were taking on one eighty-year-old man. So he opened the VW on the passenger side and somehow got across the gear shift and emergency brake and into the driver's seat. He started the car and drove to the end of the bridge and turned around, for his residence was in the opposite direction; the truck was almost exactly in the middle of the bridge. Obviously, they intended to block his passage. Somehow he squeezed the old car past the truck and the jeering men, drove to Panther Creek Road, and started up it toward his house. At one point, shortly after entering the road, he glanced in the rearview mirror to see if he was being followed.

Dick glanced too long. He was at the curve in the road too soon, going too fast. The car went straight instead of turning, and, as Dick describes it, the car found the one ten-foot-wide space in the meadow where the land is not smooth. The little car plunged into a spring and turned over. Dick somehow crawled through the window; neighbors returning from church picked him up and took him to the hospital. He had some chest lacerations, but the real damage was to his lower jaw. It was shattered—terribly shattered. Piecing together a lower jaw is one of the most difficult tasks in bone surgery. Four hours on the operating table took care of just part of the problem. By the summer of 1993, Dick Mullinix had undergone seven major operations on his jaw with world-renowned surgeons in attendance. That jaw has been hooked up and suspended by a device not unlike the chin strap on a football helmet; he has had to sip food through a straw. Fortunately, the last operation—it took seven hours—appears to have succeeded.

But Dick Mullinix's spirit is undamaged. When he is able, he confers with Bob Seay, Nelson Ross, Gay Webb, and Jim Harrison. He remains willing and able to spend hours with journalists and television producers explaining the Pigeon's problems, convincing them that Champion can, and therefore should, clean up the river.[25]

The Class-Action Lawsuit

In January 1991 a bombshell hit the region—a lawsuit against Champion was announced; the plaintiffs were asking for five billion dollars. Lawsuits were nothing new to the company; indeed, a Cocke County woman had recently tried to sue Champion for six million dollars, claiming that the company had damaged her health, but the action had been thrown out. But this lawsuit was different—different in the monetary damages demanded, different because it was a class-action suit, and different because of the details of the complaint. Dioxin was frightening people to the point that they were taking action.

The background to this litigation consisted of two other lawsuits taking place in Mississippi. There, property owners along the Leaf River, below Georgia-Pacific's pulp and paper mill, had sued the company for the toxins, including dioxin, in their water. They had won their suits. Among the lawyers taking note was Knoxville attorney Gordon Ball, who had grown up along the polluted banks of the Pigeon at Hartford. Upon examining the Mississippi cases and the judge's decisions, Ball concluded that residents along the Pigeon River, and even around Douglas Lake, had a far stronger case against Champion than the Leaf River residents had against Georgia-Pacific.

Initially, Gordon Ball suggested a contingency fee of 50 percent, defending the stiff fee on the costs of such litigation. These costs included hundreds of thousands of dollars for expert witnesses, depositions, and the services of several high-priced lawyers. "Champion," he said in a letter to *Plain Talk* defending his fee, "is a modern day Goliath that would not be easily overcome." He reminded Cock County residents that since 1986 he had represented the DPRC for nothing, although total costs for his services had run to twenty thousand dollars.[26]

On January 4, 1991, Ball made his move. J. A. and Joan Shults of Newport filed action on behalf of the property owners along the Pigeon River, the French Broad, and Douglas Lake in Cocke, Sevier, and Jefferson Counties, thus making it a class-action suit. Plaintiffs asked for five billion dollars in damages, a sum based upon Champion's earnings through the years and the damage done to Pigeon River residents. Six law firms, led by Ball's, represented the plaintiffs. In the complaint it was alleged that the mill, by polluting the Pigeon, had diminished property values, disrupted lives, and threatened the inhabitants with cancer. The brief did not pull punches. "Such conduct [by Champion] is so outrageous in character and so extreme in degree as to go beyond all possible bounds of decency and must be regarded as atrocious and utterly intolerable in a civilized society," it read in part.[27]

J. A. Shults and his wife, Joan, were the lead plaintiffs. Shults is a retired carpenter who returned to his roots in 1977, purchasing Brown's Island, a ten-acre piece of land on the Pigeon River that his grandfather had owned. In testimony, he claimed that he had believed Champion's promises to clean up the river—and he did not know then of dioxin—but Champion's failure to abide by its promises and the discovery of dioxin had destroyed all his plans and reduced the value of his property.[28] Seven plaintiffs were chosen to represent the twenty-six hundred residents along the Pigeon or the shores of Douglas Lake mentioned in the class-action suit.[29]

Preparations dragged. Again and again Champion requested delays. During this time, intense sparring occurred between the opposing attorneys and the judge. Not until September 14, 1992—twenty-one months after Ball had filed the case—did the trial get underway at the United States District Court for the Eastern District of Tennessee at Greeneville. This agricultural town of fourteen thousand about sixty miles northeast of Knoxville, seemed an unusual site for a Federal District Court. The court is located in Greeneville because its most honored citizen, President Andrew Johnson—whose home, tailor shop, and grave are in the custody of the National Park Service in Greeneville—saw to it that the court was located there. To reach Greeneville from Newport, one drives northeast twenty-six miles on State Highway 321 through attractive, rolling farm country.

The courthouse is an imposing building in a downtown that has changed little since the 1930s. The courtroom used for this trial was small, paneled, with quality government-issue furniture, and the arrangement of the room was identical to thousands of courtrooms. Behind the litigants and others directly involved sat the spectators in the four rows of seats assigned them. Mullinix, Bob Seay, Gay Webb, and other DPRC supporters tended to sit on the right side of the room; a few Champion supporters sat consistently on the left.[30]

Here in the second week of September 1992, the attorneys, jurors, judge, and spectators gathered. The press was here too—most especially reporters for the Greeneville, Knoxville, Asheville, Newport, Waynesville, and Canton newspapers. Nationwide, environmentalists and paper industry officials kept up with the proceedings. If the plaintiffs won, the results could be devastating to the paper industry. Many of its mills throughout the United States would be subjected to similar suits; Champion alone has fourteen facilities. The compensation could be so large that thousands would become participants in similar litigation.

John Deakle, a Mississippi lawyer who had won the lawsuits in Mississippi, described this as "big-time litigation. This is not for the faint-hearted." He said the Mississippi lawsuits had cost $1 million, but he had won $4.3 million for his clients. Before the Tennessee trial got underway, he told the press that he would not be surprised "by a $100 million verdict." Gordon Ball and his associates had invested between one-third and a half million dollars in the case, and Champion, by most guesses, had spent much more than that—$750,000 to $1 million.[31]

Federal Judge Thomas G. Hull presided. He was an affable, unemotional moderator who conducted the proceedings in a low key, inserting a bit of levity when things got tense; yet, his professionalism was always apparent. He imposed a gag rule on the attorneys, not allowing the press to question them when court took a recess or at any other time. He could get feisty if necessary. "You have all acted like a bunch of babies," he taunted both sets of attorneys when tempers were flaring toward the end of the five-week ordeal.[32]

The lawyers were no country hicks. For the plaintiffs Gordon Ball had brought together six successful counselors. The one who led the proceedings was Don Barrett of Lexington, Mississippi, who had been involved in "toxic tort" cases against Georgia Pacific. Three lawyers, Thomas Jessee, Gary E. Brewer, and Herbert S. Moncier, were from East Tennessee; Wade Hoyt II was from Rome, Georgia; and one, Paul Merrill, was an environmental lawyer from Tidewater, Oregon. Champion's legal defense included Louis Woolf of Knoxville, a quintessential "Philadelphia lawyer" if ever there was one, conservatively dressed in a black suit. He wore little horn-rimmed half-glasses, which he was constantly removing and putting on. He was joined by W. Kyle Carpenter, also of Knoxville. Three New York attorneys with the prestigious law firm of Skadden, Arps, Slate, Meagher and Flom added their expertise to Champion's battery of lawyers. Clerks and secretaries were also present. Both sides had rented office space nearby; at one time, in fact, they had inadvertently rented space in the same building. From the start of the trial, it was clear that no love was lost between the lawyers on either side. Perhaps it was because the stakes were so high, or possibly because of the months of dickering that had transpired since the case had been filed on January 4, 1991—a year and nine months before the trial opened.[33]

On Monday morning, September 14, 1992, jury selection began.

Within three hours, from a panel of forty-seven jurors a jury of eight was selected, with two alternates. Seven of the eight jurors were women.[34]

Although the plaintiffs originally asked for $5 billion, through court negotiations that sum had been reduced to $2.9 million in compensatory damages on behalf of the seven representative plaintiffs and $365 million in punitive damages for the other plaintiffs—somewhere between 2,200 and 2,600 landowners along the Pigeon River and Douglas Lake.[35]

One did not have to watch the proceedings for long to understand why such a court case is so expensive. A lone researcher paying his or her own expenses can only envy a money-is-no-object situation in which trained professionals pry into every facet of a case. For the plaintiffs, researchers came up with bibliographies of everything ever written about Champion's founders, about Reuben Robertson, about the mill town of Canton, about the entire eighty-four-year period in which the Pigeon had been polluted by the paper company. With the aid of the law, they obtained depositions, some in videocassette form, that were introduced at the trial. Champion executives, right up to and including CEO Andrew Sigler, thus appeared before the jurors; so did a Champion videocassette disputing news anchor Dan Rather's January 1990 comments about dioxin, Widowville, and the Pigeon River. Duplicates were made of thousands of documents, including the letter from Red Cavaney of the American Paper Institute to John Sununu, President Bush's chief of staff: "Thank you for granting time from your busy pre-Christmas schedule to meet. . . . I would also like to thank you for your receptiveness to our concerns about the creeping regulatory outreach that is jeopardizing President Bush's exemplary record as a regulatory reformer. . . ."[36]

Prior to the trial, both sides were required to file a final witness list with the court. Champion's list ran to thirty-seven; the plaintiffs' to fifty-eight and "Army officials to authenticate Red Water records." A number of Champion officials appeared on both lists. Neither side used all its witnesses, some of whom cost up to four thousand dollars for a few hours on the stand.[37]

Even before the trial was underway, the defendant (Champion) had won some significant rulings. Judge Hull threw out emotional stress claims in March. Because of the statute of limitations—which in this case was three years—damages, if any were granted, were restricted to the period from January 4, 1988, and the date of the case filing, January 4, 1991, and damage likely to be suffered in the future. Champion succeeded, to a large degree, in its bid to restrict the case to charges of trespass—not invasion by people but by chemicals—and nuisance claims that interfered unreasonably with property rights.[38]

In spite of these restrictions, problems involving dioxin, color, heavy metals, and personal injury and emotional stress were discussed during the five weeks of the trial. Champion downplayed all this, at the same time reminding the jurors of the massive changes it was making at its Canton plant, and inserting, again and again, sometimes with nuances, the mercenary aims Champion perceived in the suit: in Champion's view, the property owners were after a lot of easy money. Ignoring the reality that real estate values have risen just about everywhere over the last fifty years, the lawyers for the defendant insisted that property values, even along the polluted Pigeon and the shores of Douglas Lake, had continued to rise; ergo, the pollution had done no harm.

Although the trial lasted five weeks, the testimony was heard in just eighteen days. The whole trial boiled down to a few highly charged issues. Discussion was interrupted by conferences with the judge, by irritating questions of testimony that were allowed and disallowed, by the setting up of exhibits—245 of them in all—by recesses, lunches, and Columbus Day, by one of the jurors attending a funeral, by a professional meeting of judges that had nothing to do with the case, and by other mundane matters.

In his opening remarks for the plaintiffs, attorney Don Barrett was blunt and direct. "This whole case can be summed up in a few words—pollution for profit," he said. He repeated several times Champion's promises to clean up the river, promises that were never kept. He accused the company of corrupting the political process, of buying political favors, and of bullying EPA. Champion is "an arrogant power run amok," he lectured the jury. He said that as early as the 1930s, the plant was dumping up to ten tons a day of known poisons into the river; he accused the papermaker of dumping "red water"—liquid containing sixteen times more arsenic and forty-six times more lead than is safe—into the Pigeon. Then he mentioned the dioxins that were in the Pigeon.[39]

In his reply, attorney Louis Woolf hit the Champion argument right on the head. The environment was not the issue. The issue was whether or not property owners had suffered damage. Again and again, the three-year statute of limitations and the argument that only trespass and nuisance were involved were hammered into the heads of the jurors. Day after day of this litany had its effect.[40]

The first witness brought to the stand by the plaintiffs was well-known and widely respected Tennessee state historian Wilma Dykeman Stokely. Probably no one knows the history of East Tennessee and western North Carolina better than she. Her book *The French Broad* is a classic. While researching that book in 1954, she had interviewed Reuben B.

Robertson and asked him why the company did not clean up the river. She quoted his reply as follows: "We can't justify spending a great deal of money to our stockholders . . . [we] will clean it up when we have to."[41]

When Louis Woolf cross-examined Stokely the next day, he showed her jars of Pigeon River water, including one jar of water from near her home in Newport. The water was clear.

"Would you dare to drink from it?" asked Stokely. And Woolf said he would.[42]

The next day Woolf was met outside the courthouse by a group of eighth-graders from Newport. One of them offered him a drink of Pigeon River water from a bottle; the attorney refused. It was the best news photo taken during the trial.[43] On the second day, Dr. Douglas J. Hallett, president of Ecological International and an authority on dioxin, disputed the defendant's contention that low levels of dioxin are not dangerous. Dr. Hallett is an authority who clearly believed dioxin in any amount was hazardous. He would not eat fish from the Pigeon nor even vegetables irrigated with its waters. Dioxin was just one of three hundred chemicals being emitted by paper mills, he said, adding that Champion dumps out chloroform by the ton, and chloroform is a known carcinogen. Hallett, according to *Plain Talk*, was somewhat intimidated by Woolf.[44]

One of the high points of the trial was the testimony of Dr. Daniel Teitelbaum, one of the world's leading toxicologists. He had done his homework, having researched the Pigeon for about nine months. It was dangerous to live close by, he said, because chemicals "react upon each other in synergistic fashion," meaning that when mixed they become more dangerous than when they are alone. He said that the damage already done would take generations to disappear. Dioxin—2,3,7,8 TCDD—he said, was being discharged into the river "at close to 500 times the acceptable drinking water standard." He knew that in 1989 Champion was dumping about 5,000 pounds of organic chemicals into the Pigeon every day. (In later testimony, shown on videotape, Charles "Skeeter" Curtis of Champion admitted that in 1989, Champion released 31,000 pounds of chloroform, 15,000 pounds of phenol, 8,100 pounds of ammonia, and 7,600 pounds of acetone, "as well as seven other toxic chemicals" into the Pigeon). Teitelbaum also reminded jurors that the soil along the river was tainted with chemicals, as was the silt at the bottom of the stream bed and the floor of Douglas Lake.[45]

The defense consistently pooh-poohed the threats to health, insisting that tests showed incredibly small deposits of any dangerous chemicals in water, fish, and soil.[46]

Champion's attorney Louis Woolf being offered Pigeon River water by Cocke County eighth-grader Jason Martin. The bearded man in background is Dick Mullinix. September 19, 1992. Photo by Paul Efird. Courtesy Knoxville News-Sentinel.

The best known witness for the plaintiffs was seventy-one-year-old retired Admiral Elmo R. Zumwalt Jr., who had been chief of U.S. Naval Operations from 1970 to 1974. His testimony that some members of the Bush administration, led by John Sununu, had deliberately sought to downplay the dangers of dioxin came as no great surprise. Zumwalt's quarrel involved the use of Agent Orange, which contains dioxin, as a defoliant in Vietnam; it was, he felt, responsible for his son's death. These facts were not admissible, but on more relevant grounds, he accused Champion of unethical behavior when it tried to keep information about dioxin in the Pigeon and along its banks from the people downstream. He also stated that the evidence "is very strong that there is no known low threshold" for dioxin.[47]

Louis Woolf had on his side the reality that the study of dioxin lies on the frontier of science. This meant that he could draw up statements of worthy authorities disputing the alarming claims about dioxin made by others. When he asked the admiral why some scientists' opinions shouldn't take precedence over his, Zumwalt gave a quick answer: "Scientists in 1450 wrote that the world was flat." He also stated that many of the criticisms of his work were "politically-oriented." Woolf also raised questions about Zumwalt's integrity, reminding the jury that the admiral belonged on the boards of several corporations that were known polluters. Zumwalt's reply was that his own role had been to argue consistently in favor of safety and cleaning up the environment.[48]

Over the next few weeks, many of the details that have marked the Pigeon River controversy from the beginning came up. The condition of fish with sores and abnormalities was discussed; the fact that Champion had been fined twice—just twice—in the history of the Canton mill for pollution was brought out; scientists gave testimony that Champion knew of viable methods for cleaning the water (one method was even demonstrated in the courtroom), and the company holds the patent on one method; inhabitants along the Pigeon and Douglas Lake gave testimony about their sufferings from the pollution; and the plaintiffs discussed the alleged loss in property values. On Tuesday afternoon, September 29, the plaintiffs wrapped up their case with testimony from a mill official who admitted that dioxins might not be eliminated even after Champion had made all its improvements.[49]

Now it was the defendant's turn. Champion's lawyers continued to emphasize how the plant's massive modernization would cut the amount of water used, how the mill must monitor dioxin, limit chloroform, observe the health of fish, and restrict the amount of suspended solids discharged by the mill. They emphasized a bright future for Champion's Canton plant and for the Pigeon River. Vice-president Richard DiForio Jr. was the first Champion executive to testify in person. He insisted that the company complied with all rules and regulations and that he believed "the problem is aesthetic." In cross examination, plaintiffs' attorney Don Barrett quoted from a 1989 speech DiForio had made at a meeting of the company's managers: "We have found ways that are not excessively expensive [to remove color]. They do work. . . . Let's face it. We simply are not going to be allowed to discolor rivers." He admitted that he had made the statement, and added that he believed it.[50]

For each of the plaintiffs' experts who had testified about the dangers of dioxin and other chemicals, the defendant's lawyers brought forth authorities who disputed the claim; for the plaintiffs' witnesses who had testified to the harm done to property values by the pollution, the defendant brought forth witnesses who disputed the contention; for the plaintiffs' witness who had testified, as a practicing psychologist, that stress was placed upon residents because of the pollution, another expert was called to the stand who denied any emotional or stressful harm. By the time both sides had rested their case, the plaintiffs had called twenty-six witnesses and Champion just five. Some were colorful. A Douglas Lake restaurant owner who operated "Cowboy's Fish House" and testified for the plaintiffs called Louis Woolf a "blatant liar" for telling the jury that fish were served there that had been caught in Douglas Lake. Another witness, when asked how many bushels of corn he raised on his farm, interjected that he figured the amount in gallons, not bushels. Generally, however, very little humor characterized the trial.[51]

On Tuesday, October 6, Champion rested its case. On Wednesday, October 7, the day was spent with the judge and lawyers hammering out the judge's instructions to the jury. On Thursday and four hours into Friday, closing arguments were heard.

They were full of impassioned rhetoric. Louis Woolf said the charges against Champion were "Rumors, gossip, and hearsay." But what he said that may have had the greatest psychological effect was this: "They're not asking you to do something that will clean up the river. They're asking you for money . . . and I say they're not entitled."[52]

The plaintiffs, led by attorney Don Barrett, quoted from the story of David and Goliath in the Bible and somehow worked in the sinking of the German battleship *Bismarck* by a small British cruiser in 1940. Gordon Ball asked the jury to "render a verdict that will cause Champion and all the other Champions of this country to shudder in their boardrooms."[53]

The jurors were exhausted. Nevertheless Judge Hull took more than a half hour giving them instructions. Thirty-eight minutes after they convened to the jury room, they asked to be allowed to go home. In granting their request, the judge gave them a three-day rest because Monday was Columbus day. They met on the following Tuesday and Wednesday, and on Thursday they informed the judge they could not reach a unanimous verdict. Judge Hull asked them to return Friday morning at 9:00 A.M. to continue their deliberations. Still they could not reach a unanimous decision, and at 1:45 P.M. on Friday, October 16, Judge Hull dismissed the jurors and declared a mistrial. Six of eight jurors were for Champion; the two for the plaintiffs held out.[54]

When questioned about the jury's deliberations (the judge had authorized the released jurors to speak at will), Tina Manuel, the forewoman, explained that under the pretrial rulings the jury had to find that Champion's pollution had caused damage to the property of five of the seven representative plaintiffs, and, further, this had to be considered under a three-year statute of limitations. Six of the eight jurors had been unable to justify finding Champion guilty under the rulings.[55]

The six-billion-dollar corporation had won again.

Plain Talk expressed disappointment, suggesting that the pretrial restrictions had made it impossible for the jurors to understand the devastation the mill had done through the years to "our river and economy." And it added, "The larger question, which will never be answered in court, is why the federal and state governments allowed this to happen. There has been too much greed and too much politics for too long associated with the destruction of our beautiful river."[56]

A few weeks later, one of the jurors, Catherine Murray, who had held out for the plaintiffs, wrote an angry letter protesting the outcome. She felt that justice had not been done. She strengthened her position by mentioning one of the exhibits presented during the trial, a file that identified ninety-four hazardous substances flowing out of the pipe. "What kind of a name could you give this foamy, brown toxic soup?" she asked, and then answered, "I'm sorry but the name is Pigeon River and Douglas Lake." She was also incensed at the behavior of some of the jurors, especially one who brought a library book that she read throughout the discussions. So firm was this juror in favor of Champion, Murray wrote, she "should be investigated."[57]

Results of the Lawsuit

The story of the trial was not over yet. A settlement had to be made with the plaintiffs. On December 21 attorneys for both parties entered into an agreement. Champion was to put $6.5 million into an interest-bearing account. After the plaintiffs' attorneys had been paid, the remainder was to be used to set up a Pigeon River Endowment Fund through which Tennessee communities along the Pigeon River and Douglas Lake could finance environmental and educational projects. An already existing East Tennessee corporation would manage the fund. No compensatory or punitive damages were to be paid and no injunctive relief was imposed upon Champion.[58]

On January 19, 1993, the court conducted a fairness hearing after about forty objectors (out of twenty-six hundred landowners) protested the settlement; Judge Hull agreed and rejected the agreement. Among several reasons, the most significant was the clause that released Champion from liability from "all future claims, demands, rights of action and causes of action of every kind and character . . ." The judge also noted that by creating a charitable fund, the people involved in the class-action suit had received nothing; this was not fair to them. He suggested an agreement that would give the plaintiffs a percentage of the $6.5 million after attorneys' fees had been paid. An alternative was a retrial, which would take place in September 1993. He suggested that such a retrial would not be nearly as expensive or last as long because a video had been made of all the proceedings in the first trial, which would preclude calling in experts who charged high fees, and acceptable and unacceptable testimony had already been determined. Again, on February 3, 1993, an agreement was reached. But the settlement did not become final until March 12. Save for implementation, the great class-action suit of 1992 against Champion International Corporation was history. From $5 billion demanded to $6.5 million given, Champion's lawyers had done well.[59]

A layman studying this case might conclude that the plaintiffs had lost it before the first juror was selected. Pretrial negotiations restricted damage to a three-year period beginning in January 1989, and only trespass and nuisance charges were allowed to be considered. Other factors harmed their case: research on dioxin is so inconclusive that scientists of equal repute testified that it was or was not dangerous; Champion was in the process of upgrading its mill; and the defense pointed to the plaintiffs and insisted that they were just grubbing for easy money. The plaintiffs, to use East Tennessee jargon, had a tough row to hoe.

Certainly it is not for the historian to suggest how the plaintiffs could have structured their case more successfully. But that Champion has used the Pigeon River as an industrial sewer for nearly nine decades; that the stench, foam, color, and toxics in the stream have had an adverse effect upon the social and economic lives as well as the physical well-being of inhabitants along the river and, since its creation, in Douglas Lake; that recent and continuing scientific studies bring out convincing evidence of the dangers of toxic wastes, which may be carried as far as Knoxville's water supply—all of these factors, if highlighted at a trial, might have made a difference.

The Target Date: April 1994

The need for paper, which must be manufactured, continues; moreover, the institutions, including political entities such as North Carolina and Tennessee, that have been major players in the Pigeon River controversy, and, indeed, the conflict itself, continue on. Books must come to

Young environmentalists throwing Pigeon River water over Champion's fence and shouting, "Champion, you can't hide, We charge you with ecocide." This protest of March 28, 1993, is a reminder that protests will not stop until the Pigeon flows clear and clean. Photo by Paul Efird. Courtesy Knoxville News-Sentinel.

an end. Problems involving the river remain, but changes have taken place, and by the end of 1993, this book—except for an afterword submitted more than a year before publication—must be considered finished. It is not an altogether arbitrary decision.

The Canton Modernization Project is virtually completed, but Champion officials estimate that the retraining of personnel and the fine tuning of the new methodology and installations will take until April 1, 1994. In 1993 the company released progress reports that heralded major changes in emissions, both into the air and into the water, already taking place.

As the company entered 1993, its managers realized that the company was not free of legal matters involving the river. Even as it won the class-action suit, it was facing four separate cases: three for trespass and mental anguish, and one filed by children whose parents had died of cancer; their home was at Hartford. The company's color variance was up for review in North Carolina. EPA was watching developments.

Although in January 1993, the No. 2 fiberline went into operation, Pigeon River observers noticed little difference in the color of the water. In January 1993, a coalition of eight environmental groups, including the DPRC, PRAG, the North Carolina Alliance, the Clean Water

A kayaker demonstrates his skills below the Waterville powerhouse. The Pigeon River from the powerhouse to Hartford, Tennessee, is one of the best stretches of white water in eastern North America. So far it has been little used due to Champion's pollution. Courtesy Jim Harrison.

Fund of North Carolina, and the Foundation for Global Sustainability, vowed to fight Champion's continuing water variance. They held their press conference in downtown Canton. A very aggressive member of this coalition was the Foundation for Global Sustainability. Its dynamic young president, a veterinarian named Stephen Smith, made it very clear to officials at the Canton plant that he intended to see Champion clean up that river.[60]

To emphasize its determination, Smith's organization led a protest of four hundred to five hundred mostly young environmentalists at the Canton mill on Saturday, March 27, 1993. Cocke County school buses conveyed them to Canton, where the protesters set up a bucket brigade from the river to a fence protecting Champion's property; they tossed water over the fence. "Champion, you can't hide. We charge you with ecocide!" the protesters chanted.[61]

Dick Mullinix, ill because of his shattered jaw, conveyed his thoughts to the crowd through Bob Seay. He rebuked North Carolina for granting Champion a color variance at odds with the state's own regulations. This meant that the thirty-five miles of the Pigeon flowing from the mill to the Tennessee line, and including Waterville Lake, were being used to diffuse the color until it was at 50 color units where the river crossed into Tennessee. In spite of Champion's claims of a cleanup, "the river looks terrible, and it is not acceptable," said Mullinix.[62]

Champion and Canton officials, determined to prevent this protest from becoming a media event, remained unmoved behind their corporate walls.

The controversy continues. Champion has settled one of the lawsuits out of court; it has publicized improvements, although many Cocke County residents insist that they see little or no difference in the stream. On May 12 North Carolina once again granted the color variance for up to three years.[63]

"The Pigeon Flies Again" was the title of an article in the August 1993 issue of *Canoe* magazine. After presenting an excellent summation of the Pigeon's problems, including a description of the water discharge from the Waterville Dam, author John Manuel described his trip with Bob Benner, a forty-year veteran of Southern Appalachian waters. They embarked below the Walters (Waterville) power plant, crossed immediately into Tennessee, and continued to Denton, a tiny settlement about four and a half miles below Hartford.[64]

Benner had run the Pigeon a decade before, but remembered little about it "other than the awful color and smell of the water." Now he found it a different river. "Today," the author wrote, "there is some odor to remind us of the paper mill upstream, but it is not overwhelming." The water color they found "a little harder to gauge. In the calmer sections where you can see rocks below the surface, it looks like weak coffee. But for the most part, all we can see is blinding white spray." Best of all, Manuel's descriptions of their journey confirmed everything Cocke County inhabitants had said about the potential recreational uses of the Pigeon. It has twelve Class III and two Class IV rapids in one five-mile stretch, offering to whitewater enthusiasts thrills as well as the beauty of the Pigeon River gorge.[65]

It is turning into sort of an emperor has no clothes situation, with Champion the emperor and its supporters insisting that the Pigeon is markedly cleaner, almost devoid of color, odor, and foam—any fair person can see that, they say—while the company's opponents insist the water is still heavily colored and still smells to the high heavens. Whatever Champion has done, however much the company has spent, the DPRC insists it has not done enough.

The Pigeon River story continues.

CHAPTER 13

Where We Were, Where We Are, and a Look Ahead

I n 1992 a mystery novel was published that had East Tennessee and western North Carolina as its locale. Two of the characters in Sharyn McCrumb's *The Hangman's Beautiful Daughter* suffer because they live along the Little Dove River, which is used as an industrial sewer by the Titan Paper Company. The characters live in Tennessee; the paper company is in North Carolina and the river flows from North Carolina into Tennessee. One of the characters, Tavy Annis, develops incurable cancer; the other, heroine Laura Bruce, experiences the death of her unborn baby in her womb. Both tragedies are linked directly to the paper mill and the toxic effluents it spews into the Little Dove River. Anyone familiar with the region knows that the Little Dove is a thinly disguised Pigeon River, and Titan Paper Company is Champion International.[1]

There is a link between *The Hangman's Beautiful Daughter* and the protests of early 1993, in which members of several environmental groups closed ranks and marched upon Champion and poured Pigeon River water over the fence onto Champion property. Both are indicative of the growing concern in the national psyche over pollution. Until the 1960s local flare-ups of protest occurred, but rarely did they succeed. As we have seen, this was applicable to the Pigeon River situation. Every few years Cocke County citizens rose in protest, yet nothing was achieved. Champion kept right on polluting and even increased its capacity.

But beginning in 1982, when Tennessee first sued Champion, and continuing to the present, a marked change in national attitudes has taken place. For Champion, the progress of this transition can be followed in litigation, in pro-environmental political activity, in sustained popular opposition, in media interest, and because of scientific discoveries about toxicity in pollutants. Taken together, they exerted extreme pressure upon Champion to do something about the heavily polluted Pigeon River.

Now it is possible that none of these pressures played a part in Champion's decision to upgrade the plant at the expense, company officials say, of $330 million. On balance, however, the pressures played a role, whether they admit it or not. And even if they did not bow to all these pressures, the handwriting was on the wall and it remains there. The climate of opinion is growing, and it is growing against the polluters. If not now, soon Champion will have to clean up its act.

Court cases are running against them. In the case of *International Paper Company* v. *Ouelette* (involving New York and Vermont, but applicable to Tennessee and North Carolina), the United States Supreme Court ruled that Tennessee could sue Champion in Tennessee's courts, although the laws of North Carolina must be applied. This was, or could have been, a heavy blow to Champion because Tennessee claimed that the company violated many of North Carolina's laws. When Senator Gore applied pressure on EPA to carry out its mandate and assert the right to issue a permit to Champion, and it did, Champion sued. The company insisted that EPA lacked the power. The company lost in Federal District Court and again in the Federal Circuit Court of Appeals. Clearly, Champion's legal barricades are being weakened by court decisions.

Lawsuits are nothing new to paper companies: as heavy industry, they have personnel injury lawsuits, cases accusing them of being a public nuisance, and complex legal problems involving suppliers and customers. But class-action lawsuits accusing the companies of harmful pollution are rather new. Nowadays, occasional lawsuits are won by the plaintiffs resulting in damages running into the millions. Furthermore, it costs massive sums for a corporation to defend itself, and, even if it wins, its image has probably been tarnished.

The class-action suit brought against Champion by twenty-six hundred residents along the Pigeon River and Lake Douglas was indeed won by the company, but the original suit, asking for five billion dollars, was enough to make a C.E.O. lose sleep. There is every reason to believe that the number of such cases is going to increase, and one of these days, company officials know, the plaintiffs are going to win a whopping decision—enough to severely damage a company's financial position.

Recognizing their vulnerability, paper companies, including Champion, have always supported politicians. Certainly Champion has always had North Carolina's solons in its deep pockets. Beginning in the 1980s, some of their power elsewhere waned. Both of Tennessee's senators, Al Gore and Jim Sasser, and James Quillen, the congressman representing Cocke County, actively combated Champion. Senator Gore pressured EPA to step into the fray, and Congressman Quillen brought about a congressional hearing that was embarrassing to EPA, to Champion, and to paper companies in general. When Senator Gore supported a compromise plan at 85 color units, he was chastised by the Tennessee press; many incrementalists agreed with the senator. But Gore was not aware of the intensity of opinion in Tennessee to reject any compromise with Champion, and the error harmed his image. What about Governor McWherter? The pressure brought to bear upon him to sign the variance for 85 color units was intense, but so was the opposition. In the end, he bowed to the wishes of East Tennessee. Champion was left out in the cold. Would this have happened a decade ago, much less six or eight decades ago? Probably not. The *vox populi* is being heard as never before, and this is new.

The Pigeon River flows through a small section of North Carolina and Tennessee; population throughout its course, by modern standards, is sparse. Yet, in the past six or seven years, the national media, including *Time, Newsweek, U.S. News and World Report, Christian Science Monitor, New York Times, Los Angeles Times, Washington Post, Atlanta Constitution,* and *USA Today,* have all run stories about the fight to clean the river. More local papers, including the *Charlotte Observer, Raleigh News and Observer, Asheville Citizen-Times,* and *Knoxville News-Sentinel,* have run articles sufficient to keep the public aware of the problem over a substantial period. Even television stations in Nashville, Atlanta, Knoxville, and Asheville have run stories on the Pigeon, and the item has appeared on CBS News and once on ABC's *Good Morning America* show.

The local small-town triweeklies, especially the *Mountaineer* and *Newport Plain Talk,* played into the hands of Champion's opposition by the mere fact of their in-depth reporting of the train of events, replete with photographs and editorials.

Finally, listed last but possibly deserving first place, is the unceasing activity of Dick Mullinix, his Pigeon River Action Group, and Bob Seay, Gay Webb, Nelson Ross, Jerry Wilde, and other Cocke County citizens and their Dead Pigeon River Council. They were the letter writers, speakers, organizers, protesters, the pestilential gadflies replying to every move by Champion to defend itself. They would not quit. They were the ones behind Bach and Barnett's reports; they contacted and pressured politicians; they urged the requisite Tennessee and North Carolina departments to enforce their states' clean water laws; they contacted EPA and, along with Senator Gore's pressure, compelled it to assert its right to issue the permit. By their tenacity, they attracted and received support from the Izaak Walton League, Greenpeace, and LEAF.

What was different about all this activity—besides its tenacity—was the mere presence of these people at the regulatory agencies and in politicians' offices, either in person or through letters and petitions, and through statements to the press. These entities have always been subjected to heavy lobbying from the other side—from pro-industry politicians and industry lobbyists. What is new is the presence of a strong persuasion from opposing forces. Now, before these bureaus and politicians make decisions involving Champion and the Pigeon River, they must ask, "How will the opposition react?" Certain governors, and some state legislators, we can be sure, would be pleased if the DPRC, PRAG, and informed and angry Cocke County citizens did not exist. (Even in Haywood county there appears to be a growing number of people demanding a clean river.)

Clearly, the elevation of environmentalism in the national psyche portends increasing government actions to clean up the air, the water, and the land itself. When a movement gets so strong, industries that have fought change are forced to capitulate. Helping the environmentalists' cause is demography: the nation's population is growing. Every additional man, woman, and child demands clean, potable water. The city of Asheville is searching for new water sources and has cast covetous eyes upon the upper Pigeon River. Pigeon Forge, the shopping and recreation center near Great Smoky Mountains National Park, needs more water. Douglas Lake is the natural source, but the town fathers are skeptical of water that is contaminated by the Pigeon River. Citizens of Knoxville are aware of the Pigeon's pollution. At times in the nine decades since Champion began using the stream as an industrial sewer, that city has been troubled with water difficult to treat because of the pollutants; the river has also been suggested as a source for occasional outbreaks of illness. Most of the rapidly mounting scientific evidence about toxic wastes is bad. This means that, whether or not the dioxin scare is valid, the very existence of toxic wastes being discharged into a stream constitutes a health hazard and should be stopped.

"It is just an aesthetic problem," complained company officials and their defenders about the Pigeon River pollution. But, obviously, it is much more than that. Increasingly, society is demanding more antipollution measures from the polluting industries. Whether these companies will carry out the cleanups voluntarily or be forced to do so by government mandate is up to them.

Looking back over Champion's Canton plant history, there is very little evidence that the company has ever taken antipollution measures in themselves seriously. Such actions have really been a part of an efficiency or a modernization program. In 1985, prior to the rise of continuous opposition to the pollution, the company announced planned modernization; in 1990 it began the necessary reconstruction. As a result, the oxygen delignification process, some new treatment of water, and a process by which much of the odor is removed are resulting in a reduction in effluents. The modernization is also bringing about increased efficiency and a substantial cut in personnel—perhaps by as many as a thousand employees—with accompanying favorable consequences certain to be revealed on the company's financial bottom line.

In an ideal world, the immensely powerful pulp and paper trade—which accounts for 131 billion dollars a year—would voluntarily pool forces through its American Paper Institute and expend whatever research funds are necessary to clean up the industry's excessive pollution. Companies have argued that they have spent multimillions on pollution control, but the answer to an industry interested in results is that it has not spent enough.

In the next best of all possible worlds, an environmental president would call the executives and chemists and engineers of the pulp and paper trade to Washington and say to them: "Gentlemen, the present state of pollution caused by your industry is no longer acceptable. You must reduce your air and water emissions to acceptable standards." Under such a mandate, the industry would put forth a united effort, and if a suspension of certain antitrust regulations is necessary for such combined effort then the suspension should be forthcoming. Because this would eliminate competition, at least in terms of pollution policy, the industry should come up with new systems and new standards in short order.

Another method of forcing change is for government to pass and enforce a tough pollution tax. Such a charge, already applied in Germany, would reward the company on the cutting edge of pollution control by lowering its tax while competitors pay more. The less pollution, the less tax and the more profit. What better incentive for companies to experiment with cleaning up their effluents? Given politics and PACs, however, it is difficult to envision that the U.S. Congress would ever pass such legislation.

The real order of progress will be much more messy. Steady pressure will force the change. The pulp and paper industry will react positively only when it is impelled to by governments, and governments will only respond when the pressures for rigid enforcement exceed industry pressures for laxity. Reuben Robertson told Tennessee historian Wilma Dykeman long ago that stockholders come first, and Champion will clean up only when it has to. Andrew Sigler, Champion's present CEO, is quoted in a trade journal as saying essentially the same thing. Middle and top management are reluctant to embark upon multimillion-dollar, trial-and-error experiments when the present manufacturing process runs smoothly and produces profits. Moreover, the pulp and paper trade is so competitive that any pause in production can cost a company millions in lost sales.[2]

Chemists know that polluted water can be cleaned. At some point the industry will be forced to conduct experiments applying laboratory-proven methods to full-scale operations. Hypothetically, innovative methods could already be employed at a facility such as Champion's Canton plant. Through trial and error and fine-tuning, workable and economically feasible pollution elimination systems will emerge. These systems can be of two kinds: one concentrates on changing the production process so that it no longer creates pollution; the other works at eliminating the effluents released into the air and water by cleaning methods.

But the fundamental question of this work remains a nagging one: has all the energy expended by the state of Tennessee, by PRAG and the DPRC, by EPA and smaller groups, been in vain? Certainly these groups have caused public relations headaches for Champion. Possibly it was irritation at Stamford headquarters that led the company to launch the expensive public relations campaign at the time of the January 1988 hearings. In the final analysis, the campaign backfired in Tennessee and was an insult to Champion employees and their supporters as well as to the environmental opposition. Nothing tangible was gained on the positive side—the wheels of regulation continued to run at their same slow pace, and the granting of the permit to Champion was a foregone conclusion. It was utterly ridiculous to believe that government would force closure of a mill with a one-hundred-million-dollar payroll. Champion did lose any good will it may have had in Tennessee and, worse for the company, turned the Knoxville news media against it. Busing two thousand employees into another state to dominate a hearing, giving them yellow hats and big yellow badges to make their presence known, and leading them in cheers and catcalls was an act of sheer stupidity.

But again: were the activities of the anti-Champion groups in vain? Of course not. It is the continuity of the drumbeat that has made and is still making a difference. Because of their continued pressure, and because of the activities of such groups elsewhere, the environmental movement is growing. Champion may have expended $330 million on its modernization, but if it fails to achieve a water color at the 50-color-unit level at the Tennessee line in April 1994, then it is in trouble again, and its managers know it. Moreover, now that it has expended $330 million on improvements at the Canton plant, it cannot contemplate closing it. Like it or not, if pollution continues, Champion will hear still more calls for *really* cleaning the river. The pressure will not subside.

It is inevitable. Early in the twenty-first century, polluters, whether they are farmers, towns and cities with inadequate sewage treatment systems, or industries such as pulp and papermakers, will hear this: No excuses, no exceptions, no variances. If you take clean, clear, potable water into your facility, then clean, clear, potable water must leave it.

Afterword

August 4, 1994: The Pigeon River of western North Carolina and East Tennessee flows cleaner than at any time since the mill at Canton went on line in 1908. On April 15, David Craft, the plant's public relations officer, could proudly state that the Canton Modernization Project was an outstanding success. Water flowing across the boundary into Tennessee ran at 50 color units or less. EPA's standard, headlined the *Mountaineer,* was "no problem to Champion." Actually, the mill had been meeting the standard for several months. In happy contrast to the failure of the pilot system Champion installed in 1986 and 1987, the expensive new system surpassed expectations. "We set out to remove 50 percent (of the color) and we've taken out over two-thirds," Craft reported.[1]

In Newport and Cocke County, citizens were equally enthusiastic. Some believed that the method of measurement—a thirty-day average based upon a mathematical formula that figured color at the Tennessee line on the basis of the color leaving the pipe, twenty-six-miles-plus farther upstream—meant that the river was certain to have over 50 units once in a while. Nevertheless, they granted that the Pigeon was certainly cleaner, with little foam and much less of an odor.

The River Continues to Stir Opposition

But not everyone was so enthusiastic. Fifty color units at the state line meant that the Pigeon's North Carolina expanse, including Waterville Lake, was being used as a mixing vessel, diluting the water, foam, and odor from what it was at the pipe. Add to this process the benefits of several clear water tributaries, such as Richland and Big Creeks, and 50 units at the boundary was hardly a surprise.

Because it was known that the new system had been on line at Canton for several months, a *Mountaineer* reporter in March interviewed several residents who lived along the Pigeon. "Is the Pigeon improved?" the reporter asked. Encapsulated, their replies were "Yes, but—." "It's improved," commented Joe Davis, who had lived along the river since he was five. "They've reduced the color. I'm satisfied they've reduced it . . . (but) it's still not clean." Nor did it smell so much, although if one stood along the banks, an odor was unmistakable. Others commented that the river still looked better on days when rain diluted the water.[2]

In truth, North Carolina is still allowing Champion to pollute the Pigeon as the river passes through the state. This remains a complaint of Mullinix and PRAG as well as of the DPRC. Their rage has not subsided. "Members of the DPRC have continued to observe and take photos of the water below the mill in Canton," a DPRC bulletin reads. "*It remains the color of tea, has foam and odor*" (italics theirs). The DPRC continues to question the accuracy of the 50 color units at the state line.[3]

Another facet of unfinished business concerns the class-action lawsuit that resulted in a $6.5 million dollar settlement. So unhappy were some 200 of the class-action members that they met on May 22, 1993, and selected a committee of seven to work toward overturning the agreement offered by Champion International. Their real wrath, however, was aimed at some of their own attorneys. The objection accuses them of being high-handed, not communicating with the plaintiffs, and being too cozy with Champion's lawyers. Every two weeks the committee members met. Their class-action appeal to the settlement is to be heard by the Sixth Circuit Court of Appeals in Cincinnati, Ohio; the date set is August 5, 1994.[4]

Waterville Lake Poses a Problem

A continuing problem involving the Pigeon is the condition of Waterville Lake. For more than seventeen years, Carolina Power and Light has awaited a renewal of its permit to operate the lake and dam and the Walters power plant. As of January 1994, the company expected to have its permit, but as of this writing, it has not been forthcoming.

The reason for this is at least partly due to the controversy over the disposition of the sixty-year buildup of sludge at the bottom of the lake. It contains dioxin and possibly other toxins, mostly from Champion's effluent. What to do? The Federal Energy Regulatory Commission has suggested either removal of the sludge or capping, with a caveat—*if* fish consumption advisories are not removed by the end of 1994. The expense of either sludge removal or capping would be into the millions.[5]

At a press conference held at the Walters (Waterville) power plant on June 8, the Foundation for Global Sustainability, the Clean Water Fund of North Carolina, and the DPRC announced their petition to the EPA requesting it to investigate the lake as a possible Superfund site. They wanted tests made for dioxin before the lake and river were opened for recreation. They knew that in CP&L's permit there are provisions for recreational uses of both Waterville (Walters) Lake and the Pigeon River below the dam. (Following Champion's cleanup, both are expected to be fishable and navigable.) Among other items, CP&L will have to release water at times announced a week ahead so that whitewater enthusiasts can use the river. It must build parking areas and recreational facilities.

Champion's Publicity Campaign

The Foundation for Global Sustainability, Clean Water Fund, and the DPRC chose the date for their petition announcement shrewdly. They knew that on the following Saturday, June 11, Champion was hosting a First Annual Whitewater Shootout below the Walters power plant. It was the consummate achievement of a massive public-relations campaign Champion had launched months before. The company was determined that the public would know of its $330 million modernization; it was determined to create an image in the public mind of a clean Pigeon River. Weeks before, it had run in local newspapers a striking full-page ad showing a rafter running whitewater with the caption: He's got his river back.

Champion's public-relations staff had done much more. From the Canton plant, Champion had run a speaker's bureau, with personnel to speak to any civic group, schoolchildren, church group, or business organization desiring a free lecture. The company ran—and at this date is still running—television spots boosting Champion as a good neighbor. The company produced a videotape of the modernization. It released news reports of its purchase of eleven thousand acres of hardwoods in western Tennessee to be added to one hundred and sixty thousand acres that it already owned in the state. This, it was pointed out, would help the color problem at Canton because hardwoods create less color than pine. In April the company was named Forest Conservationist of the Year by the Tennessee Conservation League. The company boasted of how, through an agreement with the Tennessee Wildlife Resources Agency, it made "about 100,000 acres" of its land "available to the general public for hunting, fishing, and wildlife viewing." In North Carolina, Champion and the Lake Junaluska Methodist Assembly gave land for a 1.7-mile trail along Richland Creek, and from Asheville a company press release announced a new Champion program "to preserve commercial forestland sites that have historical, environmental, geological or recreational importance." The claim that this "Special Places in the Forest" program was really nothing new was supported by some examples of sites Champion had already set aside and protected.[6]

Champion neglected to mention its record in Montana during the 1980s and early 1990s. There, it and the Plum Creek Timber Company had clear-cut 1.7 million acres—an area the size of Delaware—abandoning the concept of sustained yield for ready cash: in ten years it cut what would take thirty years to grow over. They "level[ed] entire forests," reported the *New York Times*, "at a rate that had not been seen since the cut-and-run logging days of the last century."

Then they sold their 867,000 acres to Plum Creek, called by some the "Darth Vader" of timber companies. "Champion came in here promising they would be here forever, and then just overcut all the trees and left," said Dr. Thomas Power of the University of Montana. In closing its Montana operations, Champion dealt a death blow to the timber towns of Bonner and Libby; 1,500 jobs were lost. The Big Blackfoot River, site of Norman Maclean's novel *A River Runs Through It,* is one of the rivers endangered by soil erosion as a result of this rape of the forest. And, as an environmental reporter, the journalist who blew the whistle on Champion and Plum Creek lost his job.[7]

The Whitewater Shootout

Champion in Montana is one story; North Carolina and Tennessee constitute another one in Champion's wide-ranging empire. Determined to improve its image, Champion sponsored the first Whitewater Shootout to be held on the Pigeon River. David Craft, Canton's public relations officer, said the Shootout "gives us all an opportunity to show the improvement to the Pigeon River. . . . While the river is not perfect, still, significant strides have been made. . . ." He said that the kayakers "could have taken this competition to anywhere in the country. The decision on location was entirely theirs." Apparently Champion's sponsorship of the U.S. Canoe and Kayak Team since 1989 had nothing to do with the team's decision. Cocke County's point of view was expressed by Annette Mason, manager of the Newport Holiday Inn. She said she had received "many positive comments from our residents who are glad something is being done to promote Cocke County."[8]

Knowledge of the whitewater competition was first heard in Newport when Champion hosted a luncheon there in December 1993. Invited were local merchants, who listened to members of the U.S. Canoe and Kayak team describe plans for the run. They described the
wonderful rapids in the short distance from the Walters power plant
nearly to Hartford, said they had examined the river and found the water satisfactory, and held out hope for a profitable annual affair. Would
Newport merchants be willing to contribute money as sponsors? Would
individuals volunteer to handle the crowds?[9]

Altogether, Champion, which was the major sponsor, found seventeen supporters. When the day arrived—it was warm, humid and
cloudy—perhaps two hundred spectators congregated by the river near
the Walters power plant. Looking upriver, they could see clear water
flowing from the Pigeon River to the side of the building—there had
been rain and the river bed, often dry, was swollen—and muddy water
coming from the power plant gates. The water was muddy due to the
recent rains, and this worked to Champion's advantage, lightening the
usual brown color of the water, making it look like any muddy stream.
Food and drink stands and an announcer's and judge's control tower
with a public-address system had been erected; striped canvas tents
added to the festive atmosphere. Participants carrying their colorful
kayaks mingled with the crowd. Attractive sponsors' banners had been
set up on the other side of the river. As for the course, it had been carefully marked from start to finish, with an obstacle course on the river
not dissimilar to a slalom ski run.

Everything went well. No local kayakers were able to best the Olympians for a thousand-dollar prize, but other awards were given to boat-
ers who placed in various categories of competition. David Hearn, one
of the Olympians, said that he found the Pigeon "very palatable for
paddlers," adding that the increased activity on the river should help in
efforts for more clean water.[10] That statement just may carry more of a
portent about the future Pigeon River than anyone, including Champion, realizes. Once people understand the value of a clean river, they
may insist as never before that it be cleaned up and kept clean.

About noon during the festivities, Champion had some uninvited
guests. They were on the other side of the river. Laboriously making their
way down from Interstate 40, with two Tennessee state patrolmen watching from the roadside, came perhaps a dozen white-suited figures wearing
black hoods. Who were they? Soon they unfurled banners: THERE ARE
NO JOBS ON A DEAD PLANET ran one; the other, rectangular and
blue and white, read:

On the day of the Whitewater Shootout, fresh water came from the Pigeon while muddy water came from the flumes of the Walters powerhouse.

Champion
Poisoning People
for
Public Relations
Global Responsibility

At one point they turned around: letters, one on each back, spelled DIOXIN. Another banner spelled WHITEWATER CANCER. (This banner was not very good: CANCER was in white letters, and hardly discernible from across the stream.)

After a time the protesters, members of Steve Smith's Foundation for Global Sustainability, made the difficult climb back up to I-40 and left. The state patrolmen had left also.

Champion Announces a New System to Clean the River

Three days later, on June 14, L. C. Heist, president and chief operating officer of Champion, appeared at dedication ceremonies for the Canton Modernization Project. He said that it "begins the process of establishing the credibility of Champion as a neighbor that can be trusted to do what it says." He went on to say that the company had fulfilled a promise of four years before to reduce water usage (water usage had been reduced by 35 percent), to reduce the color discharge (and Champion claims the new process has exceeded their expectations), and to reduce the odor (and, indeed, much of this has diminished). Boasting of the mill as "one of the most technologically advanced and well run bleached kraft pulp mills in the world," he suggested that it "may well become the standard by which all bleached kraft mills are measured in the future." He said that EPA's proposed water standards for the industry are based on OD100, a process in use at the Canton mill.

President Heist then added a sour note: the mill had lost eighty million dollars in the last twenty-nine months. The reason for that exposé had to await two more days, as we shall see.

Then he dropped a bombshell. Here is how he began it: "We know that the people who care about this river and those who live in this valley, on both sides of the state line, expect the river to continue to improve. We acknowledge that even with the improvements that have already been made to the river with the project here, more needs to be done."

Mr. Heist then explained that Champion, through its pulping and bleaching laboratory at Pensacola and its technology center at West Nyack, New York, had developed a system it called Bleach Filtrate Recycling, or BFR. "The technology," he explained, "has the potential to eliminate almost all of the discharges to the environment from the bleaching operations at Canton." A demonstration project would shortly begin at Canton; in two years the company should know if it is feasible on a large scale. "If it works," he said, "it will remain in place and in operation." He stressed, however, that the company was not sure the system would work.[11]

It probably will work. The company has heralded the development with a vigor indicating its whole-hearted support, and its statement that five million dollars have already been spent and up to thirty million dollars may be invested in the project at the Canton mill implies an investment that is not considered too risky.[12]

In a four-page "Special Report" with color illustrations that apparently was sent to stockholders, Champion expanded upon this new technology. Titled "Closing the Loop at Champion Pulp and Paper Mills," this report describes the process. It also stated that after five years of research, Champion believes the breakthrough "opens the doors to a papermaker's dream of becoming the world's first 'closed' pulp mill—an effluent-free mill." In June 1994, the company presented BFR technology at the International Pulp Bleaching Conference in Vancouver, Canada, where it met with a positive reception. Twenty-two questions and answers make up most of the last page of this report, along with a photograph of the ion exchanger at the Canton plant, which is described as "a key ingredient of BFR technology." Suffice to say that this technology will *not*, at least not under present plans, achieve a total closed-loop system. On the positive side, the questions and answers make it clear that the Pigeon will have dumped into it still less effluent and less color. And in the future, quite possibly, a total closed loop will exist. The water that comes back into the Pigeon from the mill will be clean, clear, and pure.[13]

Two days later came the bad news, the portent of which was President Heist's statement about the mill losing $80 million in 29 months. Champion announced a 20 percent reduction in its work force, which would eliminate roughly 310 jobs. Added to a previous reduction, Champion will probably end up mean and lean at 1,240 jobs. David Craft explained that this "was not a trade-off of jobs for the environment." Modern technology, overproduction in the paper industry, and especially cheap imports were given as the reasons.[14]

Even with the cuts, Champion will remain the largest employer in western North Carolina. According to a statistical listing for 1994, furnished by Champion, as of 1994 it had 1,612 employees at Canton (prior to the announced reduction) and another 260 at the Waynesville polyethylene plant, for a total of 1,872 workers; wages and benefits for the year will be $117,233,279. Add, in round numbers, $53 million for wood chips, $19 million in freight charges, $12 million in purchased electricity, $760,000 for telephones, and $18 million for coal, oil, and bark fuel, and the impact of this mill becomes apparent. To Canton, it pays, again in round numbers, $1,200,00 taxes; to Haywood County, $1,207,000 for total taxes locally of $2,470,000.[15]

As of August 2, 1994, Champion's stock was at close to 35 points, the highest it has been in years. About the only downside to the story is the 80-million-dollar loss in Canton operations—and, let us be realistic—that may be the product of an accounting legerdemain. The plant is not going to close.

The Changing Outlook of Haywood and Cocke Counties

In the decades prior to the 1990s, little interest was manifested in Haywood County for the sporting possibilities of a clean Pigeon River. Once in a while, a recreational rafting company would run the river below the

Walters power plant, but little note was taken of it; no one bothered to fish the stream or build a pier to moor a boat. The Pigeon was dirty, foamy, and it smelled.

But something fortuitous has happened. The climate of opinion has changed. Possibilities of a cleaner river in the beautiful Pigeon River Valley may be partly responsible, but other factors are present. A "Project Pride" focuses on improving Haywood's natural beauty. Rather suddenly, people are interested in recycling. They are demanding a cleaner county. More complaints are being registered protesting ugly, cannibalized washing machines, refrigerators, and rusting junk cars that destroy the beauty of residential areas. People want a stop to junk and trash dropped where it should not be. The Pigeon gives a good example of this change of opinion.

In April 1994 a *Mountaineer* reporter, Patrick Gilseman, accompanied rafters down a section of Jonathan Creek and into the Pigeon to the Hepco Bridge near Fines Creek. This five-mile stretch of water in Haywood County has Class III and Class IV rapids and could be profitable for whitewater rafting companies. The sportsmen were pleased with the Jonathan Creek part, but "their pleasure was tempered by the amount of trash along the river's banks," Gilseman reported. And the Pigeon still smelled. "I wouldn't expect that (color and odor) in any river unless it was in Detroit," said a member of the party. Rafting company owner and guide Jerry Taylor commented that, since the modernization, the river was much better *in Tennessee.*[16]

News of the trash bothered enough people in Haywood County, and potential rafting businesses, to sponsor a first annual Pigeon Pride Cleanup. They "pulled items ranging from the bizarre to the unmentionable from the lower section of the Pigeon River in Haywood County." Eight volunteers in three rafts filled twenty-eight bags of trash, but could not pull out the tires, car engines, fenders, and gas tanks they found. And this, they emphasized, was just a beginning.[7]

Mountaineer editor Scott McLeod accompanied the rafters. He quite candidly described the Pigeon water as being still brown with a faint odor, but in the enthusiasm, these drawbacks were soon forgotten. His conclusions were positive and negative. "The river's lesson of the day," he concluded, "was one of resiliency and urgency. It was still alive, though tainted, brown and struggling. But the odds are stacked against it."[8] The last sentence seems unduly pessimistic, especially in view of Champion's announcement, made hardly three weeks later, of a new process giving promise of a cleaner river.

More good news about the Pigeon came from Carolina Power and Light. It announced continuance of a policy begun in 1993 to collect man-made trash from the 340-acre reservoir. Wood debris was still allowed through the flumes, but man-made trash, which previously had been allowed to pass through and float on into Tennessee, would be collected. CP&L's commitment was a sign of the company's good faith toward fulfilling the provisions of the impending permit.[19]

A listing of recent initiatives to clean up the environment of the Pigeon River is impressive. Community interest in a nature trail up Richland Creek; volunteer trash collection of the Pigeon River; CP&L funding for collection of man-made trash from Waterville Lake; the founding of a Project Pride to clean up Haywood County; an admission by a Champion president that the river is still dirty, and, even more amazing, the announcement that Champion is launching a system costing up to thirty million dollars to further clean the Pigeon of the mill's effluent: does all this signify a change in thinking about environmental issues in the board rooms of corporate America? Perhaps. But it is a certainty that a grass-roots change is taking place in Western North Carolina.

Moreover, the economics and demographics of Haywood County are changing, adding fuel to grass-roots campaigns for a cleaner environment. Between 1987 and the autumn of 1993, the county lost twelve hundred manufacturing jobs; add another three-hundred-plus for the new Champion reduction. In twelve years the county's school system has registered a 23 percent drop in enrollment. Young families are leaving, seeking work elsewhere. And yet, Haywood County's population has remained stable; it even grew by a percentage point in the 1980s. Who has filled the gap? Retirees, many of whom are in their forties and fifties, are opening small businesses to augment pensions already being received. While industry is more than welcome, it is no longer welcome at the price of harm to the environment. Were Dick Mullinix to begin his campaign with PRAG today, and if the river were in its 1985 condition, he would probably find less opposition and more support. Meanwhile, tourism fills the job gap left by the loss of industrial employment.[20]

Growth and Importance of Tourism

And the tourism is growing. It is hoped that the Smoky Mountain Railroad, which thrives on tourism, will come into Waynesville within a year or two. The old Balsam Inn has been reopened. Events such as the annual Waynesville Folkmoot—a festival of folk dancers from all over the world—the annual Smoky Mountain Auto Show, arts and crafts fairs, and an annual Moonlight Run in Maggie Valley are but a few of the attractions drawing tourists into this beautiful valley. Walk Waynesville's Main Street: stores catering to visitors proliferate. Even a sidewalk hot-dog vendor is welcome and doing a flourishing business. Rafting companies are scheduling regular trips down the Pigeon. Motels and restaurants have more business each tourist season.

In the summer of 1994, there is every reason for optimism in the Pigeon River Valley. "All the inns and hotels are full now, the restaurants and pubs packed and the stores and gas stations busy and the steady . . . stream of automobile and foot traffic won't die until the leaves fall," editorialized the *Mountaineer*. Because of the tourists, "what could have been a disastrous chain of events for Haywood County was softened by the growing tourist business."[21]

If things look good in the summer of 1994 in Haywood County, they look superb across the line in Cocke County, Tennessee. The *Newport Plain Talk* ran what, for Cocke County, was an amazing headline: COCKE COUNTY JOBLESS RATE RECORD LOW—the lowest level in history, at 6.4 percent. It was 16 points less than the record high of 22.4 percent in May 1983.[22]

Can this be attributed to a cleaner Pigeon River? Probably not; the citizens of Newport are certainly aware that it is cleaner than ever before. But many of the jobs are seasonal, low-paying positions in Pigeon Forge and Gatlinburg, thirty to forty miles away. Good, steady, year-round employment is still at a premium in the county. And it is a fact that the summer of 1994 is one marked by national prosperity. One can, however, sense an air of optimism in Newport, a feeling that new industries will be attracted to Cocke County now that the river is markedly cleaner, with the promise of continued improvement.

The Pigeon flows on. It is improved, but not yet sparkling clear, not yet a trout-fishing stream, not yet a river to swim in. But more than ever since 1908, there is hope that once again the Pigeon will flow pristine. Perhaps not by 1996, Tennessee's bicentennial year and the avowed date fixed by the Dead Pigeon River Council for a clean river, but surely by the year 2000. There is still hope that Dick Mullinix—that tough octogenarian fighter—may see the river clean.

Not all environmental studies can end on so optimistic a note.

Notes

1. The Mill, the Setting, and the Problem

1. *Asheville Citizen,* Jan. 29, 1961; Jan. 8, 1965; conversation with David Craft, public relations director, Canton mill, Aug. 3, 1992.
2. David Craft, "Balancing Jobs and Nature," press release, Champion International Corporation, Canton Facility, 1992.
3. James Mooney, "Myths of the Cherokee," Bureau of American Ethnology, Nineteenth Annual Report (1897–1898) (Washington, D.C.: Government Printing Office, 1900), 1: 239–40, 232–33, 299–300.
4. Interview with Jim Harrison.
5. Wilma Dykeman, *The French Broad* (New York: Rinehart and Co., 1955; reprint, Knoxville: University of Tennessee Press, 1985), 11–15, 251; Paul H. Fink, "Early Explorers in the Great Smokies," *East Tennessee Historical Society Publications* 4 (Jan. 1933): 55–96.
6. William Cicero Allen, *Centennial History of Haywood County and Its County Seat, Waynesville, North Carolina* (Waynesville, N.C.: Courier Publishing Co., 1908), 80–98; Dykeman, *The French Broad,* 35–40.
7. Allen, *Centennial History,* 22.
8. The abortive state of Franklin involved plans of land speculators and politicians more than the desires of actual settlers. See Thomas Perkins Abernethy, *From Frontier to Plantation in Tennessee* (Chapel Hill: University of North Carolina Press, 1932); also Camille Wells, *Canton: The Architecture of Our Home Town* (Canton: Canton Historical Commission, 1985), 17; and Ruth Webb O'Dell, *Over the Misty Blue Hills: The Story of Cocke County, Tennessee* (Easley, S.C.: Southern Historical Press, 1982).
9. Durward T. Stokes, "North Carolina and the Great Revival of 1800," *North Carolina Historical Review* 43 (Fall 1966): 410–11.
10. Wells, *Canton,* 20.

11. Allen, *Centennial History,* 6.

12. O'Dell, *Over the Misty Blue Hills,* 62–80.

13. Ibid.; Dykeman, *The French Broad,* 199–204.

14. O'Dell, *Over the Misty Blue Hills,* 62n.

15. Ibid., 16–24; Dykeman, *The French Broad,* 17.

16. Dykeman, *The French Broad,* 71, 188.

17. Ibid., 228, 150–83; quotation, 162.

18. Ibid, 202.

19. Paul M. Fink, "Early Explorers in the Great Smokies," *East Tennessee Historical Society Publications* 5 (Jan. 1933): 55–59, quotation 55.

20. Bureau of the Census, *USA Counties, June, 1992:* Cocke County, Tennessee, and Haywood County, North Carolina.

21. Ronald D. Eller, *Miners, Millhands, and Mountaineers: Industrialization of the Appalachian South, 1880–1930* (Knoxville: University of Tennessee Press, 1982). A different view is presented in Crandall A. Shifflett, *Coal Towns: Life, Work, and Culture in Company Towns of Southern Appalachia, 1880–1960* (Knoxville: University of Tennessee Press, 1991).

22. Shifflett, *Coal Towns,* introduction and chap. 1.

23. Ibid.

24. Dykeman, *The French Broad,* 167–74; O'Dell, *Over the Misty Blue Hills,* 195.

25. Allen, *Centennial History,* 48.

26. O'Dell, *Over the Misty Blue Hills,* 195; "Memoirs of Geo. Smathers," typescript in custody of Canton Regional Museum, 94.

27. Nelson Dunn, "The Boice Hardwood Company," manuscript in custody of the Stokely Memorial Library at Newport.

28. Ibid.; conversation with Mary Woody and Margaret Jenkins, residents of Hartford.

29. These paragraphs on the course of the Pigeon River are based upon Voit Gilmore, "The Pigeon River of Western North Carolina: Economic Exploitation vs. Environmental Quality," (M.A. thesis, University of North Carolina, 1984), Federal Regulatory Commission, Office of Electric Power Regulation, Atlanta Regional Office, *Appraisal Report: Pigeon River Basin* (Sept. 1981), and Federal Energy Regulatory Commission, Office of Hydropower Licensing, Division of Project Review, Final Environmental Assessment for Hydropower License, Walters/Waterville Project Environmental Analyses, Carolina Power and Light Company, FERC Project No. 432 (Washington, D.C., Sept. 1991).

30. Principal sources for the history of papermaking are: Dard Hunter, *Papermaking: The History and Technique of an Ancient Craft* (New York: Alfred Knopf, Inc., 1943; reprint, New York: Dover Publications, 1978); David C. Smith, *History of Papermaking in the United States (1691–1969)* (New York: Lockwood Publishing Co., 1970); Lyman Horace Weeks, *A History of Papermaking in the United*

States (1916; reprint, New York: Burt Franklin: Bibliography and Reference Series 285, 1969); Robert I. Burns, S.J., "The Paper Revolution in Europe: Crusader Valencia's Paper Industry—A Technological and Behavioral Breakthrough," *Pacific Historical Review* 50 (1981): 1–30. I have also consulted *Paper Trade Journal* from its inception in 1872 until it merged with *Pulp and Paper* in 1986.

31. Weeks, *A History of Papermaking*, 51.
32. Ibid., 66–67.
33. Ibid., 115.
34. Ibid., 119.
35. Hunter, *Papermaking*, 342–43.
36. Weeks, *A History of Papermaking*, 213–15.
37. Ibid., 234–35.
38. Hunter, *Papermaking*, 376.
39. Ibid., 391–92; Weeks, *A History of Papermaking*, 230–34; *Paper Trade Journal*, Feb. 6, 1908, 75. The making of pulp (or fiber) became an industry in itself, with the product being shipped to paper mills by the turn of the century.
40. W. H. Stebbins, "The Sulphite Process," *Paper Trade Journal*, Jan. 17, 1907; U.S. Geological Survey Water Supply Paper No. 189. A lone voice was that of David Clark Everest, president of the American Pulp and Paper Association, who expressed concern about water pollution in 1920. Smith, *History of Papermaking*, 357.
41. Robert H. Zeiger, *Rebuilding the Pulp and Paper Worker's Union, 1933–1941* (Knoxville: University of Tennessee Press, 1984). See also Richard Kazis and Richard L. Grossman, *Fear at Work: Job Blackmail, Labor and the Environment* (New York: The Pilgrim Press, 1982).
42. Smith, *History of Papermaking*, 391–418. Herty was an industrial chemist who experimented with the southern pine as a possible raw material for papermaking. Although adult pine trees have a high resinous content, he discovered that young pines did not have this condition; sapwood from yellow pines six to fifteen years old produced a nearly pure white paper. Hunter, *Papermaking*, 399. Reuben Robertson, president of Champion, is said to have used profits from the sale of Champion lands to the federal government for inclusion in Smoky Mountain National Park to further this research. Conversation with David Craft, public relations director, Champion International Paper Corporation, Canton Branch.
43. *Paper Trade Journal*, Sept. 5, 1907.
44. Weeks, *A History of Papermaking*, 298–314.
45. *1987 Census of Manufactures, Industry Series* [MC 87.1–26A]. "Pulp, Paper, and Board Mills Industries," 2611, 2621, and 2631; *Mountaineer*, Jan. 14, 1987; *Business Week*, Nov. 1, 1993, 60.

46. Smith, *History of Papermaking,* 629.
47. Ibid., 630.
48. *Paper Trade Journal,* Apr. 15, 1983; *Business Week,* June 18, 1993.

2. Enter Champion

1. Geo. Smathers, "Memoirs of Geo. Smathers," ed. Allen Roudebush for Champion International Corporation, 1990, 29; State of North Carolina, Sessions Laws, 1901, 917–18; 1907, 420–21.
2. "Memoirs of Geo. Smathers," 5.
3. *Paper Trade Journal,* Feb. 6, 1908, 37–39.
4. Information on Thomson is from *Who Was Who in America,* vol. 1, 1897–1902: 1236; William Coyle, ed., *Ohio Authors and Their Books* (New York: World Publishing Co., 1962), 631; *This Is Champion: A Proud Name in America's Industry* (pamphlet) Hamilton, Ohio: Champion Public Relations Department, 1954. *Paper Trade Journal,* Feb. 6, 1908, 36–37; July 16, 1931.
5. Discussion with Charles Moore, Sept. 14, 1989.
6. *Newport Plain Talk,* 1906 (newspaper so old that precise date cannot be determined).
7. "Memoirs of Geo. Smathers," 8–10.
8. Ibid., 12–14.
9. Camille Wells, *Canton: The Architecture of Our Home Town* (Canton: Canton Historical Commission, 1985), 20–27; *Log of Champion Activities* (in-house journal of Canton mill), Dec. 16, 1926.
10. "Memoirs of Geo. Smathers," 18–28.
11. Ibid., 54.
12. Ibid., 55–66.
13. Ibid., 44–53.
14. Ibid., 29–30.
15. Ibid., 31.
16. *Paper Trade Journal,* Jan. 23, 1908, 30; *Asheville Citizen,* Feb. 10, 1908.
17. "Memoirs of Geo. Smathers," 99–101.
18. *Paper Trade Journal,* Jan. 23, 1908, 30; *Asheville Citizen,* Jan. 23, Feb. 10, 1908.
19. *Asheville Citizen,* Feb. 10, 1908.
20. *Asheville Citizen,* Mar. 10, 1908.
21. Affidavit furnished author by Dick Mullinix.
22. *Asheville Citizen,* May 3, 1908.
23. "Company History" in *American Chemical Industry,* vol. 6 (manuscript with Geo. Smathers's memoirs).
24. Obituary of Peter G. Thomson, *Paper Trade Journal,* July 16, 1931, 24.
25. *Log of Champion Activities,* Dec. 16, 1926.
26. *Paper Trade Journal,* July 16, 1931.

27. Ibid.; *Log of Champion Activities,* Aug. 1931.

28. "Memoirs of Geo. Smathers," 109.

29. Ibid., 113.

30. *Who's Who in America, 1959–1960,* 2443; *Who Was Who in America,* vol. 4, 1961–1968: 800; obituary in the *New York Times,* Dec. 27, 1972.

31. Ibid.

32. Ibid.

33. *Log of Champion Activities,* Dec. 16, 1926; Jan. 1927; Feb. 1927; Aug. 1931; conversations with Richard Watts, curator of the Canton Regional Museum.

34. Ibid.; *Asheville Citizen,* Jan. 25, 1953; *Charlotte Observer,* July 6, 1930.

35. Interview with Richard Watts; *Newport Plain Talk,* Feb. 29, 1924.

36. Voit Gilmore, "The Pigeon River of Western North Carolina: Economic Exploitation vs. Environmental Quality," (M.A. thesis, University of North Carolina, Chapel Hill, 1984), 2; *New York Times,* Dec. 27, 1972; interview with Richard Watts.

37. Carlos C. Campbell, *Birth of a National Park in the Great Smoky Mountains* (Knoxville: University of Tennessee Press, 1969), 89–90; Michael Frome, *Strangers in High Places* (Knoxville: University of Tennessee Press, 1980), xv; 196–98; testimony of Wilma Dykeman as reported in the *Newport Plain Talk,* Sept. 16, 1992.

38. Frome, *Strangers in High Places,* xv.

39. Champion International's modernization efforts are summarized in the chronology at the front of this volume. A brief history of Champion written by W. Phalti Lawrence in 1946 for volume 4 of *American Chemical Industry* highlights the Canton mill's advances prior to that time:

> Pulp production was begun in January, 1908, in the form of sulfite pulp from coniferous wood. In April, 1908, the pulping of hardwoods by the soda process was begun, and the utilization of southern hardwoods for papermaking has continued without interruption since that date. The manufacturing of pulp from southern pine was begun in 1910, and likewise has continued without interruption. From 1910 to 1919, pine was pulped by the soda process, and in 1919 the sulfate process was adopted for pine. The Canton mill has been producing bleached pulp from southern [pine] since 1910 in the form of pine soda pulp up to 1919, and by the sulfate process since 1919. Improved multi-stage bleaching procedures involving direct chlorination were installed in 1935 for the bleaching of the pine sulfate or kraft pulp.
>
> A small groundwood unit was put into operation in 1931. For a number of years, the Canton mill produced simultaneously soda, sulfate, sulfite, and mechanical pulps.
>
> The requirements of pulp for various grades of paper, together with economic and other considerations, led to certain changes in the processing of

pulp. The groundwood operation was discontinued in 1937, the soda process for pulping hardwoods was discontinued in 1938 in favor of the sulfate process in the early part of 1947.

The manufacture of paper was begun at Canton in 1922. The facilities for manufacturing uncoated paper and paperboard at this mill was steadily increased until they surpassed 500 tons daily in the early part of 1947. . . .

By-product chemicals including chestnut extract tannin, produced at the rate of five million pounds per month; sixty-five tons of caustic soda produced daily as a byproduct of electrolytic chlorine production; tall oil and turpentine are also listed as products of Champions plants as of 1946, but the author's figures are for production of these chemicals at all Champion's plants, so a precise figure cannot be given for Canton's share of the production.

40. Champion International Corporation, *Fact Book, 1991* (Stamford, Conn.: Champion International Corporation), 6.
41. Champion International Corporation, *Fact Book, 1993* (Stamford, Conn.: Champion International Corporation), 6; conversation with David Craft, public relations officer at the Canton facility, Oct. 1993.
42. Information furnished by Champion International Corporation.
43. Ibid.
44. Ibid.
45. *Value Line Investment Survey,* Jan. 22, 1993, edition 6, part 3, "Ratings and Reports," 917.
46. *New York Times,* Aug. 12, 1984, *Business Week,* Jan. 4, 1993, 92.
47. David A. Kreuger and David P. Schmidt, eds., *The Ethics of Organizational Survival,* Proceedings of the Third National Consultation on Corporate Ethics, 1988, New York: Trinity Center for Ethics and Corporate Policy, 1989, 43–50.
48. *Paper Trade Journal,* Apr. 15, 1984, 28.

3. Pollution at Will: The First Seven Decades of the Canton Mill

1. *Newport Plain Talk,* Nov. 2, 1911.
2. Robert Heilbroner, "Reflections," *New Yorker,* July 8, 1991, 70–77.
3. Al Gore Jr., *Earth in the Balance* (Boston: Houghton Mifflin Co., 1992), 182–84, 159, 318.
4. Interview with Paul Davis, Sept. 21, 1991.
5. John Trotwood Moore and Austin P. Foster, *Tennessee: The Volunteer State, 1769–1923,* vol. 1 (Chicago: S. J. Clarke Publishing Co., 1923), 100, quoted in Ben W. Hooper, *The Unwanted Boy: The Autobiography of Governor Ben W. Hooper,* ed. Everett Robert Boyce (Knoxville: University of Tennessee Press, 1963), 85 n. 1.
6. Hooper, *The Unwanted Boy,* 6, 16.

7. Ibid., 22, 101, 162.

8. *Newport Plain Talk,* Nov. 2, 1911.

9. Ibid., Jan. 4, 1912.

10. Ibid., Feb. 20, 1913.

11. Ibid.

12. Quoted from a flawed duplicate of *Newport Plain Talk,* issue no. 51, summer of 1923 or 1924.

13. *Asheville Citizen-Times,* Oct. 15, 1931, May 2, 1959, Jan. 8, 1965.

14. "Fact Sheet About the Canton Mill's Environmental Programs," Champion International Corporation, Nov. 10, 1972, in custody of Pack Library, Asheville, N.C.; *Asheville Citizen,* Mar. 5, 1964.

15. *TVA Studies of Pollution of Tennessee River,* III, "French Broad," 16. These and following documents are duplicated reports in custody of the Reservoir Water Quality Office of TVA, Haney Building, Chattanooga, Tenn.

16. A. D. Hess and C. M. Tarzwell, "A Study of the Biological Effects of the Pigeon River Watershed," TVA, Health and Safety Department, Forestry Relations Division, 1942.

17. Ibid., 20–23.

18. Ibid., 26.

19. "A Study of Stream Pollution in Tennessee," Stream Pollution Study Board, State of Tennessee, 1943–1944, 25, 33.

20. Flawed duplicate with no date, but internal evidence indicates this was an issue of the first week of Sept. 1945.

21. *Newport Plain Talk,* July 9, 1960. The date is uncertain.

22. Ibid., Nov. 5, 1959.

23. Interview with David Craft, public relations officer, Canton facility, Aug. 1992.

24. Lowell E. Keup and R. Keith Stewart, "Effects of Pollution on Biota of the Pigeon River, North Carolina and Tennessee," Cincinnati, Ohio: Biological and Chemical Unit, Federal Water Pollution Control Administration, Technical Advisory and Investigation Activities, Technical Services Program, Feb. 1966.

25. Ibid.

26. C. E. Runas, L. E. Keup, and R. K. Stewart, "Report on the Interstate Waters of the Pigeon River," n.p.: Department of the Interior, Federal Water Pollution Control Administration, Feb. 1968.

27. Report available at Ramsay Memorial Library, University of North Carolina at Asheville.

28. Ibid.

29. "Engineer's Preliminary Report, Secondary Treatment of Industrial Wastewater, Champion Papers, Carolina Division, Canton, N.C.," prepared by Roy F. Weston, Environmental Science and Engineering Consultants, West

Chester, Pa. TVA Archives, PR-WR 10-15-8 (Champion). The statement is from the summary.

30. "Pigeon River Investigation, October, 1978," North Carolina Department of Human Resources and Community Development, Division of Environmental Management, Environmental Operations Section, Wastewater Management, Biology Unit.
31. Ibid.
32. "Draft, Pigeon River Work Plan, Introduction," included in a form letter written by Forrest R. Westall, head of the Technical Service Branch, North Carolina Department of Natural Resources and Community Development, dated July 14, 1980. Courtesy Jim Harrison.
33. Ibid.
34. David Melgaard and A. David McKinney, "Biological and Chemical Investigation of the Pigeon River, Cocke County, Tennessee," Nashville, Tenn.: Tennessee Department of Public Health, Division of Water Quality Control, Oct. 1980.
35. "Briefing Paper on the Pigeon River, Haywood County, North Carolina," Raleigh, N.C.: North Carolina Division of Environmental Management, Water Quality Section, Operations Branch, 1982; "Position Paper: Restoration of the Pigeon River: A Major Interstate River Originating in North Carolina and Flowing into Tennessee," Nashville, Tenn.: Tennessee Department of Public Health, Division of Water Quality Control, 1982.
36. "Briefing Paper on the Pigeon River."
37. "Position Paper . . . Tennessee."

4. Who Is Charles Dickens Mullinix?

1. An excellent summary of the situation is presented in Margaret I. Corwin, "Agenda Setting in the Case of a Polluted Interstate River: Champion Paper Mill and the Pigeon River," (M.A. thesis, Colorado State University, 1991).
2. Telephone conversation with Jim Harrison, Mar. 4, 1993.
3. Corwin, "Agenda Setting."
4. Ibid.; information in files of the manager of Reservoir Water Quality, TVA, Chattanooga, Tenn.
5. Much of the information on Charles Dickens Mullinix is based upon the author's long acquaintance with him.
6. Unfortunately, most of PRAG's early correspondence no longer exists. The first secretary left the organization, and at about the same time he announced that he had misplaced the files.
7. Interviews with Jim Harrison, especially those of Feb. and July 1991.
8. Interviews with Nelson Ross, beginning in Aug. 1989.
9. Interviews with Bob Seay began with a conference with Cocke County officials on Sept. 14, 1989, and have continued ever since.

10. Interviews with Gay Webb began during a meeting with him and Dick Mullinix at a local Newport restaurant in Sept. 1989 and have continued on several occasions at Webb's Wilton Springs store.
11. Interview with Jerry Wilde, Oct. 29, 1993.

5. The Legal Battles Begin

1. Alfred A. Marcus, "Environmental Protection Agency," in *Government Agencies,* ed. Donald R. Whitnah (Westport, Conn.: Greenwood Press, 1983), 184–89.
2. "Position Paper: Restoration of the Pigeon River—A Major Interstate River— Originating in North Carolina and Flowing into Tennessee," Division of Water Quality Control, Tennessee Department of Public Health, 1982.

    During 1982 several duplicated papers were produced, some of them including identical information. One of them is entitled "Restoration of the Pigeon River, French Broad Basin Program Commitment Restoration of a Major Interstate River Originating in North Carolina Flowing into Tennessee," Division of Water Quality Control, Tennessee Department of Public Health, [1982?]. Another bears the title "Presentation to the Governor's Safe Growth Committee, Status Report and Program Request Pigeon River French Broad Basin Restoration of a Major Interstate River North Carolina-Tennessee," Tennessee Department of Public Health, Division of Water Quality Control, [1982?]. The latter document includes addenda mentioned in the text, and is cited as "Presentation." McKinney and Melgaard were closely involved and may be the authors of these reports.
3. Margaret I. Corwin, "Agenda Setting in the Case of a Polluted Interstate River: Champion Paper Mill and the Pigeon River," (M.A. thesis, Colorado State University, 1991).
4. "Presentation."
5. Correspondence with Michael D. Pearigen, a member of the Environmental Division of the attorney general's office and later deputy attorney for Environment, Oct. 20, 1993; Corwin, "Agenda Setting," 41.
6. "Presentation."
7. Ibid.
8. Ibid.
9. Ibid.
10. Ibid.
11. Ibid.
12. Ibid.
13. Ibid.
14. *Newport Plain Talk,* Jan. 16, 1985; *Mountaineer,* Jan. 16, 1985.
15. *Tennessee* v. *Champion International Corporation,* 22 ERC, 1338–48, Jan. 15, 1985.
16. Ibid.

17. Ibid.
18. *State of Tennessee* v. *Champion International Corporation,* 709 S.W. 2d 569 (TENN., 1986), Apr. 21, 1986.
19. Ibid.
20. Ibid.
21. Ibid.
22. Correspondence with Michael D. Pearigen.
23. Ibid.
24. *Champion International Corporation and State of North Carolina* v. *United States Environmental Protection Agency,* 648 Federal Supplement, 1390–1400; "Supplemental Memorandum of Decision," *Champion International Corporation* v. *U.S. EPA,* 652 Federal Supplement, 1398–1400; *Newport Plain Talk,* Jan. 20, 1986.
25. Ibid.
26. Ibid.
27. Ibid.
28. Ibid.
29. 107 S.Ct. 805 (1987).
30. 850 F 2d 182 (4th Cir. 1988).

6. Cocke County Takes a Stand

1. Quotations in the following pages of Bob Seay, Dick Mullinix, Gay Webb, Charles Moore, Nelson Ross, Orville Bach Jr., and William H. Barnett are from interviews conducted over a span of four years from 1989 to 1993.
2. *Newport Plain Talk,* Dec. 26, 1986; Jan. 2, 1987.
3. Ibid., Feb. 20, 1987.
4. Orville E. Bach Jr. and William H. Barnett, "An Economic Impact Analysis on the Recreational Benefits of a Restored Pigeon River" and "A Financial Analysis of Champion International Corporation's Ability to Provide for a Cleaner River," duplicated reports, Jefferson City, Tenn.: Walters State Community College, 1987; "Addendum: Latest Financial Disclosure of Champion International Corporations, January 24, 1988."
5. David Halberstam and Al Gore have said much the same thing.
6. A copy of William H. Barnett's address to stockholders dated May 1988 was furnished me by Barnett.
7. Correspondence with Judy Webb, May 10, 1993; see also *Asheville Citizen,* May 9, 1987.
8. *Newport Plain Talk,* July 6, 1987; *Asheville Citizen,* May 9, 1987.
9. Recording supplied by Bob Seay and used with express permission of Carl Williamson and Dave Cureton.

7. A Growing Conflict, 1985-1987

1. *Newport Plain Talk,* Nov. 2, 1984.
2. Conversations with Dick Mullinix.
3. *Mountaineer,* Oct. 12, 1984.
4. *Newport Plain Talk,* Nov. 2, 1984.
5. Conversations with Dick Mullinix; the newspaper account states simply that staff members of the state Environmental Management Council had decided to recommend such a hearing to the DEM. *Mountaineer,* Dec. 10, 1984.
6. *Charlotte Observer,* May 20, 1985.
7. *Enterprise,* Jan. 3, 1985.
8. *Newport Plain Talk,* Jan. 16, 1985.
9. *Newport Plain Talk, Mountaineer,* and *Enterprise,* Jan. 30, 1985.
10. *Enterprise,* May 16, 1985.
11. Ibid.; *Mountaineer,* May 18, 1985.
12. *Mountaineer,* May 13, 1985.
13. Ibid.
14. *Newport Plain Talk,* June 17, 1985.
15. *Mountaineer,* July 14, 1985.
16. Ibid., Aug. 8, 1985.
17. Ibid., Aug. 12, 1985.
18. *Winston-Salem Journal,* Aug. 12, 1985.
19. *Atlanta Constitution,* Oct. 20, 1985.
20. *Mountaineer,* Aug. 9, 1985.
21. Ibid., Aug. 12, 1985.
22. Ibid.
23. Ibid.
24. Ibid., Jan. 17, 1986.
25. *Asheville Citizen,* July 24, 1985.
26. Ibid., July 24, 1985.
27. *Newport Plain Talk,* Nov. 8, 1985. As has been noted repeatedly, Tennessee water quality laws do not set a precise color-unit number. Instead, Tennessee laws carry the stipulation that no color be expelled into state waters that will affect aquatic life. According to Tennessee Assistant Attorney General Frank Scanlon, "You can't set a number for every river . . . in some cases 50 may be appropriate, but in other cases, 5 may be appropriate; it depends on the original color of the water and how color would affect aquatic life in the river."
28. Ibid.
29. *Mountaineer,* Jan. 22, 1986.
30. Ibid., Apr. 14, 1986.
31. Ibid., May 12, 1986.

32. Ibid.; *Newport Plain Talk,* May 12, 1986.

33. *Mountaineer,* July 16, 1986.

34. Ibid., Sept. 22, 1986.

35. *Newport Plain Talk,* Sept. 24, 1986.

36. *Mountaineer,* Oct. 8, 1986.

37. Ibid.

38. *Newport Plain Talk,* Aug. 13, 1986.

39. Interviews with Paul Davis, Sept. 19, 1991, May 13, 1993.

40. *Mountaineer,* Dec. 3, 1986; *Charlotte Observer,* Dec. 4, 1986.

41. *Knoxville News-Sentinel,* Dec. 23, 1986.

42. Ibid.

43. *Newport Plain Talk,* Dec. 17, 1986.

44. Interview with Paul Davis, Sept. 19, 1991.

45. Haynes Johnson, *Sleepwalking Through History: America in the Reagan Years* (New York: W. W. Norton and Co., 1991), 170–71; conversation with Dick Mullinix.

46. *Newport Plain Talk,* Jan. 16, 21, 1987; *Mountaineer,* Jan. 28, 1987.

47. *Mountaineer,* Jan. 29, 1987; *Newport Plain Talk,* Jan. 28, 1987.

48. *Mountaineer,* Feb. 27, 1987.

49. Ibid., Mar. 18, 1987.

50. *Asheville Citizen-Times,* May 3, 1987; *Enterprise,* May 7; May 13, 1987.

51. Ibid., Mar. 20, 1987; *Mountaineer,* May 28, 1987; June 15, 17, 1987.

52. *Mountaineer,* May 28, 1987.

53. Mountaineer, May 13, 1987; May 11, 1987.

54. *Asheville Citizen-Times,* May 10, 1987; *Newport Plain Talk,* May 13, 1987.

55. *Mountaineer,* Mar. 4, 1987.

56. Ibid., May 8, 1987.

57. Ibid.

58. Conversations with Dick Mullinix and Cocke County officials. I have heard several of these threats as recorded on answering machines. See also *Mountaineer,* May 13, 1985, and *Newport Plain Talk,* May 13, 1985.

59. *Mountaineer,* May 22, 1987.

60. Correspondence with Rebecca Allen, Nov. 12, 1993.

61. Ibid.; *Asheville Citizen-Times,* May 17, 1987; *Mountaineer,* May 18, 1987.

62. Ibid.

63. Correspondence with Rebecca Allen, Nov. 12, 1993.

64. *Asheville Citizen-Times,* May 17, 1987; *Mountaineer,* May 18, 1987, May 30, 1990.

65. Correspondence with Rebecca Allen, Nov. 12, 1993.

66. *Mountaineer,* May 18; May 15, 1987.

67. *Newport Plain Talk,* May 11, 1987.

68. Ibid.
69. Ibid.
70. Ibid., May 13, 1987.
71. Ibid.
72. Ibid., May 15, 1987.
73. Ibid.

8. The Programmed Asheville Hearing

1. For an accurate, incriminating study of corporation use of employees to prevent regulations or restrict their enforcement, see Richard Kazis and Richard L. Grossman, *Fear at Work: Job Blackmail, Labor and the Environment* (New York: The Pilgrim Press), 1982.
2. *Mountaineer*, July 3, 1987.
3. Ibid., Sept. 2, 1987.
4. Ibid., July 1, 8, 1987.
5. Ibid., Oct. 28, 1987.
6. *Enterprise*, Nov. 4, 1987.
7. *Enterprise*, Nov. 11, 1987; *Mountaineer*, Nov. 18, 1987.
8. *Appalachia* 15 (4) (Summer 1988): 423.
9. *Mountaineer*, Nov. 18, 20, 1987; *Asheville Citizen*, Nov. 17, 21, 1987; *Newport Plain Talk*, July 18, 1988.
10. Interview with Paul Davis, Sept. 19, 1991.
11. Interviews with Charles Moore and Bob Seay; *Mountaineer*, Nov. 20, 1987.
12. *Mountaineer*, Nov. 17, 1987.
13. Interviews with Bob Seay, Gay Webb, and Dick Mullinix; correspondence with Al Gore Jr., July 26, 1991.
14. *Newport Plain Talk*, Dec. 2, 1987; *Mountaineer*, Dec. 7, 1987.
15. *Enterprise*, Dec. 9, 1987.
16. *Newsweek*, May 6, 1991, 35; *Newport Plain Talk*, Dec. 11, 1987.
17. *Newsweek*, May 6, 1991, 35.
18. *Newport Plain Talk*, Dec. 11, 1987.
19. *Asheville Citizen-Times*, Dec. 9, 1987.
20. *Mountaineer*, Dec. 11, 1987.
21. Ibid., Dec. 14, 1987.
22. *Newport Plain Talk*, Dec. 11, 1987.
23. *Mountaineer*, Dec. 2, 1987, Dec. 14, 1987.
24. Conversations with Dick and Lucie Mullinix; *Knoxville News-Sentinel*, Jan. 22, 1988.
25. Conversations with Dick Mullinix.
26. *Asheville Citizen-Times*, Dec. 31, 1987.
27. Ibid., Jan. 10, 1988.

28. *Newport Plain Talk,* June 15, 1987; *Mountaineer,* June 17, 1987.
29. *Mountaineer,* Jan. 11, 1988.
30. Ibid., Sept. 16, 1987.
31. *Asheville Citizen-Times,* Jan. 10, 1988.
32. Conversations with Jim Harrison.
33. All quotations from the hearing are from "National Pollution Discharge Elimi-nation System Public Hearing, Champion International Corporation, NPDES No. NCOOO272, January 14, 1988, Asheville, North Carolina, Civic Center," USEPA-345, Courtland St., N.E., Atlanta, Ga.
34. *Asheville Citizen,* Jan. 15, 1988.

9. Overkill: The Knoxville Hearing

1. Conversations with Bob Seay.
2. All quotations from the hearing are from "National Pollution Discharge Elimi-nation System Public Hearing, January 21, 1988, Champion International Cor-poration, NPDES No. NCOOOO272, Civic Center, Knoxville, TN." USEPA, 345 Courtland St., N.E., Atlanta, Ga.
3. *Knoxville Journal,* Jan. 21, 22, 1988; *Knoxville News-Sentinel,* Jan. 21, 22, 1988; *Mountaineer,* Jan. 22, 1988; *Asheville Citizen,* Jan. 22, 1988.
4. *New York Times,* Jan. 31, 1988.
5. Discussions with Bob Seay and Dick Mullinix.

10. Dioxin

1. Pigeon River, File WR-10, TVA Offices, Chattanooga, Tenn.
2. Conversation with Bob Seay, Apr. 1991.
3. Bruce R. Barrett, Director, "EPA Environmental News, Prepared Press State-ment," Jan. 26, 1989.
4. North Carolina Division of Environmental Management, "Report: Champion Variance Review Committee," Mar. 31, 1988, 13.
5. Environmental Management Commission, In the Matter of Request for Vari-ance from Water Quality Standard Bases Effluent Limitations by Champion International Corporation, Canton, N.C., *Final Decision,* July 13, 1988, 9.
6. Ibid.
7. *New York Times,* Mar.13, 1988; *Washington Post,* Mar. 11, 1988.
8. *Newport Plain Talk,* Apr. 29, 1988.
9. Ibid., July 18, 1988.
10. Ibid.
11. Ibid., Apr. 29, 1988.
12. Differing stories are told about the invention of the name: my best information suggests three equally plausible alternatives: 1) that Bob Seay thought up the idea of calling Hartford "Widowville"; 2) that it originated with Mary Woody of the Hart-ford Post Office; or 3) a reporter for *Plain Talk* thought of the name.

13. *Newport Plain Talk,* Nov. 27, 1987.
14. *New York Times,* Sept. 24, 1987.
15. Ibid., Oct. 9, 1987.
16. *Wall Street Journal,* Aug. 6, 1991.
17. *U.S. News and World Report,* Apr. 6, 1992, 60–61; Joe Thornton, "The Dioxin Deception," *Greenpeace* (May–June 1991): 16–21.
18. *Newport Plain Talk,* Nov. 27, 1987.
19. Ibid., Nov. 1987–June 1988. Hardly an issue of this newspaper appeared without an article on the dioxin controversy during this period. See, for example, issues of Nov. 25, 1987; Feb. 3, 5, 26, 1988; Mar. 16, 21, 28, 30, 1988; Apr. 1, 8, 13, 20, 22 1988; May 2, 11, 27, 1988; and June 8, 1988.
20. *Knoxville Journal,* Mar. 15, 1988.
21. *Newport Plain Talk,* Mar. 14, 1988.
22. Ibid., July 8, 1988; *Asheville Citizen-Times,* Aug. 12, 1988; *Winston Salem Journal,* June 25, 1988; *Newport Plain Talk,* Apr. 5, 1989.
23. *Newport Plain Talk,* Mar. 28, 1988.
24. *Citizen Tribune* (Morristown, Tenn.), Apr. 24, 1988.
25. *Newport Plain Talk,* Apr. 20, 1988; interview with Mary Woody, Apr. 1993.
26. *Asheville Citizen-Times,* June 12, 1988; *Newport Plain Talk,* June 6, 1988; *Niagara Gazette* (New York), July 14, 1988.
27. *Newport Plain Talk,* Apr. 20, 1988, May 11, 1988, May 27, 1988.
28. *Newport Plain Talk,* Apr. 20, 1988.
29. *Newport Plain Talk,* May 2, 1988.
30. Federal Energy Regulatory Commission, Environmental Assessment, 1991, 75.
31. *Newport Plain Talk,* May 11, July 13, 1988.
32. "Dioxin Pollution in the Pigeon River, North Carolina and Tennessee," Hearing Before the Subcommittee on Water Resources of the Committee on Public Works and Transportation, House of Representatives, July 13, 1988, 100th Congress, 2d Session. All quotations from the hearing are from this source.
33. *Wall Street Journal,* Aug. 6, 1991, "The Dioxin Un-Scare: Where's the Press?"; *Time,* Aug. 6, 1991.
34. *U.S. News and World Report,* Apr. 6, 1992; *Reason,* June 1992.
35. Environmental Assessment, Appendix B, "Dioxin Control Analysis."

11. The Governor Rejects the Variance

1. Environmental Management Commission, "In the Request for Variance from Water Quality Standard-Based Effluent Limitations by Champion International Corporation, Canton, North Carolina: *Final Decision,*" July 13, 1988.
2. A sample's "apparent color" is the measure of color of an untreated sample of water. The "true color" of a sample is taken after any impurities are removed from the water. A measure of one unit of true color equals about 1.3 units of apparent color. Eighty-five units of true color is equal to about 110 units of appar-

ent color, or more than twice Tennessee's demand for 50 units. See *Newport Plain Talk,* Feb. 15, 1988.

3. Discussion with Gordon Ball; *Newport Plain Talk,* Apr. 27, 1988. This so-called agreement was reported in the *Washington Post,* Mar. 11, 1988, and the *New York Times,* Mar. 13, 1988, and in other newspapers.

4. *Newport Plain Talk,* Aug. 17, 19, 1988; *Knoxville News-Sentinel,* Aug. 19, 1988; *Mountaineer,* Aug. 19, 1988. Material on the Newport hearing is from these three sources.

5. Conversations with Paul Davis and David McKinney; *Newport Plain Talk,* Sept. 21, 1988; *Asheville Citizen,* Sept. 21, 1988.

6. Ibid.

7. Ibid.

8. Meeting of author with Bob Seay, Fran Ketterman, Dick Mullinix, and Charles Moore at chamber of commerce, Sept. 14, 1989; *Knoxville News-Sentinel,* Dec. 13, 1988.

9. Meeting of author with Bob Seay, Fran Ketterman, Dick Mullinix, and Charles Moore at chamber of commerce, Sept. 14, 1989.

10. Ibid.

11. *Asheville Citizen-Times,* Dec. 24, 1988.

12. Ibid., Dec. 9, 1989; *Knoxville News-Sentinel,* Jan. 8, 1989.

13. *Newport Plain Talk,* Jan. 2, 1989.

14. *Mountaineer,* Jan. 4, 1989; *Newport Plain Talk,* Jan. 13, 1989.

15. *Newport Plain Talk,* Jan. 13, 1989.

16. *Knoxville Journal,* Jan. 27, 28, 1989; *Mountaineer,* Jan. 25, 27, 28, 1989; Feb. 1, 1989. Champion ran a full-page message entitled "To the People of Canton" in *Mountaineer,* Jan. 27, 1989.

17. *Mountaineer,* Jan. 23, 1989; EPA Environmental News, prepared press statement, Jan. 26, 1989.

18. For examples, see *Raleigh News and Observer,* Dec. 24, 1988; *Citizen Tribune* (Morristown, Tenn.), Jan. 26, 1989.

19. *Mountaineer,* Feb. 6, 1989.

20. *Asheville Citizen,* Mar. 2, 3, 1989; *Los Angeles Times,* Feb. 10, 1989.

21. *Knoxville Journal,* Jan. 27, 28, 1989.

22. *Mountaineer,* Jan. 30, 1989.

23. Ibid.; *Raleigh News and Observer,* Feb. 8, 1989.

24. *Knoxville Journal,* Mar. 3, 1989.

25. *Asheville Citizen,* Apr. 26, 1989.

26. Conversations with Dick Mullinix, Bob Seay, and Nelson Ross.

27. *Knoxville News-Sentinel,* Mar. 4, 1989; *Asheville Citizen-Times,* June 25, 1988; *Newport Plain Talk,* Nov. 14, 1988; *Atlanta Constitution,* Nov. 27, 1989.

28. *Mountaineer,* Mar. 17, 1989; EPA Environmental News, Jan. 26, 1989.

29. *Asheville Citizen,* Apr. 26, 1989.

30. *Asheville Citizen,* May 2, 1989.

31. *Mountaineer,* June 21, 1989; *Asheville Citizen,* June 21, 1989; *Enterprise,* June 28, 1989.

32. *Raleigh News and Observer,* June 18, 1989.

33. *Asheville Citizen,* May 3, 1989.

34. *Enterprise,* July 5, Aug. 9, 1989; *Mountaineer,* Aug. 2, 1989.

35. Photograph in *Mountaineer,* July 28, 1989; *Newport Plain Talk,* Aug. 7, 1989; *Mountaineer,* Apr. 29, 1989.

36. *Enterprise,* June 28, 1989.

37. *Asheville Citizen,* Aug. 18, 1989.

38. Ibid.; *Newport Plain Talk,* Aug. 14, 1989.

39. *Mountaineer,* Aug. 14, 1989.

40. *Asheville Citizen,* Aug. 10, 1989.

41. *Enterprise,* Aug. 23, 1989.

42. *USA Today,* Aug. 9, 1989. On July 11 the *Los Angeles Times* ran a feature article on the controversy.

43. *Mountaineer,* Aug. 18, 1989; *Raleigh News and Observer,* Aug. 18, 1989; *Asheville Citizen,* Aug. 18, 1989.

44. Ibid.

45. *Newport Plain Talk,* Aug. 25, 1989; *Asheville Citizen,* Aug. 25, 1989; *Enterprise,* Aug. 30, 1989.

46. Ibid.

47. Ibid.

48. *Asheville Citizen,* Aug. 25, 1989.

49. Ibid.

50. *Newport Plain Talk,* Sept. 27, 1989.

51. *Mountaineer,* Oct. 4, 1989.

52. Ibid.

53. *Knoxville News-Sentinel,* Oct. 9, 1989.

54. *Newport Plain Talk,* Oct. 11, 1989.

55. *Asheville Citizen,* Aug. 29, 1989; *Knoxville Journal,* Aug. 30, 1989.

12. The Permit, the Evidentiary Hearing, and the Lawsuit

1. *This Is Champion: A Proud Name in American Industry* (pamphlet) Hamilton, Ohio: Champion Public Relations Department, 1954.

2. *Knoxville Journal,* Oct. 12, 1989; *Newport Plain Talk,* Oct. 25, 1989.

3. *Asheville Citizen,* May 20, 1988; *Mountaineer,* June 20, Dec. 2, 1988; *Newport Plain Talk,* Aug. 8, 1988.

4. "Administrative Law Judge Issues Decision on Champion International's Canton, North Carolina Wastewater Permit," *Environmental News,* USEPA, Region IV, Atlanta, Ga., Feb. 12, 1992.

5. "Requests for an Evidentiary Hearing" in EPA archives. The materials I used were in the custody of Dick Mullinix.

6. Champion news release, Oct. 24, 1989.

7. *Mountaineer*, Sept. 11, Apr. 28, 1989; David McKinney, "Pollution and the Dying Pigeon," in *The Tennessee Conservationist* (Sept.–Oct. 1989): 18–20.

8. *Newport Plain Talk*, Mar. 28, 1990; *Mountaineer*, Mar. 28, 1990.

9. Ibid.

10. *Knoxville News-Sentinel*, Mar. 29, 1990.

11. Ibid.

12. *Forbes*, May 14, 1990, 172.

13. *Canton Conversion Update* (CCU), July 26, Aug. 16, 1990. In May 1991, the title of this publication was changed to *Canton Modernization Project*.

14. *Canton Modernization Project*, Feb. 1992.

15. Ibid., May-June, 1992.

16. Ibid., May 1992.

17. Ibid.

18. *Asheville Citizen*, July 11, 1990.

19. Discussions with Bob Seay.

20. *Newport Plain Talk*, Aug. 13, 1990.

21. Ibid.

22. Conversations with Dick Mullinix and others who attended the hearing.

23. "Administrative Law Judge Issues Decision, . . ." covering statement preceding decision.

24. Ibid., 21.

25. Conversations with Dick Mullinix; *Mountaineer*, May 13, 1992.

26. *Newport Plain Talk*, Apr. 2, 1990.

27. *Mountaineer*, Jan. 7, 1991.

28. Ibid. Dozens of news items appeared during the trial that described the Shultses and their lawsuit.

29. Charge to the jury, court papers; *Newport Plain Talk*, Sept. 21, 1992; *Greeneville Sun*, Oct. 9, 1992; *Knoxville News-Sentinel*, Sept. 13, 1992. According to the *Asheville Citizen-Times* of Sept. 15, 1992, seven individuals from five families in Cocke, Sevier, and Jefferson Counties represented the group.

30. *Newport Plain Talk*, Sept. 14, 1992. Descriptions of Greeneville, the courtroom, and of Louis Woolf's comportment in the paragraphs that follow are from my own observations.

31. *Knoxville News-Sentinel*, Sept. 13, 1992; discussion with Gordon Ball.

32. *Newport Plain Talk*, Oct. 9, 1992.

33. Ibid., Sept. 14, 1992; *Greeneville Sun*, Oct. 19, 1992.

34. *Newport Plain Talk*, Sept. 16, 1992.

35. *Knoxville News-Sentinel*, Sept. 14, 1992.

36. Duplicate of letter furnished author by Dick Mullinix.

37. These lists are court documents in the case of *J. A. Shults and Joan Shults* v. *Champion International Corporation*, No. Civ. 2-91-33.
38. *Asheville Citizen-Times*, Sept. 14, 1992.
39. *Newport Plain Talk*, Sept. 16, 1992, and similar articles in *Knoxville News-Sentinel*, *Asheville Citizen-Times*, and *Mountaineer*.
40. Charge to the jury, court records.
41. *Newport Plain Talk*, Sept. 16, 1992; *Knoxville News-Sentinel*, Sept. 15, 16, 1992.
42. Ibid.
43. *Knoxville News-Sentinel*, Sept. 19, 1992.
44. *Newport Plain Talk*, Sept. 18, 1992; *Knoxville News-Sentinel*, Sept. 16, 1992.
45. *Newport Plain Talk*, Sept. 18, 1992.
46. *Greeneville Sun*, Oct. 2, 1992.
47. *Newport Plain Talk*, Sept. 23, 1992; *Knoxville News-Sentinel*, Sept. 23, 28, 1992.
48. Ibid.
49. *Knoxville News-Sentinel*, *Newport Plain Talk*, *Mountaineer*, *Asheville Citizen-Times*, and *Greeneville Sun*, issues from Sept. 20–Oct. 1992.
50. *Greeneville Sun*, Oct. 3, 1992.
51. Ibid., Oct. 8, 1992.
52. *Asheville Citizen-Times*, Oct. 7, 10, 1992.
53. Ibid.; *Newport Plain Talk*, Oct. 12, 1992.
54. *Newport Plain Talk*, Oct. 19, 1992; *Greeneville Sun*, Oct. 19, 1992.
55. *Greeneville Sun*, Oct. 19, 1992.
56. *Newport Plain Talk*, Oct. 19, 1992.
57. *Greeneville Sun*, Nov. 6, 1992.
58. *Newport Plain Talk*, Dec. 21, 1992.
59. Case of J. A. Shults, *et al.*, v. Champion International Corporation, *Order*, filed Jan. 26, 1993, United States District Court for the Eastern District of Tennessee at Greeneville.
60. Champion news release, Feb. 3, 1993. "New Settlement Reached in Champion Lawsuit."; *Newport Plain Talk*, Jan. 27, 1993; *Mountaineer*, Jan. 15, 1993; *Asheville Citizen-Times*, Jan. 15, 1993. I also have the Foundation for Global Sustainability's "2nd draft Press Release," which calls for Champion to meet 50 color units at the pipe, not at the Tennessee line; to continue efforts to remove organochlorines, including dioxin, from the mill's effluent; to accept responsibility and assist in the cleanup of contaminated Waterville Lake; and to stop using "the community of Canton . . . and the workers of the mill as economic and political pawns in an effort to avoid corporate responsibility and maximize corporate profits."
61. *Asheville Citizen-Times*, Mar. 28, 1993; *Mountaineer*, Mar. 29, 1993.
62. *Newport Plain Talk*, Mar. 29, 1993.
63. *Mountaineer*, May 14, 1993.
64. John Manuel, "The Pigeon Flies Again," *Canoe* (Aug. 1993): 17–20.
65. Ibid., 17.

13. Where We Were, Where We Are, and a Look Ahead

1. Sharyn McCrumb, *The Hangman's Beautiful Daughter* (New York: The Onyx Group, 1992).
2. *Knoxville News-Sentinel*, Sept. 15, 1992; *Paper Trade Journal*, Apr. 15, 1984, 30–31. The report is as follows: "In a speech last fall in New York City, Champion's Chairman A. C. Sigler said he doubted that American business would be spending millions of dollars to clean up the environment if it were not for government regulations. 'There's no way that any single company could deal with these issues . . . could maintain a competitive position and do that,' he said."

Afterword

1. *Mountaineer*, Apr. 14, 1994.
2. *Mountaineer*, Mar. 2, 1994.
3. Dead Pigeon River Council, Bulletin, Apr. 14, 1994.
4. Champion Class Action Committee, Bulletin.
5. *Mountaineer*, June 10, 1994; Federal Energy Regulatory Commission, "Summary," Walters/Waterville Project, Environmental Analysis, Sept. 1991.
6. Jim Carraway (of Champion International) to Nelson Ross, Mar. 24, 1994. Courtesy Nelson Ross; *Mountaineer*, Mar. 18; Apr. 24, 25; May 2, 1994.
7. Richard Manning, *Last Stand: A Riveting Expose of Environmental Pillage and a Lone Journalist's Struggle to Keep Faith* (New York: Penguin Books, 1992); *New York Times*, Oct. 14, 1993.
8. *Mountaineer*, June 8, 1994; *Knoxville News-Sentinel*, June 12, 1994.
9. Cassette recording of the meeting courtesy of Nelson Ross and Dick Mullinix.
10. *Mountaineer*, June 13, 1992.
11. Champion Press Release, "Champion Pulp Mill Dedication, June 14, 1994, L. C. Heist." Courtesy of David Craft.
12. *Mountaineer*, June 15, 1994.
13. A copy of the special report is courtesy of David Craft.
14. *Mountaineer*, June 17, 1994.
15. "Canton Mill: 1994 Statistics," courtesy of David Craft.
16. *Mountaineer*, Apr. 11, 1994.
17. Ibid., May 18, 23, 1994.
18. Ibid., May 27, 1994.
19. Ibid., May 20, 1994.
20. Ibid., Oct. 6, 1993.
21. Ibid., July 6, 1994.
22. *Newport Plain Talk*, July 1, 1994.

Glossary

acidity Any solution that has a pH of less than 7. These solutions have an excess of hydrogen ions (H+) present (Miller, *Living in the Environment*, A-39).

algae "Simple one-celled or many-celled plants, usually aquatic, capable of carrying on photosynthesis" (Miller, *Living in the Environment*, A-39).

alkalinity Any solution that has a pH of more than 7. These solutions have an excess of hydroxide ions (OH-) present (Miller, *Living in the Environment*, A-40).

ammonia A chemical compound containing nitrogen and hydrogen (NH_3), often found in fertilizers. This compound causes two problems in surface water: 1) it promotes the growth of algae and 2) it chemically breaks down through an oxygen-demanding process, thus consuming dissolved oxygen in water.

benthos Organisms that inhabit the sediments along the bottom of a body of water, where decomposition of plants and animals occurs. The respiration of these organisms contributes to the dissolved oxygen that is demanded by the river.

BOD (Biochemical Oxygen Demand) An indirect way of measuring oxygen-demanding material in a water body. It is the amount of oxygen consumed by chemicals or biological organisms. According to Miller (*Living in the Environment*, A-40), it is the "amount of dissolved oxygen gas required for bacterial decomposition of organic wastes in water; usually expressed in terms of the parts per million (PPM) of dissolved oxygen consumed over 5 days at 20 degrees C and normal atmospheric pressure."

COD (Chemical Oxygen Demand) "Measure of the total depletion of dissolved oxygen in polluted water" (Miller, *Living in the Environment*, A-41).

color units A relative measure of the ability of the stream to absorb light through reflection off colloidal and suspended particles (Davis and Cornwell, *Introduction to Environmental Engineering*, 123–24).

dioxins "A family of over 75 chlorinated hydrocarbon compounds which are known to be toxic to biological organisms" (Miller, *Living in the Environment*, A-43).

DO (dissolved oxygen) The amount of oxygen gas (O_2) in water that is available for consumption by chemical or biological processes.

fecal coliform A normally harmless type of bacteria found in the intestinal tracts of humans and other animals, it is usually found in untreated wastewater.

furans A group of flammable liquid compounds (C_4H_4O) that are generated by wood oils in various manufacturing processes.

hypolimnion The region at or near the bottom of a lake where the water is stagnant and the temperature becomes constant. The dissolved oxygen level in this region may be too low to support some aquatic species.

lignin An organic substance that with cellulose forms the chief part of woody tissues in trees (Ingram, *Glossary of Water and Wastewater Control Engineering*).

nitrates Chemical compounds containing nitrogen and oxygen (NO_3), which is produced by the decomposition of fertilizers and other nitrogen containing compounds of water. These compounds promote excessive plant growth and therefore increase dissolved oxygen demand (Davis and Cornwell, *Introduction to Environmental Engineering*, 264).

pH "The numerical value that indicates the relative acidity or alkalinity of a substance on a scale of 0 to 14 with the neutral point at 7.0" (Miller, *Living in the Environment*, A-51).

phosphates, ortho and total Chemical compounds containing phosphate (PO_4), which is produced by the decomposition of detergents and fertilizers. These compounds promote excessive plant growth and therefore increase dissolved oxygen demand (Davis and Cornwell, *Introduction to Environmental Engineering*, 264).

photosynthesis "Complex process that occurs in the cells of green plants whereby radiant energy from the sun is used to combine carbon dioxide and water to produce oxygen and simple sugars" (Miller, *Living in the Environment*, A-51).

photosynthetic activity The amount of oxygen and simple sugars that are produced by a given plant or group of plants.

planktonic organisms "Free-floating, most microscopic, aquatic plants" (Miller, *Living in the Environment*, A-51).

residual chlorine The amount of the chemical chlorine that, when added to water, is not used up in the chemical disinfection of germs in the water.

resin acids Any acid, such as abietic or primaric acids, that are found in the form of esters in rosin or other natural resins.

salmonella A genus of bacterium often found in untreated water that causes sickness if consumed by people or warm-blooded animals. These bacterium are pathogenic and are chiefly associated with acute gastrointestinal inflammation.

settleable solids Substances in water that are sufficiently large enough (ranging from 0.1 to 1.0 micrometers) to be removed by physical means such as settlement, filtration, and sedimentation (Davis and Cornwell, *Introduction to Environmental Engineering*, 123).

sulfides Chemical compounds that contain sulfur and are usually produced in surface water by the dissolving of natural deposits of sulfur salts. These compounds make water unpalatable.

synergistic effect "Interaction in which the total effect is greater than the sum of two effects taken independently" (Miller, *Living in the Environment*, A-55).

temperature A relative measure of hotness and coldness. In a river, increased temperature will increase the rate of oxygen depletion by cultivating the growth of oxygen demanding organisms (Davis and Cornwell, *Introduction to Environmental Engineering*, 265).

total coliform A group of bacterium, including fecal coliform, "whose presence in water is an indicator that the water may be contaminated with other disease-causing organisms found in untreated waste" (Miller, *Living in the Environment*, A-42).

turbidity A relative measure of the degree in which colloidal and suspended particles reflect light at a 90-degree angle from the light source. It is measured in turbidity units (TU) and related to relative particle size and density (Davis and Cornwell, *Introduction to Environmental Engineering*, 123).

Bibliography

Books

Abernethy, Thomas Perkins. *From Frontier to Plantation in Tennessee: A Study in Frontier Democracy.* Chapel Hill: University of North Carolina Press, 1932.

Allen, William Cicero. *The Annals of Haywood County, N.C.* N.p.: n.d.

———. *Centennial History of Haywood County and Its County Seat, Waynesville, North Carolina.* Waynesville, N.C.: Courier Publishing Co., 1908.

Beverley, Robert. *The Western North Carolina Almanac.* 2d ed. Franklin, N.C.: Sanctuary Press, 1993.

Brown, Michael H. *The Toxic Cloud: The Poisoning of America's Air.* New York: Harper and Row Publishers, 1987.

Campbell, Carlos C. *Birth of a National Park in the Great Smoky Mountains.* Knoxville: University of Tennessee Press, 1969.

Coyle, William, ed. *Ohio Authors and Their Books.* New York: World Publishing Co., 1962.

Dabney, Joseph Earl. *Mountain Spirits: A Chronicle of Corn Whiskey from King James' Ulster Plantation to America's Appalachians and the Moonshine Life.* Asheville, N.C.: Bright Mountain Books, 1974.

Davis, Mackenzie L., and David A. Cornwell. *Introduction to Environmental Engineering.* 2d ed. New York: McGraw-Hill Publishing Co., 1991.

Dykeman, Wilma. *The French Broad.* New York: Rinehart and Co., 1955. Reprint, Knoxville: University of Tennessee Press, 1985.

Eller, Ronald D. *Miners, Millhands, and Mountaineers: Industrialization of the Appalachian South, 1889–1930.* Knoxville: University of Tennessee Press, 1982.

Folmsbee, Stanley L., Robert E. Corlew, and Enoch L. Mitchell. *Tennessee: A Short History.* Knoxville: University of Tennessee Press, 1969.

Frome, Michael. *Strangers in High Places.* Rev. ed. Knoxville: University of Tennessee Press, 1980.

Goldman, Charles R., James McEvoy III, and Peter J. Richerson. *Environmental Quality and Water Development.* San Francisco: W. H. Freeman and Co., 1973.

Gore, Al, Jr. *Earth in the Balance: Ecology and the Human Spirit.* Boston: Houghton Mifflin Co., 1992.

Hillin, Hank, Introduction by Bill Clinton. *Al Gore Jr.: His Life and Career.* New York: Birch Lane Press, 1988. Reprint, 1992.

Hooper, Ben W. *The Unwanted Boy: The Autobiography of Governor Ben W. Hooper.* Ed. Everett Robert Boyce. Knoxville: University of Tennessee Press, 1963.

Hunter, Dard. *Papermaking: The History and Techniques of an Ancient Craft.* New York: Alfred Knopf, Inc., 1943. Reprint: New York: Dover Publications, Inc., 1978.

Ingram, William T. *Glossary of Water and Wastewater Control Engineering.* New York: Water Pollution Control Federation, 1969.

Johnson, Haynes. *Sleepwalking Through History: America in the Reagan Years.* New York: W. W. Norton and Co., 1991.

Kazis, Richard, and Richard L. Grossman. *Fear at Work: Job Blackmail, Labor and the Environment.* New York: The Pilgrim Press, 1982.

Kephart, Horace. *Our Southern Highlanders: A Narrative of Adventures in the Southern Appalachians and a Study of Life Among the Mountaineers.* 1913. Reprint, Knoxville: University of Tennessee Press, 1990.

Manning, Richard. *Last Stand: A Riveting Expose of Environmental Pillage and a Lone Journalist's Struggle to Keep Faith.* New York: Penguin Books, 1992.

Marcus, Alfred A. "Environmental Protection Agency." In *Government Agencies.* Ed. Donald R. Whitnah. Westport, Conn.: Greenwood Press, 1983.

McCrumb, Sharyn. *The Hangman's Beautiful Daughter.* New York: The Onyx Group, 1992.

McKibben, Bill. *The End of Nature.* New York: Random House, 1989.

Miller, G. Tyler, Jr. *Living in the Environment: An Introduction to Environmental Science.* 5th ed. Belmont, Calif.: Wadsworth Publishing Co., 1988.

Mooney, James. *Myths of the Cherokee.* Bureau of American Ethnology, Nineteenth Annual Report (1897–98). Washington, D.C.: Government Printing Office, 1900.

Moore, John Trotwood, and Austin P. Foster. *Tennessee: The Volunteer State, 1769–1923.* 4 vols. Chicago: S. J. Clarke Publishing Co., 1923.

O'Dell, Ruth Webb. *Over the Misty Blue Hills: The Story of Cocke County, Tennessee.* Easley, S.C.: Southern Historical Press, 1982.

O'Neil, J. Duay, ed. *Reflections of Our Heritage: Cocke County.* Newport, TN.: Cocke County Museum, 1985.

Powledge, Fred. *Water: The Nature, Uses, and Future of Our Most Precious and Abused Resource.* New York: Farrar Straus Giroux, 1982; 1983.

Shifflett, Crandall A. *Coal Towns: Life, Work, and Culture in Company Towns of Southern Appalachia, 1880–1960.* Knoxville: University of Tennessee Press, 1991.

Smith, David C. *History of Papermaking in the United States (1691–1969)*. New York: Lockwood Publishing Co., 1970.

Van Strum, Carol, and Paul Merrell. *No Margin for Safety: A Preliminary Report on Dioxin Pollution and the Need for Emergency Action in the Pulp and Paper Industry.* Toronto: Greenpeace Great Lakes Toxic Campaign, 1987.

Weeks, Lyman Horace. *A History of Paper-Manufacturing in the United States, 1690–1916.* 1916. Reprint, New York: Burt Franklin, Bibliography and Reference Series 285, 1969.

Wells, Camille. *Canton: The Architecture of Our Home Town.* Canton: Canton Historical Commission, 1985.

Zeiger, Robert H. *Rebuilding the Pulp and Paper Worker's Union, 1933–1941.* Twentieth Century America Series. Knoxville: University of Tennessee Press, 1984.

Articles, Pamphlets, Bulletins, Manuscripts, and Congressional Documents

Burns, Robert I., S.J. "The Paper Revolution in Europe: Crusader Valencia's Paper Industry—A Technological and Behavioral Breakthrough." *Pacific Historical Review* 50 (1981): 1–30.

Champion International Corporation. *This Is Champion: A Proud Name in American Industry.* Hamilton, Ohio: Champion Public Relations Department, 1954.

———. "Fact Sheet about the Canton Mill's Environmental Programs." Canton, N.C.: Champion International Corporation, 1959.

———. *Fact Books.* Stamford, Conn.: Champion International Corporation, 1991–93.

———. *Canton Conversion Update.* Vol.1, No. 1–Vol. 5, No.8 (June 22, 1989–Aug. 1993). Canton, N.C.: Champion International Corporation.

———. Numerous press releases, most undated. Stamford, Conn., or Canton, N.C.

Craft, David. "Balancing Jobs and Nature." Press Release, Champion International Corporation, Canton Facility, 1992.

Dunn, Nelson. "The Boice Hardwood Company." Newport, Tenn.: Stokely Memorial Library, n.d.

Fink, Paul H. "Early Explorers in the Great Smokies." *East Tennessee Historical Society Publications* 4 (1933): 55–96.

Heilbroner, Robert. "Reflections." *The New Yorker* July 8, 1991, 70–77.

McKinney, David. "Pollution and the Dying Pigeon." *The Tennessee Conservationist* (Sept./Oct. 1989): 18–20.

Manuel, John. "The Pigeon Flies Again." *Canoe* (Aug. 1993): 17–20.

Saylor, Charles F., Aubrey D. McKinney, and Wayne H. Schacher. "A Case Study of the Pigeon River in the Tennessee River Drainage." Nashville: Tennessee Wildlife Resource Agency, 1992(?).

Schaffer, Dan, "Managing Water in the Tennessee Valley in the Post–World War II Period." *Environmental Review* (Summer 1989): 2–14.

Schmidt, Karen F. "Puzzling Over a Poison." *U.S. News and World Report,* Apr. 6, 1992, 60–61.

Sigler, Andrew. "Good Ethics is Good Business." Kreuger, David A., and David P. Schwett, eds. *The Ethics of Organizational Survival: Managing Change in a Competitive World.* Proceedings of the Third National Consultation on Corporate Ethics. New York: Trinity Center for Ethics and Corporate Policy, 1989, 43–50.

Smathers, Geo. "Memoirs of Geo. Smathers." Manuscript. Ed. Allen Roudebush for Champion International Corporation, 1990. Canton, N.C.: Canton Area Historical Museum.

Stebbins, W. H. "The Sulphite Process." *Paper Trade Journal,* Jan. 17, 1907.

Stokes, Durward T. "North Carolina and the Great Revival of 1800." *North Carolina Historical Review* 43 (1966): 410–11.

Thomson, Peter G. "Obituary." *Paper Trade Journal,* July 16, 1931.

Thornton, Joe, and John Hanrahan. "The Dioxin Deception." *Greenpeace Magazine* (May–June 1991): 16–21.

Trippett, Frank. "Big Stink on the Pigeon." *Time,* June 6, 1988, 22.

U.S. Congress, House Subcommittee on Water Resources of the Committee on Public Works and Transportation, *Dioxin Pollution in the Pigeon River, North Carolina and Tennessee.* 100th Cong., 2d sess., 1988.

U.S. Environmental Protection Agency. *Environmental News.* Atlanta: EPA Region IV, Office of Public Affairs, occasional undated releases relative to the Pigeon River.

Value Line Investment Survey. 6th ed., part 3: "Ratings and Reports," January 22, 1993, 917.

Waldman, Steven. "Watering the Grass Roots: How to Buy a 'Spontaneous' Uprising." *Newsweek,* May 6, 1991.

Who Was Who in America. Vol. VI, 1961–68.

Who's Who in America, 1959–60.

Theses

Corwin, Margaret I. "Agenda Setting in the Case of a Polluted Interstate River: Champion Paper Mill and the Pigeon River." M.A. thesis, Colorado State University, Fort Collins, 1991.

Gilmore, Voit. "The Pigeon River of North Carolina: Economic Exploitation vs. Environmental Quality." M.A. thesis, University of North Carolina, Chapel Hill, 1984.

Norris-Hall, Lachelle. "A Social Movement Analysis of an Environmental Protest Group: The Dead Pigeon River Council." M.A. thesis, University of Tennessee, 1988.

Unpublished Material

Bach, Orville E., Jr., and William H. Barnett. "An Economic Impact Analysis on the Recreational Benefits of a Restored Pigeon River." Duplicated Report. Jefferson City, TN: Walters State Community College, 1987.

—————. "A Financial Analysis of Champion International Corporation's Ability to Provide for a Clean Pigeon River." Duplicated report. Jefferson City, Tenn.: Walters State Community College, 1987.

—————. "Addendum: Latest Financial Disclosure of Champion International Corporation, January 24, 1988."

Cavaney, Red. "Federal Government Regulatory Overreach Impacting the U.S. Pulp and Paper Industry." N.p.: American Paper Institute, December, 1990.

Champion International Corporation. "Champion and the Pigeon River." Videocassette.

—————. "CMP Video Highlights." Videocassette.

Dead Pigeon River Council. "Pigeon River Project." Videocassette.

Environmental Protection Agency. *Environmental News* 1988–1990.

Federal Energy Regulatory Commission. *Walter/Waterville Environmental Assessment.* Washington, D.C., 1991.

Federal Regulatory Commission, Office of Electric Power Regulation. *Appraisal Report: Pigeon River Basin.* Atlanta Regional Office, 1981.

North Carolina Division of Environmental Management, Water Quality Section, Operation Branch. "Briefing Paper on the Pigeon River, Haywood County, North Carolina." June 1982.

—————. "Final Report, Champion Variance Review Committee," Mar. 31, 1988.

Nashville, Tenn., Tennessee Environmental Council, n.d. "Synopsis of Major Pigeon River Studies, State, Federal, and University, 1949, 1965, 1966, 1972, 1978, 1979, 1980. Pigeon River as Impacted by Champion Paper Company Canton, North Carolina." (In chronological order, contains summations of the following Studies.) A. D. Hess and C. M. Tarzwell, "A Study of the Biological Effects of Pollution on the Pigeon River Watershed." Tennessee Valley Authority, Health and Safety Department, Forestry Relations Division, 1942; Lowell E. Keup and R. Keith Stewart. "Effects of Pollution on the Biota of the Pigeon River, North Carolina and Tennessee." Federal Water Pollution Control Administration. Cincinnati, Ohio, 1966; C. E. Runas, Lowell E. Keup, and R. K. Stewart, "Report on Interstate Waters on the Pigeon River"; John Christian Bernhardt, faculty advisor. "Biosystem Character of the Pigeon River in the Primary Stage of Recovery." University of North Carolina at Asheville, 1973; Dr. David W. Hill, director and supervisor. "An Investigation of Waste Water Sources in Newport, Tenn. & Water Quality Studies Pigeon River & Tributaries Cocke County." Environmental Protection Agency, Region IV, Surveillance and Analysis Division, 1973; North Carolina Department of Natural Resources, Division of Environmental Management, Environmental Operations Section, Wastewater Management, Biology Unit. "Pigeon River Investigation," 1978; Ibid., "Pigeon River Investigation" Oct. 1979; David Melgaard and A. David McKinney. "Biological and Chemical Investigation of the Pigeon River, Cocke County, Tennessee, October, 1980." Tennessee Department of Public Health, Division of Water Quality Control, Nashville, 1980.

Nashville News. Dick Mullinix, Nelson Ross, and Gary Davis on the Pigeon River. Videocassette.

Tennessee Department of Public Health, Division of Water Quality Control. "Position Paper: Restoration of the Pigeon River—A Major Interstate River—Originating in North Carolina and Flowing into Tennessee." Nashville, 1982.

Tennessee Valley Authority. TVA Studies of Pollution of Tennessee River, III, "French Broad." Chattanooga, Tenn., n.d.

U.S. Census Bureau. *1987 Census of Manufactures, Industry Series* [MC87-1-26A]. Industries 2611, 2621, and 2631. "Pulp, Paper, and Board Mills."

U.S. Environmental Protection Agency. National Pollution Discharge Elimination System. "Public Hearing, Champion International Corporation, Asheville Civic Center, January 14, 1988." Copies available from Neal R. Gross, Inc., Washington, D.C.

Westall, Forrest. "Report: Champion Variance Review Committee." North Carolina Division of Environmental Management, Dec. 30, 1988.

Weston, Roy F. "Engineer's Preliminary Report, Secondary Treatment of Industrial Wastewater, Champion Papers, Carolina Division, Canton, N.C." Environmental Science and Engineering Consultants, West Chester, Pa. TVA Archives, Reservoir Quality Office, Chattanooga, Tenn.

Court Decisions and Statutes

Before the United States Environmental Protection Agency Region IV: In Re Champion International Corporation NPDES Permit No. NC 0000272: *Request for Evidentiary Hearing by Dead Pigeon River Council.* Filed by Gary Davis, Attorney for the DPRC, Oct. 25, 1989.

———. Initial Decision. Filed by Thomas B. Yost, administrative law judge, Feb. 12, 1992.

———. *Environmental News.* "Administrative Law Judge Issues Decision on Champion International's Canton, North Carolina Wastewater Permit. Feb. 12, 1992.

Champion International Corporation and the State of North Carolina v. United States Environmental Protection Agency. 648 Federal Supplement, 1390–1400.

———. "Supplemental Memorandum of Decision." 652 Federal Supplement, 1398–1400. 1987.

Champion International Corporation v. U.S.E.P.A. 850 F. 2d 182 (4th Circuit 1988).

International Paper Co. v. Harmel Ouelette et al. 107 S.Ct. 805 (1987).

Shults, J.A., and Shults, Joan v. *Champion International Corporation.* United States District Court for the Eastern District of Tennessee, No. CIV-2-91-33. 1992.

State of North Carolina. Public Laws and Resolutions, General Assembly, Session of 1901, Chapter 690, 917–18.

————. Session of 1907, Chapter 298, 420–21.

State of Tennessee v. *Champion International Corporation.* 709 S.W. 2d 569 (Tenn, 1986), Apr. 21, 1986.

Tennessee v. *Champion International Corporation.* 22 ERC, 1338–48, Jan. 15, 1985.

Newspapers and Periodicals

Appalachia, 1985–89

Asheville Citizen, 1906–10; 1986–93

Asheville Times, 1986–93

Asheville Citizen-Times, 1986–93

Atlanta Constitution, 1987–93

Atlanta Journal, 1987–93

Business Week, 1986–93

Canoe, 1993

Charlotte Observer, 1987–93

Christian Science Monitor, 1987

Enterprise (Canton), 1985–94

Environmental Review, 1985–93

Forbes, 1990

Greenpeace Magazine, 1986–93

Greeneville Sun, 1992

Knoxville Journal, 1987–90

Knoxville News-Sentinel, 1986–93

Log of Champion Activities, 1922–60

Los Angeles Times, 1989

Morristown Tribune, 1987–93

Mountaineer, 1985–93

Nashville Tennessean, 1987

Newport Plain Talk, 1906–93

New Yorker, 1986–93

New York Times, 1985–93

Niagara Gazette, 1988

Paper Trade Journal, 1872–1986

Raleigh News and Observer, 1986–93

Time, 1985–93

USA Today, 1985–93

U.S. News and World Report, 1985–93

Wall Street Journal, 1986–93

Washington Post, 1985–93

Winston Salem Journal, 1985–93

Interviews, Correspondence, and Telephone Conversations

Allen, Rebecca White

Bach, Orville, Jr.

Ball, W. Gordon

Barnett, William H.

Barrett, Meschelyn

Bartus, John J.

Brodhead, Mike

Buchanan, Millie

Cates, Harold

Clark, Larry

Corwin, Margaret I.

Craft, David

Davis, Gary

Davis, Paul

Gore, Al

Harrison, Jim

Jenkins, Margaret

Ketterman, Fran

McGinnis, Sue

McKinney, David

McLeod, Scott
Merrill, Paul
Moore, Charles Lewis
Mullinix, Charles Dickens
Mullinix, Lucie
Neal, Philip
Oberst, Nancy
Oliver, George
Pearigen, Michael
Quillen, Jimmy
Roberts, Larry
Ross, Nelson
Runnion, Cindie
Runnion, Jim
Schell, Fran

Schroeder, Edwin M,
Seay, Bob
Soesbee, Gilbert
Smith, David C.
United States Bureau of Geographical
    Names
Walker, Pauline Shields
Watts, Richard
Webb, Gay
Webb, Judy
Wilde, Jerry
Williamson, Carl
Wilson, Jeanne
Wolfe, Alison
Woody, Mary

Archives, Museums, and Libraries

Canton Area Historical Museum
College of Law Library, Florida State
    University
Haywood County Public Library
North Carolina State Archives, Raleigh
Ramsay Memorial Library, Asheville
Robert Manning Strozier Library,
    Florida State University
Stokely Memorial Library, Newport

Tennessee State Library, Nashville
Tennessee Supreme Court Library,
    Nashville
TVA Records on Pigeon River in Cus-
    tody of Manager of Reservoir Water
    Quality, Chattanooga, Tenn.
Waynesville Public Library, Waynesville,
    N.C.

Index

Bach, Orville E. "Butch," Jr., 122–29; speaks
at Knoxville hearing, 204
Bach and Barnett's Report: discussion of
Part I, 122–25; discussion of Part II, 125–
29; cost of cleaning river, 126; gives legitimacy to arguments, 129; estimated
income from mill, 154; submitted at
Congressional Hearing, 223
Ball, Gordon, attorney: calls 85 color proposal "presidential politics," 212; questions EPA about dioxin, 224; lawyer representing DPRC, 230; helps with request
for new hearings, 243; brings about lawsuit, 265; costs of lawsuit, 267; closing
arguments, 273
Ballinger, Cass: at Asheville hearing, 181
Balsam Inn, reopened, 295
Balsam Mountains, 10
Barnett, Bruce, EPA official: says Champion will get reprieve, 162; moderator at
Asheville hearing, 179; moderator at
Knoxville hearing, 192–93, 197, 201; says
will approve 85 true color units, 209;
gives statistics of Champion campaign,
242–43
Barnett, William H. III, 122–29; speaks at
stockholder's meeting, 128; at Knoxville
hearing, 204
Barrett, Don, attorney for plaintiffs, 267,
272; remarks to jury, 269; arguments, 273
Bartram, William, explorer, 7
bass (fish), x, 42, 65, 149, 196; in Waterville
Lake, 220
B.E.&K. Construction Co., 175; does most
of CMP, 257
Bell, Charles, N.C.: at Asheville hearing, 181
bell ringing ceremony: at Newport, 119
Benner, Bob, raftsman: appraises Pigeon
River, 278
benthic community, 74
benthos, 73; defined, 317
Bernhardt, John Christian: supervises Pi-
geon River study, 70
Bethel community, 37; receives new water
system, 258
Big Creek, 7, 11, 15; water tested below en-
trance to Pigeon River, 243; site protested,
246–47; dilutes polluted Pigeon, 286
"Big Five" (Canton leaders), 36, 38
Big Pigeon River, 9, 60. See Pigeon River

billboards, against Champion, 155. See also
signs
biochemical oxygen demand: defined, 317
"Biological and Chemical Investigation of
the Pigeon River . . .," 73
"Biosystem Character of the Pigeon River,"
70–71
birth defects, 214, 279
black ash, 62
black liquor, 71
Black River, 11, 68, 110, 203. See also Pigeon
River
Blackwell, Oliver: Mullinix comments on,
88–89; insists problem is just color, 131; at
Canton hearing, 138; quoted, 143; explains permits, 145; announces improvements, 146; comments on failure of pilot
plant, 147; meets with county officials,
154; will drink from Pigeon, 155; comments on Champion study of Pigeon
River, 165; speaks to Rotary Club, 167;
speaks to Asheville Chamber of Commerce, 174, 175; replies to union, 176; at
Asheville hearing, 179; at Knoxville hearing, 193–94, 205; at Cocke County hearing, 232; admits Champion could clean
river, 238; admits Pigeon River too small,
246; says DPRC won, 248; on *Good
Morning America*, 250; says oxygen
delignification will reduce dioxins, 254
Bleach Filtrate Recycling (BFR): explained,
292
blind spot (pollution), 50
blue gill (fish): found in Pigeon River, 196
Blue Ridge Parkway, 17; near origin of Pigeon River, 85
BOD (biochemical oxygen demand): restricted, 69; discussed at Knoxville hearing, 193; at evidentiary hearing, 253; defined, 317
Boggan, Dr. Charles: speaks at New Year's
celebration, 237
Boice Hardwood Co., 15
Boyd, D. L., Haywood County legislator, 38
Bradburn, Max: at Asheville hearing, 183–84
Branton, William: at Asheville hearing, 182
bream (fish), 131; Andy Plemmons' experiment with, 185
breast cancer, in Haywood County, 244
Brewer, Gary E., lawyer for plaintiffs, 267

effluents. *See* toxicity; sludge; sediment; carcinogens

eighty-five color units, 149; and politicians, 281. *See also* color; fifty aluminum cobalt color units

Ekman, Carl D., 24

Eller, Ronald, 13

Ellington, Governor Buford: at I-40 dedication, 203

emotionalism, replaces rationality, 157–58

Endow, Jeff, N.C. Representative: at Asheville hearing, 181

Engineers, Army. *See* Army Corps of Engineers

Environmental Defense Fund, 76; at hearing, 222

environmental laws: proliferation of, 97

Environmental Management Commission. *See* North Carolina Department of Environmental Management

Environmental Management and Quality Assurance Administration of Tennessee, 103–4

Environmental Protection Agency: founded, 30, 58; fines Champion, 71; fails to formulate criteria, 74; empowered to enforce laws, 80; growth of, 98; urged to uphold regulatory authority, 100; asked to assist solving problem, 104; rejects permit, 110; wins court case, 110, 112–14; lags in enforcement, 117; expresses displeasure with permit, 139–41; assumes permitting authority, 144; sued by Champion, 145; orders Champion to file for permit, 146; wins lawsuit, 150; politicized, 151; announces new date for hearings, 166; issues revised draft, 170; releases dioxin study, 213; announces tests of Waterville and Douglas lakes, 220; reports Waterville teeming with fish, 220; at hearing, 222–23; failure to proceed explained, 227; proposes three years for Champion to meet standards, 240; releases new draft permit, March 1989, 242–43; DPRC accuses being denied input into permit-writing process, 245; reveals Champion plan to to reduce work force, 248; campaign successful, 284

environmentalism: elevation in national psyche, 282

EPA. *See* Environmental Protection Agency

"EPA Response Team": organized by Champion employees, 245

Epidemiology, State Department of: launches Hartford cancer study, 218

Everest, David Clark: expresses concern over water pollution, 299n40

evidentiary hearing, 249–50; preliminaries, 253–54; described, 262–63; decision, 263

external diseconomy, 125. *See* Economics

Faubian, William, 11

fecal coliform. *See* coliform

Federal Circuit Court of Appeals: hears Champion v. EPA, 114

Federal Clean Air Act. *See* Clean Air Act

Federal Clean Water Act. *See* Clean Water Act

Federal District Court of Western North Carolina: brief filed with, by Champion, 110, 145

Federal Energy Regulatory Commission: report on fish in Waterville Lake, 220; suggests removal of sludge or capping, 287–88

Federal Water Pollution Act, 108. *See* Water Pollution Control Act

Federal Water Pollution Control Administration, 69–70

Ferguson, Jeff: at Asheville hearing, 182

Ferguson, Willie: describes Pigeon River, 131

Fibreville: land for, acquired, 38; construction of, 47, 315n60

Fifty platinum cobalt color units, 30, 110, 113; favored by EPA, 134; insisted upon by Tennessee, 136; EPA questions ability to achieve, 139; controversy over, 142–44; standard to remain, 167; retained in revised draft, 170; at Asheville hearing, 179; at state line, 193, 200, 206; at Knoxville hearing, 193; considered unattainable, 210–11; DiForio says Champion can meet requirement, 247; in permit of, 248; Craft claims water meets requirement, 286